I0797517

REFLECTIONS

REFLECTIONS

ON CINEMATOGRAPHY

ROGER A. DEAKINS

GRAND
CENTRAL
New York Boston

Cover design by Shubhani Sarkar, sarkardesignstudio.com. Cover photography © 1992 Elliot Marks, courtesy of Tristar Pictures, Inc. Cover copyright © 2025 by Hachette Book Group, Inc.

Grand Central Publishing
Hachette Book Group
1290 Avenue of the Americas, New York, NY 10104
grandcentralpublishing.com
@grandcentralpub

First Edition: November 2025

Grand Central Publishing is a division of Hachette Book Group, Inc. The Grand Central Publishing name and logo is a registered trademark of Hachette Book Group, Inc.

The publisher is not responsible for websites (or their content) that are not owned by the publisher.

The Hachette Speakers Bureau provides a wide range of authors for speaking events. To find out more, go to hachettespeakersbureau.com or email HachetteSpeakers@hbgusa.com.

Grand Central Publishing books may be purchased in bulk for business, educational, or promotional use. For information, please contact your local bookseller or the Hachette Book Group Special Markets Department at special.markets@hbgusa.com.

Print book interior design by Shubhani Sarkar, sarkardesignstudio.com

Library of Congress Control Number: 2025937669

ISBNs: 978-1-5387-7150-1 (hardcover); 978-1-5387-7151-8 (ebook)

Printed in Malaysia

IM

10 9 8 7 6 5 4 3 2 1

TO JAMES

CONTENTS

PART I

PART II

PART III

PART IV

PROLOGUE

Every picture tells a story.

PROVERB

In my career as a cinematographer, spanning almost half a century, I've been lucky to play a part in telling a great many stories, whether in documentary filmmaking or Hollywood films. Since the first figurative art made on a cave wall more than fifty thousand years ago, humans have used images to visualize a story and reflect the world around them. It was a somewhat more contemporary version of this same need that drew me to sketch my early surroundings on a pad of paper, a need that evolved into photography, then finally led to producing flickering images on a movie screen.

Many people equate the craft of cinematography with creating beautiful images. In contrast, I believe the cinematographer's role is to support the story, to immerse the viewer rather than create attractive but ultimately uninvolving "eye candy." As with a cave wall drawing or an Edvard Munch painting, some images can tell a story without the need for dialogue. But, unlike a painting, other elements of a film—the writing, the acting, the production design, the editing, and so on—are of equal importance to the cinematography in combining to form a whole.

Believing in and wanting to highlight the collaborative nature of filmmaking, my wife, James, and I have hosted the *Team Deakins* TD podcast since 2020, where she and I talk to other members of the film industry, from directors and stars to cinematographers and first assistant directors to costume designers and sound recordists. We almost always begin an episode the same way, asking, "How did you get to where you are today?" It's a simple question, one that seldom produces a simple answer but always one that is interesting. As James and I have learned, there is no single path through life or into a career in film. Everyone has their own story.

Sometimes reality is too complex. Stories give it form.

JEAN-LUC GODARD

Working in the film business involves not only helping tell stories but also stumbling across them. Here's one that, like many others, I wish I had filmed but remains only as a memory. I was driving back from shooting one of my first professional jobs, a documentary in a remote part of southern Ireland. I had followed my map down a narrow road to a slipway. I could see the same road continue up the bank on the other side, but between me and it lay a wide body of water with no sign of a ferry. Gazing at me from his seat on a low stone wall that bordered a fishing shack, blacked with tar in a vain attempt to protect it from the weather, was an equally weather-beaten man and his dog. I walked over and told him I was lost. He seemed deep in thought as he lit his pipe, so I sat down and patiently waited for him to speak. What followed was the story of his life and what a rich life it had been: his wayward youth, his adventures in the merchant navy, meeting the love of his life in a strip club in London's Soho, and so much more. Finally, he emptied his pipe and gestured toward the fishing shack. "My parents lived here. I was born here, and I will die here. I can't help you get where you are going but I wish you well. Drop by if you are this way again." Ironically, the documentary I had been shooting was on storytellers.

As for my own story, it would be easy to say it was my dream to become a cinematographer from the very first time I went to the cinema, but the truth is rather different. It was a long and gradual process that led me to cinematography, one for which there was no obvious career path. And it was not until I was on a film set, looking through a camera, that I began to understand cinematography, a learning process that is still evolving today.

Art is not what you see, but what you make others see.

EDGAR DEGAS

As a schoolboy, I was drawn to the work of a wide variety of artists, from William Blake to Giorgio de Chirico, Edvard Munch and Francis Bacon to Toulouse-Lautrec, painters who sought something more than a beautiful image. I would spend hours studying photography in once-popular magazines such as *Life* or *Picture Post*, or books from the "art" section of my local library. I was mesmerized by the imagery of Julia Margaret Cameron, Walker Evans, Brassaï, Bill Brandt, Jacques Henri Lartigue, André Kertész, and Dorothea Lange. Instead of using a brush and a canvas, these great photographers interpreted the world through their lens. But my only experience behind a camera was when my brother, Bill, and I were capturing ourselves with the fish we had caught, using an ancient Kodak Box Brownie. The notion of a career with a camera did not ever enter my mind.

I loved my hometown of Torquay, in the beautiful southwest of England. In so many ways it was an idyllic paradise but, for all the happy hours I'd spent wandering the beach at low tide to gather shrimp and crabs, fishing with my dad in his small boat or simply catching mackerel off the rocks, it had not always been a happy place for me. I had watched those around me prepare for familiar lives in a familiar town, and I knew it wasn't for me. Like my Irish acquaintance, I left Torquay with little idea what I was looking for. Only at the age of thirty-five did I realize I had found it.

Everything you can imagine is real.

PABLO PICASSO

PART I

1

PARADISE

I found paradise in Devon. It was hiding behind a cloud.

UNKNOWN

My parents met during World War II. My father, William Albert Deakins, was about to embark for Germany during the last months of the war, and they decided to get married if and when he returned. My mother, Josephine, was London born and had driven an ambulance during the Blitz before serving in the Women's Auxiliary Air Force. My father joined up in 1939, at the age of twenty-one and with little experience of the world beyond rural Devon, and became an explosives expert with the Royal Engineers, serving in France before, during, and briefly after the evacuation of Dunkirk. The Engineers had been tasked with destroying or booby-trapping the bridges surrounding the perimeter of the Dunkirk evacuation, to slow down any attack that might come from Rommel and his panzer divisions. After the evacuation was completed, my father's small band of engineers were told that the time had come for them to "fend for themselves."

Deciding their best chance was to head south toward the Spanish border, my father and a mate fled on foot before the advance of the German army as it took command of the Channel coast. Dodging waves of German Stuka dive bombers, they were rescued from the beach at Saint-Valery-sur-Somme so long after the Dunkirk operation that my grandmother had given her son up for dead.

In 1941 Dad would join the newly formed Special Air Service, again as an explosives expert. His first assignment took him behind the German lines in North Africa, where the SAS made nighttime raids on supply depots, railway lines, and airdromes from their base inside the supposedly impassable Qattara Depression. Then, following the Allied victory at El Alamein, he served in Sicily as one of Major Paddy Mayne's commandoes, tasked with disabling the clifftop guns that threatened the Allied invasion fleet, not unlike a real-life version of Alistair MacLean's *The Guns of Navarone*.

My father had an eventful war. He would tell many stories, both of moments he wished to forget and others that were among the best experiences of his life.

Though my father returned to his hometown and to his father's painting and decorating business, the war years changed many things for many people. It was no different for my mother. She had little time to settle into her new life in Devon, far away from her native city, as, sadly, she developed multiple sclerosis in 1949, the year I was born. The disease progressed so quickly I struggle to remember a time before she became paralyzed. I can readily recall my father carrying her from our car to the beach or across the moors for a picnic, but I find it impossible to conjure up a picture of her walking.

As her paralysis progressed, my mother was accepted for tests at Stoke Mandeville Hospital in Buckinghamshire, some two hundred miles and six hours away. My father would drive us there for visits, and one evening we watched a play put on by the hospital staff. It was a corny story about a wife waiting for a husband who was away at war. I remember the lead actress placing a lamp on the window at sunset so that her character's husband could find his way home in the dark, but I have no idea what happened after that. We left, with my mother in tears. I was maybe five or six at the time. Only later did I realize it wasn't the story that overwhelmed her but the picture of her life as it might have been. In her youth my mother had been a model with a burgeoning career as an actress on the London stage, but that was way before I was born. She never talked to me about her role as an understudy to Anna Neagle, or her brief appearance in the 1939 film *Too Dangerous to Live*. In fact, I knew little about her once-exotic city life until many years after her death.

When my mother became bedridden, I would sit by her side as she delicately painted the birds that came to a feeder outside

the window, while I concentrated on drawing my dinosaurs, copying them from the latest *National Geographic* magazine. In the last few years of her life, when she could no longer hold a brush, I saw her less and less frequently. But I would often hear her. During the night, when my father tried to comfort her, she would scream, "I wish I were dead!" My final memory of her is looking down from the top of the stairs as she was wheeled away for the last time. She died in 1958, at the age of forty-one.

Yet a picture of my mother that dates from before I was born has followed me throughout my life. It's an image of her at a funfair in Southend-on-Sea, taken by the photographer Kurt Hutton in 1938. Rising from the seat of a ride called the Caterpillar, her dress open to the wind like Marilyn Monroe in *The Seven Year Itch*, she looks young and carefree, a side of my mother I never had a chance to experience.

When my father showed me the photo it seemed very familiar, but I would not have known it was her if he hadn't told me. First published in the October 1938 issue of *Picture Post*, the image has since taken on a life of its own. My mother seems to keep an eye on me, as I often see the picture in the most unlikely places. At the National Film School, it appeared on a poster advertising a London photo exhibition. In 1994 it appeared in the Santa Monica shopping mall, her face blown up to cover a full two floors. In 2003 she appeared on the cover of a book entitled *Woman: A Celebration*, and on a day off from shooting *1917* in Glasgow, I spotted the same photograph in a pub on the east coast of Scotland. There was my mother, frozen forever in an expression of joy.

> ***Photography can only represent the present.***
> ***Once photographed, the subject becomes part of the past.***
>
> **BERENICE ABBOTT**

Both my older brother, William, and I were more than a little confused by our mother's death, a confusion only made worse when my father almost instantly remarried. My stepmother was, I am told, my mother's best friend but, as she lived in London, we had never met. My grandparents had died, and I am sure my dad was petrified at the thought of raising his two young sons by himself. I can't blame him in the least for looking for a partner. I don't remember my stepmother's name or much else about her, other than she drank large amounts of whisky during the afternoons while sitting in front of the television. A lit cigarette rarely left her lips. One day I came home from school to find the house empty. She had recently replaced our furniture with her own, and now that too was gone. When my father came home from work, he appeared as surprised as I was but also, I sensed, relieved. It had been many years since we had been as close as we were that evening, sitting on some upturned wooden crates and watching a film, probably a gangster film with Alan Ladd and Veronica Lake, on a television that was about all we had left.

In the summer break from school, I would work on one of my father's building sites, sometimes helping to fix a leaky roof—which I remember most clearly, as I have a fear of heights—other times as a bricklayer's gofer or as a general odd-jobs apprentice. I loved working with such a diverse group of characters who took real pleasure in the jobs they did, but the work itself was not for me. As his business began to fail, my father worked longer and longer hours trying to outrun the inevitable. I am sure he felt I would eventually follow in his footsteps. So, partly for this reason and partly through loyalty to his employees, he continued to pay four or five specialist tradesmen year after year without making a profit for himself.

Yes, as everyone knows,
meditation and water are wedded forever.

ISHMAEL,
IN *MOBY DICK* BY HERMAN MELVILLE

Otherwise, I spent much of my time fishing. In the spring I would be down on the seashore before school and back again in the evening. Being by myself, the simple pleasure of watching a sunrise over the sea informed my childhood: the shadows cast across the water by passing clouds, the fin of a basking shark idly slicing through the surface (there were a great many when I was a kid), the shrill call of an oystercatcher announcing the arrival of spring, or a ganett diving on its prey.

It was only in my teenage years that I grew to enjoy the company of a group of like-minded friends, all of whom were older than me and already working for a living. Peter was a hairdresser, Luke a signwriter, Phil a shoemaker, Martin a house painter, and Graham a onetime champion motorbike racer who worked at the local china clay quarry. In the autumn months I might ride passenger with Graham through the narrow lanes of Devon to find remote, untouched fishing spots, or a group of us might spend the night fishing for conger eels, lighting a fire to cook some mackerel while watching the skies for Yuri Gagarin and UFOs.

On winter evenings our group might be seen fishing off the harbor breakwater or holed up in the sea anglers' clubhouse to keep warm while sharing a beer or two. Or more. In Devon, recreation revolved around drinking, and what was true for aimless youth was just as true for the adults around us. Late one night, while walking around the harbor on my way home, I came face-to-face with my math teacher, who was weaving toward me from the opposite direction. I worried about meeting him at such a late time of night and me having had an "underage" drink, but I had no need. It was well past closing time, and he was hardly in a state to recognize me. I was glad he was a no-show at school the following day, though I did feel sorry for him when I read the evening paper. Shortly after we crossed paths, my teacher had fallen in the harbor. It was only by chance that someone was there, sober enough, to fish him out.

After playing at the Town Hall in 1964, Mick Jagger of the Rolling Stones described Torquay as "a great town. But I shouldn't think there's much to do in the winter." He was being polite. The winters could be grim, but summers in Torquay were alive with tourists and music. Eric Clapton and the Yardbirds came that same summer, while The Who followed them to the Town Hall in 1966, only for Pete Townshend to smash his guitar onstage and start a fire.

At the height of the summer season, the town could also be rough. I was at a social gathering for visiting foreign students at a local church hall when the vicar was viciously stabbed, as was the manager of a club I occasionally drank in after the pubs had closed. On leaving a concert by the Kinks at Torquay Town Hall with my brother and a friend, we got into a fight with some sailors from a naval warship anchored in Torbay. It climaxed with my friend being thrown through the front window of a shop displaying TV sets. He ended up sitting among the televisions surrounded by broken glass but, amazingly, without a scratch on him.

My brother eventually settled down to work in my dad's hardware store, finding religion in a church that seemed to me more akin to a doomsday cult. Later in life, when I was living in London, I attempted to deal with my own lingering anger at our mother's death through twice-weekly visits to a therapist—until he gave up his practice, informing me in parting that he just couldn't take all the sad stories he was having to listen to every day, mine included. I believe he left London and joined a commune in the wilds of Scotland, which seemed like a good idea.

TOWN HALL
CASTLE CIRCUS, TORQUAY.
TORBAY MANAGEMENTS PRESENTS A
SUMMER SPECTACULAR
STARRING THE DEDICATED FOLLOWERS OF FASHION
THE KINKS
LATEST No. 1 HIT "SUNNY AFTERNOON"
THE TRAVELLERS ★ THE LAST-TIK-BAND
THE PACKAGE DEAL ★ THE REACTION
PLUS FABULOUS MOD FASHION PARADE
TUESDAY 16TH AUG.
8-1 A.M. LATE LICENSED BAR TILL 12.30 A.M. TICKETS 10/-
Promoted by L.M.D. ENTERTAINMENTS LTD.
COMING SATURDAY 20th AUG.
THE WHO
Town Hall Torquay
EXPLOSION '67
THE
CREAM
Tuesday 15 August
Late Licensed Bar till 12.30 am
Admit ONE 10/6
8 pm — 1 am
Town Hall Torquay
SUMMER SPECTACULAR
★ THE KINKS ★
PLUS FOUR TOP SUPPORTING GROUPS
Tuesday 16th Aug. 1966
Fully Late Licensed Bar and Buffet
Admit ONE 10/-
8 pm — 1 am
TOWN HALL TORQUAY
Fabulous
RECORDING Stars
the
WHO
+ Supporting Band
SAT. 17th JULY
Advance Tickets from
Victor Gifts VICTORIA PARADE
(HARBOUR SIDE)
TOWN HALL
TORQUAY
FRIDAY, 26TH JULY
JOHN SMITH PRESENTS
THE FABULOUS
★ FLEETWOOD MAC ★
– FEATURING –
PETER GREEN
– PLUS –
DUSTER BENNETT
(ONE MAN BLUES BAND)
Also SUPPORTING GROUP
TICKETS 8/6 in advance from:
A. E. ORME, 5D FLEET STREET, TORQUAY.
AND USUAL AGENTS.
FRIDAY, 9TH AUG. – JOHN MAYALL

There's a funny little cat / With a tummy nice and fat. /
He's won picture fame... / Felix is his name.

"FELIX KEPT ON WALKING"
BY ED. E. BRYANT (LYRICS) AND HUBERT W. DAVID (MUSIC)

Images of Felix the Cat (the first animated film star), Mickey Mouse, and Popeye might well be my earliest memories. My brother and I would climb up a rickety wooden ladder to the dusty, low-ceilinged attic where my father readied the projector he had brought back from Germany at the end of the war. Afraid of heights, I dreaded the climb, but what I experienced there in the dark helped me overcome my fear. The machinery would whir, the light would flicker, and Felix or Popeye would come to life. Reels of cartoons could be rented from our local post office and came with a film splicer, which was just as well, as our projector would snap the film and leave it with more taped-over breaks than clean frames. My favorites, such as *Felix the Cat at the North Pole* or Mickey's debut film, *Steamboat Willie,* were from the 1920s, but some things never get old.

Like many in the UK, my father had bought our first black-and-white TV set to watch the Queen's coronation in 1953. Until he began to spend all his time at work, in the evenings and on weekends we would watch films together, American noir with such great titles as *The Asphalt Jungle*, *Kiss of Death*, *On Dangerous Ground*, *They Live by Night*, or, my favorite of them all, *In a Lonely Place*. But as time went on, my brother and I were left to our own devices.

There were then five cinemas within walking distance of Torquay town center, including the Empire, the Odeon, the Colony Cinema (the first in town to be equipped with CinemaScope, when it was still known as the Electric Theatre), and the Tudor (now a family-run museum filled with antiques). This meant I always had a wide range of films to choose from. Options on any given weekend could include the latest *Carry On* film (in which I had little interest), Anthony Mann's *The Fall of the Roman Empire*, Peter Sellers in *I'm All Right Jack, Zulu* starring Michael Caine, Stanley Kubrick's *Dr. Strangelove* (it's hard to put into words the effect that film had on me at the time), and even an occasional import from Italy or France. On our first date, a girlfriend asked to see *The Sound of Music* and proceeded to cry through almost the entire film. The power of film?

Beyond its proper cinemas Torquay was also briefly home to a film club that showed films on a portable 16 mm projector in the beautiful Art Deco showrooms of the Gas Board on Torquay's high street. The first films I remember seeing there? Jean-Luc Godard's dystopian *Alphaville*, Chris Marker's post-apocalypse *La Jetée*, and Peter Watkins's *The War Game*, which staged the effects of a nuclear explosion over London in horrifying detail. Using grainy black-and-white images captured by handheld cameras, *The War Game* exposed the sheer pointlessness of the British government's planning in case of nuclear attack. Two women who were sitting in the front row of the mock-up cinema fainted when the bomb exploded over the East End. Reactions such as theirs pressured the BBC to ban the film for the next twenty-five years.

Harrowing as *The War Game* was, I considered myself lucky to have seen it. I had watched Sergei Eisenstein's agitprop masterpiece *Battleship Potemkin* by then, with its famous montage scene of the massacre of civilians on the Odessa Steps, but found *The War Game* even more remarkable in both its content and its filmmaking. Not every film had to be a fairy tale or beautiful to look at. It could also be angry; the camera could shake, and the image could be grainy. In 1967, Watkins's film won the Academy Award for best documentary, which always struck me as curious. The whole film was made with nonactors and staged as if a report on events that were real, but was it a documentary? Either way, there's no other film quite like it today. *Perhaps we really have learned how to love the bomb?*

My bleak view of life was not helped by the news that dominated the '60s, but despite my occasionally excessive drinking and all the days and nights spent fishing rather than in study, I did well at school. I even topped the religious studies class without attending a single lesson. I asked that we study both Buddhism and Karl Marx alongside the Bible and was sent to stand in the corridor for my sins. When it came time to join the outside world, I didn't have the slightest clue what I would do. My headmaster and a career guidance counselor suggested I seek employment in a bank.

Whether I was inspired by my father's stories of foreign lands or a need to leave some bitter memories behind, I became desperate to leave home. I loved film, but film was not a career choice. It was simply something that *other* people did.

Every child is an artist.
The problem is how to remain an artist once he grows up.

ATTRIBUTED TO PABLO PICASSO

I spent many of my school hours painting pictures of things I had observed: a lonely woman waiting on a station platform with a child in her arms, an elderly couple in a park shelter, or simply the waves crashing on a beach. My art teacher, George Roper, was nicknamed "Stringer" for the way he would twist a noncompliant pupil's hair. (The French teacher was called "Hitler" for similar reasons. French was the only exam I failed, and I had the bruises to prove it.) Mr. Roper was not only a brilliant watercolorist but the only person who impressed on me that life was short, and I should be sure to find what I wanted to do with it.

More to avoid a job at the bank or return to the building site than anything else, I decided to apply for a place at a university or an art college. But by the time I dragged myself away from fishing for long enough to decide where to apply, it was too late for a university place. Art college—which, as the name suggests, was entirely devoted to painting, sculpture, pottery, printmaking, and graphic design—was my only option. After a rejection from my first-choice school for, somehow, being "academically too well qualified," my father helped me find one that was still open to applications: Bath Academy of Art. For the first year of study, a prediploma year, I would have to pay my own way, but I would be able to obtain a grant if I continued on to the three-year diploma course. The paintings I had done at school under the guidance of Mr. Roper secured me a place, and my father agreed to an advance on the wages he would pay me for future work I would do on one of his building sites. He still fantasized I would come to my senses, get this "art thing" out of my system, and straighten out for good.

Let me ask you something, what is not art?

ATTRIBUTED TO EDGAR DEGAS

Bath Academy, then based in Corsham, Wiltshire, was very much an "art" college. The first winter I experienced there in 1968 was very cold and it snowed heavily. But that didn't deter one student in the fine arts department from arranging his bed on the lawn outside the administration building and lying down on it naked to become just another snowdrift. It might have been his form of expression, but maybe I was in the right department after all. It was in the graphic design department where I first discovered I had a skill for composing a photograph and, more important, that this gave me creative satisfaction. Both things are related. *Why would you develop a skill if you found no satisfaction from exercising that skill?* There were a number of inspirational tutors who found their way to the college, such as the painter Michael Craig-Martin, the concrete poet John Furnival, and printmaker Jack Shirreff, but it was through the photographer Roger Mayne that I discovered my pleasure in taking pictures.

If you can't feel what you're looking at, then you're never going to get others to feel anything when they look at your pictures.

DON McCULLIN

But photography was not a recognized discipline at Bath Academy of Art—and, of course, I was not Roger Mayne. Most people would have seen Roger's historic documentary-style photography of London's Southam Street, if nowhere else, on the cover of a Morrissey single or Colin MacInnes's novel *Absolute Beginners*. But great photographer that he was, even he needed the income from a teaching position to survive (Roger would say he couldn't teach anyone *how* to take a photograph). It was a fantasy that I could make a living with the kind of photography that interested me. I was drawn to photojournalism rather than the world of advertising and graphic design. I had no interest in helping to sell vacuum cleaners or dishwashers. Between classes, I stole off with the darkroom key to have a copy made at the local hardware store. I wanted to work on my own projects at night, without the distraction that comes from a room full of students. During the day, I would hitchhike to Bristol and spend hours photographing the city's backstreets, or to Bournemouth, where I'd sleep on the beach to shoot yesterday's abandoned deckchairs silhouetted against the sunrise. I photographed Corsham's stately buildings and avenues of trees at night, using lengthy exposures and the multiple flashes of a borrowed battery-powered flash unit. On nights I was not taking photos or watching the moon landings on the common-room TV, I was often working in the darkroom.

The presence of an art college in Corsham inspired the opening of a small independent cinema, which would show both contemporary films and some of the major classics by directors such as Jean-Luc Godard, Ingmar Bergman, Akira Kurosawa, and Francois Truffaut. But it was the more angry and visceral films, such as Jean-Pierre Melville's masterpiece *Army of Shadows* or Sam Peckinpah's *The Wild Bunch*, that left me in awe of what could be achieved by a master of the craft. Westerns had begun to change dramatically in the 1960s, and though I loved Sergio Leone's *The Good, the Bad and the Ugly* and *Once Upon a Time in the West*, it was *The Wild Bunch*, set in a violent, rapidly changing American West before World War I, that felt especially relevant to the world of Vietnam and the Manson murders. As Peckinpah was to say of John Huston, he "tried not only to tell a story but to make some kind of statement." My father loved Westerns, especially any that starred either Joel McCrea or Randolph Scott, so *Ride the High Country* (also called *Guns in the*

Afternoon) was a favorite of his. I'd also seen the much-underrated *Major Dundee* in the cinema. But it wasn't until I was at college that I connected these three films to the singular vision of one director.

As graduation approached, few options for my future presented themselves. I'd discovered a love for still photography and had begun to consider pursuing documentary filmmaking as a natural extension of that work. But that seemed like a daydream. There was the rumor of an old 16 mm film camera somewhere deep inside the college vaults, but I had failed in my attempts to even set my eyes on it. After all, I was at an art school, and neither film nor photography were art. Which is probably why, to this day, I have a problem with the word "art."

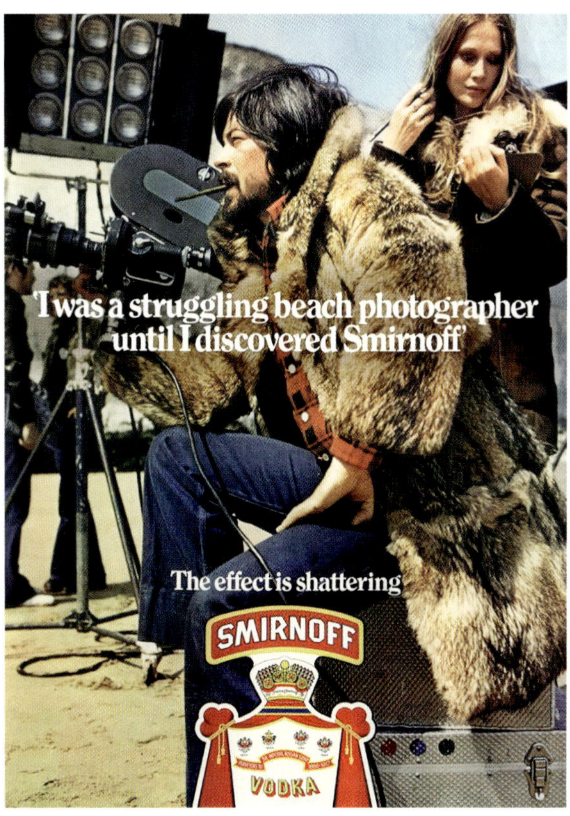

My belief in myself was diminished even further when I went in search of a part-time summer job as an alternative to my father's building site. I applied to be a beach photographer on the Torquay seafront, taking Polaroid pictures for tourists enjoying their summer holidays. Shortly after I was rejected for that job, an advertisement for Smirnoff vodka appeared on billboards across the country. It showed a young man, obviously a film director, beside a movie camera. He was smoking a cigar and accompanied by a beautiful girl holding a clipboard. A caption read, "I was a struggling beach photographer until I discovered Smirnoff." The picture seemed to say it all. I was not even that struggling beach photographer.

Bath Academy's rather imposing principal, Rosemary Ellis, offered little hope when we met to discuss my future. I confessed to her that I had no idea what I would be doing in the real world, but I knew it would in no way involve a bank or graphic design. She asked me why I had attended art college in the first place if not to pursue a career in art and design. I had no answer.

> *Whoever wants to know something about me…*
> *they should look attentively at my pictures*
> *and there seek to recognize what I am and what I want.*
>
> **GUSTAV KLIMT**

It was only by chance that a fellow student read of an exciting opportunity. The National Film School, a unique government-sponsored institution, now known as the National Film and Television School, was set to open in Beaconsfield, to the north of London. Its first class would consist of twenty-five students seeking training for the film industry. It seemed like a pretty good idea, but with only twenty-five places available I did not have high expectations. In truth, loving film was probably not the only reason for me to apply to the NFS, as my fear of a nine-to-five job still haunted me.

What had I to lose?

2

A SECOND CHANCE

Filmic: Relating to or characteristic of motion pictures

DICTIONARY.COM DEFINITION

After getting my rejection letter in the summer of 1971, I called for an appointment with the head of the film school, Colin Young, and took the train to London to ask him why. I was so nervous. I was shaking by the time I walked into our meeting. All I remember was having a strange discussion with Colin as to what makes an image "filmic." He pointed to a framed photograph of a dray horse on the wall behind his desk: "That is filmic!" The image was taken with a long exposure so the horse and the cart it was pulling were blurred while the background was sharp. *It's out of focus! How is that filmic?* I expected I had blown my chance but, as I left, I was met by Tony Gurrin, who would become head of the school's sound department. He assured me if I applied again next year, I would be offered a place. I caught the train back to Corsham with a little more hope while trying, without success, to decipher what Colin had said. To this day I cannot define "filmic."

But what to do for a year?

Again, I was called to the office of Rosemary Ellis, this time not to receive a reprimand for wasting my place at her college, but to suggest a job as a photographer. An arts center in North Devon, run by her friend John Lane, wanted to create a contemporary photographic record of the area and of a way of life that had changed little since the end of the war but was now rapidly catching up with the outside world. Or, more correctly, the outside world had begun rapidly taking over North Devon in the shape of tourism and holiday homes.

I remain immensely grateful to Rosemary for guiding me to the Beaford Arts Centre. I was not the ideal person to take on the project, which needed someone far more self-confident and outgoing than me. But I did my best, and in hindsight, my initial rejection by the National Film School was a blessing in disguise. The year I spent wandering the country lanes of North Devon offered me the perfect space in which to gather my thoughts and to find my eye, which is a pretentious way of saying to record images that reflected the world I was looking at in the way that I saw it. I discovered how pictures could tell a story and that it was the stories that drew me to create pictures.

As Tony Gurrin had assured me, my second application to the National Film School, which included a script I had written about a homeless woman in Torquay as well as photographs from North Devon, was accepted. But the school—a campus built around Beaconsfield Studios, a place whose glory days were well behind it by 1972—was hardly what I expected. The studio had been in operation since the silent era and once served as home to the Crown Film Unit, which began making government-sponsored documentaries during World War II. It continued in that role until the newly elected Conservative government shuttered the unit in 1952. But, despite the studio's prestigious history and its newfound purpose, it was in a dilapidated state when I arrived. I felt lucky not to have been accepted as one of the National Film School's first twenty-five students.

If I knew how to take a good photograph,
I'd do it every time.

ROBERT DOISNEAU

Though the school hadn't really been ready to open, its founding director, Colin Young, had seized the moment, while there was a Labour government backing the project. Born in Glasgow, Colin had served as head of UCLA's School of Theater, Film and Television beginning in the mid-'60s, when its students included Francis Ford Coppola, Paul Schrader, Haskell Wexler, and other future luminaries. Through the NFS he hoped to provide British filmmakers with similar educational opportunities.

I doubt even Colin's most dedicated students at UCLA spent as much time in the studio as some of my film school classmates and I did, though this was at first more by necessity than by choice. My tuition fees were again paid by my local council, and I had a little spending money left from my year as a photographer. Even though I decided to live near the studio rather than in London, I still could not pay Beaconsfield rent. Some fellow students found themselves in a similar bind. Happily, there were some unused offices on the studio lot. Why not sleep on their floors?

It was the perfect solution, if an unsanitary one, at least at first. Within a short time, the school supplied us with beds and bedding and fixed up the bathroom facilities. The NFS also supplied lunch on weekdays, so I would need only to account for supper, which usually consisted of a pint and a pie at the local pub, or a fish-and-chip takeaway. On weekends, while most every other student left for London or home, I stuck around.

Despite Beaconsfield Studio's ramshackle condition, the school had, by its second year, been supplied with most of the necessities of filmmaking. There was an array of camera and lighting equipment. The stages were basic and probably not up to today's strict safety codes, but they worked. We were not instructed in how to use all the equipment, as the course—or what course there was—was not so technically oriented. We made our first short films using 16 mm cameras, taking turns at directing, shooting, recording sound, and other tasks, learning as we went. Colin very much believed in leaving students to their own devices. Once I became familiar with how the equipment operated, I grew to like the anarchic nature of the school.

Which isn't to say we learned everything on our own. One of my most valuable lessons came from Charles Lagus, though I didn't fully realize it at the time. A cameraman who'd worked on the '60s police procedural *Z Cars*, Lagus charged us with lighting a set that represented a backstage dressing room with multiple makeup mirrors, each of which was outlined by the familiar pattern of bare light bulbs. He left after setting the exercise up, asking Charles Stewart, famous for his work with Ken Loach and on the documentary series *World in Action*, to take over during his absence. I had decided that the lighting was quite fine as it was, but Stewart suggested that we were not working on a documentary. On a feature I would have to light the scene.

So, light it I did. I wasn't unhappy with what I had done, but it all felt a little unnecessary. Then Lagus returned. "That's nice, but it looked pretty good to me with just the natural light coming from the practical bulbs," he said, "Just because you can light the shot doesn't mean you should, or you must." It was amusing that the documentary veteran expected narrative films to have an obviously artificial look. But Lagus's advice was probably the most important lesson I learned while at the National Film School.

Over the length of the course, we were each allowed a large sum of money—our training was said to cost the same as for a jet pilot—to invest in our own productions or contribute to the productions of our fellow students. Most students used the opportunity to make a film that would gain them employment in the outside world, a showreel if you like, and because of that they would look for the best craftspeople to work with them on their projects. As I had no experience, I could not expect to be one of the chosen few, so I decided I would make my own.

I shot my first effort, a short documentary about the homeless veterans who'd gather at the Salvation Army in London's Waterloo neighborhood, on Super 8. For the soundtrack, I had my girlfriend at the time sing the World War I standard "When This Lousy War Is Over." My second film was a 16 mm black-and-white short that I directed with the same girlfriend playing an actress who

was readying herself to go onstage and having a nervous breakdown, an interesting exercise as she was an actress herself.

For a third project I returned to the Devon countryside to film a documentary about the Tiverton Stag Hunt, which I called *A Farmer's Hunt*. Stag hunting, like all hunting with hounds, had become controversial by the early 1970s. It's a topic about which I have mixed feelings. Intellectually, I'm against it. But I've also seen the important role such hunts have played in rural society, uniting the community in a big event. As with my photographs, I wanted to document a tradition before it disappeared.

Film is a reflection of the world we live in, not an escape from it.

SAM PECKINPAH

Still waiting for other students to ask for my "expertise," I decided to try my hand at directing my own fictional story. I had often imagined what all those old people who retire to the seaside would talk about all day, so I wrote some Pinteresque dialogue for two women as they sat together on a bench facing the beach. I hired two well-known London theater actresses to play the parts, and a friend agreed to record sound. Very early one morning my friend and I drove to the seaside in a van with the two actresses we had arranged to meet in the West End. It was soon obvious that my "cast" felt they were slumming it (as they most certainly were) and didn't care too much for the notes from their director. But I persevered. After a couple of takes in which all I could hear was "acting," I suggested they just read the lines. "Imagine you are reading from the telephone directory." The result was so deadpan it was perfect, exactly what I had in mind. It's also probably why this was my last directing gig!

With this short drama I had now photographed four very different films. My camerawork on these led directing students to hire me as their cinematographer and, by the time I finally left film school in 1976, I'd shot fifteen films. These varied considerably in content and tone and included everything from a 35 mm comedy short shot in Switzerland, to a poetic exploration of the work of the painter Paolo Uccello, to a documentary about the development of a park in the East End of London. I even shot a gangster film, inspired by Jean-Pierre Melville's *Le cercle rouge* and *Le deuxième souffle*, though our film paled in comparison.

I left in 1975 well prepared for a job in the film business. *But what job? And where?* One bit of advice I received took me aback. A governor of the school suggested I seek work as a production assistant in Plymouth, at the local television station closest to Torquay. With luck and hard work, he suggested, I might make my way up to camera operator in seven or eight years. Whether this was a serious suggestion or a deliberate attempt to rile me up I have no idea, but within a decade I'd worked as a cinematographer on a film the governor in question produced. Whether it was intentionally motivational or not, to this day I am indebted to David Puttnam for giving me such uninspiring advice. Instead of Plymouth I decided to try my luck in London.

I was and still am not someone comfortable among strangers, but having no money can be a tremendous source of motivation. During one of my attempts to scare up work, I stumbled on an opportunity that was far bigger than I expected. Having knocked on a door unannounced, I was ushered into the offices of one of the independent production companies that then peppered Soho, servicing industrial documentaries and what were once called "pop promos," later referred to as "music videos." Its director, Chris Boger, agreed to watch a tape of my work at that very moment. This was unusual. He turned to me after what felt like half an hour of silence. "I think your work's great, but I'm not doing any pop promos at the moment." I began to wonder if I'd wasted my time. But, at least, I could reflect on overcoming my nerves to get this far. As I rose to leave, Chris added, "I'm doing my first feature film."

"Well, let me shoot that," I said, seizing the moment. Thanks to some recent work I'd done on a corporate documentary, I had a union ticket (much to the despair of the union hierarchy, whose president had made an agreement with the National Film School—if you get a job you get a ticket), a necessary requirement to join a professional production, even a low-budget one such as this. After taking a moment to consider what I had said, Chris offered me the job right there and then. I was twenty-seven, and it seemed too good to be true!

It was only after I'd accepted the job that I learned what the project was. *Cruel Passion* was what might be called soft porn, though its literary source material, Marquis de Sade's 1791 novel *Justine*, set it apart from *Confessions of a Window Cleaner* or the *Carry On* series. I left the meeting elated at the opportunity and confident in my ability to pull it off but also wondering what I'd gotten myself into. Luckily for me, the start date was extremely close, giving me little time to worry, especially once Chris and I began scouting out locations, assembling a team, and planning what we would shoot and where. In seemingly no time, I found myself in my car and on my way to the first day of shooting.

Both then and now, I aim to arrive on set before the general crew call, to allow myself some quiet time to prepare myself mentally for the challenges ahead. I see it as disrespectful of the cast and crew to arrive late and to arrive unprepared. (Later in my career, I worked with a director who was habitually late to set and often unaware of the scenes we would be scheduled to shoot. After the film turned out well, which was a testament to the cast and crew that supported him, he called me to talk about his next project. Having arranged to meet for coffee, he arrived more than forty-five minutes late. The first thing he asked me: Could I work faster?)

For our first day on *Cruel Passion*, a one-room cottage had been constructed among the trees on the backlot at Bray Studios, where many Hammer Film productions had been shot in previous decades. I had not seen the set before that day, so I was using my early arrival to consider what I'd need to light it. Two other crew members, many years older than me, arrived a few moments later. They introduced themselves to each other as the first assistant director and the standby set carpenter. Neither took notice of me. Then they began to talk about the ex–film school student who had been hired by the director and would obviously be gone within a week. He was not only lighting the picture but also operating the camera. What was the industry coming to? If my body hadn't been frozen in fear I would have surely gone home.

The first AD turned to me, and only then did he ask who I was. I blurted out that I was the ex–film school student. Then I turned to the carpenter to ask that he rig a spreader between the walls of the set and as close as possible to the ceiling. I required this beam to hold a maximum of two small open-face lamps, so there was no need for anything substantial. Turning back to the first AD, I requested he send a runner to the local pharmacy to get me some aspirin. When the carpenter and the first AD left, still well before the crew call time, I looked around for a secluded place in which to throw up.

The rest of the first day went fairly well, although I found I had good cause to be nervous—just not for the reasons I'd anticipated. Later in the schedule I almost burnt to a cinder while filming a graveyard dream sequence. An overzealous effects supervisor loaded a coffin with plastic bags filled with gasoline which, had they all ignited, would have blown away anyone standing within fifty feet of the grave. As it was, my camera crew and I were briefly engulfed in a dramatic fireball, which, luckily for production, we captured on film. It was after episodes like that the more hardened, long-time film workers began to accept me, if not respect me.

I could not have known it at the time, but my experience of working with few resources at the National Film School prepared me for some of the other challenges of *Cruel Passion*. Much of the film took place in candlelit spaces, so I needed to create the effect of flickering flames. While there are now many reflective materials made expressly for film use, they didn't exist in the 1970s. Instead, I used thermal blankets, the kind that you use if you're going on an expedition. Crinkling them as I bounced light off their reflective surfaces created a convincing firelight effect. With limited resources, I had to ask myself, "How can I do this cheaply and with something I could find at a hardware store or a haberdashery?" Even now, working with much bigger budgets, I find that's often still the best solution.

Released in some parts of the world as *The Marquis de Sade's Justine* or simply *Justine*, *Cruel Passion* starred Koo Stark, who would later become a tabloid fixture thanks to her relationship with Prince Andrew, and later still a respected photographer. On one memorable day, an October day and as cold as hell, Koo was required to fall seminude into a lake as her character attempted an escape from what were in reality the director's Doberman pinschers. Getting the shot required me to film her while sitting alone in a rowboat. By the time we were done, Koo was all but a block of ice. I had to fish her out before she was. Like the rest of us, maybe even more than the rest of us, she experienced the discomforts of low-budget filmmaking firsthand.

When posters for *Cruel Passion* began to appear in London, I found myself hoping my name wasn't on them. But in truth, I would have still taken the job. It's not a film I would do now, but back then, I really needed a break. Within a few months of leaving the National Film School, I'd gotten a chance to work as a professional. I had no idea at the time, however, it would be the last narrative feature I'd work on for the next six years.

AROUND THE WORLD

A tourist with a typewriter.

CHARLIE MEADOWS, IN *BARTON FINK*

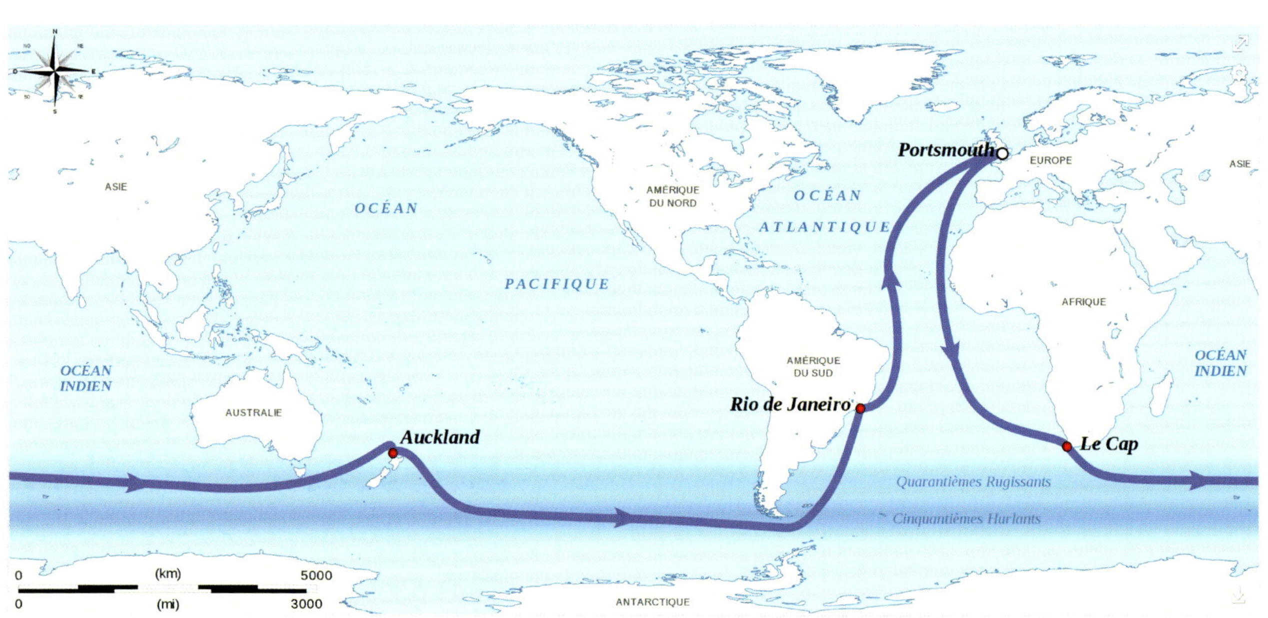

Moving into documentaries wasn't part of any grand design for my career, but it undoubtedly helped that I had a passion for them. My passion and that the UK feature film industry in the 1970s (*Cruel Passion* notwithstanding) remained something of a closed shop to anyone who had not worked their way up through the grades. Documentary filmmaking, on the other hand, was another story. British documentaries came into their own in the 1960s and '70s, thanks to groundbreaking shows such as the investigative news program *World in Action*, the globetrotting cultural anthropology series *Disappearing World*, and a boom in films about social issues. What's more, their producers were more open to working with recent film school grads with relatively short résumés—and even smaller salaries.

While my focus had been on still photography, I aspired to become a photojournalist. Film school didn't squelch that ambition so much as transfer it from a still frame to a moving image, thanks in large part to Colin Young's emphasis on documentary filmmaking. I admired the work of filmmakers like Albert and David Maysles and D. A. Pennebaker, whose use of lighter cameras and synchronized sound popularized the cinema verité movement in the 1960s. I especially loved the long observational films of Frederick Wiseman and those of French director Jean Rouch. His 1961 documentary, *Chronicle of a Summer*, opens with a discussion between Rouch, codirector Edgar Morin (who coined the term "cinema verité"), and fellow filmmaker and Holocaust survivor Marceline Loridan-Ivens about whether it was possible for subjects to be themselves on camera if they knew they were being filmed. I'd think about that scene a lot during the next few years.

My first job on leaving the film school had been with another film school veteran, director Ben Lewin, and sound recordist Eddie Tise (both destined for long film careers) on *Welcome to Britain*. It was a look at the British immigration system shot verité style, centering around the work of Reuben "Mr. Fixit" Davis, who would arrange a sweatshop job in the garment district of London, as well as a visa through a fake marriage, for immigrants from Pakistan and elsewhere.

Seeing is different than being told.

AFRICAN PROVERB

My second assignment would involve covering a different sort of confrontation. A filmmaker and activist, Antonia Caccia, conceived *Chimurenga—The War in Zimbabwe* as a firsthand look at the Rhodesian Bush War, a years-long struggle for control of the country now known as Zimbabwe. As with her previous film, *Last Grave at Dimbaza*, the first to document apartheid in South Africa, Antonia received funding from the African National Congress, the chief opponent of South Africa's government. That film made her persona non grata in both Rhodesia and South Africa, but she had a workaround: pair a two-person film crew with a journalist who would work under the cover of shooting a wildlife documentary.

It briefly looked like the film would fall apart. Sound recordist Diana Ruston and I set off to meet with a journalist in the Rhodesian capital of Salisbury (now Harare) and create a plan together. Nothing in film school prepared me to be a covert operative but, when our initial contact was thrown out of the country, Diana and I were left stranded in the unfamiliar capital city of a country in the grip of a civil war, with nothing but sketchy credentials as cover.

Enter Bruce Palling. Now a widely respected food writer, Bruce was familiar with dangerous locales, having spent time covering the Vietnam War. Somehow, the ANC connected us and we arranged to meet at a café in the city. We found Bruce, sitting at a table among a group of war correspondents discussing their work. *The Bush War was winding down. There would be a settlement soon. The story was getting stale. Where would each of them go for their next front page?* Lebanon seemed the favorite.

Why were we, two wildlife filmmakers, sitting in full view of the street with this group of cynical war correspondents? Wouldn't it appear suspicious? It seemed a crazy way to start but, having met up with Bruce, we discussed our options. Our permits allowed us to film in game parks and animal reserves in the north and west of Rhodesia, but all Bruce's acquaintances resided elsewhere. It would have to do.

First, we drove our bright yellow rental car (inconspicuous in its conspicuousness) to Fort Victoria (now called Masvingo) to film the Great Zimbabwe National Monument, the ruins of a Bantu city dating from the eleventh century. Despite its well-documented history, the ardent white supremacist prime minister Ian Smith had deemed Great Zimbabwe to have been built by the Arabs rather than by indigenous Africans. The government's racism went so deep it wanted to rewrite history to suit its vision of the world. Next, we traveled toward the city of Bulawayo, stopping on the way at a small motel for the night.

We ordered a meal at the bar and got talking with the owner of the place, who was a longtime resident of the country. He left us as we sat down to eat and only reappeared as we were about to turn in for the night. Transformed from a chatty barman to a soldier in uniform, albeit a rather sloppy one, he placed his high-powered rifle behind the bar and asked if we wanted a drink, seemingly eager to tell anyone who might listen what he had been up to. As he described it, it had been a successful night's work. He and some friends had been in the bush hunting Kaffirs, their name for the ZANU nationalists, as if it were just another day at the office. We quickly left the next morning for Bulawayo, where our interview subjects included a girl who could only watch as the security forces raided her family home; swinging her cat around their heads, they beat the poor animal to a pulp against the wall.

We headed east, in the opposite direction to the game parks we were supposed to be filming. The white European settlers typically traveled in armed convoys, but we felt this would draw attention toward us. And, besides, wouldn't a convoy be a more substantial target for a band of armed guerrillas than a vehicle traveling alone, however boldly colored? As we drove, Bruce suggested the three of us had to make some tough choices. Should we drive as fast as possible in expectation of an armed attack? (Yes!) Should we slow down on dirt roads that might contain IEDs? (There was no consensus on this one!) And what about when a dirt road split into multiple choices? The Vietcong, Bruce told us, would place a stick at a fork in the road to tell any of their number which direction was safe. *Were Joshua Nkomo's ZAPU or Robert Mugabe's ZANU freedom fighters using the same tactics? If we found a stick, would we even be able to tell which direction it indicated? Or was it simply a stick?*

Somehow, close to the border with Mozambique, we reached a mission station hospital run by a doctor whom Bruce had met in Vietnam. An elderly farmer was sitting on his sickbed, in the midst of telling us how he had been abused by government forces, when he suddenly stood up and gestured toward the window. "You should be filming them!" he cried. Outside, among the trees, we saw dozens of Rhodesian soldiers, many wearing ski masks and in camouflage, marching toward Mozambique both armed and ready for combat. We then heard planes passing overhead and flying east. We'd arrived on the day Rhodesian troops engaged in their first major raid on ZANU training camps on the other side of the border. We were miles from where we were supposed to be, so to avoid endangering the mission station staff or their patients had we been discovered, we left as quietly as we could. We had been lucky up to now, but it wouldn't last.

While staying for a night on a farm owned by another of Bruce's more liberal friends, but temporarily managed by an Afrikaner, we woke to the sound of soldiers surrounding the farmhouse. The manager had decided to inform the local authorities that he suspected the so-called wildlife photographers staying with him were not who they claimed to be. We were under arrest for being in a restricted area and told to follow the army convoy back to its base in Chipinga, where we faced the guardhouse.

Fortunately, none of the troops joined us in our now-well-traveled yellow rental car and, fearing the soldiers would impound our footage and target our interview subjects, we gathered our sound tapes and film reels, intending to bury them somewhere, anywhere, alongside the road. When our military escort disappeared behind a sharp bend, we seized the opportunity. I dumped our material inside a storm drain and quickly covered it with dried grass before scurrying back to the car. We hit the accelerator and rounded the bend to fall in line behind our captors. Thankfully, they seemed none the wiser.

To our surprise, we weren't jailed but given comfortable accommodation and invited by the soldiers to join them for drinks at the bar. They were all young and friendly, and especially so to Diana. They described the opportunities that had brought each of them to Rhodesia, in their minds a country and a people that the world misunderstood and that they were now fighting to protect. It was as if they were trying to win us over to their side. One young man had been in Rhodesia for only a matter of months. In Liverpool he'd been an unemployed laborer on the dole, or "signwriting for the Queen," as it was ironically known among those without work. Now he was a lieutenant in the Rhodesian army, speaking derisively of what he called "the old country."

Like the others, he had only unkind words for all that he'd left behind. England was going down the drain thanks to James Callaghan, socialism, and too many immigrants. They spewed an all-too-familiar fantasy, but the beer was cold and welcome, and we did our best to keep our opinions to ourselves. Maintaining our cover story, Diana stressed that the nature film we were shooting was a lucky break—and maybe our only chance of employment in a brutal industry (a lie that at least had a kernel of truth to it, and Diana was very convincing). After some questioning the next day, we were given instructions to report to the home affairs department in Salisbury.

We didn't head there directly, however, stopping first to retrieve our footage and recordings, which were miraculously still hidden in the storm drain. But we needed to find a way to get them safely out of the country. As we made our way to the capital, via the much longer but safer route through Bulawayo, I recalled seeing a business under Indian ownership on the main shopping street that specialized in beautiful carpets from Pakistan and Afghanistan. Suspecting its owners might have little sympathy for Ian Smith and Rhodesia's white nationalist government, I delicately approached them, expressing interest in their wares and buying a small carpet to boot. Could they send the carpet to the UK, I asked, so I did not have to hand-carry it, and maybe I could add something more personal to the package? The two shopkeepers, cautiously friendly, agreed. Whether they knew the "more personal" item was film footage I couldn't tell, but I suspect they did. It was just a simple cardboard box, but I had forgotten to remove a label on the outside that read "KODAK."

Either way, the package arrived safely in London not many days later. Told to leave the country but not told *how* to leave, Diana and I boarded a train for Botswana. Our plan was to meet up with our director, Antonia Caccia, in the capital city of Gaborone and continue filming in the refugee camps along the border. In the middle of the night our train crossed into Botswana, leaving us to watch the Rhodesian border post recede into the darkness behind us. It was engulfed in flames.

We are tied to the ocean.
And when we go back to the sea—whether it is to sail or to watch it—
we are going back from whence we came.

JOHN F. KENNEDY

Back in London, in the autumn of 1976, I had the good fortune to meet Chris Menges, a cinematographer then best known for his work on the early Ken Loach classic, *Kes*. I was eager for any advice he could give me but, after I screened some of my work for him, he only asked how many more there were like me leaving the National Film School. Chris had worked as a freelance documentary cameraman for producer Charles Denton at Associated Television, and I suspect it was on his recommendation that I received a call from Denton asking me if I could take a meeting about a boating project. At the time, I assumed it would be a film about Donald Crowhurst, a sailor who'd apparently taken his own life during the first single-handed yacht race around the globe, having fabricated logs of a journey to within sight of the winner's line that he could not live up to. Crowhurst, who never ventured out of the Atlantic Ocean, had sailed his yacht from Teignmouth (hence his boat's name, *Teignmouth Electron*) on October 31, 1968. His ill-fated adventure had been big news in the South Devon seaside town, and I had followed the story closely.

However, it was not Crowhurst that Denton wanted to make a documentary about but John Ridgway, who'd gained fame in 1966 by rowing across the Atlantic with his partner Chay Blyth. Ridgway had since founded the John Ridgway School of Adventure, which remains in operation in the Scottish Highlands, and planned to compete in the second Whitbread Round the World Race, now known as the Ocean Race. It was Denton's hope to produce a film about the stress on people working in extreme conditions by embedding a two-person film crew with John on his yacht.

Around the World with Ridgway was an opportunity I could not pass up, even if getting the job required lying about my sailing expertise. Well, not so much lying as waffling around the producers' questions. I told them I came from Torquay, had grown up around boats, and was well qualified for the job. Then I let them draw their own conclusions. In truth, my sailing experience stretched no further than time spent on my father's dinghy (which invariably failed to get off its mooring or soon capsized when it did). Also, I could not swim. Nonetheless, they believed me. And why shouldn't they? I was from Devon, birthplace of John Hawkins, Walter Raleigh, and Sir Francis Drake, the first ever Englishman to circumnavigate the globe. When I joined Ridgway at his school it became obvious how little I knew, but by then it was too late. I had the job.

To keep it I had to learn the ropes, literally. After some preparation, I joined John and the rest of his crew on a test sail from Cape Wrath on Scotland's northern coast to the north of Ireland and toward Madeira. Still a work in progress, John's boat wasn't prepared for the hurricane-force winds we encountered. (Not as well funded as some of the other fourteen captains, John had to change the name of his boat from *English Rose VI* to *Debenhams*, the name of the now-defunct department store sponsoring him.) After taking down all but a small staysail to keep the boat from rolling, we went below to wait out the storm. Everybody was seasick. Everybody. We began passing around a bucket. Though ill myself, I started filming, not wanting to let such a moment pass. Despite my obvious inexperience, "Anybody who can film while being sick," John told me as he retched, "is all right by me."

Noel Smart, a staff cameraman at ATV who had dearly wanted my role, joined me as a sound recordist after my original partner had to drop out on doctor's orders because of his extreme seasickness. Noel was an experienced yachtsman, which was a good qualification, but he did have to learn how to work a Nagra tape recorder. Space was at a premium aboard John's fifty-seven-foot ketch, and everyone—other than the skipper and his wife, Marie Christine, who came along for the ride—had to pull their weight on watch. For Noel and me, every day of the nine months we spent preparing for and shooting *Around the World with Ridgway* required us to work as both filmmakers and crew members. Both these tasks could be exhilarating but were also exhausting. Our regimen was four hours on, four hours off. Sometimes things would happen while we were on watch that we wanted to film but couldn't because we were sailing the boat. Other times, after a hard shift, Noel and I would have to persuade each other to get out of our bunk beds, put on our wet-weather gear, and shoot.

I was filming in the aft cockpit as K1218, *Debenhams*, left Portsmouth on August 27, 1977, in a light rain. Over the following seven weeks we endured a storm in the Bay of Biscay, the intense, airless heat of the doldrums, days of eerie calm without a breath of wind, and, probably the most nauseating part of the entire journey, the constant pounding of the boat as we tacked into the southeast trade winds of the South Atlantic. Our first stop was Cape Town, South Africa, which provided welcome relief but a bracing jolt of political reality. I ended up spending quite a bit of time at the yacht club next to the marina where we moored *Debenhams*, and I got to know one of the barmen quite well. One night, when no one else was around, I asked if he fancied a game of snooker. "No," he replied. "I can't touch the snooker table." It was a sickening feeling to, once again, come face-to-face with the reality of apartheid.

Later, we were invited to a "braai," an all-day, all-meat barbecue (and almost always a drunken piss-up) central to white South African culture. Our crew included two brothers from Scotland who were turned away. Why? Because their grandmother was from India. We all walked out. Sure, we met a lot of white people who were very nice, like the Russian countess who made me strawberry pavlova in the kitchen of her mansion overlooking the Cape but, as in Zimbabwe, you could see they were living a lie. As for ourselves, by simply sailing into Cape Town, we had all become guilty of condoning apartheid. And, while at the start line for the second leg of the race, less than nine miles away lay Robben Island, where Nelson Mandela had been imprisoned for thirteen years in a cell measuring seven feet by nine.

Momentarily seduced by the Cape Doctors, warm, southeasterly winds that carried us to the front of the race for the first and last time, our passage to New Zealand involved surviving some of the journey's most dangerous stretches—and its most thrilling. Our navigator for this leg, Captain Tom Woodfield, who had spent nineteen years in Antarctic waters on a naval research vessel, reckoned we could save time by sailing on the Great Circle Route, which would be shorter and might give us an advantage over a more northerly trajectory. But this would mean leaving the latitudes of the Roaring Forties and sailing into the Furious Fifties (whalers would have it that "at 40 degrees, there is no law, but at 50 degrees, there is no God") or even dropping down as far as the Screaming Sixties, winds that travel, unbroken by any land, around the Southern Ocean.

I have exceptionally good eyesight, an advantage in both cinematography and sailing. Because of this, I usually stood watch at the bow to scan the horizon for icebergs. I loved it. Being in that position, with the yacht behind me and nothing but cresting waves or the occasional dolphins ahead, it felt like flying. Years later, when I watched *Titanic*, I found Leonardo DiCaprio's "King of the world!" scene a bit embarrassing, but I also understood how he felt.

Spotting icebergs in a snowstorm usually means they're not that far away and, as there is always more ice below the surface than above, it's best to give them a wide berth. With a full rig, sailing at ten or fifteen knots and with sails frozen into sheets of ice that crack as they come down, it takes quite a lot of effort to make a yacht change course. On one occasion I was reducing sail with Dick McCann, the youngest member of our crew, when a wave caught us and swept Dick over the rail of the foredeck. His safety harness kept him out of any real danger, and I pulled him back onboard with little difficulty. But when we finished our work on the foredeck and I went to unbuckle my own safety harnesses (I always used two), both safety harnesses were hanging free. For sure, it was my lucky day.

We sailed on until one morning, while on watch, I saw something I couldn't understand. I turned to Noel to voice my concern. "We are in a gale, but the sea is calm. That white line across the horizon. What is that?" As we got nearer it became obvious: We were sailing into a bay of ice. *This was no longer yacht racing.* Tom took a reading of the sea temperature. At almost 30°F, it was below the freezing temperature of fresh water. The sea would freeze over at 28.4°F. Soon growlers, ice chunks the size of cars, began bumping against our fiberglass hull. Noel and I wanted to film, but the boat was now in danger.

The ice was here, the ice was there / The ice was all around: / It cracked and growled, and roared and howled, / Like noises in a swound!

SAMUEL TAYLOR COLERIDGE, *THE RIME OF THE ANCIENT MARINER*

A book of Coleridge's poems was the only reading matter I carried with me on the voyage, and by the end I knew *The Rime of the Ancient Mariner* by heart.

As we tacked into clearer water, Noel and I left our watch. When I returned with my camera, Ridgway was taking over the helm. We backtracked out of the ice, heading north and losing all the advantage our more southerly route might have given us.

The race plan was for all the yachts to spend Christmas in Auckland and, as we rounded the tip of New Zealand's North Island, I could smell cut grass wafting off the coast, a welcome sign we were near. (Even all these years later, I think of that moment whenever I pass a freshly mown lawn.) But, as we sighted land, an intense storm blew up out of nowhere and, by nightfall, we were, again, a long way from our goal. We finally docked more than thirty-two hours later, alongside the high-tech racing machines of some of our fellow competitors. The Auckland before us could have happily fitted into the 1950s of my Devon childhood, a sleepy English town on the far side of the world. Though I returned to New Zealand with James in 2003, and experienced how vibrant and multicultural Auckland would become, in 1977 it felt as if we had stepped out of a time machine.

It was in Auckland that the project almost disintegrated. Neither producer Richard Creasey nor I wanted *Around the World with Ridgway* to be simply about yachting. Nor was that the brief I had been given by Charles Denton. John, on the other hand, wanted a flattering film. He spent stretches of the voyage trying to influence the film's depiction of him by dictating what we were allowed to film, even demanding he be present during all interviews with his crew members. The tension between these two goals escalated, and both Noel and I came close to walking off the project. Only Richard's intervention, and a truce that made it clear I could shoot what I wanted to shoot, thrashed out during a discussion that John refused me permission to film, kept us aboard.

The tensions between John and his crew, as well as the crew and the filmmakers, do play out in some of the film's more memorable scenes, but knowing he was being filmed, was John being himself? Were the crew? To quote Tom's *Yachting World* review of John's book about the experience, "as skipper his priorities were as confused as the seas to be met in the Southern Ocean. Caged afloat, this showman adventurer...tormented by the possible cost of every sound around him frequently became wretchedly depressed."

Later in the voyage, John would deliver a speech lashing out at his crew (ironically, a scene he encouraged Noel and me to film), criticizing their body odor, and accusing them of being "freeloaders" for not having "contributed one penny toward the voyage." He saw them as in debt to him for the opportunity he'd given them. Later I'd occasionally hear echoes of his attitude in the directors who thought of films as "theirs" with little regard for the grips humping the gear to the top of the mountain.

Beyond Auckland, across the Pacific Ocean, Cape Horn stood waiting for us. Some 5,000 miles (8,147 kilometers) later we rounded the Horn without incident, sailing through on a cool breeze in spite of the Horn's dangerous reputation.

Albatrosses greeted us as we tacked through the sound that separates the East and West Falkland Islands, past Fox Bay and San Carlos—names made infamous by the Falklands War in 1982—before docking at Rio de Janeiro on the very day Carnival began.

It is a mild, mild wind, and a mild-looking sky; and the air smells now, as if it blew from a far-away meadow; they have been making hay somewhere under the slopes of the Andes, Starbuck, and the mowers are sleeping among the new-mown hay.

CAPTAIN AHAB, IN *MOBY DICK* BY HERMAN MELVILLE

Debenhams
HENRI LLOYD

SAMBA AND LIBERATION

I'm still patient until patience gets tired of me.

ALAMIN ABDULATIF, ERITREAN SINGER

***Debenhams* was an alcohol-free zone, and we were mostly living off dried food supplied to us** as part of a sponsorship deal (though an occasional flying fish that landed on deck added some spice to our menu, and I'd smuggled aboard a bottle of wine and some leftover Christmas cake to celebrate with as we rounded the Horn). Now we were in the middle of an ongoing feast. I spent many nights at Carnival during our stay, sometimes filming and sometimes just reveling in it. One night, Rio Yacht Club hosted a cocktail party for all the crew members of the yachts, but they obviously had no experience of ocean racing crews celebrating. The night ended with everyone in the swimming pool—including the skipper of *ADC Accutrac*, Clare Francis—being gassed by local police in full riot gear.

A time such as this would never come again, and Noel and I made the most of it. A wealthy British banker decided to show the crew of *Debenhams* the real Rio, which involved a tour of nightclubs and brothels that beggared the imagination. The banker had a woman—specifically, a paid companion—for every day of the week. One, in surprise, asked him, "What are you doing here? It's not your night!" There were only a few of us who took the journey with this guy, and no one had any intention of participating in the brothels' services. Besides, we couldn't even afford the cost of the beer! The banker, however, bought a round in every club. One brothel was dressed as if from the boudoir of Louis XVI's wife, Marie Antoinette. Another was like an immense barn with human-size canary cages hanging from the ceiling, containing nude dancers of all races, from which the clientele could make their selections. It was the definition of decadence, and after one last cold beer we headed back to our yacht.

At each port of call I would send back the footage we had shot. From Rio I drove down the coast to the ITV news office in São Paulo to send off my package. This was quite a trip in itself; São Paulo was a vast city unlike any I had experienced. I eventually found my way to the right office, only to discover no one had any idea what I was talking about. But, regardless, they sent off my exposed film and I made my way back to Rio.

I anxiously waited to hear from the cutting room. In Auckland I had been informed that my previous months of work had all looked very dark. In fact, the images might not even be usable. I had checked the camera but could find nothing wrong, and I had left Auckland wondering if I was shooting for no reason. Thankfully, before we sailed out of Rio, I received word that all was well. It was not until I was back in London and visited the cutting room that I found the cause of the problem. I looked at the screen of the flatbed editing machine and could see that the print was indeed very dark. But it was dark not just within the frame but across the sprocket area as well. If the negative was at fault, it would show only in the picture area of the print, so this was a print defect. The print stock was fogged, and I had spent four months worrying about nothing.

By the time we returned to the Solent we had circumnavigated the globe, sailing more than 26,780 nautical miles to do it. During those 161 days, 5 hours, 5 minutes, and 23 seconds aboard *Debenhams*, the world could often feel very small. As I was about to go on watch in the vastness of the Pacific, our navigator informed me we had reached Point Nemo. Named after a character in Jules Verne's *20,000 Leagues Under the Sea*, it's known as the "oceanic pole of inaccessibility." Simply put, it's the furthest spot from land anywhere on Earth. Interesting, I thought, as I climbed on deck and looked down to see a Coke bottle float by. This was January 1978. I wonder what it looks like now.

Even on this remote patch of blue was a reminder we'd inevitably be returning to civilization. For all the difficulties of life at sea, the end of our voyage filled me with mixed emotions. I remember vividly the Capital Radio jingle blaring out of the speakers in the cabin to introduce the London traffic news as we sailed into the English Channel. I thought then of Bernard Moitessier, the French yachtsman who'd been leading the single-handed Golden Globe Race when he decided to opt out in the home stretch, choosing instead to sail to Tahiti after sending an explanation via slingshot to a passing ship: "because I am happy at sea and perhaps to save my soul." At that moment I knew how his soul felt.

Back at home I began to think about what I'd experienced, three very different countries in very different stages of development as well as a lot of blue, but also the things I had missed out on during my time at sea. Somewhere, among the rolling swells and screaming winds of the Southern Ocean, a friend had sent a message to me over the ship's radio. It read, "May the Force be with you!" I had no idea what she was talking about!

It was a bright cold day in April, and the clocks were striking thirteen.

THE OPENING LINE OF GEORGE ORWELL'S NOVEL *1984*

It was April and my arrival home seemingly confirmed some of my misgivings about resuming my old life. As often happens in the film business, I found another toothbrush by the sink, my girlfriend having moved on in my absence. Perhaps it's fortunate, then, that I scarcely had a moment to get used to my life in London before packing my bags. Richard asked if I'd be interested in working on a documentary with Sarah Errington about Eritrea, a country locked in a war for independence with Ethiopia since 1961. He was attempting to start a series of documentary films that reflected the news in a more personal way, and I didn't hesitate to say yes to this first effort. A reporter who'd stayed in Vietnam after the fall of Saigon (she had been in the Associated Press darkroom processing film when the Vietcong arrived in the office), Sarah seemed to me the closest the era had to Gertrude Bell, the nineteenth-century explorer-writer-diplomat-historian.

With the addition of sound recordist Eddie Tise, our small team was complete. Africa lay ahead. But, having flown into Khartoum, we were asked to shoot a news story in aid of the famine that was again distressing the western part of the Sudan. In a remote desert hospital, we filmed the human casualties of the crisis, including a young boy who had no limbs. His arms and legs had been so withered by hunger that the medical team removed them as simply as if they were made of papier mâché. The Italian doctor who was caring for him told us that no one would adopt such a child, that they would have to return him to his parents and, as they would have no use for him or any way to care for him, he would die. When the piece was set to air in the UK, the union stepped in. As we were a freelance crew we were only sanctioned to film in Eritrea. What we had shot outside of that agreement could not be shown. I'm still speechless.

We essentially had an open brief shooting *Eritrea—Behind the Lines*, no agenda beyond filming with the Eritrean People's Liberation Front. But first we had to get there. Bureaucracy in Khartoum was eventually overcome by Sarah, gentle as a kitten but intimidating when angry, bursting into the Sudanese Minister of the Interior's office to demand our travel permits. We were on our way, first boarding a flight to Port Sudan, before taking a taxi down the Red Sea coast to Tokar.

From here we would hitch a ride on one of the many Mack trucks moving supplies across the border into Eritrea. Our truck, like the rest, traveled the desert and mountain roads by night for fear of enemy planes. Sarah sat inside the driver's cabin while Eddie and I perched atop the stacks of supplies beneath the starry sky, clutching onto our film gear as the unwieldy vehicle lurched its way toward the border. We slept under acacia trees during the day and followed the tracks of previous supply trucks across the desert sand at night. Once, woken by what I thought was rain, I opened my eyes to see that it was blood from a lamb our driver was slaughtering for the cook pot, which was to be the last meat we were to eat for some weeks.

Later, after we left Eritrea and crossed back into Sudan, we were served a memorable curry in a dusty border town where camels roamed the street. Having lived for some weeks on a kind of fermented pancake called injera, chips, and the occasional boiled egg, this was more than a special

treat, but to this day I'm not sure if it really was goat curry. Was it made from the puppy we played with as we ordered our meal? The waitress had disappeared with the puppy in tow. Apart from a single yelp coming from the kitchen, we never heard from it or saw it again. Or maybe we did.

When we arrived at the EPLF's main base we were prevented from filming, and it took a few days until our hosts determined we were not CIA spies. Sarah and I had met with the leaders of the EPLF in Rome, but here in the field things were different. After our release we were encouraged to document their training camps, where hundreds of girls with shaved heads made green by an antilice formula learned to fight using wooden rifles, and the hospital built deep inside the mountains. All this was interesting, and quite visual, but we wanted to visit a more traditional Eritrean village, to capture the EPLF's attempts to make their case to the people. Which was how we ended up in Zager, close to the Ethiopian front line and on hills that overlooked Asmara.

In Zager we filmed daily life in what appeared to be a peaceful village: Farmers hoed their fields and tended their cows while the women gathered firewood or drew water from the well. Peaceful, that is, until children harvesting sorghum in the midday sun were interrupted by a MiG jet and a phosphorus bomb that exploded in the air above them.

We followed Teke, the village elder, and some of the EPLF teachers to their meetings among the eucalyptus groves (held there to be out of view of enemy planes). Other than a daily visit from the Ethiopian Air Force, these meetings were the most interesting aspect of life in the village, as the freedom fighters attempted to persuade a rural Christian community to support their Marxist ideals. We were always accompanied by our "translator," a primary school teacher in civilian life who now carried a Kalashnikov, and our work was overseen by another member of the EPLF who had been studying law at Harvard before being drawn into the fight for his country.

Once the fighters trusted us, we were taken to visit the front line that overlooked Asmara, though, to our frustration, we were prevented from filming what we saw. Russian tanks sat out on the plains below us while their crews shaved in the early-morning sunlight. As we were warned by our guide, and exactly on time, a mortar barrage rocked the defense line, and we were ushered across a field riddled with angry plumes of black smoke to an underground bunker made of stout tree trunks. After we settled in to wait out the barrage, Eddie began playing chess with some of the EPLF soldiers, while every now and again a mortar round would shake the roof and cover the board with dust. Watching Eddie blow off the dust and resume the game, I found myself thinking, *This is a long way from Torquay.*

Later, the night sky was lit up by explosions, and the soldiers we had observed shaving were brought into the action. We did not know it at the time but the Ethiopian army, spearheaded by a column of Russian tanks and armor, were in the coming days to take control of almost every part of Eritrea. Sarah, Eddie, and I discussed our options. Should we stay and film? Before making that decision, we found we had no choice. A Land Rover pulled up to our shelter, and our EPLF minders whisked us off to Sudan and safety. While we had not completed our work, I appreciated the exit from who knows what. But, as we sat in the safety of Sudan, enjoying our "goat" curry, I thought about the villagers who, if they were to remain in place—and they had little choice but to remain in place—could well suffer Ethiopian reprisals. And neither we nor the EPLF could do anything to help them.

Our journey to Khartoum and home was a memorable trip, and not just for the endless taxi drive across the desert or the midnight stop for tea in a Bedouin tent deep inside the sand dunes. In the short time we had been in Eritrea, Khartoum had changed. What had been a bustling city was now beginning to close in on itself. Less music echoed in the streets, and the mesmerizing Sufi Whirling Dervishes no longer whirled. As our flight left for home, I thought of Ray Bradbury's short story "A Sound of Thunder," in which a hunter travels back in time and, by accident, alters the future into which he returns. It felt we too had trodden on a butterfly.

To leave the UK we had filled out a carnet, a customs form stating exactly what equipment we were temporarily taking out of the country and what we would be returning with. To our customs official at Heathrow our film had left the UK in a raw state and was returning having been exposed to light. Did that not change its value? he asked. I questioned his thinking: "Perhaps. But there is only the possibility of an image. Its value depends on what we might have filmed and how good a cameraman I may or may not be. Until the negative is developed and the film seen by an audience, how can we know?" Thankfully, with a grunt and a shrug of his shoulder, he let us through.

The heart sees before the eye.

SUDANESE PROVERB

It wasn't long before I traveled back to Sudan, to a country controlled by an ever more repressive Sunni regime. Directed by Chris Curling, *Worlds Apart: The Southeast Nuba* focuses on some of the tribespeople who make their home at the foot of the Nuba Mountains. They'd been documented before by Leni Riefenstahl in a pair of exploitative books in the 1970s, transposing the manipulative imagery of her Nazi propaganda films to its new setting in Africa's Sudan. I don't believe we ever intentionally crossed any ethical lines, certainly not the lines Riefenstahl crossed, but our presence itself was disruptive, and that in turn became part of the film's story.

Sudan had been ruled by an Islamist government since gaining independence in 1956 but it was, at first, Islam with a light touch rather than the strict Sharia law of later years. Religious and social change were slow to come to the Nuba in the remoteness of Kordofan province, but we, no doubt, accelerated it. The people we filmed traditionally wore only body paint, but after our arrival the government sent in truckloads of clothes and, sometimes with armed soldiers in support, attempted to force them to cover themselves. The Nuba were confused by this. Since Riefenstahl had brought them notoriety, tourists had been drawn to their nakedness. They had been paid to remain in their state of innocence, but now the government was insisting they cover themselves. Later, James Faris, an anthropologist who had been one of the first to study the Nuba and assisted on the film, expressed regret over his involvement, though we were pretty sure all those Bermuda shorts and lime-green skirts the government supplied would wind up in the markets of Malakal or Melut no matter what the authorities hoped.

On our arrival in the village of Kau, we had been held in a small compound, able only to listen while the Nuba's seasonal festival, made famous by the Magnum photographer George Rodger as well as Leni, took place in the village beyond its walls. The Sudanese government didn't want any more attention brought to the Nuba and only bowed to pressure from the BBC once their festival had ended. I suspect they knew full well that, with the hot dry season having begun in earnest and the temperature rarely falling below 90°F, there was little activity in the village. Chris once suggested I film a man sitting under a tree because he was picking his nose. And he was serious.

It offended Jim that Chris decided to pay the village to stage another version of the festival we had missed and to film some of the more secretive rituals on a very long lens. At the same time, our work was being monitored by agents of the Sudanese security service, and this government scrutiny became as much a part of the film as the body painting and the ritualistic, but brutal, bracelet fighting. It was far from the "man in harmony with nature" style of ethnographic documentary that Jim had imagined. But, though it was as exploitative as any outside view of a culture must be, what Chris Curling edited out of all the footage we shot was a lot truer to the reality of the Nuba in the early 1980s.

Unlike on previous assignments, I was now working with an assistant. It takes a certain kind of person to leave home and to live rough for months at a time, but Barry Ackroyd was both young and eager. I worked with Barry on several documentaries, including one made previously for Chris in India, *Reflections in a Peacock Crown*, also in the *Worlds Apart* series, and another that followed Van Morrison and his band on tour in Ireland. Barry soon began to shoot documentaries himself before going on to be a very successful cinematographer, working on *The Wind That Shakes the Barley*, *United 93*, *The Hurt Locker*, and *Captain Phillips*, among many others.

Our journey took us by small plane down the course of the White Nile and on a long drive; once again I rode on the top of a supply truck, this time with Barry into South Kordofan. Finally reaching

Kao, Barry and I spread some foam matting on the dirt between three mud walls that had once held a roof. We cooked on a small propane stove, and once we managed to rent a Land Rover, we washed in water we collected in jerry cans from a nearby well.

One morning we were cleaning our camera equipment and loading magazines when Barry spotted some tiny clear scorpions that had hidden under one of our cases. I brushed them aside as if they were harmless and went to fire up the stove for breakfast. In the refuse trench next to the stove I encountered a large black scorpion, one that looked truly dangerous. But no! Jim cautioned, "That's not a problem. It could give you a nasty bite, but it's the small clear scorpions that are the ones you need to watch out for. They are deadly."

The next night, Barry slept in the open, far away from our ruin and on an Indian charpai, a wood-and-rope bed he had specially made to raise him off the ground. When, around dawn, the dogs began to bark, I went to see what was going on. What looked like a tire track zigzagged its way beneath Barry's bed and ended at the foot of a giant Bao Bao tree some fifty yards away. A large python had holed up in its branches. Dogs barked at it and a group of young men yelled and threw sticks, while Barry slept peacefully through it all.

Barry was in his element and was willing to help with any task, but I found it odd he always volunteered to fill our water cans and clean the vehicle. One day I accompanied him to the well, and the attraction immediately became apparent. The well was the only source of water for the entire area, so each morning there would be a long line of naked young women, clay pots balanced on their heads, making their way down the same road Barry was driving. On the return journey to the village Barry, being a gentleman, would fill the Land Rover with passengers. The girls were all smeared with sim-sim oil and a rich red ocher, so when they got out of the Land Rover, having been squashed inside the cabin as well as riding on the footplate, the imprints of their body parts left the vehicle looking like a modernist work of art.

Stigma against mental illness is a scourge with many faces, and the medical community wears a number of those faces.

ELYN R. SAKS,
THE CENTER CANNOT HOLD: MY JOURNEY THROUGH MADNESS

The last documentary I worked on and codirected with Jon Sanders (a sound recordist I knew well and who would later produce and direct his own independent feature films) would be *Then When the World Changed*. This was a Channel 4–commissioned expansion of a previous film we had made about patients with schizophrenia. For the new film, Jon and I followed seven patients through their treatment in a psychiatric hospital over the course of many weeks, observing them in the common room, interviewing each individually in different emotional states, and sitting in with doctors as they discussed each patient's diagnosis. We found we had far more time to talk to them one-on-one than any of the overtaxed doctors, and we learned many details they'd missed.

We discovered, for instance, that one longtime resident of the ward had avoided Nazi Germany's persecution of the Jews by hiding in a barrel on the deck of a freighter. She had not seen her family since that day forty-five years ago and had no idea what happened to them. While Jon and I sat in on another assessment session, a doctor asked a nurse when the patient in question had last been seen without medication. She'd been taking eight different drugs, many of them first prescribed to her more than ten years previously. The doctors no longer knew who the real person was underneath all that medication.

One case troubled me even more than the others. Visiting a recently released patient in her dilapidated fourteenth-floor tower block flat, Jon and I found her in a terrible state. She was drunk, vomiting all over herself, and completely alone. Jon began running the tape recorder, but I couldn't bring the camera up to my shoulder to film her. It felt voyeuristic and wrong. So, I cleaned the lady up as best I could before Jon and I cooked her a meal. Then we interviewed her and had her describe to us what had just happened, including her impression of our arrival at her door. It was in no way as powerful as the visual of when she opened the door, but, maybe, it showed her more respect.

So many sad faces and so many sad stories. Some made it into the final film, while others, too personal to use, were left on the cutting-room floor. It came as no surprise when my therapist closed his practice and left London for a commune. To become intimately involved in the lives of people that I knew I would leave behind when a project ended made me uneasy. I had that same feeling when I left Eritrea, and now it was much closer to home. Even with the best intentions, were we not exploiting our subjects? I had no regrets about my time shooting documentaries, and I have great respect for many being made today, but for me it was time to move on.

I'd remember this time when working on *Barton Fink*, in which John Goodman, playing a psychotic working-class salesman, tells Fink, "You're just a tourist with a typewriter. I live here."

5

INTO THE MUSIC

In another time / In another place.

VAN MORRISON, "ASTRAL WEEKS"

During my days of knocking on doors unannounced, I had made contact in 1976 with a small film service company based in Soho called Solus Enterprises. The partnership included Jack Hazan, the cinematographer and director of *A Bigger Splash*, a film about David Hockney, and its editor, David Mingay. They were working on their next project, *Rude Boy*. It was there that I first met Dick Pope, who was just making the transition from assistant to cameraman and would become a good friend. (In fact, our careers seemed to develop in tandem over the years, a highlight being when we attended the Academy Awards together in 2015 as fellow best cinematography nominees, he for *Mr. Turner* and me for *Unbroken*.) On my return from Zimbabwe, I had used the office at Solus as a base to organize myself for the around-the-world yacht trip; after that adventure, I returned to see if the company could send any work my way. I was now the proud owner of an Éclair NPR 16 mm, a backup camera that I had left packaged in cellophane for the entire voyage and came as part payment for the job. It no doubt helped my acceptance to the company that I had my own camera and that I was willing to add it to Solus's equipment pool.

Being freelance can be quite depressing when the phone doesn't ring. And while few assignments came directly to Solus, rather than to its individual partners, it was good to have a base in Soho, even if only for somewhere to sit with a cup of tea when there was no work.

It was Dick who came to my rescue and kept me solvent by hiring me to operate a second camera on the occasional documentary or a concert featuring bands such as the Clash or Whitesnake. *Around the World with Ridgway* had given me a profile as a cameraman, so other work gradually began to come my way, including a documentary about the footballer Jimmy Greaves and his struggle with alcohol, and another for Michael Radford, the ex–film school student with whom I'd later work on *Another Time, Another Place*, *1984*, and *White Mischief*.

Mike's *Van Morrison in Ireland* followed the famed singer's tour of Belfast and Dublin in February 1979. Although almost entirely a concert film in its present form, we shot some wonderful footage with Van and the band, including scenes of the maestro walking up Cyprus Avenue in Belfast and meeting, for the first time in many years, the window cleaner with whom he once worked. Here he was, up a ladder and still cleaning windows.

I especially miss a scene we shot at a dark Italian restaurant one evening outside Dublin that didn't make the final cut. We were having dinner with the band when Mike suggested we start filming. My first thought was there was not enough light, but my assistant, the always imaginative Barry Ackroyd, had a solution. Seeing the dining tables were already lit by candles, he went into the kitchen, returned with a whole box of them, and proceeded to line them up along the middle of the table. In lighting we use the term "footcandle." The term almost explains itself: A footcandle is the amount of light that falls on an area one foot from a standard candle, so this was the perfect place to test the formula. Quite simply, on 100 ASA film stock and shooting with an aperture of 2.8, one hundred footcandles are required for a "correctly" exposed negative. The twenty-five candles Barry sourced from the kitchen gave a great light but burnt down so quickly he had to constantly keep adding more to keep my exposure steady. Once the dinner was over, the table looked like something out of a Salvador Dalí painting, with candle wax frozen in place as it dripped down on its path to the floor.

Back at our hotel, Van decided to stage an impromptu concert in the lobby and, having uncovered the piano that the manager had attempted to conceal, proceeded to wake the entire building. Only some of the guests considered it a great treat to be serenaded by no less a singer than Van Morrison at one in the morning. It is a pity nothing from these scenes made it into the final cut, but the concerts were brilliant. Van was playing in his hometown, Belfast, for the first time in years, in front of ecstatic crowds, and in Dublin, where we shot a concert that contained probably the best-ever version of "Moondance."

After I returned from Ireland I headed for Great Yarmouth, a faded resort town on the Norfolk coast once famous for a cold-smoked herring known as a bloater. With the fish long gone, Yarmouth

was servicing the North Sea oil boom and a rock and roll revival festival. Curtis Clark's *Blue Suede Shoes,* part documentary and part fiction, features acts with names like the Flying Saucers, Freddie "Fingers" Lee, Matchbox, and the Rockabilly Rebels, all of whom fed off the raw and raucous energy of a Norfolk crowd. One act even culminated with a singer taking an axe to a piano—shades of Pete Townshend!

My lighting for the film was simple. Not only what we could afford, I felt it looked right for the "cheap and cheerful" setting. But it did not involve any backlight. Curtis's wife, Penny, who was the producer, called me into her office after a first day of filming. "Some of your fellow cameramen are complaining about your lighting. They say you are not using any backlight," she informed me. Backlighting was a standard for concert films at the time—fill the stage with smoke and punch light through it to silhouette the band. This would not be the last time I received, and ignored, a complaint about an absence of backlight. Or smoke.

Around this time, I began shooting pop promos, now more elegantly called "music videos," which, thanks to the introduction of MTV in 1981, began to explode in popularity. I was still concentrating on documentary work, but I enjoyed shooting the few promos that I did, including those for Karla DeVito, Tracey Ullman, the Belle Stars, Lene Lovich, Status Quo, Kirsty MacColl, Genesis, Robert Wyatt, and Meat Loaf, among others. For the directors Godley and Creme, recording artists in their own right and famous for their band 10cc, I shot Herbie Hancock's "Rockit" and Eric Clapton's "Forever Man."

And it was a music video that led me to America for the first time in 1982, though not for long enough to form many lasting impressions. My memory now of Marvin Gaye's video of "Sexual Healing" is of a mad rush of filming during the day and an exploration of the Sunset Strip at night.

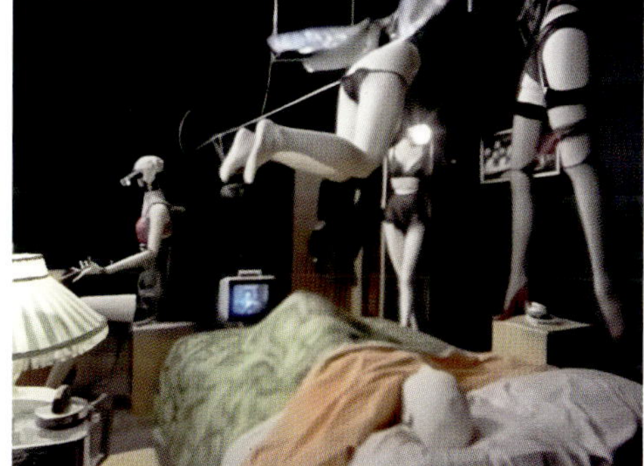

Thankfully, Marvin Gaye was not an early riser, so my assistant and I had plenty of time to recover from our first night's escapade. On our last day we decided to drive up the Pacific Coast Highway and take in Malibu, have lunch sitting by the blue waters of the Pacific, not thinking how far we were from LAX and how long it would take us to return our rental car. We made the flight just as the doors were closing, hoping the film we had shot made it on the plane with us.

As with "Sexual Healing," most shoots were fast and cheap without a lot of prep time, often in challenging situations that varied from one extreme to another, from running around with a handheld camera to lighting a stage set with laser beams. They could also go on all day and all night, the longest I ever worked being something like thirty hours straight. On that shoot a producer turned up after the first fifteen hours with a suitcase of cash and convinced us, in truth easily enough, to keep going even though we were already half asleep.

I had seen Ray Davies and the Kinks play in Torquay, so it felt quite odd to find myself working on a film the singer was directing, *Return to Waterloo*. We shot as if it were a documentary, jumping on and off a train to capture elaborate dance routines staged on station platforms with little chance of being able to return for a second take. It was kind of crazy, but it was also a good way to discover ways to shoot fast and work instinctively. And it was fun.

Two of my favorite experiences in the music world came while working on documentaries about the roots of jazz. One featured traditional kora players of the Gambia and another the contemporary music of Jamaica. The latter included filming the producer and recording artist Lee "Scratch" Perry as he smoked spliffs the size of cigars in his Jamaican studio and the wonderful ska band the Skatalites, jamming in their garage on a Sunday morning after I had almost overdosed on a mix of sinsemilla and a Cuba Libre the night before. Whether my hangover had any effect on the footage or not, what I shot that Sunday became a standalone episode within the series. And it was while filming in Kingston's Trenchtown that I accidentally wandered into a turf war between two rival gangs. But that's a whole other story.

The Malcolm Mowbray–directed documentary *Capital City* was a little less fraught. We shot all around London, but an afternoon concert at Alexandra Palace was the highlight of both the film and all my concert experiences (other than sleeping in a field to "experience" Jimi Hendrix's penultimate gig at the Isle of Wight Festival in 1970). I'm a big blues fan, so I was starstruck by a lineup that included B.B. King, Chuck Berry, and Muddy Waters. I stood onstage with a handheld camera, a 35 mm Arriflex BL that weighed around fifty-five pounds with a fully loaded thousand-foot magazine, as close to each performer as I could manage. In a moment I'll never forget, B.B. King turned to me while riffing on his guitar, Lucille, and said, "That camera's got to be heavy." I agreed. After shooting his set for over half an hour I surely knew it was.

> ***The beautiful thing about learning***
> ***is nobody can take it away from you.***
>
> **B.B. KING**

In 1983 it was time for me to move on. It was shooting a variety of small documentaries with Mike Radford, including his *Van Morrison in Ireland*, that led me to my first feature film since *Cruel Passion*.

Another Time, Another Place was Mike Radford's adaptation of a recently released novel by the Scottish writer Jessie Kesson, set in rural Scotland during World War II. The film concerned the complex relationship that develops between three Italian prisoners of war and the wife of an isolated crofter fifteen years her senior. We chose the beautiful but bleak Black Isle on the east coast of Scotland, to the north of Inverness, for our location, a place where the weather can change from one hour to the next. We had the entire cast, led by Phyllis Logan, on call for the length of the shoot, and all our locations were within easy reach and available to us on any day.

In the mornings Mike and I would have an early breakfast together and confirm, based on the weather outside and the forecast for the day, which scenes we would shoot. The crew would rendezvous at a crossroad in the middle of the Black Isle and there receive directions to what would be the first scene of the day. That might have been the bothy or a potato field, a cornfield or the barn. If the weather felt right, we might cover the ground with cotton wool and pretend it had recently been snowing. One night we waited in the hotel bar for a local farmer to telephone when his cow was about to give birth so we could film the event with Phyllis playing the midwife. Luckily it all happened before we had been in that bar for too long. I asked myself, "Are all films going to be like this? Everybody staying in the same place, going to the pub together in the evening and talking about the movie. Being able to choose what you shoot in the morning depending on the weather. If this is the way films are made, maybe this is for me!"

That it's never happened since would come as a shock to few people in the film industry. But in 1983 *Another Time, Another Place* showed during the Directors' Fortnight at the Cannes Film Festival and led to yet another experience I could not have even dreamt about as a boy.

6
BIG BROTHER

Who controls the present controls the past.

GEORGE ORWELL, *1984*

It's tempting to say the time was right, but Orwell's novel is, unfortunately, always timely, as the years to come would further confirm.

It was on April 4, 1984, when we shot John Hurt writing in Winston Smith's diary the words, "April 4th, 1984—From a dead man, greetings," though we didn't realize our schedule would lead to this somewhat stunning coincidence.

When Mike offered me the chance to shoot *1984* I was taken aback. I had shot only one independent feature with him and that had involved minimal location lighting and no studio sets. The film had not even been shot on 35 mm as, to save money, we had used Super 16 mm. My only other on-set experience of a feature film (I certainly wasn't going to suggest Mike see *Cruel Passion*) had been when I shot some behind-the-scenes footage of *Pirates of Penzance* for an arts program with Mike. I hadn't been encouraged by what I had seen. Not that I wasn't impressed by Douglas Slocombe's high-key, direct lighting; it was the industrial, almost impersonal, way the set was run that seemed counterintuitive to the kind of filmmaking I pictured being part of. Later, Mike told me that a TV series I had shot, *Wolcott*, had reassured him that I was up for the challenge of *1984*. I didn't let on that I had no such confidence in myself.

Mike hoped to shoot *1984* in black-and-white, but the realities of production and finance made that impossible. So, wanting a look that would convey the grimness of the dystopian Britain Orwell renamed "Airstrip One," we worked to figure out the next best thing. Our friends at Kays Laboratories in London helped us employ a technique first used by Kazuo Miyagawa for Kon Ichikawa's 1960 family drama *Her Brother*. Miyagawa had extensive experience in film labs and gave *Her Brother* a desaturated look that he called "silver tint." Our main problem: Miyagawa never told anyone how he achieved his results.

Kays accepted the challenge of cracking it, applying what we now call "bleach bypass" to our footage's positive print. Silver crystals, which act as a catalyst for the development process, were retained in the print emulsion by skipping the bleach bath that would usually remove them and keep the colors of the image truer to life. By remaining in the print, the crystals act as a black-and-white layer in the emulsion, resulting in an image with more muted colors, a high contrast ratio, and an intense black. We were thrilled with their work, which allowed Mike and me to create a visual analogue for a joyless world defined by fear.

To complement the process, I used very little bounce light, though this was, and remains, my usual approach. I wanted the harder look created by a single directional light source falling into deep shadows. And *1984* is one of the few films for which I severely restricted the colors of my light sources. Whether shooting night scenes or interiors, I wanted to keep the color of the light neutral or a little cold (or bluish). The only color contrast within the film is the warmth of the Telescreen projections and the bucolic Golden Country.

With our look established, we set off to find appropriately joyless locations. Scouting is done either by a production designer, a specific department, or, as has been my more usual experience, by the director, accompanied by the production designer and the cinematographer. Sometimes, I simply venture out on a day off to get ideas. Which was how, when walking around the East End of London on my own, I came across Beckton Gasworks. This sprawling industrial complex had

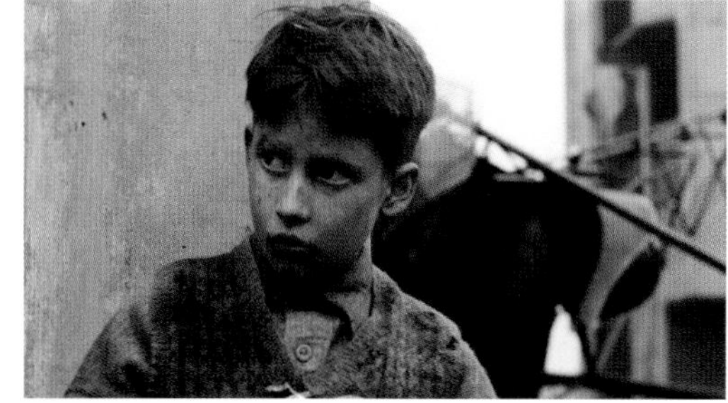

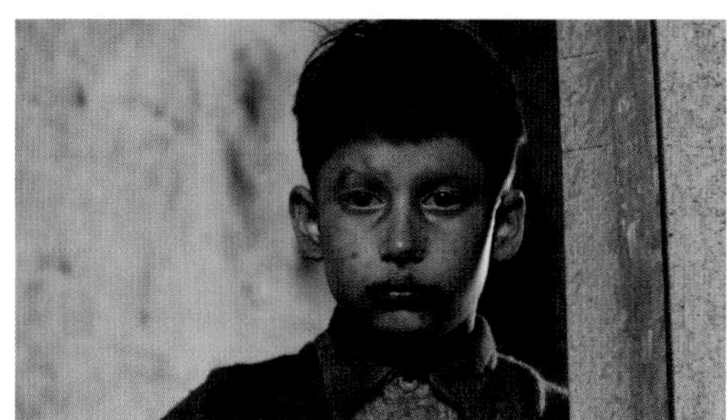

opened in 1870 but for the previous eight years had been left to rot. Its dilapidated state certainly looked joyless. After looking at my Polaroids and making a quick scout, Mike embraced the location. You may recognize Beckton from a more popular film shot there some time after *1984*, Kubrick's *Full Metal Jacket*, in which the gasworks stood in for Vietnam.

Finding the rats proved to be a greater challenge. When our animal handler took the cloth off the cage he had brought to the production office, Mike and I were confronted by a lab rat, a snowy white animal with luminous pink eyes. We asked him how he thought a white rat might be appropriate to Orwell's vision. "We could dye it black," he replied. "And the pink eyes?" asked Mike. I expected him to suggest the lab rats could be fitted with contact lenses, but no, he agreed to bring us sewer rats, as big and as black as he could find. I have no idea how he caught them, nor do I want to know, but knowing it would take time to film the rats, I asked my friend Dick Pope to help us out. Unknown to Dick, I was asking him to take close shots of rats. Unknown to me, Dick shared a common fear with the main character in *1984*, Winston Smith. Inside Dick's personal room 101 were rats.

Telescreens of various sizes project propaganda masquerading as news everywhere from private dwellings to crowd-filled public places, like Victory Square. To find out how we could create them, we turned to special effects expert Charles Staffell, whose career stretched from *Henry V* through *Superman*. Talking to Charlie was a little daunting as I could tell he was straining to be

patient with two unknowledgeable but enthusiastic beginners. He had so much experience in the world of effects, while both Mike and I had, let's just say, none!

We discussed what Charlie could do in terms of back projection and front projection, what our options were to shoot everything "in camera" (rather than adding postproduction effects work to the image we had captured on the set), what restrictions there would be in terms of the space required for the projection system, and the time it would take to set up. A technique nearly as old as movies themselves, back and front projection involves filming actors against screens with previously filmed images projected onto them, either from the front or the back. Both have advantages and disadvantages. Front projection produces the stronger image but, as its name implies, also requires finding ways to project the image at an angle that avoids hitting the set and the scene's actors.

Further complicating matters, our actors would sometimes have to sync their performance to some specific cues in the playback or to match precisely what was being shown on a screen behind them as if the image was being beamed in from cameras observing them in real time. We'd also need to rewind the footage during the shoot to accommodate multiple takes. All this was new to both Mike and me, but once we had some understanding of the complexities involved, we broke down what we could shoot on location, what needed to be shot in a studio, and how much time it would all take.

We achieved our playback images in several ways, mostly using front or back projection but on some sets just regular televisions housed in a frame of the same style and shape as our larger Telescreens.

On one occasion, we inserted the image as a glass shot, a once-popular technique that dates back to the silent era and was used on *All Quiet on the Western Front* and *Ben-Hur* among many others. The camera was set to photograph a landscape in the East End of London. On a large piece of glass, held at forty-five degrees to the lens and in the foreground of the shot, both the framework supporting the Telescreen and the buildings beyond were painted in perspective to the existing landscape as it appeared through the lens. The playback image of Winston Smith confessing was then projected to fit the screen area as it appeared on the glass—care being taken that each element of this composite shot was held in focus—and the shot captured entirely in camera. Five extras walked through the midground, and a helicopter hovered in the sky, but much of the image was simply painted on the glass. How differently such shots can be achieved today.

We filmed the elements that were to be played back well in advance of principal photography to allow time for the processing and editing of the footage. As we wanted these images to convey a distressed texture, we reshot our playback footage off a CRT television screen. This embedded the scan lines inherent with that system in our image. Using filtration, we added a warm brown tone that contrasted with the predominantly cold look of the live-action footage.

One location proved especially difficult to figure out. We were to film a pair of large crowd scenes in the ruins of Alexandra Palace, an entertainment facility built in the Victorian era and more recently renovated before a fire virtually destroyed the main structure in the summer of 1980. (The fire started at night, and I happened to have been filming Capital Radio's Jazz Festival there that same afternoon.) In *1984*, it remained literally a shell of its former self, and so provided an ideal stand-in for the public rallies of Airstrip One's Victory Square.

But Victory Square would be dominated by two towering versions of our Telescreens, and we had not settled on how this would be achieved. It seemed the one time in the film that we would have to resort to bluescreen and insert the image in postproduction, but neither Mike nor I wanted this. So, I took Charlie aside and naively asked him if there was a way we could simply project the images as would be done in a cinema. Was there a projector that would give me enough light? It was hard to gauge Charlie's reaction sometimes as he often seemed a little grumpy, but that was just his way. We made some tests.

To create the forty-five-foot-tall Telescreen images, Charlie used his carbon arc projectors. But as bright as they are, the carbon arcs barely moved my meter when projected from the required distance of seventy-five feet onto a white screen. Instead of being the brightest element within the frame, the images were in danger of being completely washed out. Charlie realized that front-projection material would reflect more efficiently than white, but it would not allow us to shoot at an angle to it. However, there was a paint used on hazard signs that might serve our purpose when applied to the screen. It was a compromise but, sure enough, my meter did now register an exposure, and the reflective surface gave us some latitude to shoot at an off angle to the screen. The effect was similar to the experience of modern 3D or IMAX screens, which also have a silvered surface and reflect light at varying intensity depending on the angle of the viewer to the image.

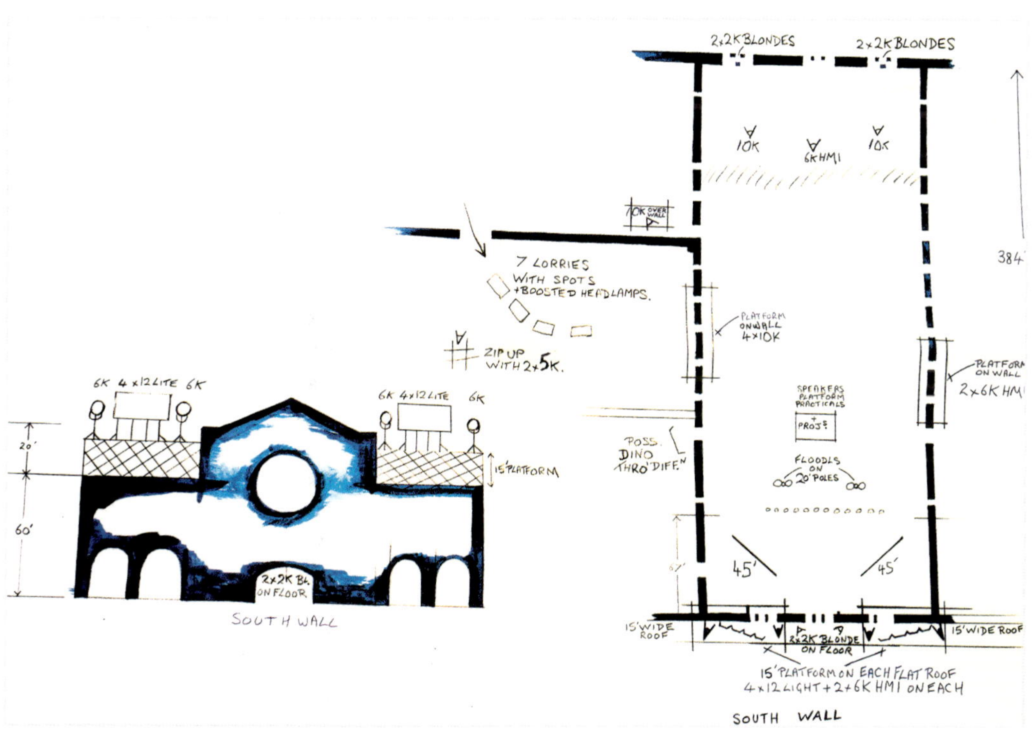

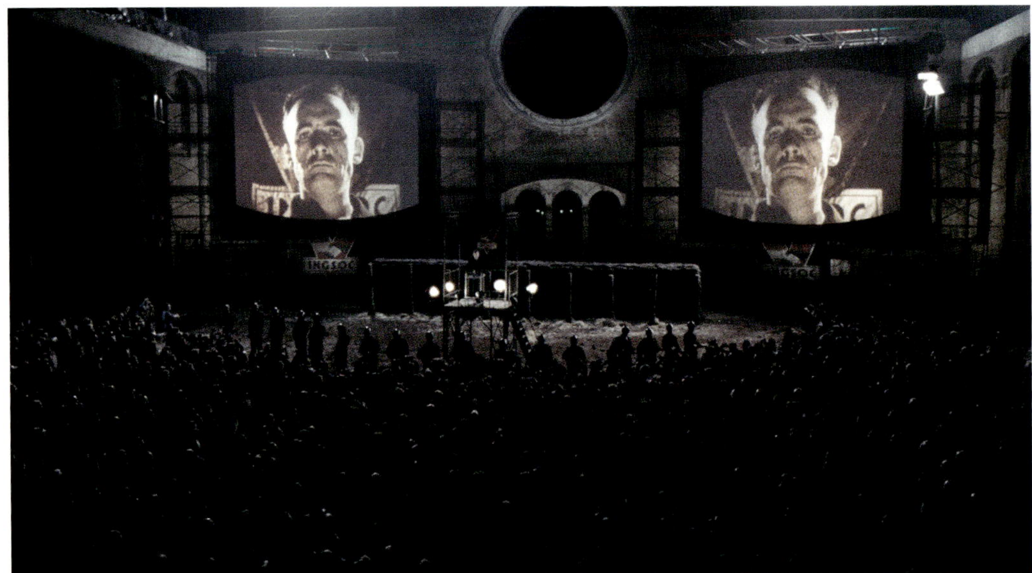

The lighting in the playback footage of the speaker had to match what we'd film on the set, which was shot many days later and under very different conditions. This was just one of many reasons I drew a schematic of the location lighting well in advance. The irony of shooting with the playback in camera was that if the camera and the projector were fully in sync, I would see it only as a very faint image through the eyepiece, if at all. Both the camera and the projector had 180-degree shutters so, when they were in sync and both fully open, the maximum amount of light passed from the playback screen onto the film. But when the camera's reflex mirror reflected through the viewfinder what the lens was seeing, the projector's shutter was closed, and no playback image was

visible through the camera. In the days of no video assist or a way to play back a take, it felt a bit like flying blind.

In spite of all his wizardry, Charlie was not entirely happy with the film because he didn't approve of, or maybe just didn't understand, our aims. After we shot and processed our first playback footage and Charlie saw what we wanted him to project, he went apoplectic. Why would we want to use such a trashy-looking image? He had been in the business for more than forty years, he had so much more experience than two ex–film school students, and he had no intention to work on a film that, he felt, had little regard for quality. But Mike knew what he wanted and was adamant that it was to be done his way. This was Orwell's grubby, retro-futuristic version of 1948, rather than the gleaming future of *2001: A Space Odyssey* (on which Charlie had also worked), but Charlie was never convinced.

Other scenes presented different challenges, some of them also Telescreen related. Since my early exercises at the National Film School, with Charles Lagus and the makeup mirrors, I have asked myself one question before addressing a scene: Where is the light coming from? The answer is not simply an aesthetic choice but involves the practicalities of a set or a location.

For the office of O'Brien, the Inner Party member played by Richard Burton who serves as antagonist to John Hurt's Winston, we built a set onstage. For both this set and the prison cell, Charlie required a large area to accommodate his back-projection system. Not only would each entire set be reflected in the glass in front of the playback screen, but I needed to limit any direct light from hitting the image and washing it out. Although I tend to prefer a light source, such as a window or a practical lamp, that will more easily project light into an actor's eyes, for these and similar sets I had to take a different approach. That approach was to ask the art department to build a softbox into the ceiling of each set, which would allow me to project a pool of soft light onto the actors and control what fell onto the Telescreen behind them.

If you are a man, Winston, you are the last man.
Your kind is extinct; we are the inheritors.

O'BRIEN, IN *1984*

The torture room (the Ministry of Love) posed a similar challenge to O'Brien's office, though it did not involve a Telescreen. The staging of the scene required shooting in every direction, including a pivotal moment in front of a mirror. To reach into the actors' eyes at that moment would be hard with a source coming from above, and would be a compromise that I wasn't willing to make. Again, I asked the art department (collaboration between the cinematographer and the production designer during the prep period of any film is so crucial) to build a light source into the set, this time a high window that ran almost the entire length of one wall. This would place Richard Burton, who had most of the dialogue, in a soft frontal light while leaving John Hurt, lying on the torture bed, in

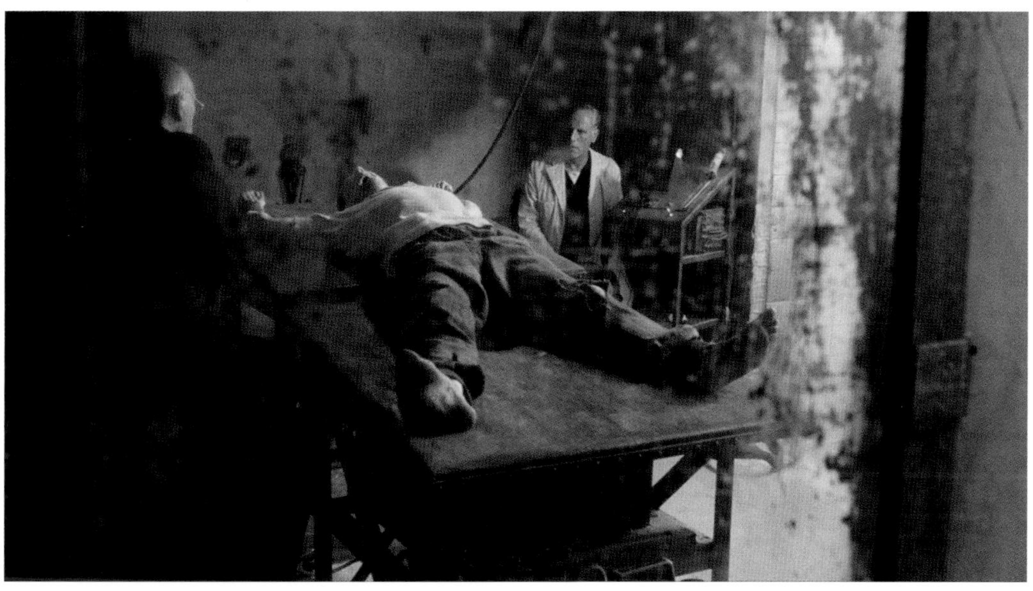

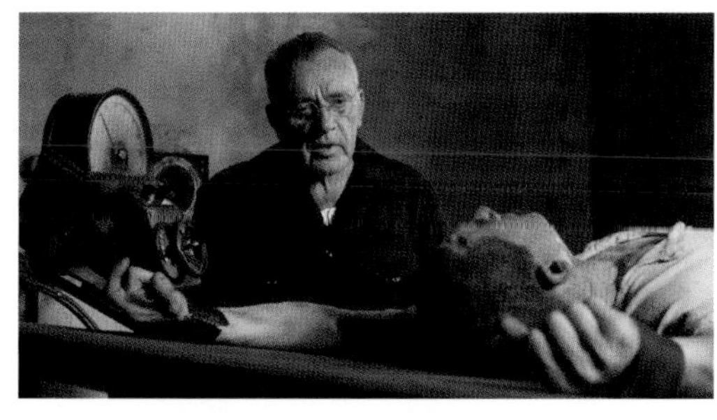

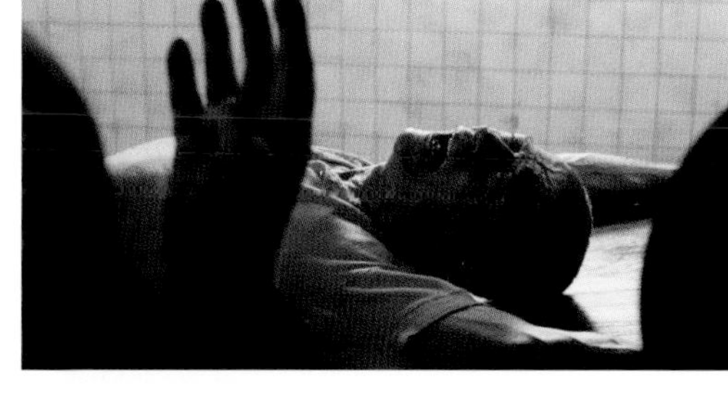

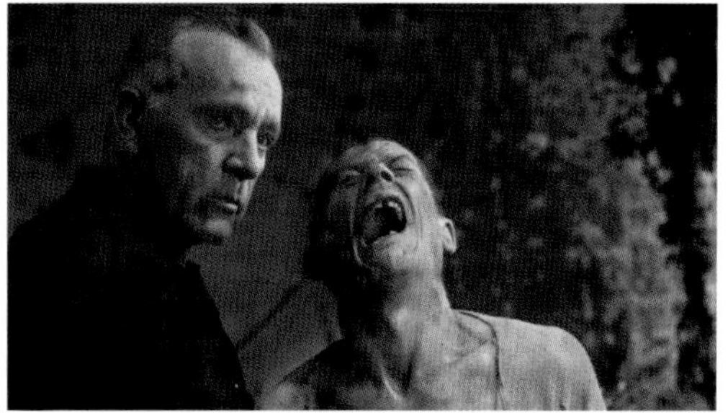

semi-silhouette. Only at the point Winston Smith is introduced to his own face in the mirror would it be fully visible in what would become a soft sidelight.

It was through such simple challenges that I developed my way of lighting, an approach that was naturalistic but also gave me flexibility as a camera operator. And it was through these day-to-day challenges that I developed a way of collaborating with a team. Many of them had been with me on documentaries and pop promos rather than having worked their way up through the feature world. My gaffer John Higgins, nicknamed Biggles, I had met on a Genesis pop promo, and *1984* was our first, but by no means our last, feature film together.

Shooting *1984* was complicated and stressful but also, despite the dark material, a lot of fun. Mike was a joy to work with, largely because of the passion and integrity he brought to the film. There were times during *Another Time, Another Place* when he had serious doubts about the film. It was not Ermanno Olmi's film *The Tree of Wooden Clogs*, which he always made reference to. Was it even any good, let alone anywhere close to the film he had dreamt it would be? By the time a film is cast and starts production, it takes on a life of its own and becomes a product of all the elements that bring it in front of the lens. Our process did not change from *Another Time, Another Place* to *1984*, but we did have more time. Mike focused on rehearsing with the actors and determining exactly what he wanted from a scene before we set the camera. Occasionally, rehearsals would last for hours. Once, Mike locked the stage door to keep the producer at bay, while we rehearsed all morning and into the lunch break. By the time we began shooting it was well into the afternoon, but we still managed to complete the day's schedule, and without going into overtime. This showed me the value of having a plan before you start rolling the camera rather than just shooting your way into the scene.

We also shot the entire film in camera, shooting images that with today's technology are more often given over to visual effects. It's a shame because the thrill of doing it for real on the day just can't be beat. Not just photographing the set and the lighting but the entire image in combination with the performances. One of the least recognized but most important aspects of a cinematographer's job (and, by extension, that of the shooting crew) is to help provide an immersive reality for the film's actors, a secure and welcoming space in which they feel free to do their work. Without the characters the actors create, there is no film.

The experience of shooting *1984* also helped teach me not to compromise the way I like to work because of what other people think about my ability. A line producer on the film had a low opinion of me and—reviving memories of *Cruel Passion*—was particularly skeptical that I could cope with a film of such scale as both its cinematographer and camera operator. Not only did he imagine an operator would be taking over after a day or two, but he also insisted we carry a full second unit camera crew for the entire shoot—I suspected as a backup, as we had no need of them otherwise. One day, a geared head turned up on set. A geared head is operated using two revolving handles, wheels that control both the pan and tilt axis of the camera. Most camera operators used them in the past, when cameras were far heavier, but, even now, they can be an effective tool in the right hands. Our line producer assumed an ex–film school student wouldn't know what to do with one, and he came to watch, or should I say gloat.

Feigning my gratitude, I had my camera grip make the swap with my regular fluid head, also referred to as a friction head, manipulated using just a single pan bar. We got the shot and I turned to my first assistant, Andrew Speller, and asked that the geared head be returned. I didn't see a need for it again that day. The train we were shooting had crossed through a static frame, and I had simply locked off the wheels. While in film school, I'd practiced using a geared head until I could attach a pen to it and sign my name, something cinematographer Gerry Turpin (operator of *Peeping Tom* among many other films) had told me was the traditional way to prove one's competence. I was not carrying one on *1984* to save money and for no other reason.

1984 earned strong reviews, but that might have not been the case if we hadn't avoided a potential disaster before its release. Because of the additional silver left by the bleach bypass process, heat could build up in the gate of a projector and cause the print to burst into flames. Had we not warned projectionists to make sure their equipment maintained a sufficient gap, we might have had serious problems. I can't imagine the image of movie theaters burning across the UK would have been good for the film, or any of our careers.

As for my own career, it had taken me a long time to find myself. Behind the camera, as a film's cinematographer, I felt a confidence that had previously eluded me. But it was only while shooting *1984*, while standing on the western edge of Salisbury Plain looking toward a landscape of gently sloping hills slowly coming to life in the early-morning sunlight, when I recognized myself as that cinematographer.

Behind me was a parking lot, but it was the view ahead that mattered, the location that director Michael Radford and I had chosen to represent the Golden Country, as described by George Orwell in his masterwork *1984*. This was the idealized vision of England dreamt of by the story's protagonist, Winston Smith. It fell to our production designer, Allan Cameron, to build a gloomy corridor that had no place in such a bucolic landscape. My job, as the film's cinematographer, was to shoot it in such a way that it matched the sets we had built onstage back in London.

The crew arrived early to build the hallway and, at the end of it and facing to the west, a door to the dreaded Room 101. Later it would contain Winston Smith's worst fears, but for now it served as the entryway to his dream. The work done, we broke for lunch early, readying ourselves to take full advantage of the afternoon light for our shoot. Ordinarily this would have been just another meal break—a boxed lunch, a quiet cigarette, and a few moments of slumber. But this day was different, for a couple of reasons. We had the location for only one day, and because we were working with a limited budget, we had no individual trailers, no catering tent, and only a single portable toilet. That left our well-known stars, John Hurt and Richard Burton, to make the best of it along with the rest of us.

They did so without complaint, seated on the grass verge of the parking lot eating their boxed lunches with the rest of the crew. I'd first seen and admired John Hurt alongside Derek Jacobi in the TV series *I, Claudius* and, more recently, playing John Merrick in David Lynch's film *The Elephant Man*. Richard Burton, on the other hand, had begun his career in film before I was born! Here was Alexander the Great from the film of the same name, Jimmy Porter from *Look Back in Anger*, Mark Antony from *Cleopatra*. And here was Alec Leamas from Martin Ritt's haunting film version of John le Carré's *The Spy Who Came In from the Cold*, one of my all-time favorite films, just a few feet away, chatting casually with us on a fine spring day in the English countryside. It was a moment I've not forgotten. I knew then that I had found what I had been looking for.

What exactly we talked about that day disappeared in the moment, but I remember an earlier event a little more clearly. A few days after joining our production, Richard Burton sent word he would like to talk with the entire crew once shooting had wrapped for the day. It made for an intensely nervy afternoon. Famous actors are often preceded by their reputations, and Burton certainly had one. As we all gathered sheepishly outside his trailer, which was no more than the

holiday caravan an elderly couple might take to the English seaside for a weekend break rather than that more often seen on a Hollywood shoot, we feared we were in for a bollocking. What were we doing wrong?

Richard Burton appeared, stooping to exit through the low door of his trailer and be confronted by a sea of worried faces. His first words? "Thank you." Could he hear our collective sigh of relief? Then he elaborated, "These last few days have been among the best experiences of my life. When I came on set and saw so many young faces looking at me, it terrified me. So, I wanted to take a moment to thank you all for making me feel so welcome and for being so supportive. I'm truly happy to be working with you all and especially so on such a project as this. Again, thank you. I will look forward to seeing you all tomorrow."

Even now, I am deeply moved when I think about that moment, especially remembering Burton passed away before he could see the finished film. It was a wonderful thing for him to say, and it was said with such sincerity. It not only made me realize someone of his stature could be as insecure as the rest of us but why he was. (It also showed me the power of graceful behavior—something that you don't always see on a film set.) Together we were a team, each of us trying to do our best for a director and a project that we all really cared about. Not Richard Burton, nor any one of us, wanted to let the team down.

I was energized by the fear that came with the challenge. I liked being part of a team, which is an essential part of the process, and I liked having the responsibility of fulfilling a director's vision while running a crew of technicians. But by many, I was still considered an outsider. I had not worked my way up through the industry ranks, which was the normal path in the 1970s and early 1980s, much as it had always been. But how was I to know? It was a happy accident that had led me to the National Film School, and into an industry I knew little about.

I had also learned that as soon as you pick up a camera you must be prepared for compromise. There are many elements involved in shooting a film. Things that can always be done better. But what is better?

7

LOVE KILLS

I'll never look like Barbie. Barbie doesn't have bruises.

NANCY SPUNGEN, IN *SID AND NANCY*

Although I had seen the Clash in concert when working with Dick and knew of the Sex Pistols—who could have not been aware of that notorious Bill Grundy interview and their provocative songs such as "Anarchy in the UK" and "God Save the Queen"?—I was deep into filming an around-the-world yacht race by the time punk rose to prominence. Like *Star Wars* and a great many other things, I missed the release of the Pistols' first album and the band's infamous live shows after they added Sid Vicious as bassist. But the impact of punk could still be felt when we were making Alex Cox's dramatization of the fatal romance between Sid and Nancy Spungen in 1985. It was natural that a kind of "punk chaos" set the tone for the shoot.

With Gary Oldman cast as our Sid and Chloe Webb as our Nancy, it soon became quite clear this would be a kind of spontaneous filmmaking—and quite the opposite of *1984* or the more recent *Defense of the Realm* I had shot for executive producer David Puttnam. We were operating with very little money, working from a script that was open to variation, and often shooting on locations without permission. And when we did have permission, it might be for something quite confined rather than what it expanded into. For example, at one fancy central London hotel our location manager had arranged for us to shoot in a suite on the second floor and nothing more, but the scene soon spread its wings into the main lobby and, once we had outstayed our welcome there, up to the roof. To work quickly and to give myself more control over the frame as a scene "progressed," both Alex and I agreed I should shoot much of the film handheld. This, in turn, influenced the way Biggles and I approached the lighting. Often, we needed to light a scene quickly and allow for shooting in all directions, so we began to construct various ring lights and batten strips of household bulbs, both cheap and easy to rig. To save on gel, and if we had no dimmer system, we might connect the bulbs in series, thus reducing the voltage to each and warming the color they would emit. Apart from our concert scenes, we used very few conventional film lights on

Sid and Nancy. It was a way of working that I was moving toward before this experience, but this film certainly had a significant effect on how I developed my approach to lighting.

For one scene we re-created the Sex Pistols' infamous Silver Jubilee celebration during which the band performed "God Save the Queen" aboard a boat, in mockery of Queen Elizabeth II's own celebration of her twenty-five years on the throne that was to happen on the Thames a few days later.

Like the Pistols, we were confronted by the river police, and at least some of their boats featured in the film were not an intended part of the scene. Like the 911 call that someone made to the fire brigade when we were shooting outside a theater in New York City, the chaos added to the scene's production value. The shot of Sid and Nancy leaving the melee was lit using only the fluorescent tubes underneath the walkway, which Biggles had purposely rigged, and I shot it handheld simply walking backward with Chloe and Gary, doing focus myself and panning to County Hall as the couple passed out of frame. And, because our shoot was being closed down by the police, we had time for only a couple of takes. Despite the rush, I love the feeling of the shot, especially when combined with the music of Pray for Rain.

We also shot our own version of "My Way," this time in a West End theater, loosely based on the original video but with a heightened nod to the romance of the piece and with a foretelling of its ultimate end. Nancy is shot but the two of them still manage to walk away as if in a dream. Andrew McAlpine, the film's production designer, Biggles, and I chose a simple stairway of fluorescent tubes for what was one of the few formally staged scenes.

He's a fabulous disaster. He's a symbol, a metaphor, he embodies the dementia of a nihilistic generation. He's a fuckin' star.

MALCOLM McLAREN, IN *SID AND NANCY*

Otherwise, much of the film was made on the fly, literally. We took a skeleton crew to Paris, flying in at dawn to shoot Sid and Nancy experiencing the sights of Paris. After dark and before taking a flight back to London, we shot a scene involving Sid's agent, played by the film's co-producer, at a café across the street from the famous Moulin Rouge cabaret venue. As on so many other occasions, we obtained permission to shoot from the proprietor of the café only when we turned up with our cast and equipment. I was working with one assistant, David Bryant, and Biggles served as our sole electrician, carrying a basic lighting kit of four Red Heads, small and lightweight 650-watt open-face lamps that I was used to using on documentaries. It was all our small plane could accommodate. Both Gary and Chloe spent the day in full makeup and in character. In truth, Gary spent the entire shoot with his hair extensions and in full punk mode, whether on set or out for a beer in San Francisco. Crazy and brilliant. It was a world away from shooting *1984*.

Soon after our day in Paris we left London for New York's JFK airport, disembarked in the late afternoon, and piled into a van to begin scouting a wide variety of locations I had never seen before in a city I was experiencing for the first time, places including the Chelsea Hotel, Times Square, Alphabet City, and a methadone clinic. Not least, we scouted the Jersey Shore in search of a location for the film's dreamlike final scene, in which a spectral Nancy joins Sid at a pizza parlor in the middle of nowhere with the city skyline in the background.

At close to midnight, we wearily gathered for a production meeting to finalize our plans for the seven o'clock call time scheduled for the next morning. Moments later Dave Bryant burst in. "I just want to tell you the camera truck is outside, and the driver is nowhere to be found. The fuel tank is leaking, and the vehicle holds twenty-eight gallons of diesel fuel. Or it did. Much of that is now running down the street. We have unloaded all the camera equipment but it's sitting on the pavement." Dave meant the sidewalk in Brit talk, and the mix-up between the meaning of these two words would often cause problems for us while shooting in the States. "Simon," he continued, referring to our second assistant, "and I have nowhere else to put it. Oh! And it's beginning to snow. And you think we're shooting at seven tomorrow morning? I don't think so. But that's up to you. For myself, I'm going to bed. Or I will be if you can tell me where I'm supposed to be sleeping tonight." It had been a long day.

The following day, a little later than planned, we began filming a few scenes at the storied Chelsea Hotel, the site of Nancy's death. It was there that I first met Bill O'Leary, then a practical electrician but now a gaffer, with whom I've worked in America whenever possible. Bill is quiet, focused, easygoing, and especially gifted in embracing unorthodox ways of lighting. These qualities served him well on *Sid and Nancy*, a film on which we used a wide array of unusual practical bulbs (gag lights), either hidden to augment an existing source or as a visible addition in the shot. This included, at Billy's suggestion, a single red bulb in the back of a shot as if marking an exit. (Slipping a single red bulb into a shot became something of an inside joke. You might spot them in *Fargo*, *The Hurricane*, and others.)

Anywhere, but especially on locations, distractions can slow the work. Alex had a lot of friends in New York, and the day we shot on the Chelsea stairwell turned into an unexpected social gathering. I admit I can get annoyed at these sorts of things when I'm trying to set the camera and to light. Unable to hide my frustration, I took our first assistant director, Betsy Magruder, aside and asked, "Can you get rid of that woman who's leaning over the balcony there? I mean, it's really hard to concentrate when you've got all these people hanging around!" She turned to me and replied, "That woman? That woman's Raquel Welch."

From New York we moved to San Francisco where, among others, we shot the scene in which Sid talks to the Pistols' frustrated road manager Phoebe (played by Debby Bishop) in the back of a taxi. This was, like much of the film, a spur-of-the-moment decision that somehow worked out. We filmed the scene over a lunch break with Alex spontaneously hailing a cab and nonchalantly asking the driver if he could accommodate an unusual request. We needed to use the cab for filming, and all he needed to do was hold on while we made a few adjustments, then simply drive us across the Bay Bridge. I taped a piece of muslin on the roof of the cab and with my free hand—my right hand was holding the camera on my shoulder—aimed a "sun gun," a handheld portable lamp, at it to get a bit of reflected light in the actors' eyes. Alex recorded the sound, and I can't remember if he was in the trunk or wedged beneath the actors' legs. Either place was quite unusual for a director.

One of the most memorable scenes in *Sid and Nancy* comes late in the movie. The shot encapsulated the look and tone of the film, which varied from the dark and realistic to the poetic and surreal. It figured prominently in the film's trailer, and a still image from the scene served as its poster in much of the world, becoming synonymous with its doomed love story. But was it planned?

On the morning of the shoot, Alex, Abbe Wool (who cowrote the screenplay with Alex), and I were, as usual, traveling together to the location. We were scheduled to shoot a scene in which the couple meet with their drug dealer, played by Xander Berkeley, in an area of downtown LA that could stand in for New York. With the alleyway already on our minds, the romantic moment took shape as we drove. At first it was Alex who suggested he needed a shot of the couple embracing in the alley. Then it was Abbe who suggested they be surrounded by trash and that, maybe, it should be falling from the sky

as well. Alex warmed to Abbe's idea, and I added my own contribution by suggesting that the moment would be more poetic if we were to shoot in slow motion. It would be as if, for them, time had slowed.

I can't remember who suggested we put dustbins in the mix, but I knew then it had to be shot in slow motion. To capture metallic dustbins falling through the frame in a way that would feel weightless and poetic, rather than angry and violent, we'd needed to shoot at least at seventy-five frames per second. The higher the frame rate, the slower the projected image; 120 fps would be even better. It seemed a simple idea, but I would never have imagined that renting a high-speed camera in Hollywood, the center of the world's movie industry, would prove so difficult.

Because we didn't need to shoot sound, a non-sync Arriflex 111, which could shoot up to 150 fps, would do, but production had to call every single rental company in LA before finding one. When the camera finally arrived on set—and who knows where it came from—David put it through its paces: faster and faster! 50 fps, 75 fps, 100 fps, until an awful crunching sound told us the film was being shredded by the camera's mechanical claw. Eventually, David managed to get the camera to run perhaps twenty feet of film through the gate at 120 fps, before we heard the same awful sound. It would have to do.

Without any time to prepare for the shot, the dustbins and the trash were simply what our prop department had managed to find on the morning of the shoot. Between each take, everything had to be gathered up and carried to the roof from which it would be thrown. We'd run the camera and, when it came up to speed, cue the trash, but by the time it entered the frame the camera would have jammed. The first time I worked in LA, shooting the "Sexual Healing" video, we'd used our own equipment brought over from London. This was only my second time shooting in LA, and it wasn't living up to my expectations. But everyone took a turn to haul those trash bins up the six flights of stairs. Eventually the camera ran for a full take, and that is the one you see in the film.

But luck was sometimes on our side. One shot of Sid calling Nancy from a pay phone somewhere in the American West takes place against a skyline at magic hour (the time between sunset and darkness, or between first light and sunrise), as seen through the window of a harshly lit diner. For the scenes of the band on the road we had a tour bus that we drove to El Centro in *southern* Southern California, east of San Diego and near the border with Mexico. Alex and I wandered around the town looking for inspiration. "Well, that café is great. Let's try it." Once again, we simply asked the owner for permission, gave him some money, and that was that. We needed to film a few shots inside, but I saved the one through the window for the moment the sun set below the horizon and was blessed with a wonderfully surreal pinky sunset. To capture a simple shot like this for real is a thrill you don't get on a stage against a backing or an LED screen.

For the scenes in Sid and Nancy's room at the Chelsea Hotel we worked on a set in Los Angeles. This gave us time to rehearse in the quiet of a stage and have control over the environment, such as when Sid flicks the cigarette that causes the curtains to catch on fire, which we shot in slow motion to, again, give it a dreamlike feel. I love it when Gary lights a second cigarette and throws the lit match into the flames. It was something he did in the moment and one of the subtleties that makes his performance so brilliant, a piece that illustrates the intensity Gary and Chloe brought to their work.

Looking at the film now, I regret the way I lit some parts of it, particularly this set. Preparing the scene in which Sid and Nancy's dealer comes to their room, I got too obsessed with lighting each of the three characters. I rigged 1K Fresnel lamps on top of the set walls to make everyone in the scene clearly visible. I rarely work in that way, setting a lamp where there is no justification for it to be, and I see now that it would have been better to play one character in silhouette, or deep in shadow. But when you are under pressure and in the thick of things, it can be hard to stand back and look at what you're doing from the outside.

PLAY

I recognized my tendency to overlight when under pressure quite early on in my career, and it's something with which I still struggle. Thankfully, by the time we got to one of *Sid and Nancy*'s final scenes I'd suppressed that urge. The scene of Nancy's death appears more naturalistic and motivated, using the cold, green light of the hotel room's fluorescent bathroom fixtures, the sharp pattern of an exterior streetlight, and a flickering television from the apartment window next door. It's minimal and raw, and I believe it's one of the best scenes I've ever shot, one in which the performance and the camera are fully in sync. I wish I had had the guts, and the clarity of vision, to take a similar approach throughout *Sid and Nancy*.

I had learned a lot. There is not always a need to draw a storyboard or plan out the shots in detail before the day of shooting. I enjoyed the challenge of a "run and gun" approach, though "chaotic" might also be a valid description and experiences often seem rosier in reflection. While it can be fun and exhilarating to shoot this way it is only so when you have a director, such as Alex, who is always in the story, rather than searching for something, anything, they have not thought through. No film is ever perfect, and we made plenty of compromises on *Sid and Nancy*. But the film is successful in its blend of the real and the unreal, especially in its final scenes, where the ugliness of Nancy's death gives way to Sid's fantasy of a reunion against the Manhattan skyline. The day we filmed, a low cloud hung over the Twin Towers and the cold grayness of the day provided a striking contrast with the pink neon sign reading simply PIZZA. On a sunny day the scene would have been entirely different, and, once again, we got lucky.

Not counting the whirlwind "Sexual Healing" shoot, *Sid and Nancy* was my first real trip to America. I decided to stick around for a bit and spent five or so weeks exploring California and the American Southwest. Though America was growing on me, I had no idea when, or even if, I'd be back.

Instead, it was three films I shot in Kenya during this time that remain among the most influential in my life.

8

AFRICAN STORIES

The eye never forgets what the heart has seen.

AFRICAN PROVERB

Written and directed by Harry Hook, *The Kitchen Toto* takes place against the backdrop of the Mau Mau rebellion of the 1950s in Kenya. I liked the script because it didn't attempt to simplify the story into bad guys and good guys. The film succeeds in conveying the situation's historical complexities by concentrating on the experiences of its few characters and limited settings, but what could have been a thoroughly pleasant experience was marred by personality conflicts and, above all, poor planning.

We were shooting in the Kakamega forest area, in the far northwest of Kenya and not far from the border Kenya shares with Uganda. Because we were on the equator, the daylight, in theory, lasted twelve hours. But with the surrounding forest being both dense and tall, the number of hours we could shoot using natural light proved to be far more limited. And Kakamega was called the last tropical rain forest in Kenya for a reason. Every afternoon we would have intense thunderstorms, some of which would bring hail that covered parts of the jungle in two or three inches of ice. It often made filming impossible.

The main location for *The Kitchen Toto* is a plantation house where the title character, Mwangi, played by Edwin Mahinda, works as a houseboy to a white policeman. We'd get a couple of exterior shots in the morning, be forced to break for lunch when the thunderstorms came in, and move inside during the afternoon. That may sound simple enough, but because the storms were so intense, we'd have no natural light coming through the windows when we came to shoot our interiors. Not that we could shoot much when it was pelting down, as the corrugated iron roof made recording sound impossible.

One storm was so violent that the dining tent began to blow away as if it were a yacht's spinnaker. It floated skyward while ten or more crew members held on to one of the guy ropes. All of them, including Biggles—who is quite a large man—became momentarily airborne before a brief lull in the wind sent them crashing back to earth. On we went, intent to keep on schedule, even though I informed the production that some footage could not possibly match what we were shooting in bright sunlight. "That's because you have no idea what you are doing. Haven't you got a sunshine filter?" To our producer, everything looked fine on our low-quality VHS dailies tapes. Only when we were back in London did it become obvious to everyone that some of the footage was, indeed, unusable.

Night work presented a different sort of challenge, particularly as the thunderstorms always seemed to arrive just as we were rigging our lighting. One afternoon Biggles was attempting to position a lamp high in the branches of a large fig tree when lightning began flashing all around him. We were shouting at him to get down, especially since he was holding a large metal lamp and running a cable from the tree to a generator a hundred feet away. What's wrong with this picture? Nothing was worth the risk he was taking, but Biggles just wouldn't stop until he had finished securing the lamp in place. Today a safety officer would shut down the entire unit until a dangerous storm like that had passed by—as happened to us on a number of occasions when we were shooting *Sicario* in New Mexico—but there was no such position in the Kakamega rain forest.

Though we did not have a large crew, accommodation was a challenge in such a remote spot. But as luck would have it, there was the Golf Hotel, which, as the name suggests, fronted a golf course that had been hacked out of the jungle. The drab concrete block was a work in progress, but with help from our electricians, it gradually came to life, never more so than on a Saturday night when the entire cast and crew gathered in the disco. Naturally, the Samburu warriors who were serving as extras in the film came along. These nomadic cattle herders, close relations to the Maasai, wear their hair in long braids which, like their bodies, they color with a rich red ocher. When we first began shooting, they had all gotten sick eating from our catering tables. The combination of chips, avocado, and chocolate pudding upset stomachs used to milk, cows' blood, and raw meat. From then on, the caterer supplied food better suited to their specific diet. Whether on or off the set, the Samburu wore their traditional dress, which was not much, and they always carried their throwing spears. They are also renowned for their dancing. Much like a scene from a John Ford Western, they were asked to put their spears behind the bar before they took to the dance floor. Once disarmed they began their singular traditional dance moves, which consisted of jumping up and down, in a frenzy getting higher and higher, while remaining on the same spot. All to the sounds of Bananarama or Wham! and under the disco ball lighting supplied by our electrical department. Which, I have to say, was some of their best work.

> *You wouldn't by any chance have a chocolate-covered lobster?*
>
> **ALICE DE JANZE, IN *WHITE MISCHIEF***

White Mischief, which reunited me with *Another Time, Another Place* and *1984* director Michael Radford, showed another side of the colonial misadventure. Set during World War II, the film depicted a real-life murder case involving the "Happy Valley set," a group of aristocrats who took up residence on the shores of Lake Naivasha in Kenya. While scouting around the lake, Mike and I walked into the home of an older couple from Scotland, a Tudor-style mansion built out of Scottish granite and surrounded with a beautiful, well-manicured rose garden. They'd taken their little bit of Scotland and transferred it to the shores of Lake Naivasha, where hippos wandered around instead of sheep. It gave us a glimpse into the mindset of the affluent and decadent Brits of our story who could ignore a war that was tearing Europe apart and, with their amphibious planes and crates of champagne, turn Naivasha into their personal playground. No matter how much you read about colonialism, it's only when you see the lasting effects of its arrogant history firsthand that it really hits home.

Working with Mike again was a no-brainer after *1984*, though *White Mischief* required a much different look. The sun-drenched film depicts a beautiful place forcibly taken over by ugly people incapable of appreciating it. While looking out over Lake Naivasha, a character played by Sarah Miles sums up their attitude completely as she watches another dawn come up over Lake Naivasha: "Oh God. Not another fucking beautiful day."

In many respects Mike and I took an approach opposite to *1984*, which relied heavily on the claustrophobic atmosphere created by a locked-down camera. Instead, we emphasized floating camera moves that connected characters within the same shot, movement motivated less by what was happening within the frame than by the sense of the scene. We wanted the camera movement to appear light and effortless, but shooting scenes in this way required careful blocking and actors that would work to specific camera direction. Many of the shots also involved rigging a crane on which I could ride and laying tracks for some lengthy moves, which could be particularly tricky on irregular terrain. One scaffolded platform that we constructed for a shot that followed a car up a hill and revealed the Rift Valley began to collapse as soon as I mounted the crane. It was a miracle we got the shot. Normally we would have used a much larger crane that would have required less of a build, perhaps a remotely operated camera head as well, but to have either for a single shot in Kenya meant having to rent it for the time it would take to ship it back and forth from the UK. We were no longer in Shepperton Studios.

> *Reminds me of my safari in Africa. Somebody forgot the corkscrew and for several days we had to live on nothing but food and water.*
>
> **W. C. FIELDS**

White Mischief ends with a sequence in which Greta Scaachi's character, Diana, rides through the bush, ending her journey at a cocktail party taking place among the gravestones of a cemetery beside the glistening water of Lake Naivasha. Diana leads the camera to reveal the cemetery and the characters we have got to know during the film with a movement that is typical of what Mike wanted throughout the film. But the movement then becomes even more dreamlike, ending as she sees a vision of her murdered lover enjoying himself among the other guests, helping to blur the line between the real and the unreal. It seemed a bookend to both my experience in Kenya and that of the country that the final image is a close shot of a servant holding a tray of champagne, played by the same young actor who had been our *Kitchen Toto* star, Edwin Mahinda.

Over the 1980s, I would shoot a variety of films ranging from the stylized noir of *Stormy Monday* to the brooding British spy thriller *Defense of the Realm* and the period drama *Pascali's Island*, set on a Greek island during the fall of the Ottoman Empire. Some were good experiences, and some were not so good. It was shortly after returning from Greece that I left a film with a multitude of problems that, for me, epitomized the indulgent side of filmmaking, from an unprepared director to a cast with specific ideas as to how I would photograph them. One actor suggested he would only be shot on a 50 mm lens, and an actress insisted I use an Obie light (a frontal light invented for Merle Oberon by her husband, the great cinematographer Lucien Ballard, to soften the scar tissues left over from a car accident), cosmetic lighting for which she had no need and nor did the film.

Since the release of *1984* I had received several approaches from American directors, but either I had been busy, my visa application had been turned down, or a studio had vetoed my hiring. I decided it was time to take a chance. I flew to LA to look for work.

It took some time, but an offer eventually came my way. A "prestigious family comedy," as my agent described it. I wandered along the beach in Santa Monica thinking through my options—being by the sea always seems to clarify my thoughts. It had the expectation of an enjoyable shoot with a fine cast of actors. Should I say yes? No sooner had I turned the offer down than my agent, who had begun to doubt my sanity since I had left the last project, received a call from Bob Rafelson. Would I be interested in a film about Richard Burton (another son of Torquay) and John Hanning Speke, two Victorian explorers, and their search for the source of the Nile?

Would I? Bob Rafelson was one of the most influential directors of the 1970s. *Five Easy Pieces* and *The King of Marvin Gardens* are two of the best American movies of that or any other era. If I had not been in Los Angeles, if I had not left one film and turned down another, I would have never been available to meet with Bob, nor would I have been free to work on his film. *A happy accident? Who knows?*

In this wilderness you will find only Allah's terrible whimsy.

ARAB CHIEF, IN *MOUNTAINS OF THE MOON*

I often don't know why I'm approached for a job, and *Mountains of the Moon* is no exception. I suspect Bob wanted someone out of the UK as we were shooting part of the film there. Perhaps a cameraman who had documentary experience. Chris Curling, who I had worked for in India and the Sudan, came aboard as an associate producer and anthropological advisor, but Bob told me he had no idea we had worked together. Perhaps he had seen *1984* and it was as simple as that.

Bob was a larger-than-life character. He had a reputation for having a temper, and everyone had heard stories about him hitting producers and having other eruptions. Perhaps he had mellowed by the time we met, as I saw only flashes of Bob's dark side. I loved working with him. He told tall tales that were impossible to believe until we discovered that, yes, he was telling the truth. One time we were in this small plane flying across a wide expanse of seemingly empty bush, and he said, "Ah, a friend of mine lives on a ranch down there. I recognize it. I was walking across Kenya and I met him down there." He had never mentioned any of this before. Suddenly, there was a ranch and we were buzzing around his mate somewhere in the wilderness to the edge of Mount Kilimanjaro.

Bob loved exploring. We hiked for hours along the border with Tanzania, between lines of trenches and barbed wire left over from World War I, before coming across a perfect crater lake that appeared out of nowhere. On the northeast border, we traveled with Kenyan soldiers as guards until they refused to go any further. "Somali bandits" was their reasoning. Bob asked, "Should we press on?" I replied, "Well, yeah. We're here, aren't we?" In another era he might have been Richard Burton searching for the source of the Nile. I love exploring too, though the trip did stir my fear of heights. Scouting the far-flung areas of Kenya by plane reminded me of my last trip with Chris Curling, following the White Nile from Khartoum into South Kordofan. Our bush pilot in Sudan told me that most in his profession don't live past fifty because of crashes, something you don't want to hear when as far as you can see there is only desert.

For a final scout we flew up to Lake Turkana in the northern part of the country. The area is pretty much a desert where the lake is surrounded by the cones of multiple volcanoes, though I don't think they're active anymore. We wandered around looking for an establishing shot we could use for a scene set in a nearby village, and we happened on a wonderful spot looking down toward the lake over the straw roofs of some huts. I asked Bob, "This would be good, wouldn't it?" before our guide said, "Yes, this was built for Vilmos...Vilmos..." I finished his thought: "Vilmos Zsigmond?" I asked, not expecting to hear the famous cinematographer's name. He said, "Yeah, that's it. For a car commercial." And I thought we were in the middle of nowhere. Vilmos's car commercial brought back memories of that bobbing Coke bottle at Point Nemo.

I asked Dick Pope if he would come on the project and shoot second unit of the expedition. I knew Dick had experience working in Kenya with Chris Curling on his *Worlds Apart* series and that he would be a perfect fit for this project. I was relieved when he said yes, and I couldn't have made a better choice. Dick seemed in his element. He would disappear into the wild with his own caravan of extras and return, days later, with two or three beautiful shots. Not dozens of images but just what you really want from a second unit.

That *Mountains of the Moon* was a passion project for Bob made it all the more embarrassing when, after some scenes early in the shoot, it briefly looked like I didn't know what I was doing. While we were still in the UK we filmed a scene in which Burton, played by Patrick Bergin, attends a dinner party with members of the Royal Geographical Society, and we needed to light the dinner table as it would have been in the 1850s, with candles. I couldn't do what Barry Ackroyd had done for me in Ireland, so Biggles made up some rigs with little bare bulbs to boost the candlelight in the most naturalistic way I could think of, though there still wasn't a whole lot of light. When the dailies came back only the candle flame was well exposed while the characters appeared as green shadows in the inky blackness surrounding them.

Sitting next to Bob and producer Dan Melnick in the screening room, I pulled out the lab report. These reports assign a number to the density of each of a negative's three color layers (red, green, and blue) from the intensity of light required to make the print. I was shooting with an Agfa stock that I rated at 320 ASA and would usually print at 31 across the average of all three colors. That's a little overexposed (27 being considered a midlight), but the heavier negative allowed me to maintain a good black in the shadows. When I looked at the sheet I saw a much higher number, 45 or 50. The image had been printed down from where I had exposed the negative by as much as two stops. I called the lab, and the timer came to the phone, "Oh, on the sheet you said 'candlelight.' That's what I printed for." I suppose that made sense. Not looking at the rest of the frame, he'd printed for the flame. I was much happier when we screened the proper version the next day. And so was Bob.

It's sometimes tricky to create a naturalistic look while still lighting the actors in ways that will do justice to their performances, and candlelight once made that even more challenging. During one scene in *Mountains of the Moon*, Burton passes a single candle over the naked body of his wife, Isabel, played by Fiona Shaw. There was no way I could shoot with the candle by itself unless I had one with a triple wick, but that would have involved dropping hot wax all over our lead actress.

Biggles came up with a solution—a boom pole with a 60-watt bulb hanging from the end of it. At 25 percent of its regular voltage, it matched the color temperature of the flame, and Biggles simply followed the path of the candle while keeping the bulb just out of shot. I'm always happy when we can find the simplest solution to a problem, and this was a trick we'd return to several times in the future. Cinematography is a wonderful blend of creativity, technical know-how, and problem-solving. I still think it's quite a nice-looking scene, although with modern film stocks and faster lenses, let alone the capabilities of digital cameras, I would be able to use the single-wick candle and nothing more.

In spite of the remote locations and complicated logistics, the shoot in Kenya went smoothly thanks to line producer Terry Clegg, whose careful planning allowed us to travel to all the places we'd chosen during our scouting. Filming, on the other hand, wasn't always so easy. Our most difficult scene appears early in the film when Somali waranle (warriors) attack Burton and Speke's expedition as they camp on the beach, which we shot on the shore of Malindi Bay.

I always want to create lighting that has a plausible source and consider simulating moonlight for night scenes to be something of a cheat when there is any other possibility, but it's sometimes unavoidable. Here we had fires outside and oil lamps inside the expedition's tents, not much to light the entire scene, but even so, I did not want to use moonlight. That the explorers couldn't see their attackers until they were feet away was part of what made the moment so fearful.

I think Bob had originally hoped to shoot the entire sequence by firelight but then resigned himself to a more conventional approach. "Well, where are you going to put the moonlight?" he asked me. "I'm not going to use moonlight," I told him. By this point Bob had become quite trusting but he still wanted to understand what I was going to do, replying, "So, how are you going to light it?" I explained the campfire and oil lamps approach. "What about the landscape?" he asked. We'd chosen the spot in part because of the miles of sand dunes surrounding it and Bob naturally wanted to see them in the film. But we had seen them, I reminded him. We'd shot a scene with Speke arriving back at the camp in the late afternoon, having been out hunting.

Bob remained skeptical about the darkness I was proposing, but he went with it. To increase the effect of the natural sources, Biggles and I created some practical lights using a variety of incandescent bulbs that came from the hardware store and could be used in multiples, either mounted on short wooden battens or inside purpose-made rectangular metal dishes. We buried the dishes in the sand, so that they were hidden from the lens, and angled them toward the focus of the shot, which they bathed in a soft but directional light while still appearing to come from the campfire or the tents.

It's not what you light—it's what you DON'T light.

JOHN ALTON

When Burton escapes the confusion of the battle and retreats across the dunes I began to wonder if not creating a moonlight source had been a mistake. Biggles was the one who suggested we use Maxi Brutes (lamps that hold twelve or eighteen sealed-beam 1,000-watt PAR 64 bulbs) and dim them down to look like firelight. I was skeptical at the light being so frontal to the camera but, by placing the lamps directly on the sand, we found the light would rake the patterns the wind had made in an interesting way while separating the characters from the dunes behind them. It was a technique that I carried with me until using it again on a much larger scale, and hopefully to better effect, for *Jarhead*.

Filming *Mountains of the Moon* stretched from Liverpool's Victorian docks to Kenya's Rift Valley. Scenes involved anything from a genteel game of croquet to a more concerning encounter with lions. The lions, supposedly tame, were maneuvered into our frames by two slightly built young lads banging sticks on rusty sheets of metal. But I suspect the lions had already been well fed as they were not remotely interested in us or our film.

While shooting on more remote locations the cast and crew were housed in a tented camp. It was as if we were on safari, sitting around the campfire in the evening with beers and watching our dailies from a VHS tape on a small television. But remote as we were at times, I wished it were more. Bob was in the radio tent for some time one evening and as he left, he called me over. "The studio wants a word." Fearing the worst, I lifted the radio receiver. "Deakins? Your dailies are too yellow. Too yellow!" I had no idea what the voice from the studio was talking about. The negative was being processed in London, and I would have known had there been a problem. "Where are you?" I asked, as politely as I was able. "How are you viewing them?" "I'm in my car on the Pacific Coast Highway. On my TV in the back of my car." Maybe, I suggested, the TV might be at fault (it was 1989 after all), or maybe the connection cut out. Either way I returned to the campfire shaking my head. Bob looked over as I sat down. "Hollywood," he said as he returned his gaze into the fire.

We shot Speke's discovery of Lake Victoria on our last day in Kenya. Only it wasn't. During our scouting we had found a beautiful overlook a short drive from Homa Bay on the eastern shore of the lake, and we had mapped out a single shot that would require a small crane. As the camera position involved a long hike up the almost vertical hillside that drew us to the shot in the first place, it took a while for our reduced shooting unit to get ready. Everyone mucked in and we made the shot in the midafternoon sunlight, which, as the sun set into the shot, was always our preferred time of day.

"OK?" Bob asked, after we made the shot. Of course, there was no video assist or playback at this time, so a director had to trust the operator more than today. The shot worked fine, but I was not sure if the lake was entirely visible as the air was thick with haze. I suggested that we should wait and see if it cleared. To cut a long story short, it never cleared. Our small unit stayed in a hotel (a charitable description) on Homa Bay for several days, carrying the camera up to the crane every morning, readying the cast with their props, hoping the sky would clear and the lake be fully visible. Bob disappeared after that first take. We knew precisely what was wanted, so he had no reason to stay. Besides, Jack Nicholson was flying back from London to LA in a private jet. Bob could get a free ride, so off he went.

That left us to the lake flies—which can be so bad you don't go outside after dark, and are known to have killed fishermen by smothering them in their swarms—and a bar with warm beer. One day turned into two, two into three. Until one evening our barman told us, "The farmers in Uganda burn off their fields at this time of year. That is why it's so smoggy. It might clear if the wind changes." "Do you think it might?" "Not at this time of year, no. It always blows across the lake from Uganda." The first take is the one in the film.

Making *Mountains of the Moon* wasn't all hard work all the time. It's not often that I get a chance to fish on the job, but I take advantage of opportunities when I can. On a meal break while shooting at Lake Turkana I hooked a large Nile perch. As I was playing the fish, Bob was having his regular lunchtime swim. The El Molo people who lived by the lake were once crocodile hunters, and the guide who had taken me out on his boat commented that the rock Bob was swimming toward was called Crocodile Island. We considered breaking the line to pick up Bob before it was too late, but that would have meant losing our fresh lunch. Besides, we didn't want to disturb Bob's midday relaxation. We arrived back at camp and cooked the fish, which was large enough for everyone to enjoy as a treat before beginning that afternoon's work—including Bob, who returned safely.

Later, Bob would call *Mountains of the Moon* the favorite of his films. I think *Five Easy Pieces* is his masterpiece and that elements of *Mountains of the Moon* don't quite come together. But it was an experience that stays. Shooting three films in Kenya was like exploring the history of colonialism, traveling back in time from the Mau Mau rebellion to the hedonism of the Happy Valley set to the first European exploration of the country, before it even became a country. It was not until after World War I that the area became known as the Kenya Colony and two million acres of land were given over to settlement for those who had been in "imperial service."

Mountains of the Moon saw part of that history from one narrow, Eurocentric point of view, but as I learned about Sidi Mubarak Bombay, the WaYao guide emerged as a more interesting subject for a film. Enslaved as a boy and raised in India, where he became fluent in Hindi, it was Bombay, played beautifully by Paul Onsongo in *Mountains of the Moon*, who led Burton and Speke to their discoveries. It was Sidi Bombay who guided Henry Morton Stanley in his search for David Livingstone. In 1873, Bombay walked across the continent from coast to coast with Verney Lovett Cameron. He was given a medal by the Royal Geographical Society but was never invited to England to receive it. That's a story.

You go away for a long time and return a different person—you never come all the way back.

PAUL THEROUX, *DARK STAR SAFARI*

After Kenya, I did return to America to shoot, but to a very different part of the country. *The Long Walk Home* is a fictional story set during the 1955 Montgomery Bus Boycott, the yearlong protest of Alabama's segregated public transportation system set in motion by Rosa Parks's refusal to give up her seat to a white passenger. The film shot in Montgomery using historic locations and even some of the original buses. It was the sort of film I had always hoped to work on, one with human characters that took an insightful perspective on real events, although, like *Mountains of the Moon*, one that also felt the need to place undue emphasis on the perspectives of its white characters. Even then, so many years after the bus boycott took place, our filming *The Long Walk Home* stirred up ghosts in that part of America. While scouting the film we'd approach homeowners and be told we could use their homes to shoot in—until they found out what the story was. "Uh-uh. Not in my house."

I don't want your children to grow up scared of mine.

ODESSA COTTER, IN *THE LONG WALK HOME*

My next film was also about America but shot largely in Thailand. Originally scripted by Richard Rush, *Air America* began as a satirical take on the true story of the CIA's clandestine airline, which operated inside Laos and Cambodia during the Vietnam War transporting guns and drugs. Rush, who had a gift for dark comedy, originally planned to direct the film himself. When this didn't work out, the script ended up in the hands of producer Daniel Melnick and became a vehicle for Mel Gibson and Robert Downey Jr. I'd worked with Dan on *Mountains of the Moon*—in fact, Bob Rafelson was set to direct *Air America* at one point—and we got on very well. I'd also liked director Roger Spottiswoode's 1983 film *Under Fire*, in which Nick Nolte plays a photojournalist working in Nicaragua. Its tone and politics felt like a good match for the *Air America* I imagined we'd be making. It felt like the right project.

What's considered psychotic behavior anywhere else is company policy.

GENE RYACK, IN *AIR AMERICA*

The bad omens started in preproduction, when a rare earthquake threatened to destroy our production office on the twelfth floor of a hotel in Chiang Mai, and they continued as we scouted the film by helicopter. Roger, Dan, production designer Allan Cameron, aerial unit director Marc Wolff, and I were passengers in a Thai Air Force Huey helicopter, no doubt left behind at the end of the Vietnam War, flying out of Chiang Mai to scout the mountains to the north and west of the city. The clouds lay low in the sky and, after a long time seeing nothing *but* clouds and the dark shapes of the mountains below, it seemed to us that we were lost. But, as the Thai pilot spoke little English, it was hard for us to know for sure. To cut a long story short, we landed in a Hmong village nestled among the mountains, where we were greeted by a people who looked to be in full ceremonial costume, though these were apparently their everyday clothes. Our pilot proceeded to spread a map and ask one of the elders to point out where we were. What village was this? I never did hear an answer, and we took off without seeming to know more than we had before we landed.

This was at least a colorful life experience, but our return trip was much less enjoyable. As we flew back toward Chiang Mai in a direction that seemed at best a guess, Marc gestured to the fuel gauge. He was concerned that the needle hovered around the full mark, indicating the Huey had not used any fuel during all the hours we had been circling the mountains. The copilot tapped the gauge, the needle dropped to zero, and a red light began to flash. *How far are we from the runway? Should we fly in fast in the hope that, if we run out of fuel, our inertia will take us in? At least we would be close to the ground if we crash! On the other hand, if we gain altitude, we might be able to glide our way to the runway.* It was a bizarre conversation to listen to from the back of the Huey, but we somehow landed safely.

The scouting trip set the tone for what would be one crazy shoot, which stretched from October 1989 through February 1990 in Thailand, the UK, and Los Angeles. *Air America* involved working with the largest crew I have come across before or since—or ever want to come across again. I felt the film could have been shot handheld using a single camera with long takes that concentrated on the characters rather than the action, but the director took the opposite approach.

It's not that I don't ever see a place for multiple cameras, as one scene on a dirt runway illustrates. A giant cargo transport, a DC-130, flew into Chiang Mai one afternoon having, reportedly, flown directly from where it was in use in South America. In what use was the subject of much speculation. The pilot, a real American cowboy, came to scout the runway in the middle of the jungle where we expected him to land his "bird." He took one quick look at its length, pointed to a spot in the dirt where he would stop the plane, and disappeared into the nightlife of Chiang Mai.

When the plane circled the field the next morning, we were waiting with eleven cameras set to where our pilot had made his mark. We were close but not too close. Maybe. Should we shoot on longer lenses? No, that would only weaken the shots. The pilot brought the plane in; it taxied slowly toward us and stopped within a foot of the mark. Once our assistant director gave the all clear, we had the shot, and the plane took off on its journey back to whatever it did in South America. Had we known the pilot had had to be dragged out of bed that morning, after a night on the town that, for him, had hardly ended, we might have made a different decision as to where the cameras would be!

This was a good use of multiple cameras, but I prefer every scene to have a specific visual perspective rather than showing the audience a series of random shots that, however beautiful, don't further the story. Even when shooting action scenes, I like to remain focused on what's needed rather than a series of options that will never be used. Action can have a point of view: Witness the distinct identities of both Henri-Georges Clouzot's *The Wages of Fear* and William Friedkin's 1977 remake, *Sorcerer.* Roger Spottiswoode is an ex-editor (who worked for the great Sam Peckinpah), and he likes to have a lot of footage when he gets to the cutting room. He is the director and that is his prerogative, but I might never have signed on if I had understood this.

Dan had hired me, and he wanted to make it work, but Roger clearly did not value my input or like me operating the camera. I realized just how low his opinion was of me when, some four weeks into the shoot, we were watching dailies: tedious coverage of a convoy of trucks wending its way through the jungle, mortar rounds exploding and troops in camouflage responding, action shot multiple times, on multiple lenses, and with multiple cameras. It was footage that I didn't remember shooting—a cinematographer's nightmare. Only then did it dawn on me that the crew was even larger than I had initially thought. An "action" unit, being directed by a stunt coordinator, had been shooting for almost as long as our first unit. While a second unit is not unusual on a film like *Air America*, it was odd that the film's cinematographer—that is, me—had not been consulted.

The final scene of *Air America* involved another helicopter, this time shooting on a Los Angeles freeway using nine cameras. When the production wrapped, I returned to London harboring grave doubts about the business and my place in it. Doubts that led me to move back to Devon. As luck would have it, I found a flat in a location where I had often imagined I would one day like to live. I made an offer (OK! I admit it. I did use my *Air America* earnings, so I shouldn't complain too much!), and in little more than a month I was back in Devon. I got out my paintbrush and attacked the walls of my new home. *Air America* could and should have been something very special, but instead of a satirical black comedy in the vein of *M*A*S*H*, it turned into a wacky buddy action comedy. We started with a good script and the budget to do the story justice. How could you tell?

And then the phone rang.

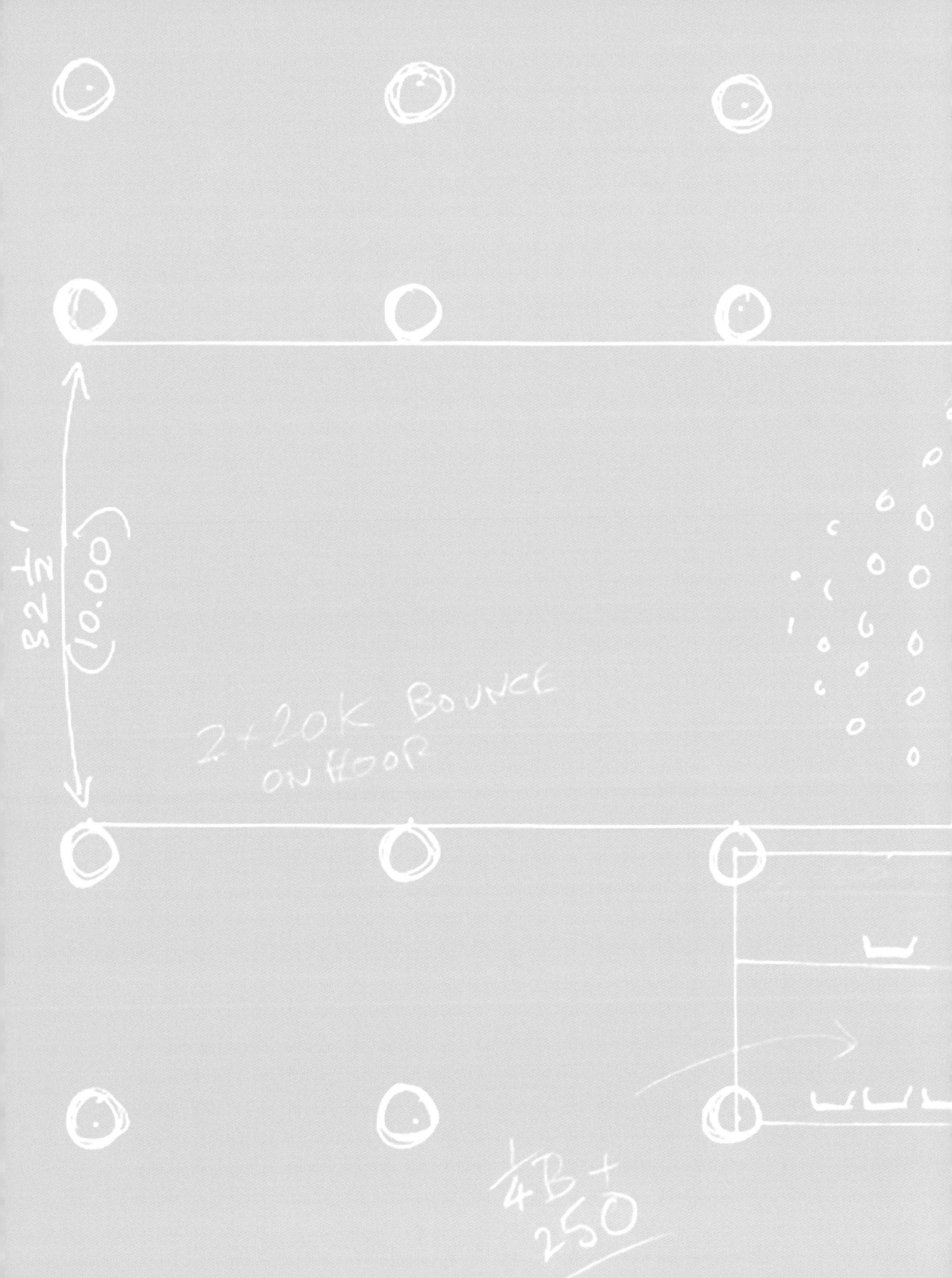
32 ½'
(10.00)
2 + 20K BOUNCE
ON FLOOR
¼ B +
250

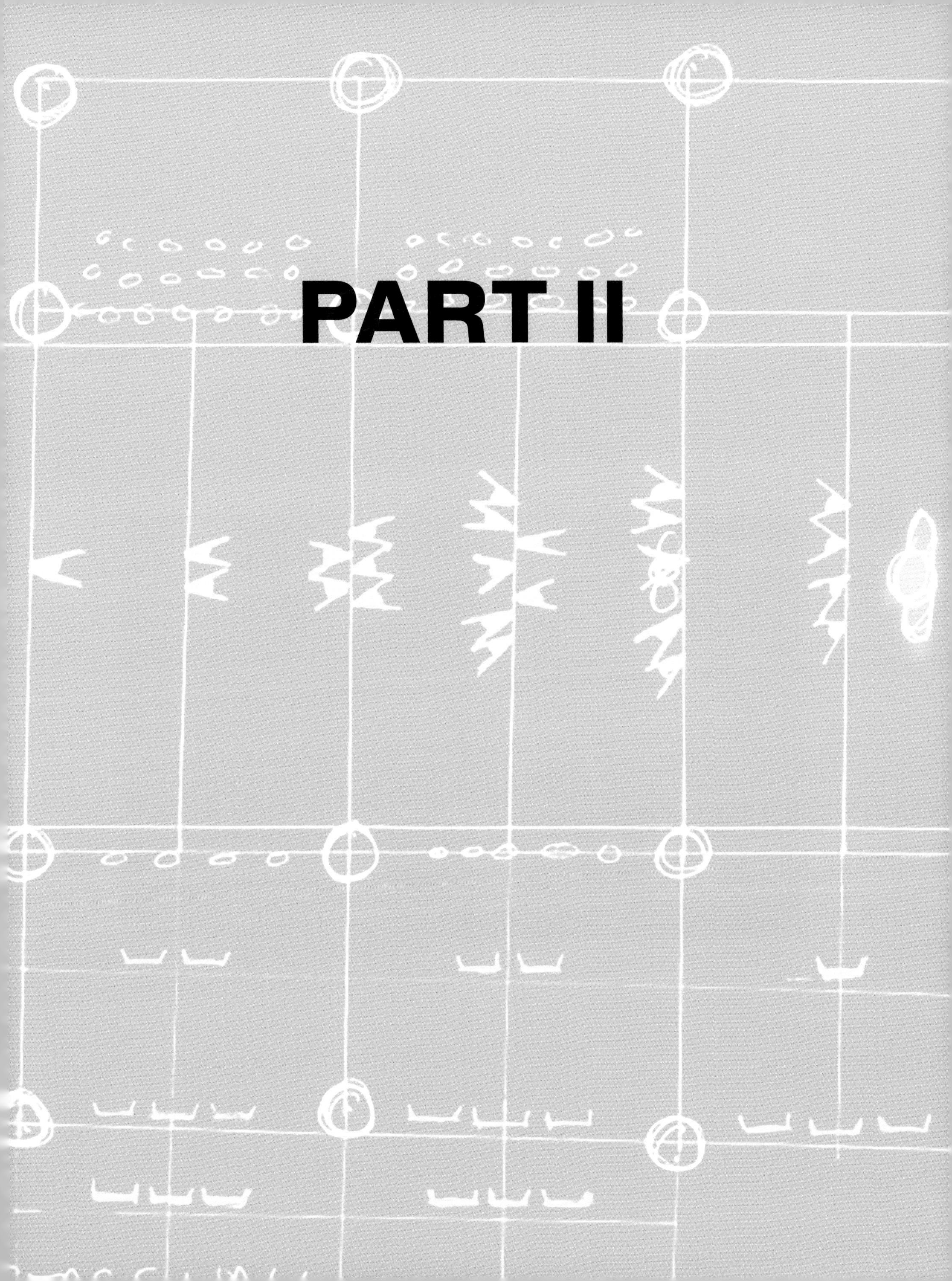

PART II

TWO BROTHERS

Look upon me! I'll show you the life of the mind!

CHARLIE MEADOWS, IN *BARTON FINK*

It was my agent calling to tell me about a script, though it probably wasn't the right project for me. "It doesn't make much sense. It's like two different movies. About halfway through it changes into something that doesn't match what it sets up."

I asked who the director was, then remember hearing the shuffling of paperwork.

"It's two brothers. I don't know them. Joel and Ethan Coen." I asked for the script to be sent over right away.

That Joel and Ethan Coen wanted to meet came right out of the blue. They'd only released two films—*Blood Simple* and *Raising Arizona*, with a third, *Miller's Crossing*, soon to follow—but I thought the two that I had seen were the work of highly imaginative filmmakers. And *Barton Fink* was nothing if not imaginative, filled with references to old Hollywood, American literature, and World War II–era politics, some of which I got and other parts I didn't.

The Coens were in London and, my Devon flat still being a work in progress, I was as well. So, we met up for tea in Notting Hill. The brothers were not at all how I'd imagined they might be. Just a couple of young chain smokers with long hair—Joel's was particularly long and curly back then—rather quiet and unassuming. They were also very much in sync about the material and their approach to it, so much so that one would finish the other's sentences. What had been a pleasant conversation wound up after an hour or so leaving me with little idea what would happen next—until my agent rang and told me production would start in June. I would be meeting up with the Coens in Santa Monica for five weeks of prep.

It was years before I understood why they'd hired me (or that I wasn't the only cinematographer they interviewed in London that day). *Barton Fink* was to be shot nonunion in a union town, so a European cinematographer would fit that bill. Joel later told me they had put in a call to *Air America* director Roger Spottiswoode to find out how I worked, and he'd given them a scathingly bad report. He told Joel and Ethan I liked to operate the camera myself, was not a fan of second units, that I did not like shooting with multiple cameras or with zoom lenses, and that I preferred working out the shots in a scene before the day's shooting began. Joel laughed when he told me this; it was exactly what the brothers wanted to hear.

Barton Fink was my introduction to the idea of working from storyboards (line drawings of each shot). Before that, on *1984*, *Sid and Nancy*, *Pascali's Island*, and *Defense of the Realm*, I had worked with the director to figure out how we would cover a scene during a blocking rehearsal. Almost without exception, this would take place on the morning of the shoot. The process could take an hour or more, sometimes, as was the case on *1984*, even longer. During the five weeks of prep I had with the Coen brothers in Los Angeles, we scouted locations, discussed the look of the film, and drew storyboards together with their regular storyboard artist, J. Todd Anderson. On subsequent films with Joel and Ethan, I would not always be involved in the initial process of creating the storyboards but, at the very least, we would review them together before production began in earnest.

The first shot of *Barton Fink* is also the first shot I worked on for Joel and Ethan, though what you see is different from what we had initially conceived. The film opens in a New York theater at the premiere of Fink's latest play, *Bare Ruined Choirs*, a drama set among working-class New York fishmongers. We used the Orpheum Theatre in downtown Los Angeles to stand in for a Broadway house and storyboarded a series of small, close shots to open the film: the fly counterweights moving, the stagehand reading his paper between actions, then, finally, a close shot on John Turturro that swings around to reveal the stage and the play's cast taking in the audience's applause. While scouting the location, I asked if we might connect these individual shots into one flowing camera move and was taken by surprise when the brothers agreed to try it. I think they knew we could easily shoot the individual setups if the move proved impossible but, not yet having any reason to have confidence in me, they asked that I prep the shot the day before.

I knew we could pull it off, but we'd need the right equipment, so I ordered a Louma crane. Invented in the early 1970s but only slowly coming into common use, the Louma was the first telescopic camera crane arm to incorporate a remote head with a video assist monitor from which the camera could be operated. Where traditional crane arms would generally require a human operator mounted behind the camera, the Louma made this unnecessary and expanded the sorts of shots we could create. It was the most maneuverable lightweight crane I knew, and we rigged it on our location at the same time as Billy O'Leary set up our simple lighting. Since I met Billy in New York, we had become good friends. He had worked as my gaffer on *The Long Walk Home* and had also joined Biggles and his crew in Thailand for the *Air America* experience. It gave me confidence to have him with me on *Barton Fink*, as not only was he a good electrician, but he could also understand my most wayward sketches.

I arrived at the theater early on the first shoot day, as did much of our crew. We had the camera up and ready soon after the scheduled call time. While waiting for the actors to finish with makeup, hair, and wardrobe, we had plenty of time to rehearse the crane move with Joel and Ethan. After the actors arrived, we completed the shot in one or two takes, without Joel or Ethan suggesting we cover the action with static shots. Leaving the camera on the crane, we shot the two other angles we needed for the scene, and by late in the morning we had completed the scheduled work for the day. At one point Ethan asked me to slow down (something I have yet to be asked to do by any director but the Coens, before or since) or the lunch that had been prepared by the film's caterer would go to waste. I was relieved. It had been my first day of shooting with the Coen brothers and I had avoided being physically sick. In truth, however nervous I might be, I have learned to bury myself in my work, and my confidence grows from my work.

But every day brought a new challenge, and my next was in the main ballroom aboard the *Queen Mary*, the retired British ocean liner that had been converted into a floating Long Beach hotel. We had our storyboards, so I knew this location called for a shot that would track through the ballroom as if it were Barton's point of view, before stopping on a static shot of his agent sitting with some dinner guests and cutting to a close shot of Barton. To accomplish this long, winding move across what was by no means a smooth floor, I had arranged for a specialist operator, Mark O'Kane, to be hired along with his Steadicam rig. I'd used the Steadicam on pop videos and Mike Figgis's *The House*, but it was still a relatively new tool for me. Invented in the 1970s, it had become overused in the 1980s. But applied properly, as in Hal Ashby's *Bound for Glory* or Elem Klimov's *Come and See*, it could both create a unique and powerful effect and be useful in challenging locations. But our long moving shot only added to the difficulty of the lighting.

Using even a minimal rig inside such a sensitive space as the *Queen Mary* presented problems. Today I would almost certainly use one of the many lightweight lighting balloons to project the soft, central light source I was looking for, but, in 1990, those were still years in the future. By removing some of the recessed lighting fixtures, Billy and our key grip, Brian Reynolds, devised fixing points to suspend a rig over the dance floor, but this would allow only for the lightest of units. Conventional film lighting was out of the question and, because I wanted the light source to be both warm and soft, dimming an array of household bulbs struck me as the simplest solution. Though it was a technique I had used many times in the past, here it would be on a much larger scale.

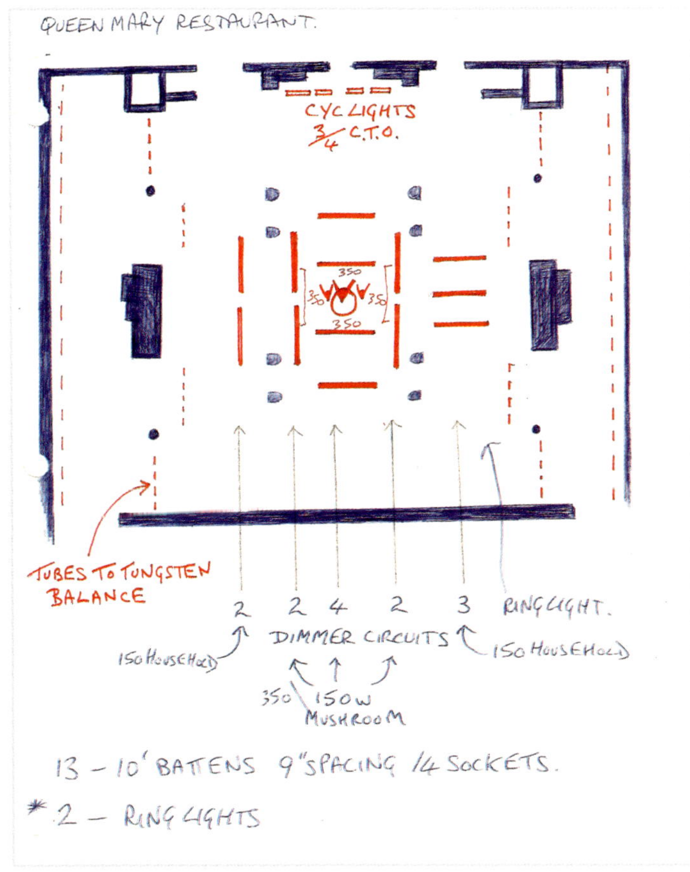

To avoid the walls becoming as bright as the center of the ballroom, Billy and I turned to an off-the-shelf hardware-store item, the R30 mushroom bulb, which is both directional and, at that time at least, available in a range of wattage. We mounted 150-watt bulbs, spaced nine inches apart, on thirteen ten-foot-long wooden battens. To accentuate the central brightness of the dance floor we used two small wooden rings mounted with 300-watt mushroom bulbs. Each of the more than two hundred bulbs faced directly down from the battens, which we rigged to a simple pulley system to be able to raise and lower them easily. It was quite an affair to assemble, but once we got it in place, the light it gave off worked well and, thanks to having each line of bulbs on dimmers, it was totally controllable. We were told by our minders that in all the time the *Queen Mary* had been used as a film location they had never seen anything quite like it!

We shot the scene at the *Queen Mary* bar using still more household bulbs, specifically a row of 100-watt globes rigged above and between the two characters and softened with a layer of tracing paper diffusion.

I use regular hardware-store items to save money but also because of the way I think about light. I see practical lights—a fluorescent tube or a bare bulb—as tools of equal importance to more specialized film lighting. It's a practice I embraced long before *Sid and Nancy*—even bringing it to documentary work—and one that I've maintained on far bigger-budget films such as *Blade Runner 2049*.

When I sometimes (quite often, in truth) have doubts about the improvised kinds of things I come up with, I am reminded of an article in *American Cinematographer* magazine on John Alonzo's lighting of *Chinatown*. Alonzo was brought in by Roman Polanski to replace Stanley Cortez because Polanski found the great cinematographer's methods too predictable and slow. Like myself, John Alonzo had experience as a documentary cameraman, and when it came to lighting the sets for Polanski's film, instead of the conventional film lights Cortez had been using, he reverted to the minimalistic style and simple tools with which he was more familiar—tracing paper and household bulbs. That was in 1974. Nothing is new.

We repurposed another real-life location for the lobby of the Hotel Earle, where Barton lives while in Los Angeles. The Wiltern presented a different set of challenges. The job of transforming the theater into the lobby of a hotel that had seen better days fell to production designer Dennis Gassner, but his hard work would be for nothing if it couldn't be seen, and the script called for a shaft of sunlight. We had an early call, but Bill O'Leary and I arrived about an hour before that to finesse our lighting in the quiet before the rest of the crew arrived. I'd planned on bouncing two 12K HMI lamps off two 4' × 4' mirrors set on opposing sides of a balcony above the reception desk, but it soon became clear that the short throw of the lamp did not allow for the clean sharp beam of light we were looking for. We called the rental company and ordered a Molebeam, a lamp that produces a sharp parallel beam of light, which turned up in rapid order. The effect looked good, but it was not sunlight. It produced a sharp beam, even more so when bounced off a mirror, but it didn't have the intensity I was after.

The clock was ticking, and we needed a solution. On Billy's suggestion we again called the rental company and asked if they had any HMI PAR lamps. These were quite new to the market and neither Billy nor I had used them before—few had—but our rental house had two, and we took a chance. The lamps arrived as I watched Joel and Ethan working

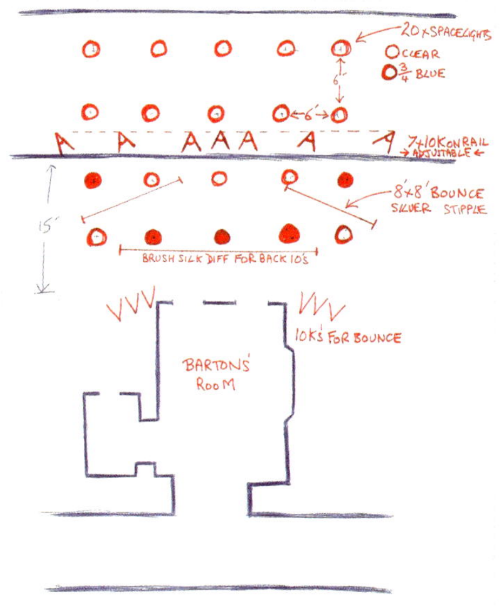

with the actors on a blocking rehearsal, and Billy quietly moved them into position. As the actors left the set for a final makeup and costume check, Billy struck up the two lamps and aimed them at our mirrors. To this day I don't think the Coens or anyone else was aware that all the equipment going up and down those stairs was to achieve a "simple" sunlight effect, or of all the stress I felt trying to pull it off. If the PARs had not worked as well as they did, I would have resorted to one of the other sources. The result would not have been as I had in my mind, but sometimes such compromises are unavoidable.

Much of *Barton Fink* takes place in Barton's hotel room and the corridor outside. For Barton's room we worked on a stage in Culver Studios, whereas the corridor was constructed in a Long Beach warehouse. Ideally, we would have used the same stage for each, but the sheer scale of the corridor made it beyond the scope of our Culver Studios stages.

The hotel room scenes take place at various times of day and differ considerably in tone. Though I briefly considered treating each quite separately, this began to feel heavy-handed and time-consuming. (A cinematographer must always be mindful of a film's schedule when choosing a lighting plan.) For Barton's room, playing the changing daylight in the world outside would be enough to shift the mood without dramatically altering the lighting within.

We mimicked the effect of skylight percolating into the room with an array of 10K Fresnel lamps positioned above the backing and diffused with brush silk. Additionally, we set three 10Ks on either side of the window to bounce off silver stipple reflectors and bring soft light in from the sides of the set. I also laid a white sheet on the stage floor outside the windows to lift the ceiling with the bounce it provided. This kind of flexible lighting plan allowed me to easily adjust the quality, intensity, color, and direction of the light without shifting the rig. The sunlight effect for the opening shot of the room was simply created using a single direct 10K lamp, rather than the daylight-balanced, narrow-beam HMI PAR. At the flick of a switch, I could go from sunlight to night or any step in between, saving both time and money.

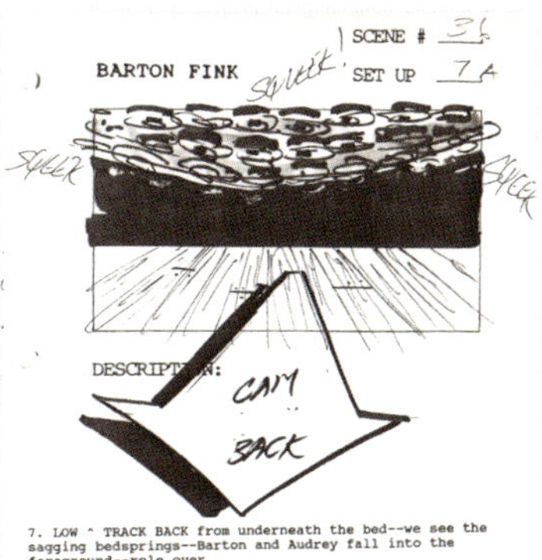

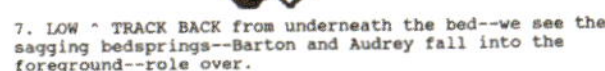

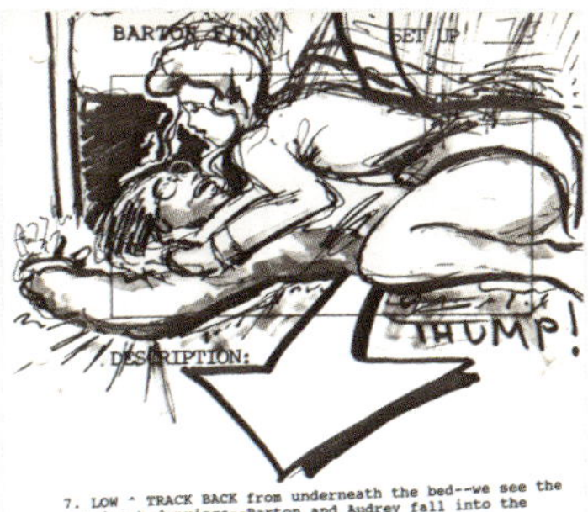

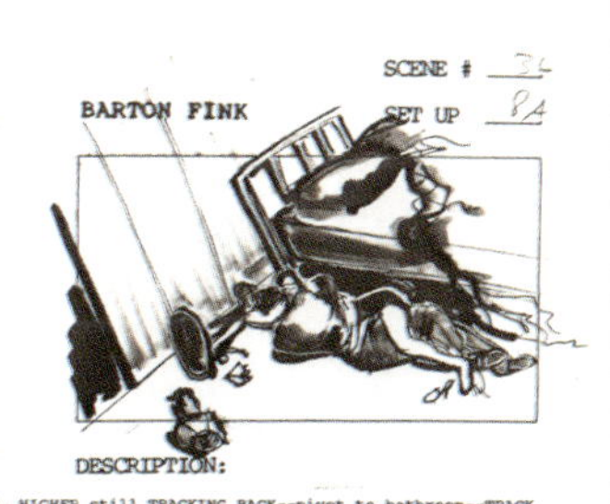

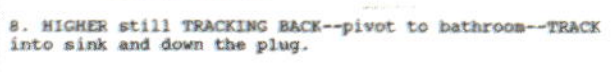

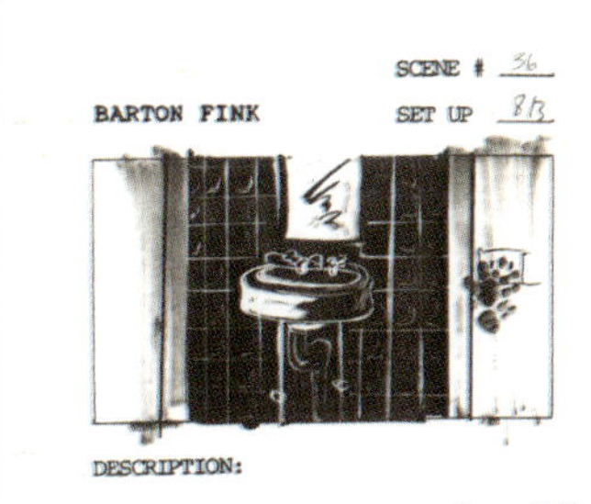

J. Todd Anderson

Like classic noir, shadows played just as important a role as light and, to create pools of light rather than an overall wash, the choice of practical lamps (the desk and floor lamps) was crucial to the look. There was little space to add additional lights, but by hanging them from above the set, I could use a 1K or a 650-watt Fresnel lamp to bounce light off two- and three-foot muslin reflectors and augment the practical sources for a close shot, while keeping the floor clear of clutter for the actors and camera to work in.

Some of the camera moves that Joel and Ethan proposed required some creativity, particularly when one involved tracking into a bathroom, up to a sink, and down its plughole, as it did during a sex scene between Barton and Audrey Taylor, played by Judy Davis. It's quite an extreme, and wonderful, variation on the train going into the tunnel. But, as you see from the comparison between the storyboards and the shot, things change. The storyboards act as a marker for what is essential to the scene, but they are not set in stone.

We accomplished this seemingly singular move by marrying two shots together. For the first we used a small Fisher jib arm and a Power Pod Classic remote head, an unusual combination at the time. The Power Pod Classic was the first compact remote head and as good as there was for working in tight spaces. I'd use it regularly after *Barton Fink*, sticking with it even after new devices superseded it in popularity.

During prep, first assistant cameraman Scott Ressler figured out how to keep the image sharp during what was for him a particularly difficult shot, by shortening the focus range of the 40 mm lens we were using—we had no need for the lens to focus to infinity—and tying a knotted string below its front element. As the camera moved down toward the sink, the knots helped him gauge the diminishing distance between the camera and the plughole.

When the screen goes black the film dissolves into the second shot that descends the pipe as seen through an Innovision probe. This is essentially a narrow tube with a fisheye lens at the end of it, the

same piece of specialized equipment we used to photograph the keys of Barton's typewriter as they hit the paper. To extend the apparent length of the pipe, I had a small card painted with concentric circles, leaving a gap between it and the far end. Beyond the probe's circular view of the card, I bounced light to rake the interior of the actual pipe as if the source were coming from the distance as represented by the concentric circles on the card. Not the most elegant solution, but simple.

For the film's most striking sequence, the hotel fire, Dennis built two matching hallway sets so we could shoot on one as the other was being set up, and the paper from any burn shot being replaced. (Incidentally, the length of the set was extended using a photograph of the built hallway pasted on the end wall in a similar way to the pipe.) Our effects team rigged the set walls with perforated gas pipes that zigzagged all the way down the passageway, allowing us to control the way it burnt via a series of valves. That didn't mean it couldn't be a little dangerous. The actors, my dolly grip, and I had to coat ourselves in a fire gel, and those of us not on camera wore asbestos suits. But because the effects team was so good and rigorously showed all of us how the effect was being done, everyone felt very comfortable. For the tracking shots, I handheld the camera on a wheeled rig made of speed rail, essentially lightweight pipe, that was alternately pushed or pulled by Bruce Hamme, our dolly grip, with whom I would work on almost every subsequent film until he retired in 2017. Today, this sequence might be done in VFX, but would it look as exciting as it was to shoot with real fire?

Barton Fink's final scene would become one of its most discussed, so let me just say right away that I don't know what's in the box. (And I don't think Joel and Ethan know, either.) But I *can* shed some light on one element of the last shot. The pelican diving into the water, just before the film cuts to the credits, is there because we were lucky to catch a bird (a real bird as opposed to a digital bird) diving into the water.

Sometimes, it's as simple as that.

J. Todd Anderson

Soon after *Barton Fink* wrapped, I headed to Baltimore to scout for playwright David Mamet's third film as a director, *Homicide*. For this film we drew storyboards for the major sequences but, as the locations were chosen late in preproduction, these illustrations bore little relationship to where we would shoot. Nor did the ambition behind the storyboards reflect the tight schedule we were up against. On the other hand, John Sayles made his own simple sketches for every scene of *Passion Fish*, depicting the size of a frame or the movement of the camera. The final film closely reflects the intent behind John's drawings even though it is not a mirror of them. *Barton Fink* adhered far more closely to the original storyboards, and I was struck that the finished film contained all but a handful of our shots. The Coens had achieved this using one hundred thousand feet of film stock, no doubt a tenth of what we had shot on *Air America* and a pure fantasy on most mainstream productions.

Coming from the instantaneous nature of documentary shooting to working with a preconceived plan might seem restricting, but I can't say I have ever felt that. But there is always an exception to every sweeping statement like that. M. Night Shyamalan and I spent many weeks storyboarding *The Village* together and based everything we drew on the locations and sets we knew we would shoot on. It was a surprise, and sometimes frustrating for both the actors and me, that what we shot mirrored exactly what we had conceived beforehand. That, to me, is a little too restricting.

But before *Passion Fish* took me into the bayous of Louisiana, my life took an unexpected turn in the badlands of South Dakota.

BADLANDS

Hard to believe, huh?
It used to be all theirs, clear on up into Canada.
This is what they got left with.

FRANK COUTELLE, IN *THUNDERHEART*

Directed by Michael Apted, *Thunderheart* is a mystery set in the 1970s starring Val Kilmer as an FBI agent of Sioux heritage who's sent to a South Dakota Native American reservation to investigate a murder. Kilmer's character has spent much of his life covering up his Native American roots and, in some respects, the film felt to me like a natural follow-up to *Homicide*, in which Joe Mantegna's character takes on a case that forces him to reexamine his Jewish identity. Mike Apted alternated between narrative films and documentaries throughout his career, and *Thunderheart* was a fictionalized version of a story he explored in *Incident at Oglala*, which documents a fatal conflict between the FBI and members of the American Indian Movement.

Filming took place on the Pine Ridge Lakota reservation, where the actual events unfolded in the 1970s, with some characters being played by local members of the Lakota people who remembered the history well. We'd shoot action that felt a bit too Hollywood, only to be told the real events were so much worse. It's a credit to Mike that none of the Pine Ridge residents raised objections. They felt like he was making an earnest attempt to tell a truthful story.

Shooting with Val was never less than interesting and often involved coping with his eccentricities. Once we were filming with him and Ted Thin Elk, who plays the character of Grandpa, in a vast and empty landscape with, as far as we could tell, nothing around for miles. Val had told us, "Nobody can stand in my eyeline." Fair enough. Some actors are very particular about where the crew stand so, to Val's wishes, everybody had to get behind the camera. I was operating, with Eric Swanek as my first assistant and Andy Harris serving as his second, which was the first time Andy and I worked together. Mike and the rest of the shooting crew were all lined up behind a large diffusion we erected as a blind.

All Val should have been able to see out of the corner of his eye was the camera and my head. But we were about to roll when he pulled away from the frame. "No! No, I can't. There is still somebody in my eyeline." We all looked around. *Really?* Way, way out toward the horizon you could just barely see a kid sitting on the back of a pickup truck, the child of a rancher who was probably out looking for his cows. Val insisted, "I can't shoot with that kind of distraction. It's all I can see." So, we sent a production assistant out in a vehicle, which took some doing since we had cleared the set for Val's eyeline, and the nearest transport was far away. As this was all playing out, Bruce Hamme (our dolly grip, who I had met on *Barton Fink* and stayed with me for *Homicide*) whispers to me, "Does Val ever act in the theater? Does he have the audience turn their backs to the stage?"

While scouting, it was obvious that South Dakota's great landscapes, the badlands that go off into infinity, would present problems at night. Without completely losing the naturalism we were going for, I required a single source rather than an approach that might make it feel as if there were multiple moons. We'd chosen a location for Grandpa's trailer that looked out over a beautiful view of the badlands and was close to a rise that would serve as a spot from which Val's character, Ray Levoi, would keep watch. It was at the top of this rise that I could position a moonlight source, but what kind of light could we possibly use?

We could erect a high scaffold tower and rig individual lights on it, which would cost a lot of money, eat up a lot of time, and make daylight filming impossible on any consecutive day. Instead, I convinced the production to rent a Musco light, a mobile floodlight usually used to light sports events and stadiums. It was something of a leap of faith as I'd never used a Musco before, but Billy O'Leary called to find out the specs on the unit, and we thought we could make it work. At its full height of one hundred feet and parked on the top of our hill, we found we could mount a heavy diffusion across the lower two rows of the Musco's sixteen individual lamps, flooding them out to spill a soft light across the landscape below the unit while spotting in the two upper rows of four lamps to directly light the badlands in the distant background. We finished one shot, a pan across the landscape toward our moonlight with the Musco truck above the frame line, and breathed a sigh of relief. We felt confident that we'd made the right choice—until it rained.

Dry and chalky, the landscape of the badlands readily reflects light—except when it rains. What had looked mystical and ghostly was now invisible. I peered into blackness and suggested to the assistant director, Chris Soldo, that we take an early meal break. Sure enough, it had stopped raining when we returned at around eleven o'clock. We *could* resume shooting, but the badlands had yet to dry out. It was then that Billy suggested that the generator would need refueling. The Musco had been left on during the break and the genny had run low. All this took time, but I was aware that it was taking a little more time than was usual. Finally, Billy turned to me and asked if he should fire up the light. At that point I knew for sure he had been diplomatically filling time. The landscape had dried out; we completed the night's work on time and went on to shoot another badlands exterior with no further holdup.

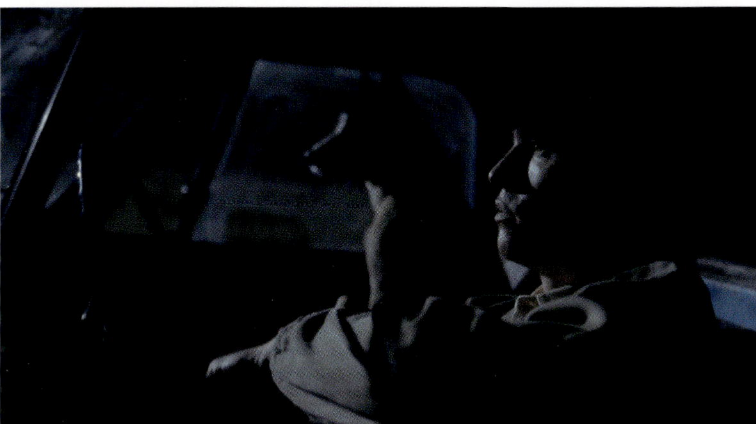

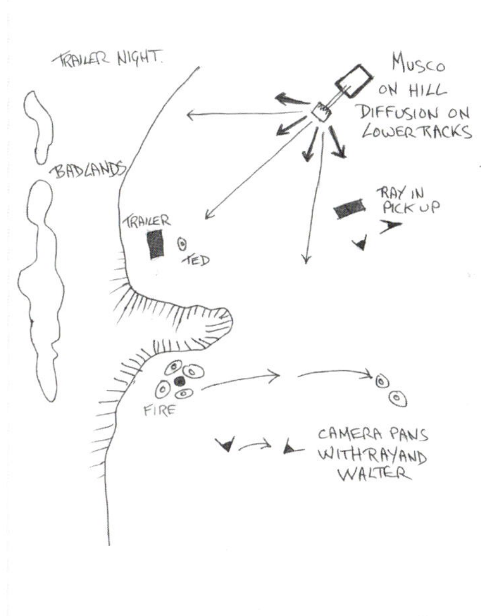

On a shoot like *Thunderheart* you get to know your coworkers quite well. We'd rented out virtually every motel room in the small South Dakota town of Kadoka, which we turned into our home base for the film. I love shoots like this, and I enjoyed using what downtime I had to explore the landscapes of South Dakota, driving to the Black Hills as well as to the Devil's Tower in nearby Wyoming. Having no distractions ensures that everyone on board the movie cares about what they're doing and is willing to sacrifice the comforts of their home life for the length of the project. It's a situation in which everyone works closely together and often shares some free hours together.

One person I always work particularly closely with is the script supervisor. Not only the director's right hand, the script supervisor—or continuity person, as they are known in the UK—is a key ally when it comes to deciding on a shot or when reference must be made to a shot or scene that has been completed days or weeks previously. *Thunderheart*'s script supervisor was named James Ellis.

Born in New Jersey, she spent most of her childhood there and on the island of Ocracoke in North Carolina. At the University of North Carolina at Chapel Hill, she studied classics and began creating multimedia shows for the university with friends. This sparked an interest in working in film, which in turn led to a job at DuArt, a New York–based film lab where she had a chance to learn from the best but hit a glass ceiling when she asked for a raise. After DuArt, James worked as a postproduction supervisor before, when filling in for an absent coworker, she segued into the role of a script supervisor, which in turn led to feature films and commercials. It was my luck that a commercial had brought her to Michael Apted and South Dakota.

They broke my TV.

GRANDPA SAM REACHES, IN *THUNDERHEART*

While on *Thunderheart* James and I had one date, though we sometimes can't decide whether it counts as a date or not. One Saturday (a rare two-day weekend of no shooting or scouting), we drove an hour to Rapid City, where we took in a double feature of *Robin Hood: Prince of Thieves* and *Terminator 2*. (I didn't care for either, but James liked *Terminator 2*.) We ate at an Italian restaurant, which felt luxurious compared to Kadoka's grocery store. Afterward we talked all the way back to the motel, not only about the movie we were working on or those we'd just seen but about all sorts of things that pass through your mind on a long, late-night drive. Though we met in the badlands of South Dakota, it was *Thunderheart* and our love of film that had drawn us together.

James and I married, in Hong Kong, in December of that same year. She's both a professional and creative partner as well as a personal one. (We use the Team Deakins name for our collaborative efforts for good reason.) Perhaps because we met as collaborators on a film set, we have always worked well together. Over the years, we have built up a method of working that, at this point, is accepted by production. We come as a team. From the initial reading of the script through prep, shoot, and post, we work side by side. James fully understands the technical side of the process, so she will coordinate with production, VFX, the post supervisor, the AD department, and our crew to ensure we have what we need and that there is a clear communication with all the departments. Because we've worked through the script together, she knows exactly what I am trying to achieve visually. She will view the dailies each morning and make sure there are no surprises! It's a bonus that we get to share the life experiences of the movies we work on together.

Never work with animals or children.

W. C. FIELDS

Though it was a rarity that we could work on the same project when James was still scripting, *The Secret Garden* presented an early opportunity. Agnieszka Holland was shooting her adaptation of the classic children's story in the UK. As it was her first time in the country, she readily brought on James as her script supervisor. We enjoyed the experience of being in England together and working with Agnieszka, though making the film wasn't without a few speed bumps.

A key character in the story is the robin who leads the heroine to the secret garden of the title. For the film, this involved using a specially trained English member of the species. But when our American Zoetrope producers viewed some early test footage of the bird, they were confused. "What is this?" "A robin." "That's not a robin. A robin is bigger than that." "It's what we have in England." "How will an audience know *this* is supposed to be a robin?" We were filming an English classic in England, so we had, quite logically, been training a European robin, but it transpired that the English variety is, of course, far smaller than its American namesake. But we stayed with the original robin because, although they explored the option, the production couldn't secure a permit to import the American bird. If the producers had waited a few short years for special effects to catch up with their demands, they could have had any robin they wanted. There would have been no need to spend weeks training it to land on a garden spade, and the bird could have talked.

Apart from those I met in Africa, who became fascinated with my balding head, I'd never had to deal with kids at all. But the younger members of the cast took easily to James and, by extension, to me, meaning I often had to shoo them away from the camera when it was time to shoot. Despite the famous admonition never to work with children or animals, we found both quite pleasant. The English summer proved otherwise, but that's another story.

"THE SECRET GARDEN"
113
A74
3
DIRECTOR AGNIESZKA HOLLAND
CAMERA ROGER DEAKINS
DAY-EXT
276

11

THE INVERSE SQUARE LAW

That gag's got whiskers on it!

SMITTY, *ARGUS* REPORTER, IN *THE HUDSUCKER PROXY*

From the fairy tale of *The Secret Garden* I returned to the world of the Coen brothers. *The Hudsucker Proxy* takes place in a kind of stretched reality, a fantasy world built from the familiar elements of 1950s New York. I saw it as a joyful challenge to light, particularly some of its more elaborate sets. But it was also a hugely ambitious film and, as we began to prep and shoot before Christmas 1993, I think we all began to harbor doubts that we would pull it off. Joel and Ethan were working with their biggest-ever budget. Designed once again by Dennis Gassner, the full-scale sets were like something out of a Fritz Lang movie and built to completely fill our stages in Wilmington, North Carolina. At a scale of 24:1, even the model of the New York of *Hudsucker*, beautifully crafted by Mark Stetson and his team, filled a large stage. Some of the scaled buildings were so tall that our effects team, using a motion control rig, had to shoot them lying on their side.

Hudsucker was the most complex technical challenge I had confronted since *1984*. The sets alone seemed daunting enough, let alone the number of large locations we had to scout and prep; many of them, like the Merchandise Mart and the Blackstone Hotel, were in Chicago. Yet when we returned from the Christmas break all the elements began to click into place, and the shoot took on the more relaxed and focused atmosphere I'd already begun to associate with Joel and Ethan's sets.

One afternoon on the set of *Barton Fink* the lights had gone out and I asked Billy O'Leary what was going on. He seemed unusually evasive. When "God Save the Queen" began to play over the speakers and a single lamp came on, I knew why. It was my forty-first birthday! In the darkness Billy provided, production had laid out a proper British teatime spread, complete with a butler bearing a silver tea set and cucumber sandwiches. Similar routines happened on *Hudsucker* as well. Birthday cakes would arrive to surprise a crew member and a band might play during our lunch break. You took your work seriously shooting with the Coen brothers, but there was always time for a laugh.

Though the film is set in the 1950s with some dark themes, a noir look was not what I had in mind for *Hudsucker*. The film is a parable and a romance, so to offset the heightened sense of reality that would come from the exaggerated sets and wide lenses, I felt the lighting should be more naturalistic and reflect an overcast, wintry New York. A cool soft light approach felt appropriate to the story; it would complement Dennis's wonderful expressionist sets and minimize any additional lighting I might need on the floor. This was important, not only to save time but because of the nature of the sets: the multiple reflective surfaces and the wide, even carpets that would become a confusion of shadows if lit by any source other than a window.

The cavernous boardroom from which Hudsucker founder Waring Hudsucker, played by Charles Durning, takes his fatal leap, is one of the sets that everyone who's seen the film remembers. Knowing the entire set would be in the frame at some point, including being reflected in the mirror-like surface of the boardroom table, Dennis and I had built into the ceiling what was essentially a large diffusion panel with a surrounding soffit. Just as on *1984*, I was choosing to light the space rather than a series of individual shots.

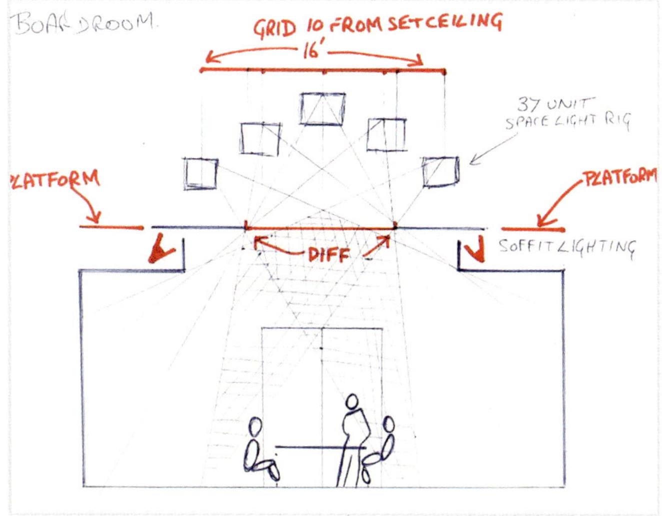

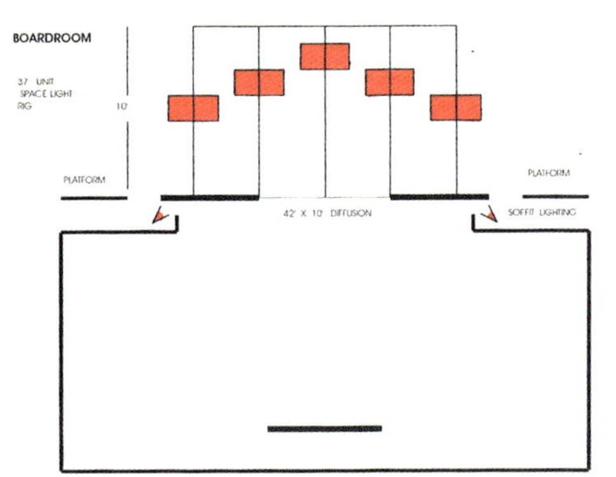
BOARDROOM
37' UNIT
SPACE LIGHT
RIG
10'
PLATFORM
PLATFORM
42' X 10' DIFFUSION
SOFFIT LIGHTING

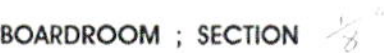
BOARDROOM ; SECTION

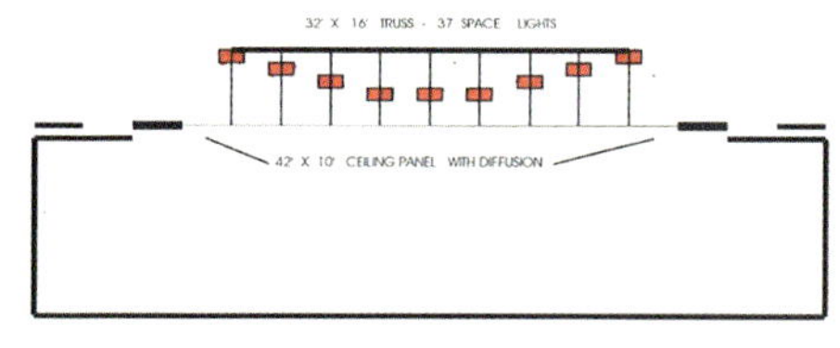
32' X 16' TRUSS - 37 SPACE LIGHTS
42' X 10' CEILING PANEL WITH DIFFUSION

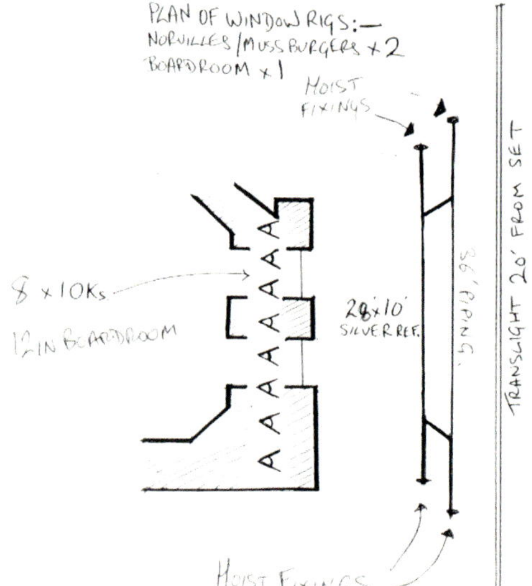
PLAN OF WINDOW RIGS:—
NORVILLES / MUSSBURGERS × 2
BOARDROOM × 1
HOIST FIXINGS
8 × 10Ks
12 IN BOARDROOM
28' × 10'
SILVER REF.
36' PIPING
TRANSLIGHT 20' FROM SET
HOIST FIXINGS

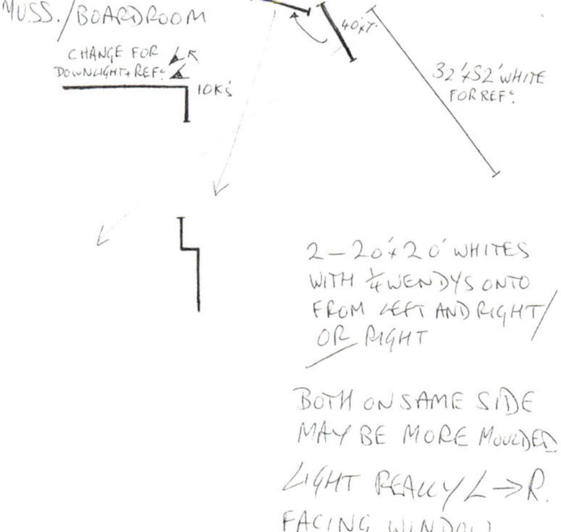
MUSS./BOARDROOM
CHANGE FOR
DOWNLIGHT + REF.
10Ks
40 × 7
32' × 52' WHITE
FOR REF.
2 — 20' × 20' WHITES
WITH ¼ WENDYS ONTO
FROM LEFT AND RIGHT /
OR RIGHT
BOTH ON SAME SIDE
MAY BE MORE MOULDED
LIGHT REALLY L → R.
FACING WINDOW

A large set is the same as a small set, only bigger. Light works in the same way on both, and all that changes is the size and number of the units required and the practicalities of rigging them. Here, the practicalities took precedence. Spacelights are a staple for film productions. Often used in multiples of a hundred or more to create a soft overhead source that emulates daylight, they're both easy to rig and cheap to rent. While not the most efficient way to project light into a set like this, they would provide a soft and easily controllable source. Besides, we had far more pressing challenges to concentrate our efforts on and which needed more specialist rigging.

For daylight to reach into the set through the windows of the boardroom we mounted 10K Fresnel lamps above the ceiling and bounced them off a purpose-made 28' × 10' reflector that was rigged on chain hoists above the Translite backing (a photographic backdrop). We used a similar lighting pattern for both Norville's and Sidney Mussburger's offices, though for these we needed larger reflectors and even more 10Ks.

All this worked quite well for the daylight scenes, but dusk was another matter. I nearly came unstuck trying to light a scene between the film's naive hero, Norville (Tim Robbins), and the scheming Sidney Mussburger (Paul Newman). I wanted to create a warm pool of light where Tim was sitting while keeping the walls and far side of the room dark, so that Paul would appear as a silhouette against the backing, only walking into the light to confront Norville. I began the morning rigging 1K Fresnel lamps to bounce off gold reflectors, while the rest of the electrical crew added blue gel to the Maxis lighting the Translite outside the window, which was no small task in and of itself. The more I struggled with the reflectors, the more I hated the result.

By midmorning I realized I was flogging a dead horse. I needed a change of plan. I approached Joel and Ethan in the production office and apologized for the delay. I asked if the crew could break early for lunch, promising everything would be ready when we came back if I could keep working with a few electricians. I was more than a little surprised how relaxed they were about the deal. I would be ready after lunch? That's fine. Let's have lunch then.

We stripped the gold reflectors out of the way, and in place of what had become a complex rig we hung three Chinese lanterns and angled them in such a way that they formed one single source when viewed from where Tim was seated; we placed the one nearest to him highest and dropped the other two down toward the window. Then we covered the sides of the lanterns facing the window with Blackwrap to avoid any reflection in the glass, before going to lunch ourselves. The process took less than thirty minutes and taught me a lesson: When a plan needs so many little fixes to make it work, there is something fundamentally wrong with the plan. It's better to cut your losses. This was the only time I have made such a dramatic lighting U-turn on a shooting day—and, of course, I was very lucky it was with Joel and Ethan.

The Hudsucker Building was based on Chicago's Merchandise Mart, and the set extended with a central tower and clockface using a model. Dennis Gassner built the room behind the clockface as a separate stage set with working machinery and a high tier of walkways connecting it all together. Until late in the film, we see the large clock only from the outside. Then the climactic action moves inside where Moses (Bill Cobbs), the good clock keeper, uses a broom handle to pause time. This prevents Norville from falling to his death but also leads to a fight between Moses and the evil janitor Aloysius (Harry Bugin). You have to see the film to understand!

The clockface is backlit when seen from

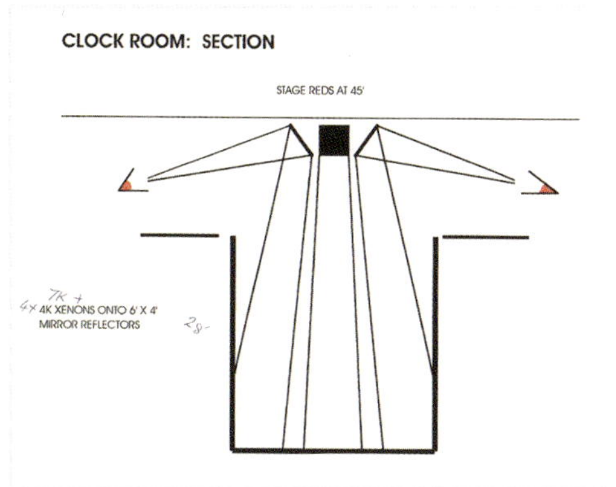

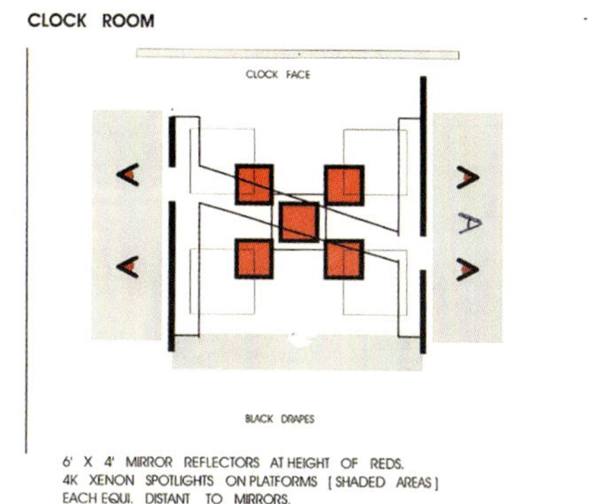

the front, so I simply used a festoon of 100-watt household bulbs, controlled by a single dimmer unit, to justify that look. My first instinct was to use these same bulbs as the only source for the set, but I would have a hard time controlling both the falloff of the light and the hot spots around the bulbs. Besides, the soft, warm glow of the bulbs alone felt emotionally wrong for a scene that was both surreal and violent, nor was it the best way to enhance the graphic nature of the machinery behind the clockface. The scene and the set called for a more dramatic, almost theatrical approach. So I decided to keep the clock lights very warm and contrast this with a cold snap of light from above, a kind of "God" light.

The height of the clock room presented a challenge as, although there was ample space on the stage to each side of the set, it left little room to bring in light from above. I asked Dennis to leave just enough space above the set so that we could create an illusion of a sharp beam of light from above using mirrors. Specifically, Billy suggested we bounce four 4K Xenons (though he also rigged a higher-wattage Xenon)—at the time the sharpest, brightest lamps on the market—off four 4' × 6' mirrors. With 6' × 4' mirrors at an angle of forty-five degrees to the Xenon lamps, their beams would start out at approximately four feet square, widening out only as dictated by their distance from the reflector.

As the inverse square law dictates, the further away the lamp, the more even its light falls over a measured distance. So, by using mirrors and lengthening the throw of the lamps, we were also evening out the light between the top and bottom of the set. The inverse square law is a very useful tool when considering how you want your set to be lit. If, for instance, you want a person standing at a window to be that much brighter than another deep inside a room, you place your source close to the window. Conversely, if you want both people to be lit to the same intensity, you place your source as far away as is practical.

The Hudsucker Proxy's producers included Joel Silver, who was taking a rare step away from action movies. Joel was incredibly supportive through the whole process, but when he joined us to watch dailies in the evening, after his first appearance on the set, I could feel him growing increasingly uncomfortable in his seat next to me. Frankly, he made me uncomfortable by just sitting next to me but, with his eyes still glued to the screen, he said, "Roger, what the fuck am I looking at?" Without turning to him I replied, "You did read the script, Joel, didn't you?" Though it's since been reappraised and embraced—rightly, I think—*The Hudsucker Proxy* baffled most critics, and audiences stayed away. If this was a test of whether the Coens' sensibility could play to a wider audience, they seem to have failed it.

The last scenes of *Hudsucker* took place on the backlot in Wilmington, Carolina—exterior shots with fake snow that froze. It was that cold. Joel, Ethan, and I sat around a burning brazier while Tim did his thing in a crane shot I was operating remotely. After a long, complicated shoot, we were exhausted but sad for it to end. Like *Barton Fink*, it had been one of those jobs.

It was still a surprise to find it was on Tim Robbins's recommendation—or was it his insistence?—that I came to be offered my next film. In truth, I wasn't a huge fan of Stephen King's horror stories. I probably wouldn't even have read the script if James hadn't insisted. "It's not what you think," she said. James was right.

12

REDEMPTION

Nothing left but all the time in the world to think about it.

RED, IN *THE SHAWSHANK REDEMPTION*

***The Shawshank Redemption*, written by Frank Darabont, is one of the best scripts I have ever** read. But even a great script takes a lot of hard work to bring to the screen.

Shooting began in June 1993 with Frank directing his first high-profile feature. *Shawshank* would be a challenge for anyone. We worked on alternating six-day weeks and often for fourteen-hour days. A lack of momentum hurts the morale of any crew, most of whom want to keep busy rather than stand around kicking their heels, so it's important to come to set with a plan. Shooting went slowly, so slowly that rumors began to circulate that the film would be shut down, and to keep on schedule scenes began to be cut from the script. But I was the one looking through the camera, seeing for the first time those remarkable performances as an audience would see them. From the first few days of the shoot it became obvious that the film would be special.

Though I knew them to be as frustrated as I was, Tim Robbins and Morgan Freeman were both true professionals, key in keeping up the morale of the entire crew. Some actors get engrossed in their characters and rarely talk with anyone behind the camera, but not Morgan. He would be telling the most raucous joke right up until Frank called action. One day, during a scene with the parole board, he stopped in midflow to give the most moving performance on camera, then completed the punchline after the camera had cut. I was amazed. James took over as script supervisor during the latter part of the shoot, and she found it hard to stay focused on her job when watching some of Morgan's performances.

To match the Shawshank State Penitentiary of King's novella, *Rita Hayworth and Shawshank Redemption*, we needed to film at a prison in a rural setting with a sizable yard. We found one in Mansfield, Ohio, the site of the Ohio State Reformatory. Built between 1866 and 1910, the reformatory had been in use until 1990, just three years before we began filming, and a number of ex-cons were still around to tell us of their experiences. It was a grim but ideal space. It offered almost everything we needed except for the central bullpen, a cell block with tiered floors that opened onto an interior courtyard.

Working from the beautiful designs of Terry Marsh, the production built a set in a disused factory not far away from the reformatory. This suited our purpose, but there were a number of serious issues that needed to be confronted, not the least of which were the resident pigeons and the building's walls of glass. Leaving the set open to the inconsistencies of the daylight would create all sorts of problems, so the entire factory would have to be blacked out at some cost to production.

To have any chance of lighting through the three-floor window at one end of the interior courtyard, I asked that the set be positioned with the maximum floor space between it and the factory wall. I suggested the set be offset so that there was space outside the windows of the cells belonging to the two main characters, Andy and Red, so that we could build a platform for lighting and make our lives easier if and when we needed to float the wall. But the one three-floor window, however large, would provide only a limited source of light for any shots deep inside the set. I preferred to stay away from turning on the practical lamps for the daytime scenes, as I wanted a distinct look to each time of day, so Terry and I discussed building skylights into the ceiling of the set, leaving enough room between the set and the roof of the warehouse to accommodate some lighting. The complexity of the rigging and lighting of the set, along with the pigeon wrangling, had probably not been factored into the original budget.

We primarily shot *The Shawshank Redemption* in script continuity, meaning we filmed each scene in the order it appeared in the script. This approach can be advantageous artistically to both the cast and director, but returning to sets and locations as needed, rather than filming all the scenes within them at one time, creates some logistical and technical challenges. It also creates additional costs. To negotiate these issues with production, and for many other reasons, I was happy to have Billy O'Leary as my gaffer again. *Hudsucker* had included some of the most difficult technical challenges we had faced on any of our eight films together, so it was a blessing he was able to travel to Mansfield with his great rigging gaffer, Richie Ford, and his regular key crew members.

To facilitate shooting in continuity and allow flexibility within the schedule, Billy and I developed a plan to light the set and leave it standing, which was another production cost but one with no cheaper alternative. We had to shoot both day and night scenes on this set and needed to keep what we did for one unobtrusive in the other. Daytime scenes required large sources we could project through the skylights and the cathedral-style window, for which we used Maxi Brutes. We spaced a series of these lamps to form large panels the size of each window and skylight. We affixed blue gel to the barn doors of all the lamps, hung diffusion outside the glass window, and stretched diffusion panels that would stand in for glass across the skylights. Fortunately, because we were working in Ohio's rust belt, the nearby manufacturing district included a plant that could provide us with a cloudy polythene product tough enough to withstand the heat of our lamps, neutral in color, and, most important, cheap.

For the nighttime interior we worked closely with the set dressers to come up with a style of practical light that would work for both the design and lighting of the set. In the main bullpen area, I wanted overhead practical lights that both shaped the light and, with the right bulb, I could use as my only source. On the walkways or inside the cells, I was looking for one that would be visually correct but would offer me some place to add a "gag" light behind it. The cage lights fit that bill. For each fixture, we threaded in an additional power supply so that we could add a double-ended halogen bulb, of either 150 or 250 watts, to the side facing away from camera. To fix these bulbs in place Billy used green plastic-covered garden wire, stiff enough, when soldered to each end of the bulb, to hold it in position. I wouldn't recommend using this type of wiring, or an open bulb, if the light is to ever be used at full intensity, but here we kept it dimmed down as a warm source that blended with the bulb seen on camera. If you look closely, you can see a slight double shadow, which always bothers me.

The prison set was rigged and lit to be available to shoot at any time, but the location offered another logistical challenge. The most efficient way to light the interiors of the State Reformatory was to use HMIs, which are both powerful and daylight balanced. But lighting through the windows from outside—something that seemed obvious to me—created a problem for our day scenes scheduled to shoot in the prison yard. And we were shooting in script order: inside one day and outside the next. Finding a way to accommodate this required a little scheduling magic from our first AD, John Woodward. It also required a great deal of overtime for the rigging crew. We were lighting with around twenty-five lamps, so each time we shot inside the reformatory we had to re-erect the scaffold and order anew all the HMIs. These HMIs were not a widely available lamp in the summer of 1993, so they had to be shipped in from a variety of rental houses far away from central Ohio. Shooting in continuity came at a cost.

We shot the day exteriors without additional light unless the natural daylight changed so much that I was forced to use lighting to match one shot with another. John had tried to build some flexibility into the schedule so that we could shoot as many of our exteriors as possible under cloud cover, but there is never enough. It proved to be a much different experience to that on *Another Time, Another Place*, when Mike Radford and I could shoot any scene on any day.

> *I guess it comes down to a simple choice, really.*
> *Get busy living, or get busy dying.*
>
> **ANDY DUFRESNE, IN *THE SHAWSHANK REDEMPTION***

There was one long exterior scene between Tim and Morgan, the "get busy living" scene, that we had to shoot on a specific day. When that day came, the weather refused to cooperate. The sky stubbornly remained blue when we wanted clouds.

After talking this over with Frank, and having no alternative to shoot, we staged the scene against a wall that remained in shadow for most of the day. It was preferable to working under a full sun, but as the sun rose in the sky it illuminated more and more of the prison yard and dramatically altered the color and intensity of the light reflected onto the actors. To prevent this, we stood up large baffles that allowed only the skylight into the area in which the scene was being played out, which was fine for certain camera angles but not for everything. Luckily, the middle of the scene played in closer shots that we could more easily control, and we held a single wide angle for late in the day, when the opposite wall acted as a flag to put our characters in shadow while the sun cast a dramatic shadow on the background.

I was shooting *Shawshank* utilizing naturalistic lighting, motivated camera moves, and a minimal range of lenses. Wide shots were made on a 28 mm or 32 mm and closer shots on a 40 mm or a 50 mm. I think these lenses are closer to natural vision, and I like an audience to feel present in a scene, not looking at a character as if on a long lens from far away. If I had shot the closer angles of this scene on longer lenses, a 65 mm or an 85 mm, it would certainly have been more forgiving. Less of the background would have appeared in the shot, and what did could have been put out of focus. But I never saw shooting this way as an option. You establish a style and keep to it.

Seemingly simple scenes are often more complex than they appear, as proved to be the case when we shot the prisoners laying down pitch on the roof. For one shot we needed a Giraffe crane with an arm spanning thirty-two feet, while for a final shot we needed the smaller Aerocrane with a sectional arm of approximately thirteen feet. Each crane would carry a camera I could operate remotely, so we did not have to worry about the extra weight it would take for an operator to ride the Giraffe. But the Giraffe alone weighed 2,821 pounds without accessories, which required us to shore up the roof from the floor below as it was hardly in shape to support the crew, much less the weight of the crane.

Once we mapped out a rough scheme of the shooting, we found that the Giraffe could be hidden from view during the second section of the scene, so we rented scissor lifts to carry the equipment up to the roof, and we were set.

The moment when the convicts relax with their beers is an example of how efficient these tools can be even in the simplest settings. The scene involves a slow track and panning shot to establish all the characters in place, followed by a series of static closer shots, all of which had to be filmed in the same soft, end-of-day sunlight.

When you work with a remote head on a small jib arm such as the Aerocrane and a dolly grip as good as Bruce Hamme, you can be extremely efficient in repositioning the camera from one shot to another without allowing the momentum of the shoot to slow. A good dolly grip will notice when an actor is out of position or when a move is slightly different than in a rehearsal, and this system allows them to rapidly compensate. All of which has become easier with the introduction of miniature onboard monitors, but no technological advance can replace the human touch.

It seems to be common knowledge I don't care for one of the most iconic shots in *The Shawshank Redemption*—but like a lot of common knowledge this simply isn't true. As originally planned and storyboarded, Andy's prison escape would have been a much longer sequence, one that included a train passing by the prison walls and him chasing down a boxcar, another ten or twenty shots. It was more than the fastest of crews could complete in one night. By the time we had filmed Tim emerging from the sewer (I had extended the length of our set pipe by using a trick from *Barton Fink*, painting concentric circles on a card) and wading in the stream, we knew we were in trouble. We needed a shot to end the scene. We already had the camera on the Giraffe crane, so one of us, I can't remember who, suggested taking it to its full height and shooting a top shot of Andy breathing in fresh air. It would become an iconic moment.

Here's the *only* thing that annoys me about it: We had a Lightning Strikes, essentially a lamp that you can flicker like lightning. Billy was manning the remote control to the lamp as I operated the camera when Frank said, "Oh! Let me do that." Then he took the remote control, and began pressing it over and over, like a kid with a new toy. I said, "Frank, it's just going to be one long flash!" And it almost was. But who am I to argue with the many who love that shot exactly as it appears in the movie?

Lightning strikes in the same places all the time.

BORIS ZAKHARIN

At this point, it might sound as if my career had kicked into high gear. In some respects, it had. My work, especially on *1984*, *Sid and Nancy*, *Mountains of the Moon*, and *Barton Fink*, had established my reputation. I'd been welcomed at the American Society of Cinematographers' clubhouse, where I'd met Gordon Willis, Owen Roizman, Haskell Wexler, and others whose work had inspired me. Conrad Hall had complimented me on *Barton Fink*, and I doubt he could have imagined how much that meant to me. I'd even met Stanley Cortez, cinematographer of *The Magnificent Ambersons*, *Shock Corridor*, and *Night of the Hunter*, who'd become a fixture at the clubhouse in his retirement and often scolded me for not wearing a tie. But esteem doesn't equate to job security in the film business. After completing the shooting of *The Shawshank Redemption*, I was to be fired from my next two projects. And in between those unhappy experiences *The Hudsucker Proxy* was released to a decidedly tepid response.

A cinematographer can be fired from a project for any number of reasons. Perhaps the cinematographer had never been the director's choice but had been imposed on them by a producer. When a shoot is behind schedule the cinematographer might be the first to go, a warning to a director to go faster or a message to the studio that production is doing something to solve its problems. A cinematographer may be fired by an actor, more often an actress, who doesn't like the way they are being photographed. It may be that the director and cinematographer just don't see eye to eye. Not only had Stanley Cortez been fired from *Chinatown* by Roman Polanski but, on *Doctor Zhivago*, David Lean replaced the great Nicolas Roeg (cinematographer on *Fahrenheit 451* and *Far from the Madding Crowd*, and director of *Walkabout* and *The Man Who Fell to Earth*) with Freddie Young. But to know all this did not make it any easier. My self-doubt returned with a vengeance. But on meeting with Conrad Hall, he laughed it off. Since being introduced to him at the ASC clubhouse after the release of *Barton Fink* we had become friends. Now, at the same venue, this time for a celebration of the ASC award nominees for cinematography in a feature film, he told me, "You're no one in Hollywood until you've been fired at least three times."

Not being familiar faces to a majority of members of the ASC, James and I were privy to some personal opinions about my cinematography:

"...It's easy when you can shoot everything in natural light. Yes, *Shawshank* looks good and deserves its nomination, but there was no lighting involved and cinematography is about lighting."

"...*Shawshank* was shot like a documentary, not a feature film..."

Being asked who I was once again recalled my experience on *Cruel Passion*. Who am I? I am the cinematographer you are talking about!

I was flattered that so many members of the ASC thought *Shawshank* involved little lighting, and perhaps theirs was the greatest praise. They couldn't tell that the major interior was a lit set. That not only was the real prison interior dark at any time of the day, but just getting an exposure was often impossible without lights. Besides, we were working long days, and with the actors' guaranteed turnaround, our start times were forced later and later as the week progressed. By Friday we could be shooting a day scene well into the night. Despite the wishes of our production department, we had no option but to light both the set and the location.

Because *The Shawshank Redemption* began to "find traction," as they say in Hollyweird, we were off to the award shows—or maybe not!

When I found out I had been honored with the ASC annual award for a feature film, I was on the roof of a parking structure in Minnesota, where it was the middle of the night and the temperature had fallen to twenty degrees below zero.

13

TWENTY BELOW

Oh geez...

JERRY LUNDEGAARD, IN *FARGO*

I can't remember ever being so cold as we were shooting *Hudsucker* in Chicago, but Joel and Ethan's follow-up would lead us all into a freezer. When they told me about their next movie, they weren't sure I'd be interested. After the commercial disappointment of *The Hudsucker Proxy* they decided to return to their roots, not only with a low-budget film but one that would shoot in their native Minnesota. In the middle of winter. Why wouldn't I say yes?

I loved Joel and Ethan's script for *Fargo*, but it was only while scouting the film with them that I fully understood their vision for the film. The brothers would often look at a location, then pace back and forth before suggesting to our production designer, Rick Heinrichs, "It's a little too interesting." Spots deemed "too interesting" included the hallway of a Radisson hotel. "It might work if we took the picture off the wall," suggested Joel. "Or removed those two chairs," Ethan pitched in before Joel suggested the couch might also go.

Joel and Ethan talked about shooting in a more observational way than our previous collaborations. The camera almost becomes a character in *Barton Fink* and *The Hudsucker Proxy*. It rarely stops moving, whether motivated by the action within the scene or not. With *Fargo* they wanted an approach more akin to a Ken Loach film, where the camera remains planted in a static position, panning only when the action demands it. Where we used wide lenses on *Barton* and *Hudsucker*, for *Fargo* we'd rely on longer lenses, in keeping with the observational approach...or so we said.

It's nice having a guiding concept, but rules are made to be broken. For our very first shot, of Steve Buscemi's character burying a case of money in deep snow by a fence, we laid eighty feet of track. But we did use a 40 mm lens, which was a departure from the wider lenses of their previous films. This and other choices would give the film a more naturalistic feel even though the dolly was not banished to the truck.

We shot *Fargo* in the first months of 1995, a cold winter but one stubbornly light on snow. Finding consistently snowy landscapes forced us to move some locations further and further north, until we were almost into Canada. We knew we might be shooting elsewhere when an elusive snowstorm hit the location we'd chosen for the opening shots, so one weekend we marked off each camera angle with a wooden stake, writing on them the lens length and camera height. Sure enough, when snow finally arrived we were locked into shooting at an interior location, but Robin Brown, my onetime assistant and now a standby operator (I have always operated myself but the union demanded I carry a standby), was there to capture the moment.

Elsewhere, we had to make our own snow, including for the overhead shot of the frustrated Jerry Lundegaard (William H. Macy) trekking back to his car in the middle of a parking lot. Our effects team had laid down chipped ice overnight, but the lot was not originally intended to be so barren as it appears in the film. After we removed the glass from a window in the office block that overlooked the lot, I could look down at Jerry's car as it was being moved into position and the driver walking away on a predetermined path. All that remained was a lonely car with a single set of footprints leading from it. I asked our assistant director, Michelangelo Csaba Bolla, to hold off bringing in the other cars until Joel and Ethan could see what I was seeing. Although logically it didn't make any sense for the parking lot to be empty on a workday, they agreed the shot was stronger. Their only concern was what to do with the dozens and dozens of cars that had been brought in to fill it.

As is common practice with the Coens, we were working from a storyboard. Other cinematographers might feel that the amount of preparation the brothers do leaves them only to "paint by numbers," but I don't find that at all. If anything, you can be more open to what happens on the set because you already know the essential elements that will make the scene work in the edit. Prep can free you to concentrate on the challenges of the day or the happy accidents it might bring. Not every director works this way, and I also love working with no safety net, as I might on a documentary. But the Coen brothers' films are hardly documentaries, even if *Fargo* pretends it might be.

The night shoots presented the most difficult challenge. In particular, the scenes set on desolate stretches of highway with no obvious light sources other than those produced by the vehicles. I considered shooting establishing shots at magic hour, with just enough light in the sky to see the horizon or, alternatively, using Musco lights to define the landscape. Each approach had its pros and cons. But why not embrace the darkness? It would look more menacing and, while we would see the snowscape only in the headlights of the cars, the contrast with the bleached white of the daytime scenes would be quite dramatic.

Joel and Ethan signed off on the plan, and Billy O'Leary and I lit the driving scenes with lights attached to the front bumper of our picture vehicle facing the road ahead and a four-foot fluorescent tube resting on the hood to light the characters. In the static scenes we hid 650-watt Fresnel lamps beside the vehicles and bounced a little red light onto our cast. A bonus? The inky background allowed us to shoot many of the close shots during the daytime without suffering the cold of the location, in a garage and with simply black drapes surrounding the car. The pity was that to get breath coming from the actors' mouths, heaters were not an option.

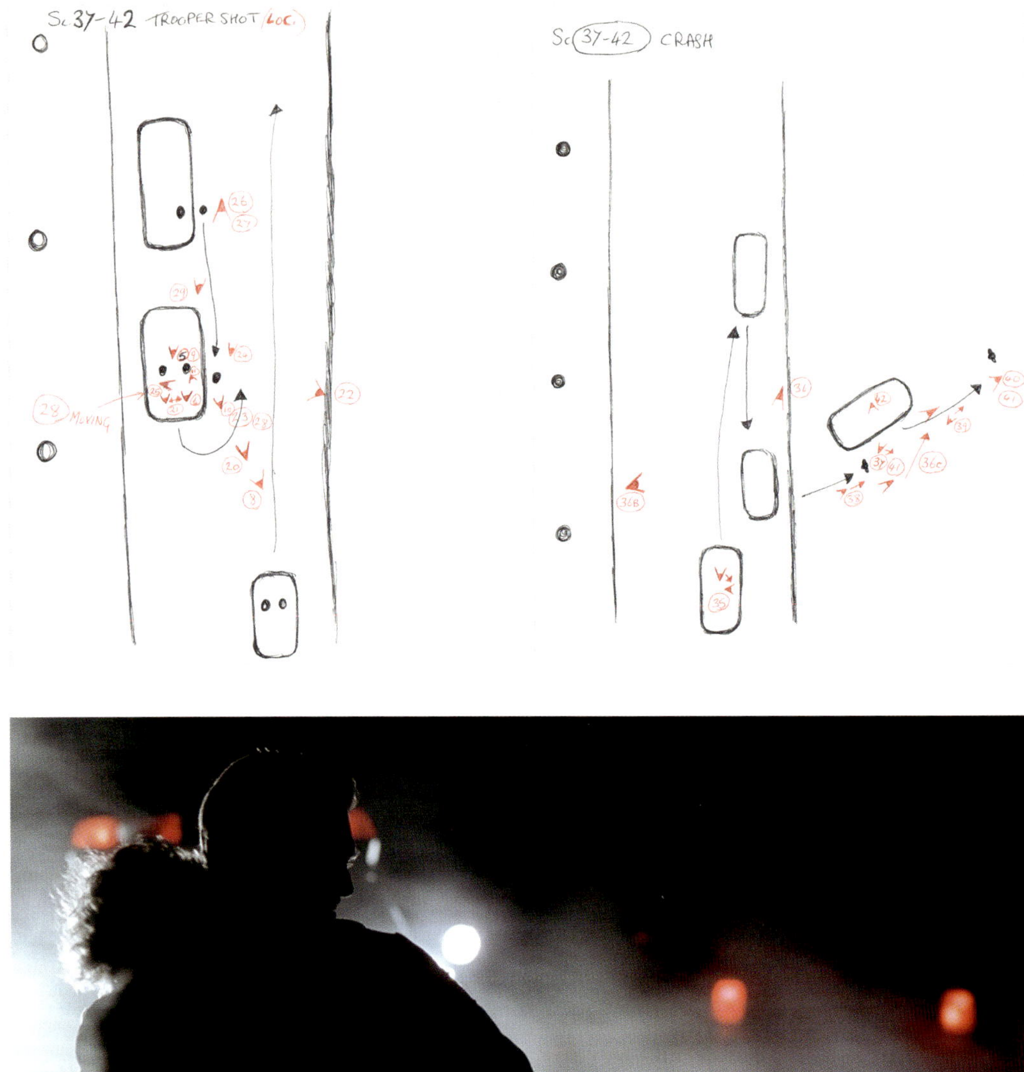

From the storyboards I would do a breakdown of the more complex scenes and display each shot in an overhead view. From these diagrams the AD and I would order the night's work, giving each shot an allotment of time to complete. Sharing this information with Billy and Mitch Lillian—possibly the best key grip in the business and who I was working with for the first time—allowed us to function as efficiently as possible in quite extreme conditions.

Although the snowscapes and the night driving provide the more memorable visuals, the film is really about characters and the settings they inhabit, making our location choices crucial. The bars, Jerry's office facing onto a busy highway, the airport parking lot, the Lundegaards' home, and others (none of them "too interesting") helped establish who these characters were. Lighting the actors and locations in a simple, naturalistic way seemed right, and using practical lights and carefully selected window treatments—blinds, curtains, sheers, and so on—helped achieve this. In other ways it recalled working on *Sid and Nancy*, only my lighting techniques had become even more minimal and reliant on purpose-made gag lights, such as ring lights or a strip of household bulbs, rather than traditional film lights. As had been my practice since *1984*, I made a drawing of each location that illustrated all the changes and additional lighting I required.

Shooting the scene at the wood chipper went well, with the addition of a large amount of strawberry jam. To reset the chipper and the "bloodied" snow was time-consuming, but, luckily for our schedule, the Coen brothers were comfortable with only a single good take of each setup. The action that followed out on the ice could have been more difficult. Ethan walked out to make sure it was safe. I have no idea what would have happened if we'd lost a Coen brother midshoot.

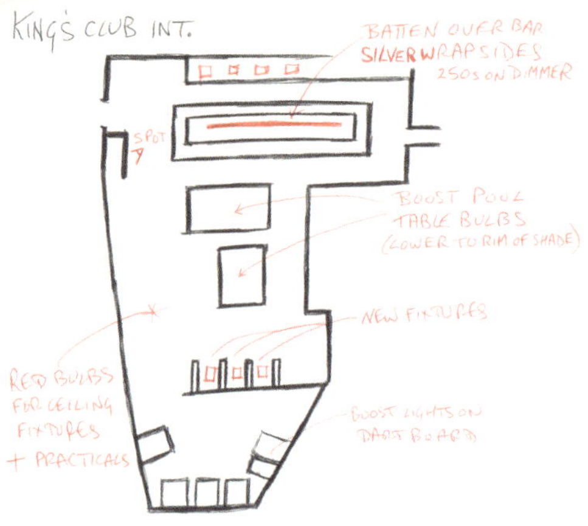
KING'S CLUB INT.
BATTEN OVER BAR
SILVERWRAP SIDES
250s ON DIMMER
SPOT
BOOST POOL
TABLE BULBS
(LOWER TO RIM OF SHADE)
NEW FIXTURES
RED BULBS
FOR CEILING
FIXTURES
+ PRACTICALS
BOOST LIGHTS ON
DART BOARD

EXIT

POLICE

When Peter Stormare ran away from camera and fell down, a price number appeared prominently marked on the soles of his boots, which now faced the camera. It was a mistake, but as it made everyone laugh, the brothers left it there for the closer shot.

Despite the cold and the film's low budget (not including the expensive boots), we'd enjoyed working on *Fargo* but in no way could have anticipated it would go on to become such a well-loved and critical favorite. When shooting a film, it's hard to foretell what lies in its future.

If I do not speak out and resist, I am an accomplice.

SISTER HELEN PREJEAN, IN *DEAD MAN WALKING*

Tim Robbins and I had gotten along well making *The Hudsucker Proxy* and we had shared a mutual frustration on *The Shawshank Redemption*. He approached me to work on a film he was directing, though he wasn't sure I'd want to do another prison movie, and one with a minimal budget. In truth, I had turned down a director who'd asked me to simply re-create what I'd done on *Shawshank*. But where *Shawshank* had the qualities of a fable, Tim wanted to keep *Dead Man Walking* stark and realistic. He even said to me that it might look ugly. Or, at least, mundane. While I liked the script and Tim's concept for the film, I also felt like it had a great deal to say about the morality of the death penalty, depicting both sides of the argument without preaching to either.

We shot *Dead Man Walking* using deliberately anonymous lighting, and I saw my job to serve the performances, to keep the focus on the characters rather than on any visual flourishes. That we were working with a low budget provided another good reason to keep it simple. I count both *Dead Man Walking* and the next film I worked on, *Courage Under Fire*, among my most satisfying professional experiences, yet, apart from dealing with weighty topics, they couldn't be more different.

14

THE FOG OF WAR

Imagine a life without consequences.

SPECIALIST ILARIO, IN *COURAGE UNDER FIRE*

Set during the then-recent Persian Gulf War and informed by some real events, *Courage Under Fire* depicts conflicting accounts leading to the death of a helicopter pilot, Captain Karen Walden. Meg Ryan had signed on to play Walden and Denzel Washington to play Nathaniel Serling, the lieutenant colonel charged with determining whether Walden deserved a posthumous honorary medal. Scripted by Patrick Sheane Duncan for director Ed Zwick, it touched on themes both timeless and timely, since the role women should play in combat was a much-debated topic at the time.

Production was denied any military cooperation, so all the armory, such as one of many tanks seen in the photo of Mitch Lillian, me, and Billy, was provided to the film by private individuals. It's kind of scary what's out there.

The nighttime tank battle was complex, but the film's extensive helicopter sequences led to more lengthy preproduction conversations. We shot-listed the alternating versions of the *Rashomon*-influenced story. Then we broke down each camera angle, deciding on those we could achieve for real by my operating either inside or hanging outside of a flying helicopter. On *Air America*, I had done a lot of hanging outside a helicopter, filming Mel Gibson in the copilot seat as we flew over the mountains north of Chiang Mai and Mae Hong Son, and it was one of the few things I really enjoyed about that film. My fear of heights never kicks in when I'm shooting like this. As James has suggested, looking through the lens removes me from reality.

The space inside a Huey was limited, especially with our full cast of characters, so we needed another option. Production's initial concept of shooting on a stage against a bluescreen would have been expensive, and given the intricate way sunlight plays inside a flying helicopter, I did not see how it could be made to feel real. I thought back to a sequence in *Air America*, one that involved a Huey crashing into the jungle. Our effects supervisor on that film, George Gibbs, mounted a helicopter on a gimbal on the flatbed of a truck and, with Mel Gibson and Robert Downey Jr. in the cockpit and me filming from the back or a side seat, we simply drove the rig into the jungle.

I talked over the same idea with *Courage Under Fire*'s effects super, Paul Lombardi, and we pitched it to production. It saved on a studio rental and on a company move, so they were happy with that and, luckily, our location department found a raised dirt road from which, with the additional height of the rig, it would appear in camera as if the Huey were flying. Shooting on the rig with Andy Harris, who was now my regular first assistant, and me strapped outside the copter felt scarier than when we were really flying. But it was good to shoot every angle in camera and find the two approaches, on the truck and in the air, blend together seamlessly.

SUPER
MAN

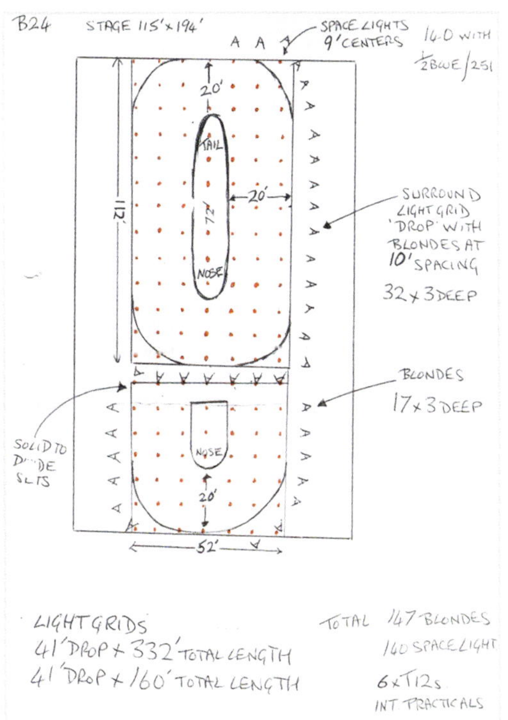
B24
STAGE 115'×194'
SPACE LIGHTS
9' CENTERS
14.0 WITH
½ BLUE/251
20'
TAIL
20'
112'
72'
NOSE
SURROUND
LIGHT GRID
'DROP' WITH
BLONDES AT
10' SPACING
32×3 DEEP
BLONDES
17×3 DEEP
NOSE
20'
52'
LIGHT GRIDS
41' DROP × 332' TOTAL LENGTH
41' DROP × 160' TOTAL LENGTH
TOTAL 147 BLONDES
160 SPACE LIGHT
6×T12s
INT. PRACTICALS

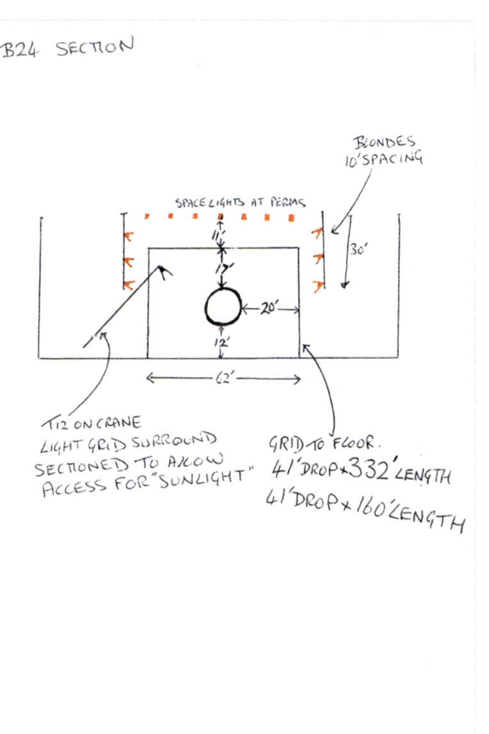
B24 SECTION
BLONDES
10' SPACING
SPACE LIGHTS AT PERMS
11'
17'
30'
20'
12'
62'
T12 ON CRANE
LIGHT GRID SURROUND
SECTIONED TO ALLOW
ACCESS FOR "SUNLIGHT"
GRID TO FLOOR.
41' DROP × 332' LENGTH
41' DROP × 160' LENGTH

EMPTY
37,201
MIDSHIP
TURRET

PHIL: *Remember that story in* Life *magazine?*
The one about Eddie Rickenbacker?
Him and his crew ran out of fuel over the Pacific
and were drifting in a raft for twenty-four days.

LOUIS ZAMPERINI: *They made it, right?*

PHIL: *Yeah. Most of them lost their minds, but they made it.*

UNBROKEN

Filming the aerial sequence in *Unbroken*, some eighteen years later, presented a similar challenge. Having discovered that there was no longer a B-24 Liberator that was flying, we looked for an alternative. Production suggested mounting a fuselage on a gimbal and shooting it in a parking lot, but that would leave us open to the weather and the constantly varying angle of the sun. Finally, we opted to shoot onstage, surrounding the set with a light box of diffusion, backlit by an array of 160 Spacelights and 147 2K Blondes, while creating our own sun via a T12 Fresnel lamp on a crane arm.

In those eighteen years since *Courage Under Fire*, visual effects had evolved. With a little "persuasion," our ILM effects team agreed to forgo the use of a bluescreen and comp in exterior imagery using the foreground structure of the plane as their matte line. To shoot toward a bluescreen would have severely restricted the light I could have projected into the plane from what would be the natural source, so it was key to keep open to view the entire width of the light box. Today, both these alternate methods (whether from *Courage Under Fire* or *Unbroken*) of shooting inside a flying machine can be superseded by an LED video wall, more often called the Volume. This can certainly take the danger out of the process, but I don't think there is yet an alternative to simply driving that helicopter into the jungle.

15

THINGS CHANGE

Just like a dream experience,
whatever things I enjoy will become a memory.
Whatever is past will not be seen again.

THE DALAI LAMA, IN *KUNDUN*

For *Courage Under Fire* I relied heavily on my documentary experience, and I suspect, though I've never confirmed, that played a role in Martin Scorsese's decision to hire me for *Kundun*. The film Marty planned to shoot about the Dalai Lama, with a cast of nonprofessional actors, could not have been more different from one set during a war and starring Denzel Washington and Meg Ryan. I happily signed on to the film, and James would join us as script supervisor. We'd come to treasure our time in Morocco, a truly once-in-a-lifetime experience.

That's not to say the location didn't present difficulties or the shoot went entirely smoothly. The production was based in the city of Ouarzazate ("The Door of the Desert") and operated out of Atlas Studios. When I first arrived to scout with Marty at the beginning of June 1996, beyond two signs—one reading ATLAS STUDIOS and the other OSCAR HOTEL—lay open desert broken only by the stooping figures of women making bricks out of the bare earth and leaving them to dry in the sun. I found out later this was being done in anticipation of our film needing stages, essentially airport hangars with tin roofs and dirt floors, within which we'd construct the sets.

By the time James and I returned, less than two months later, the "stages" were up, and production designer Dante Ferretti's sets were nearing completion. Though they were wondrous, I occasionally had to cut an opening to make them visible in camera. For instance, Dante and his team had painted the ceiling of the assembly room, a cavernous space with no apparent light source, with the most beautiful of Buddhist motifs. I hated defacing it but, much as I dislike top light, I saw no alternative approach to accommodate the wide tracking shots that our director wanted. Besides, the ceiling would never be seen by the camera, so I asked my Italian key grip, Tommaso Mele, to cut some holes in the murals that I could pretend were skylights.

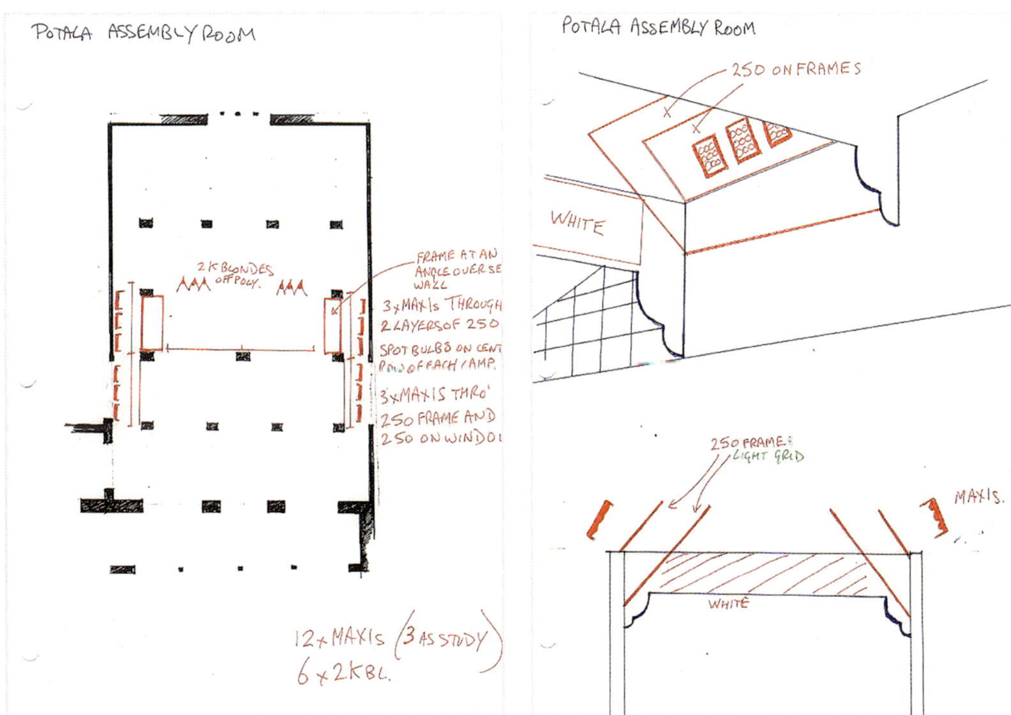

Skylights are a traditional feature of Tibetan architecture, and our sets incorporated many of them. Billy O'Leary and I adopted a consistent style of lighting for each that used a cutoff pyramid of diffusion with an open top. The angled sides of this diffusion were lit using an array of Maxis, in the case of the assembly room, and 2K Blondes, for the smaller skylights, to mimic the soft ambience of the sky, while the opening above allowed me to occasionally introduce a stronger source as if it were direct sunlight. To get a sharp beam, as in the Amdo farmhouse where the infant Dalai Lama is discovered, we rigged a mirror above the set—referencing the clock room on *Hudsucker*—and hit it with a 6K HMI lamp that we worked off a stand on the floor.

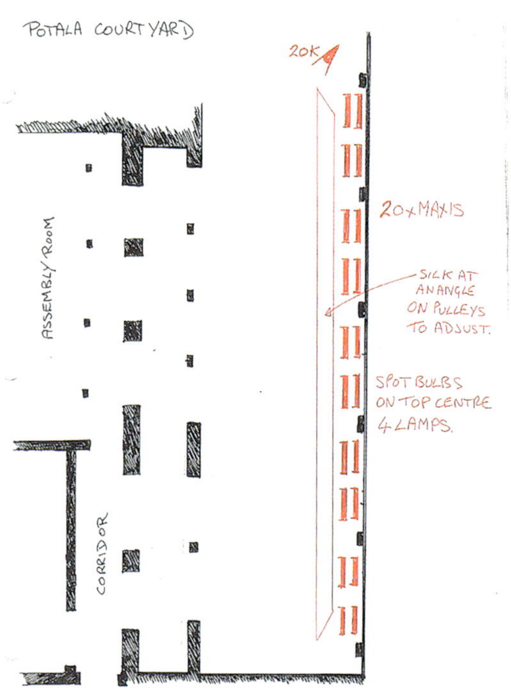

AMDO FARMHOUSE

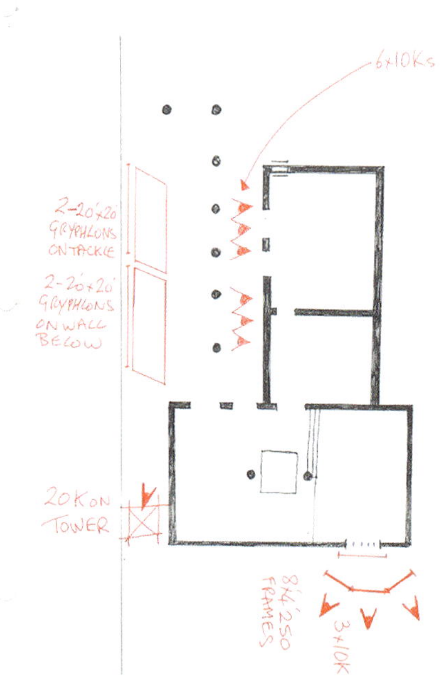
6x10Ks
2-20'x20' GRYPHLONS ON TACKLE
2-20'x20' GRYPHLONS ON WALL BELOW
20K ON TOWER
8x4' 250 FRAMES
3x10K

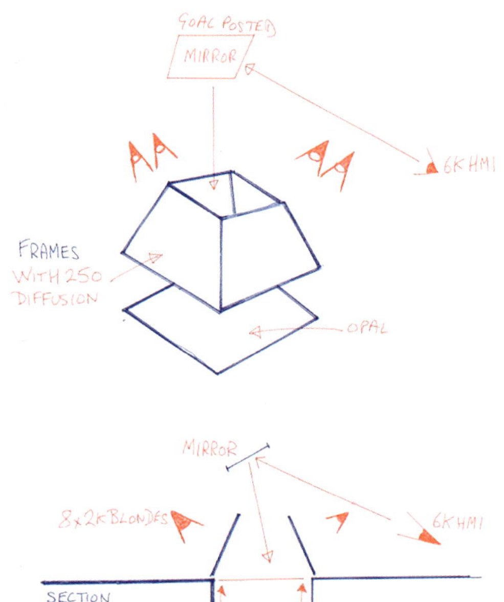
AMDO FARMHOUSE SET: SKYLIGHT.
GOAL POSTED
MIRROR
6K HMI
FRAMES WITH 250 DIFFUSION
OPAL
MIRROR
8x2K BLONDES
6K HMI
SECTION
OPAL DIFF.

The Tibetan cast came from a wide variety of places. Many were from Dharamsala, but a Tibetan who played one of the Dalai Lama's advisors ran a newsstand in New York City, while another had been an advertising executive in San Francisco. They were a diverse group, but they shared a culture and a passion to reflect their traditional way of life, which had been disrupted when China annexed the country in 1950. A famously peaceful people, some became worried about the direction of the film after seeing the violence in Marty's previous work. Others were a little shocked at his quite colorful language when a shot wasn't working as he wanted. I suspect Marty didn't realize how many of his cast could speak English.

Lobsang Lhalungpa, our technical advisor, left Tibet in 1947 and since 1989 had lived in Santa Fe, New Mexico, which he felt was most like his home world. Similarly, many of the Moroccan locations reminded our cast of Tibet; some were brought to tears by the sight of the mud-built farmhouse that we chose to stand in for the real birthplace of the Dalai Lama in Amdo province. With the High Atlas Mountains as a backdrop, a fortress, said to have been occupied by the French Foreign Legion, could easily appear as a Tibetan monastery.

Our Tibetan cast never complained. They were there for the sake of the Dalai Lama. On many days they stood in 110-degree heat, dressed in heavy Tibetan costumes. Craft service would come around with bottles of water and some cheese sandwiches for the crew, but the camera crew and I would send them back, suggesting that if the Tibetans got nothing, then we would have nothing. More than food, the Tibetans wanted yak butter tea. When production arranged for this to be brought, morale improved appreciably.

The Tibetans stayed in a hotel in the center of Ouarzazate that gave them free rein in the kitchen on Sundays. James and I were delighted to be invited to join them for Sunday dinners, which provided a nice break from the bland set catering. Other members of our crew brought their native cuisine with them as well. During prep, Billy and I had been anxiously waiting for our lighting package to arrive as we were keen to start work. The grip and electric trucks were driving from Rome, and when they finally arrived, our Italian grip crew began unloading what, to them, were the most important items on the vehicles: boxes of pasta, cooking utensils, the largest cheeses I've ever seen, and a pizza oven.

We had a seventy-five-day schedule that ballooned to 103 days. Though *Kundun* was not on the same scale as other films with shorter schedules, it involved child actors. Four actors played the Dalai Lama at various points in his life. As soon as we ran the camera the youngest did more crying

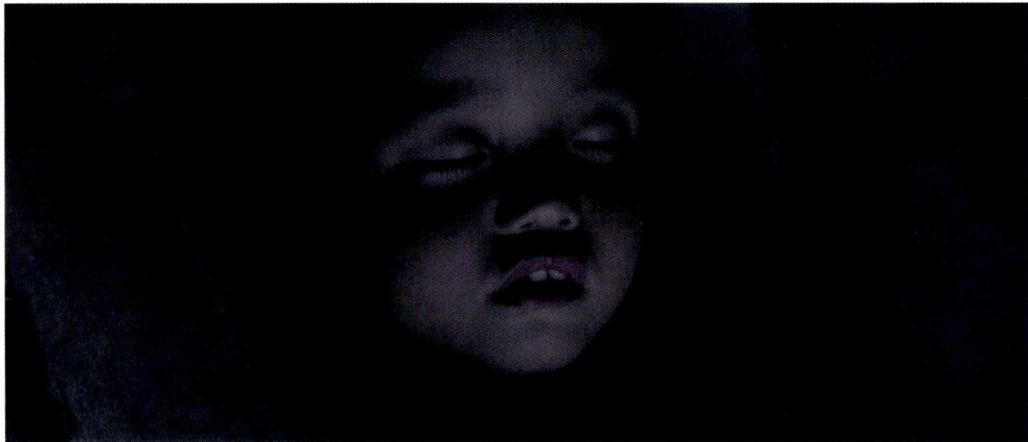

than any child I have ever encountered or want to encounter. We even tried to shoot him from inside a blacked-out hide, distracting him by dangling puppets and cardboard birds in front of his face using a long nylon thread knotted to the end of a boom pole. Nothing seemed to work unless he was sleeping. Marty's long-serving editor, Thelma Schoonmaker, did a wonderful job with the footage we gave her.

The bulk of our crew came from Italy and the UK. But in addition to Billy and a few of his New York team, I had with me Bruce Hamme as dolly grip and Andy Harris as first assistant camera. Andy and I had first met when he was working as Eric Swanek's second assistant on *Thunderheart*. I later worked with Eric on *Shawshank*, but when he had to leave due to a prior commitment, Andy took over. We have been working together ever since. Andy is a Jersey boy whom James knew well from her New York days. He had never traveled outside of the United States before *Kundun* and was quite reluctant to do so. Consequently, I had struggled to convince him that Morocco would prove to be the experience of a lifetime, one he would regret if he turned me down.

After checking out our relatively modest camera package, Andy boarded an early flight to Casablanca and disappeared off the map. Our production office in Ouarzazate was in a panic, having heard nothing from him through the night and late into the following morning. The office had assumed the worst, as the route from Casablanca to Ouarzazate involved crossing the High Atlas Mountains via a very treacherous road. In truth, Andy had been picked up by a taxi, arranged by production, at the airport in Casablanca, but the driver spoke no English and did not know which hotel he was taking Andy to—though, luckily, he knew the town. Andy got into the car, and they set off into the pitch-dark night. Had he been aware then of the sheer drops to each side of the road as it wound its way across the mountains, Andy might have found the drive even more "exhilarating." Arriving in Ouarzazate in the middle of the night and after being turned away by others, Andy checked himself into the first hotel that agreed to give him a room. In the morning the hotel guided him to the production office of a television series that was also basing itself in Ouarzazate and they in turn sent him on his way to our production office—after a leisurely breakfast.

Traveling—it gives you a home in a thousand strange places, then leaves you a stranger in your own land.

IBN BATTUTA (1304–1368)

When he finally arrived, the Italian staff began sobbing, acting as if he had been lost forever, because they assumed he *had* been. From that day on they called him "Andy of the Desert," and he has since become an avid traveler. In retrospect, he was quite lucky. One taxi had dropped an older Tibetan lady in another village altogether, remote and in the heart of the High Atlas. It was only via gossip a day or two later that the production office learned where she was and could send a vehicle to retrieve her.

During preproduction, Marty gave me a copy of Melissa Mathison's script on which he had written notes and drawn a bird's-eye view of both the camera position and movement he envisioned for each of the various scenes. In the mornings he would leave it to me to ready the shot and only come to set when called for by our AD, Scott Harris. Whether intentionally or not, if what I had set up deviated at all from what Marty had in his mind's eye, I was in trouble.

Marty once told James that he liked editing films more than shooting them. He seemed uncomfortable in the desert, and talking about movies appeared to help. James would try to stump him by thinking of a movie he had never seen, but she never could. When he would mention a movie James hadn't seen, he'd say, "Oh, I'll get you a VHS!" There wasn't much to do in Ouarzazate, so we watched them all, even *Shakes the Clown*. Only later did James learn from the production office that every time Marty asked for a movie, the staff had to find someone in Italy to hand-carry it through Moroccan customs as, if sent on its own, a VHS tape would never have made it. Those in the production office were not so fond of the "name a movie" game that Marty and James played!

The sets that together formed the mazelike Potala Palace had been built to accommodate a long tracking shot through the corridor leading to the assembly rooms, but no consideration had been given to how we could track with a dolly on uneven stone paving slabs. Early in prep I managed to convince production to hire one of the best Steadicam operators for the length of the shoot, Peter Cavaciuti. Peter had been a friend since we had worked together on the Eric Clapton video "Forever Man," and this kind of shot was why I had asked him to be with us.

Peter and I had practiced the camera move before asking for Marty to come to the set and, as I felt we were ready, we immediately went into a full rehearsal. I was watching the live feed with Marty on his monitor and, I guess wondering why I was not operating, he turned to me and asked how we were accomplishing the shot. I said it was Pete and his Steadicam. Marty was taken aback. "Really?" he said. "He's good! I would not have known." Later Peter would work with Stanley Kubrick on *Eyes Wide Shut* and with Sam Mendes and me on *1917*. As I said to Marty, he is one of the best.

Night scenes set around the Buddha were lit using small halogen bulbs hidden among the votive candles. But most of the other sets required much larger rigs, and the throne room is just one example.

Billy and I lit this using an array of twenty-four 10K Fresnel lamps bounced off gold stipple reflectors. Our rigging crew hung a series of scaffold tubes as high above the set as possible.

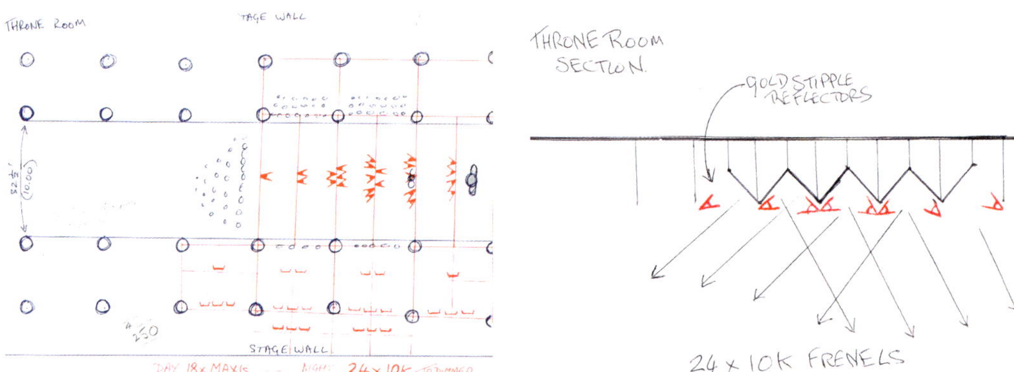

As our "stage" was not load bearing, these were supported by goalposts hidden behind drapes the art department had supplied to look like authentic columns. The 10K Fresnels were set to project light both toward and away from the throne but always parallel to the chamber. Between them hung a series of 16' × 4' gold stipple reflectors set at forty-five degrees to each row of lamps. The gold stipple focused the bounce into the central area of the set rather than allowing it to spill out in all directions, as it would off a matte white reflector, and the light from multiple lamps blended into one another to create a large, soft source. In conjunction with dimming the lamps, the gold of the reflector warmed the light to the same color temperature as the votive candles on the set. The Maxis referred to in the diagram were rigged for the daylight scene, between the Tibetans and the Chinese general, that shot at a later date on the same set.

Every day, residents of Ouarzazate would queue up outside the studio in the hope of getting a job on the production. I was lining up one shot of the young Dalai Lama underneath a red cloth when a production assistant brought in a small boy from the street named Mohammed to work as a stand-in. I immediately placed the red cloth over his head and aimed a fully spotted 10K Fresnel toward him. Though he spoke no English and was quite overwhelmed he soon became engrossed with everything he was seeing. It's easy to forget how exotic filming can appear to someone on the outside.

On Fridays we had "Dollar Day," when crew members put a dollar (or dirham) in a hat for a winner-takes-all draw. It was probably Bruce who wrote Mohammed's name on a note and put it in the hat. As luck would have it, his name was drawn. It was difficult to convince the boy that the prize, $70 or $80, was his to keep as he had never seen that much money in his life. When it really sank in that this was his money, he flat-out fainted. Mohammed and his dad, a local goat herder, went off smiling that evening.

The set usually had security that restricted access to outsiders. But one day in Casablanca, as we were shooting some of the montage shots depicting the Dalai Lama's journey to China, the system apparently broke down, allowing two or three Chinese "officials" to confront some of our cast members. Wearing long trenchcoats and homburg hats, they looked so obviously like spies that they might have been from central casting. But despite their comical appearance they were quite serious. "Why are you betraying the Motherland?" they shouted in the face of one of our cast members. This actor, who had studied as a monk and had found it difficult to pretend anger for a scene earlier in the shoot, now took a swipe at one of the officials, flooring him. He told us later he had been thinking of all the family members he had lost when the Chinese invaded Tibet. The Motherland! He was one of the gentlest people on the set, but even he had a breaking point. He told James, "I've spent years as a monk getting rid of anger. It's hard to find it." But find it he did. The same Chinese "gentlemen" had previously been to our production office while we were still based in Ouarzazate but, irony of ironies, we had been at a distant location shooting a scene depicting the Chinese takeover of Lhasa.

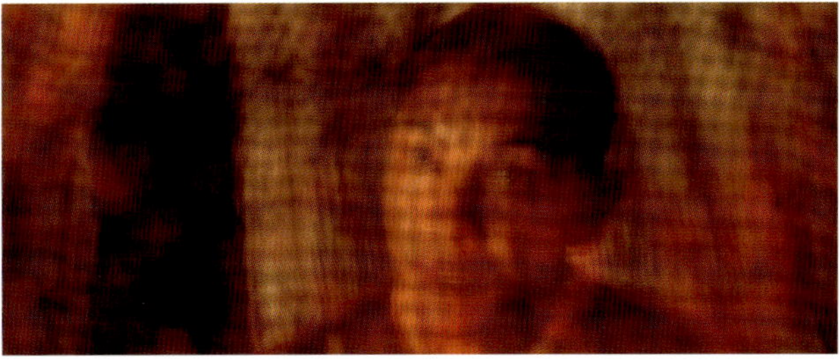

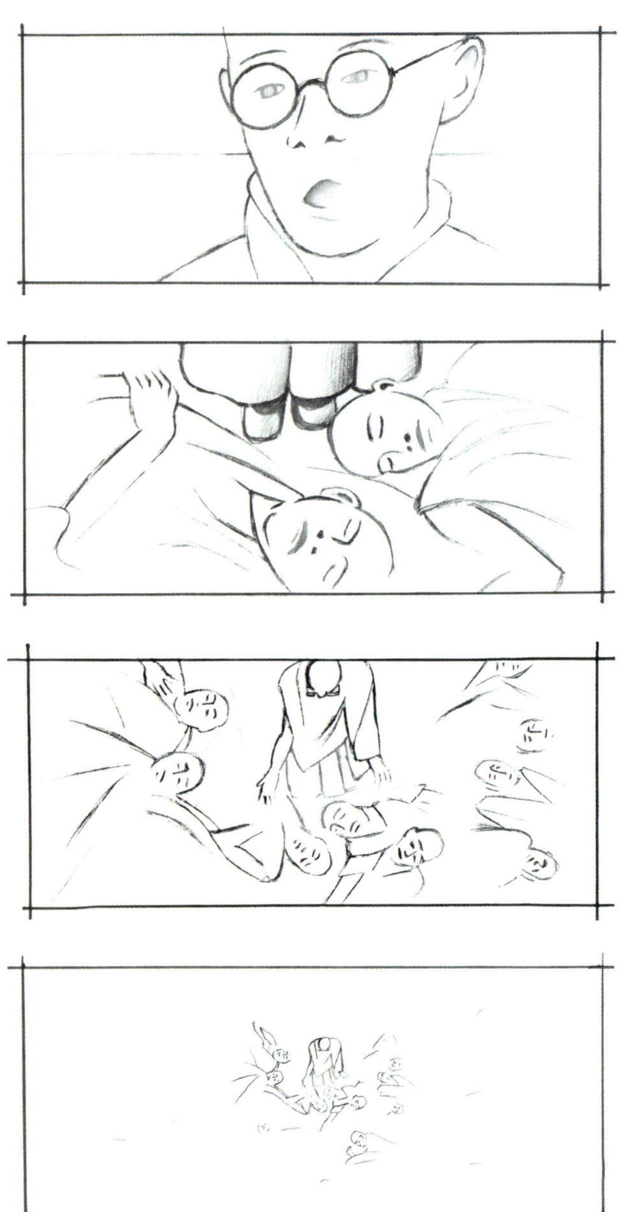

Late in the film, the adult Dalai Lama (Tenzin Thuthob Tsarong, the Dalai Lama's grand-nephew in real life) has a nightmare in which he stands in the middle of hundreds of corpses, monks he imagines are to be killed by the Chinese. I had once achieved a similar camera move to the one Marty envisioned using a massive construction crane, but that had been a boom down and shot on a wide lens. For the camera to start on a close shot of the Dalai Lama's face before tilting down to the bodies at his feet and slowly rising to reveal a wide tapestry of death, it required a more delicate tool set: the seventy-five-foot, Russian-made Akela (at the time the largest camera crane available and before a drone was an option) in combination with a Cooke 18–100 mm Varotal zoom lens. Our production was hesitant to transport such an expensive item as the Akela, along with its accompanying technicians, from Europe to the edge of the Sahara for a single shot. But I was not going to be the one to tell Marty we could not make that shot.

Without the extras we needed, or the Akela getting us as high as Marty wanted, the final frames had to be extended in post. This was the first time I had used the Akela, and it was a pure coincidence that the second time was for our first shot on the next project, *The Big Lebowski*—to follow a tumbling tumbleweed down an LA hillside.

Kundun includes a wide variety of imagery and lighting that ranges from the warmth of the candles to the chill of the night scenes. I wanted to play with the contrast in color a little more than I might in another film. *Kundun* is a dream, a kind of visual poem, so I felt this gave me license. But I did want to keep it within reality, and I often obsess over the smallest of details. A single bare light bulb contrasts the romantic candlelight of the film's earlier moments with encroaching modernity.

Production finished in Casablanca, which stood in for Peking. After so many days and weeks in Ouarzazate, where the food selection was sparse, we immediately sent out to McDonald's for our night shoot's supper. In fact, we ordered from McDonald's for the next four nights rather than eat from the catering truck. I don't think McDonald's hamburgers had ever tasted so good—maybe not since I returned from the yacht race—so good that Tenzin ate three and went back for more.

Kundun was detested by the Chinese government, and the film received only limited release elsewhere. Looking back, I remember a comment widely attributed to Disney CEO Michael Eisner—"The bad news is that the film was made; the good news is that nobody watched it." But another

quote seems more heartfelt, this one from cinematographer Fred Elmes: "Whenever possible, shoot the films that you care about, because those are the ones where you'll do the best work." Given the chance to work on *any* Scorsese movie, *Kundun* would be my pick. It's not a traditional narrative story or a history of Tibet, violent or otherwise, but a melancholy tone poem to a changing world.

James and I had experienced another country, an eclectic mix of cultures, and shared the shooting of a film together. The good and the bad. By the time we left Ouarzazate many of the Moroccan cafés and carpet stores featured a picture of the Dalai Lama alongside that of their king. The Tibetans had that effect on people.

16

THE DUDE ABIDES

It's good knowin' he's out there. The Dude.
Takin' 'er easy for all us sinners.

THE STRANGER, IN *THE BIG LEBOWSKI*

***Kundun*'s schedule had expanded to 103 days, but we** still made it home by Christmas. Joel and Ethan had waited patiently to finalize prep and location scouting for their next film, *The Big Lebowski*, which was scheduled to shoot before the end of January 1997, so we hit the ground running. I was happy. For all its challenges, *Fargo* had been a fun shoot, and they had become two of my favorite collaborators. Their new project, not a surprise with the Coens, was "something completely different," as Monty Python put it. The script read like a cross between *The Big Sleep* and a stoner comedy, making it hard to picture exactly what sort of movie it would be. That had been true of *Fargo*, but with *The Big Lebowski*'s many moving parts, plot strands, and red herrings I wasn't sure what to make of it. But I knew it would be interesting.

That *The Big Lebowski* also offered a chance to work with Jeff Bridges made it even more exciting. In the early 1970s, Bridges appeared in Peter Bogdanovich's *The Last Picture Show*, Michael Cimino's *Thunderbolt and Lightfoot*, and John Huston's *Fat City*, all of which helped shape my appreciation of film. To my mind, they're still three of the greatest American films.

I was in Torquay when I saw *Fat City* for the first time, having been rejected as a beach photographer and yet to start on the next stage in my life at the National Film School. Back then, Torbay cinemas served as a test market for some films before they went into wide release, but I'm not sure *Fat City*—with its gritty depiction of boxers living in Stockton, California, and Conrad Hall's shadowy cinematography—played that well based on the screening I attended. The cinema was almost empty, save for a few old people who were most probably there to get out of the incessant rain of an English summer and have a short nap. I like to think those who stayed awake were as deeply affected by the film as I was. Now, twenty five years later, Jeff Bridges was the Dude.

Sometimes a film's look comes together at different points in preproduction. On *Barton Fink*, the Coens and I had five weeks of prep together, scouting locations and discussing what worked for them and what didn't. It was during these conversations, standing on real locations, that I started to see how Joel and Ethan pictured the film. Though decidedly different films, we went through a similar process on both *The Hudsucker Proxy* and *Fargo*, but because I arrived late to *Lebowski* I had some catching up to do.

The Big Lebowski provides a fine example of how the most seemingly simple locations can prove to be

THE BIG LEBOWSKI
SET LIGHTING DEPT.

EQUIPMENT ORDER:

SET: TRUCK PACKAGE

DATE: AS OF 1/17/97

RENTAL PERIOD: WHOLE SHOW

Quanty :	Item:	special notes:
~~1~~ 2	18K HMI COMPLETE	SILVER BULLET
~~2~~ 3	6K PARS COMPLETE	ARRI
4	1200 HMI PARS	
2	575 HMI FRESNELS	
2	200 HMI PARS	
2	BABY 10K'S	
2	BABY 5K'S	
2	BABY JURNIOR'S	
6	407 BABY'S	
6	TWEENIE'S	650W GLOBES
8	BLONDE'S	
8	REDHEAD'S	
2	PAR 64'S	WIDE/MED./SPOT
6	SNUBNOSED PAR CAN'S	WIDE/MED./SPOT
6	500W PAR GLOBE'S	3MED./3SPOT
6	1K NOOK'S	
2	1K BABY SOFT LIGHT'S	
2	TODA LIGHT KIT'S	
1	LOWEL K-5 KIT	
1	MINI FLO KIT	
6	FLICKER GENERATOR'S	GREAT AMERICAN
4	12K STAND-ALONE DIMMER'S	WITH CONTROLER &150'DMX CABLE
4	2K VARIAC'S	
4	1K VARIAC'S	
2	CABLE CART'S	
2	HEAD CART'S	
1	ELECTRIC TACO CART	
4	SUPER CRANK STAND'S	
2	CRANK STAND'S	
8	JR. STAND'S	STEEL

MON. P.M.P. AS DIAGRAM (REVERSED FOR RT. HAND DRIVE !!!)
SOBAC - AS SEEN.

TUES. BEACH: 3B LIFT ON HEIGHTS IF POSS.
4 x TOWERS (10' OR THEREABOUTS)
4 x DINOS ON TOWERS TO FLICKER.
POSS 2 TO HIDE.
12 - 2K BLONDES (AS R.H. RIG IN BOWLING ALLEY)
LIFT + B.B. FOR P.C.H. SHOT.

WED. MALIBU BEACH HOUSE.
POOL LIGHTS AS DISCUSSED)
TWIN. FLOURESCENT TUBES AS DISCUSSED,
POWER AND FIXING TO APEX OF CEILING *

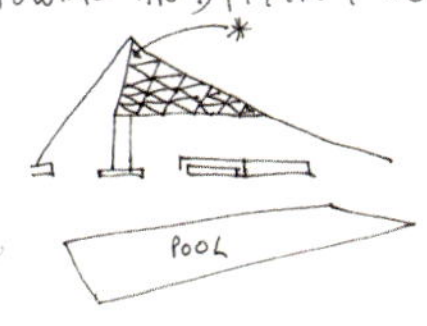

FRIDAY LARRY'S HOUSE - INT PRACS AND CHERYL'S ON DAY

EXT. 2 LIFTS ETC AS DISCUSSED

MERCURY → 18KS + 6KS ON STREET
ENDS - FLOODS ON HOUSE PORCH
LIGHTS IN HOUSES NEXT DOOR

surprisingly difficult. A bowling alley, the gathering place for the Dude and pals Walter (John Goodman) and Donny (Steve Buscemi), served as a central location. You might think finding a working LA bowling alley at the beginning of 1997 for a story set in 1991 would be easy, but no. After several dead ends, we settled on the Hollywood Star Lanes on Santa Monica Boulevard. It looked the part and, just as important, was closed at the time, which allowed us the freedom to prep and to shoot both interiors and exteriors. But lighting its thirty-two-lane space would take time and money.

Billy O'Leary joined me once again, and we knew from the first time we laid eyes on the place it would need to be rewired. Few of the existing light fixtures worked. Those that did were caked in years of accumulated grime, rendering them virtually useless. It would have been possible to approach each shot separately, by moving lamps as needed, but it is my practice on most films to light each scene in a way that requires little relighting when shooting the coverage. Besides, on *Lebowski* we had little time for changes. We'd need to light the alley in its entirety, and we had only a short time to get it done.

And there was another complication. Because we'd be shooting some scenes in slow motion, filming at 120 frames per second rather than the usual twenty-four, we'd need to light for a level almost two and a half times brighter than normal. And that was not the only issue. Some fluorescent lights flicker. Changing the speed of the film going through the camera's gate offsets the sync between the shutter and the flicker of the bulb, creating a strobing effect. You can avoid this by shooting at certain high speeds paired with specific shutter openings, but we wanted to change speed within the shot.

To do this and maintain an even exposure you can adjust the shutter opening or the lens aperture. As changing the shutter opening can also affect the strobing of the image (see *Band of Brothers* for an example, which used the strobing for effect), we rented a speed aperture compensation unit. And we still had to swap out the alley's old-style magnetic ballasts for flicker-free electronic ballasts, while we added more fixtures to increase the light level. That's the work you sometimes need to do to make an everyday location look as if it hasn't been altered at all. But once we had everything in place we could shoot quickly, adding little beyond a handheld reflector

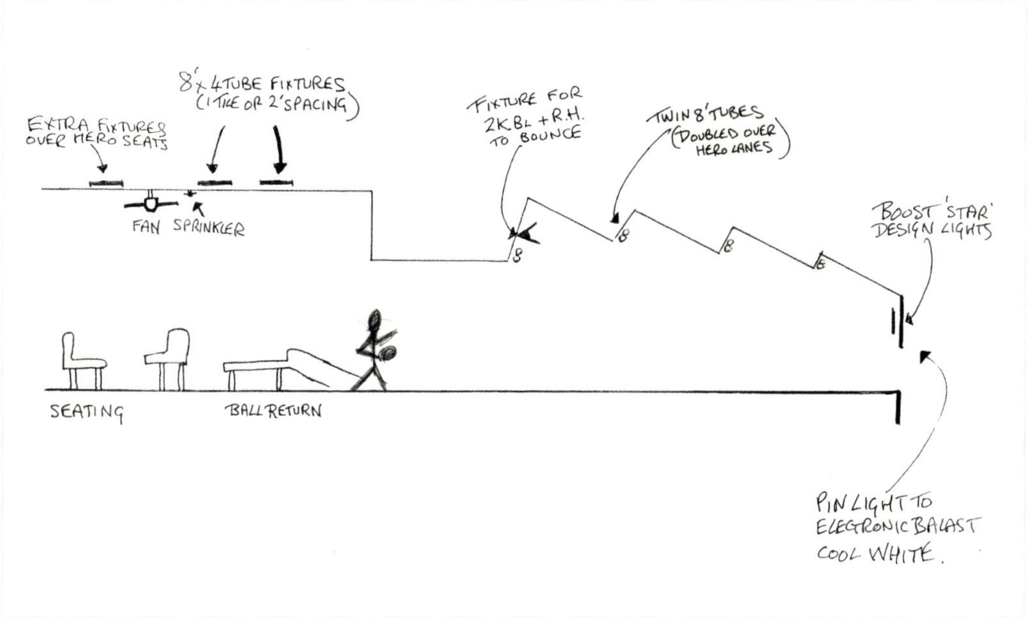

8' x 4 TUBE FIXTURES
(1 TILE OR 2' SPACING)
EXTRA FIXTURES OVER HERO SEATS
FIXTURE FOR 2K BL + R.H. TO BOUNCE
TWIN 8' TUBES (DOUBLED OVER HERO LANES)
FAN
SPRINKLER
BOOST 'STAR' DESIGN LIGHTS
SEATING
BALL RETURN
PIN LIGHT TO ELECTRONIC BALAST COOL WHITE.

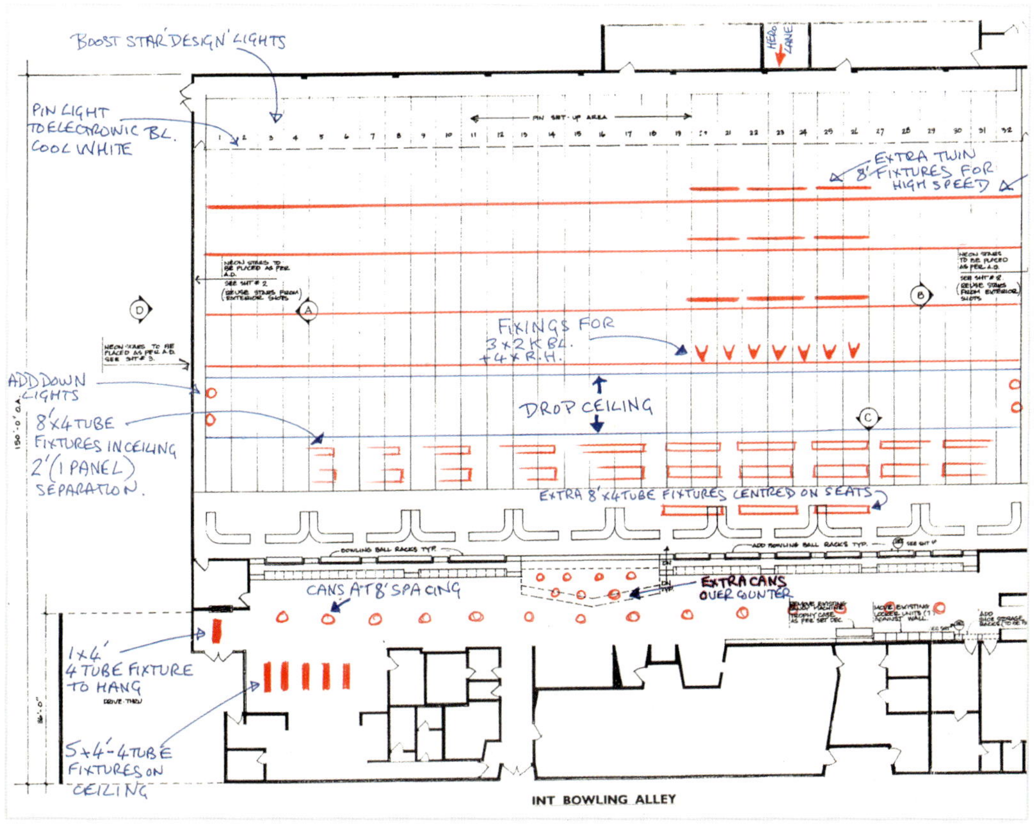

BOOST STAR' DESIGN' LIGHTS
HERO LANE
PIN LIGHT TO ELECTRONIC BL. COOL WHITE
PIN SET-UP AREA
EXTRA TWIN 8' FIXTURES FOR HIGH SPEED
FIXINGS FOR 3 x 2 K BL. + 4 x R.H.
ADD DOWN LIGHTS
DROP CEILING
8' x 4 TUBE FIXTURES IN CEILING 2' (1 PANEL) SEPARATION.
EXTRA 8' x 4 TUBE FIXTURES CENTRED ON SEATS
CANS AT 8' SPACING
EXTRA CANS OVER COUNTER
1 x 4' 4 TUBE FIXTURE TO HANG
5 x 4' - 4 TUBE FIXTURES ON CEILING
INT BOWLING ALLEY

BIG LEBOWSKI

CAMERA EQUIPMENT FOR "THE BIG LEBOWSKIE"

1 ARRI 535 B CAMERA
1 GROUND GLASS 1.85 ?
1 B/W CCD VIDEO ASSIST
4 400' 535 MAGAZINES
6 1000' 535 MAGAZINES
1 EYEPIECE EXTENSION
1 EYEPIECE LEVELER
1 EYEPIECE HEATER
1 SLIDING BALANCE PLATE COMPLETE
1 STUDIO FOLLOW FOCUS UNIT COMPLETE 2-SPEED
1 WHIP, LEVER, KNOB
1 4X4 ARRI MATTE BOX MB-16
1 SET HARD MATTES
1 EYEBROW
1 REMOTE SWITCH
1 PRESTON REMOTE FOLLOW FOCUS UNIT W. CABLES ARRI MATTE / PRESTON W/ POD
1 4X4 CLAMP-ON MATTE BOX
1 HAND HELD BASE
1 LITTLE LIGHT
1 9" MONITOR W. CABLES
10 4X4 FILTERS
1 SET ZEISS HI-SPEED PRIMES (18,25,35,50,85mm) T1.3
1 ZEISS 14mm T2.1
1 ZEISS 28mm T2.1
1 ZEISS 32mm T2.1
1 ZEISS 40mm T2.1
1 ZEISS 65mm T1.3
1 ZEISS 135mm T2.1
1 200mm NIKOR T2
1 DIRECTORS FINDER
4 SUPER BLOCK BATTERIES
2 BELT BATTERIES
1 RONFORD 2000 FLUID HEAD
1 ARRI GEAR HEAD 2 – LARGE WHEELS
1 STANDARD TRIPOD
1 BABY TRIPOD
1 HI-HAT
1 SPREADER

PANCROS

CRANE DAYS:– Sc 74 BOWLING ALLEY
Sc 1 HILLSIDE
Sc 42 AUTOCIRUS
Sc 57 DREAM #2
Sc 26 SIMI VALLEY
Sc 3 EXT. RALPHS
Sc 50 LARRY'S HOUSE
Sc 19 VENICE
Sc 55 MALIBU BEACH PARTY
TECHNOCRANE Sc 22 STORYBOARD 6 X (8)

EYEMO :– BOWLING ALLEY
MAUDS LOFT

POORMANS STAGE :– EXTRA 50MM, 60MM + 2ND CAMERA

SPEED APERTURE COMP :– Sc 55 MALIBU BEACH
Sc 33 BOWLING ALLEY
Sc 56 MALIBU BEACH HOUSE
Sc 58 BLUE SCREEN WORK

18–100 MM ZOOM Sc 33 BOWLING ALLEY
Sc 56 BEACH HOUSE
Sc 76 CLIFFTOP

STEADYCAM :– Sc 34, Sc 74 BOWLING ALLEY
Sc 58 P.C.H "PLATE" SHOT

LOW ∠ PRISM Sc 56 MALIBU BEACH HOUSE

RADCAM (SKATE BOARD RIG) Sc 6 BOWLING ALLEY SHOT (1)
CALL MARK CENTKOWSKI INNOVISION 310 394 5510 Sc 57 DREAM #2 SHOT (11)

to bring out a cast member's eyes or add a highlight to a bowling ball. Like so many situations, from *Shawshank* to *Kundun*, production might balk at the initial cost of a piece of equipment or a lighting rig, but when it saves shooting time, it saves money.

Shooting inside and outside the bowling alley went smoothly, and only one or two shots proved to be head-scratchers. We wanted to push behind a ball as it rolled toward the pins, and our little motorized skateboard had trouble catching up with the ball. What to do? Bruce Hamme suggested we set the camera on a soft pad, and he would push it down the lane at the end of a forty-foot pole. And for the point of view from inside the bowling ball, Mitch Lillian and Bruce simply mounted the camera on a revolving spit, offset it on the dolly, and tracked alongside the alley. The black "hole" was added as an overlay later.

The simplest solution is most often the best!

A POPULAR VERSION OF OCCAM'S RAZOR

Keep it simple, stupid!

THE U.S. NAVY'S "KISS" DESIGN PRINCIPLE

We worked hard to keep the bowling alley scenes naturalistic, but *The Big Lebowski* freely departs reality at several points. We shot the fantasy sequence—in which the Dude rents shoes from Saddam Hussein, descends a staircase stretching to infinity, and joins Maude Lebowski (Julianne Moore) in a bowling-themed, Busby Berkeley–inspired dance sequence—in a Santa Monica airport hangar. Because the hangar didn't have a load-bearing ceiling, as a studio would, Mitch had a truss built to span the set and hold our lighting rig. I wanted the sequence to appear as if it were illuminated by a single soft source but keep the light from spilling beyond the set and allow the background to fall into darkness. The solution was an array of 1K Fresnel lamps rigged in an overlapping pattern that imitated a soft source, just as a ring light or a strip of household bulbs might, but that would also act as a directional source. This approach was not dissimilar to lighting the ballroom in the *Queen Mary* but one with an even more focused pattern of lamps than the R40 bulbs. I would return to the same technique many times in the future, including for the concert scene in *O Brother, Where Art Thou?* and for Wallace's office in *Blade Runner 2049*.

To isolate the set, we draped the walls with black cloth, but to give some sense of a night sky beyond we created stars using small pieces of front-projection material to make them shine. In fact, we used material I had left over from *Shadey*, a bizarre British comedy reviewed as a "cult film looking for a cult," for which I had attempted to turn an elevator into a spaceship. As for that film, lighting the projection material required only a small source placed close to the camera lens, so dim that it made no difference to the shot otherwise. And to run the camera down the alley between the legs of the girls we again fell back on Bruce's low-tech solution, his soft pad and a forty-foot pole.

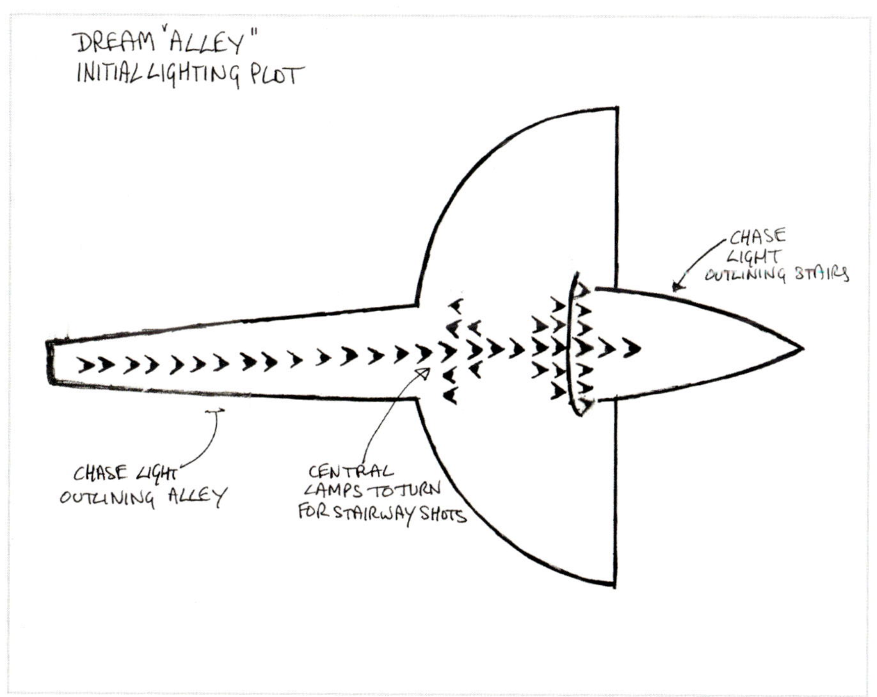

That rug really tied the room together.

THE DUDE, IN *THE BIG LEBOWSKI*

We shot the exteriors of the Dude's bungalow on location, but, as the Coens wanted a specific layout, production designer Rick Heinrichs built its cluttered interior as a set. It also had to look dirty and uncared for, so Billy and I took steps to emphasize this with our lighting, for example using a single bare bulb in the bathroom. It's always a balancing act when shooting a movie. It needs to look good, but what does "good" mean when depicting places that aren't pretty? I used to have long conversations with Conrad Hall about this topic. How do you draw an audience in while staying true to what the scene needs? Just because it may look lovely doesn't mean it looks right.

Driving scenes are always time-consuming if they are shot for real, out on the street. It's necessary when you are shooting car to car or the characters interact with their surroundings, but there are scenes that can be shot onstage and faked, using a technique called "poor man's process." I find this quite fun to do, especially when a film is not supposed to be completely naturalistic and the scenes take place at night.

For *Lebowski* we used rotating lights to mimic the passing streetlamps. Behind the car a series of dollies tracked back and forth with small red and white lamps standing in for the taillights and headlamps of the surrounding traffic. With every lamp on a dimmer, a simple setup can create quite a complex interactive pattern of light.

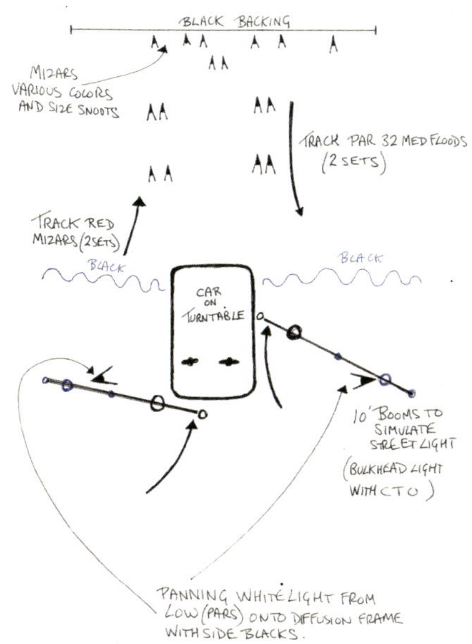
BLACK BACKING
MIZARS VARIOUS COLORS AND SIZE SNOOTS
TRACK PAR 32 MED FLOODS (2 SETS)
TRACK RED MIZARS (2 SETS)
BLACK
BLACK
CAR ON TURNTABLE
10' BOOMS TO SIMULATE STREET LIGHT
(BULKHEAD LIGHT WITH CTO)
PANNING WHITE LIGHT FROM LOW (PARS) ONTO DIFFUSION FRAME WITH SIDE BLACKS.

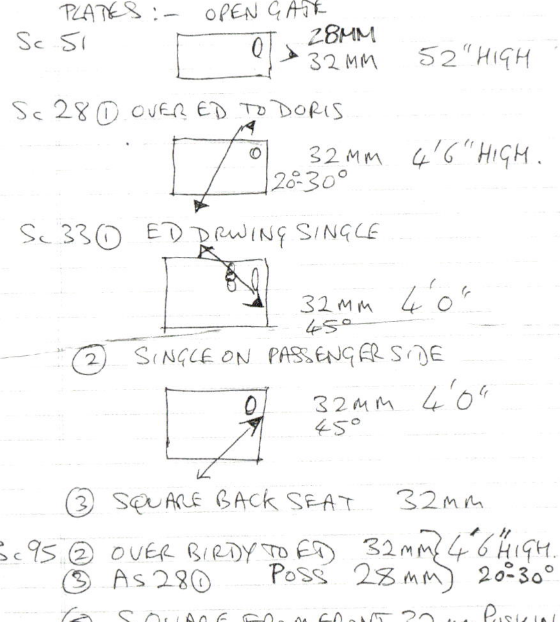

PLATES :- OPEN GATE
Sc 51 28MM 32MM 52" HIGH
Sc 28 (1) OVER ED TO DORIS
32MM 4'6" HIGH.
20°-30°
Sc 33 (1) ED DRIVING SINGLE
32MM 4'0"
45°
(2) SINGLE ON PASSENGER SIDE
32MM 4'0"
45°
(3) SQUARE BACK SEAT 32MM
Sc 95 (2) OVER BIRDY TO ED 32MM 4'6" HIGH.
(3) AS 28 (1) POSS 28MM 20°-30°
(5) SQUARE FROM FRONT 32MM PUSH IN
FLAT PLATE AT 18 F.P.S. SWERVE
POSS REF.N PLATE AT 45° FRONT

On the other hand, for the daytime car work in *The Man Who Wasn't There* (a film I will return to later) we used a combination of live-action points of view and bluescreen work (one of the advantages of shooting a black-and-white film in color) for which we had shot background plates in advance. Onstage, Mitch rigged a rotating arm, much like we had done on *Lebowski*, but that held a large leafy branch at its far end rather than a lamp. The gaffer, Randy Woodside, rigged a lamp, a 5K Fresnel, at the center of the circle of rotation so that it cast the pattern of sunlight across the car's interior. As we could play back our chosen background plates on a monitor, Mitch and his grip crew could time the shadows cast by the revolving greenery as if the car were traveling past the trees in the plate. This technique would not have been an option for a black-and-white film noir shot in the 1940s and '50s, hence their use of the back-projection technique we had embraced for *1984*. Bluescreen became the preferred technique in the late 1950s (one of the first and most famous uses was for John Sturges's *The Old Man and the Sea*, shot by the great James Wong Howe), and back projection is rarely, if ever, used today. Things have changed again since we "faked" our driving shots on *Lebowski* and *The Man Who Wasn't There*, and today these can be shot entirely in camera, on a virtual reality stage.

It's hard to believe it now, but *The Big Lebowski* debuted to mixed reviews and tepid box office in March 1998. At the time, this didn't come as that much of a surprise. It's an odd film, a stoner noir that undoubtedly confused those expecting another *Fargo*. Though it found a second life, it wasn't until James and I were consulting at Pixar a few years later that I realized what a beloved cult film it had become. Pixar's animators had decorated their workstations to reflect their tastes, with a *Star Trek* theme or a favorite sports team as well as a shrine to *The Big Lebowski*, complete with bowling paraphernalia and a palm tree.

I felt a sense of whiplash going from a stoner comedy to *The Siege*, a mainstream Hollywood movie with Ed Zwick that attempted to imitate Gillo Pontecorvo's epic *The Battle of Algiers*. *Courage Under Fire* had found a reasonable balance between a commercial drama and a film that dealt with a real-world situation. With *The Siege*, Ed would attempt the same, but with a story that depicted what might happen in the event of a terrorist attack on New York. While I can't entirely disagree with reviews that criticized the film for a sense of self-importance or for ultimately trying to be all things to all viewers, I think it works as a cautionary tale of how democracy under stress can easily morph into a fascist state. We made the film a couple of years before 9/11, yet the FBI and CIA ended up making many of the same mistakes Ed, Lawrence Wright, and Menno Meyjes's screenplay anticipated—blowback! The film's happy ending might be the most Hollywood thing about it.

I worked for a third time with Denzel Washington, alongside director Norman Jewison on *The Hurricane*. Like many directors of his age and experience, Sidney Lumet being the prime example, Norman didn't do many takes once he felt he had what he wanted, and, for me, the shoot was a pleasure. But the script of *The Hurricane* often embellished Rubin Carter's story. It smoothed over his marital infidelities and the thornier aspects of his past. Consequently, the finished film met with controversy when it arrived in theaters at the end of 1999. As much as I like the film and admire Denzel's performance, I think true stories should be just that. A less-sanitized version of Carter's life would have been far stronger. Whatever his faults, Carter deserved the fair trial he never got.

ALL OTHERS
TOWARDS AUDIENCE

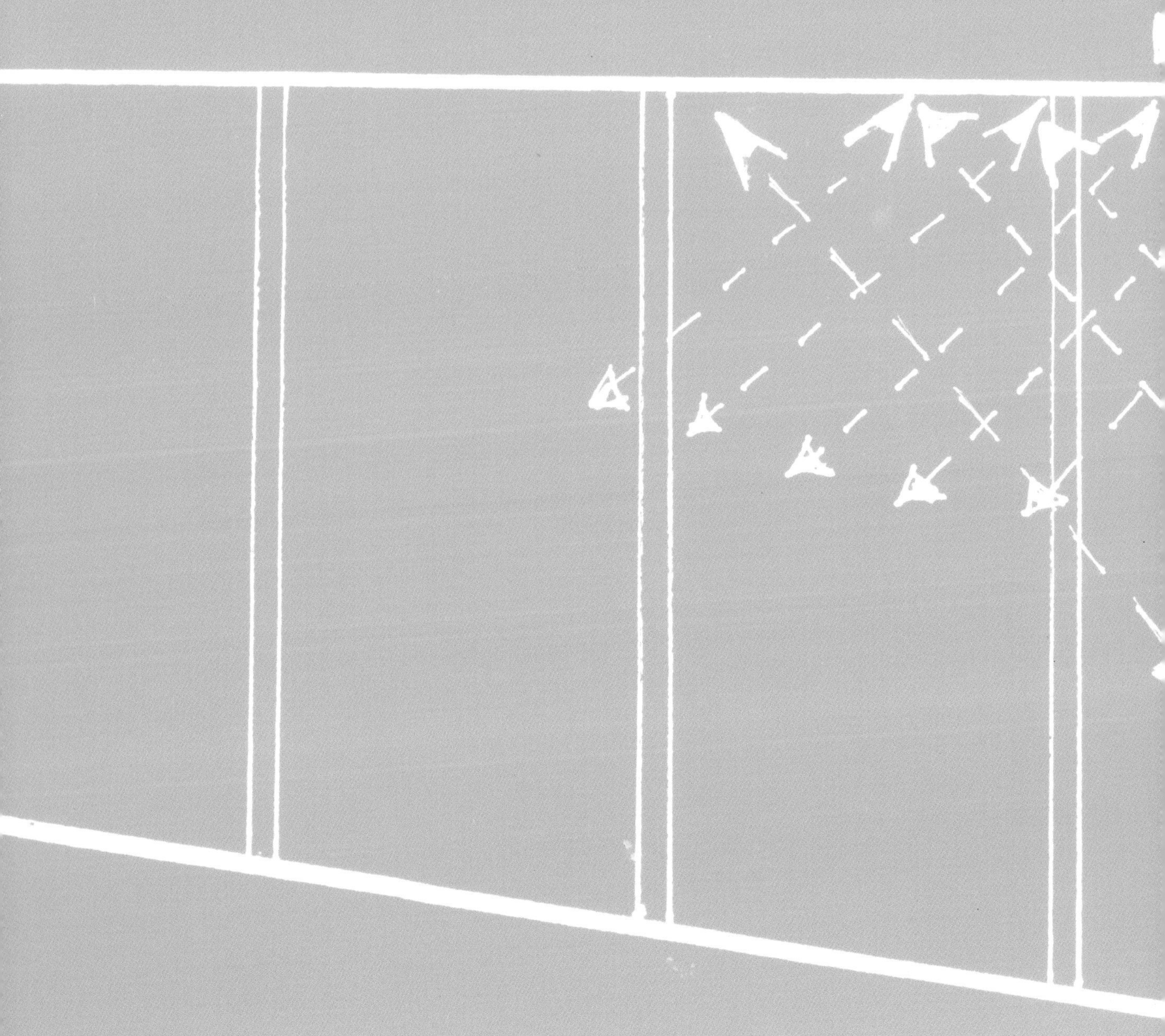

PART III

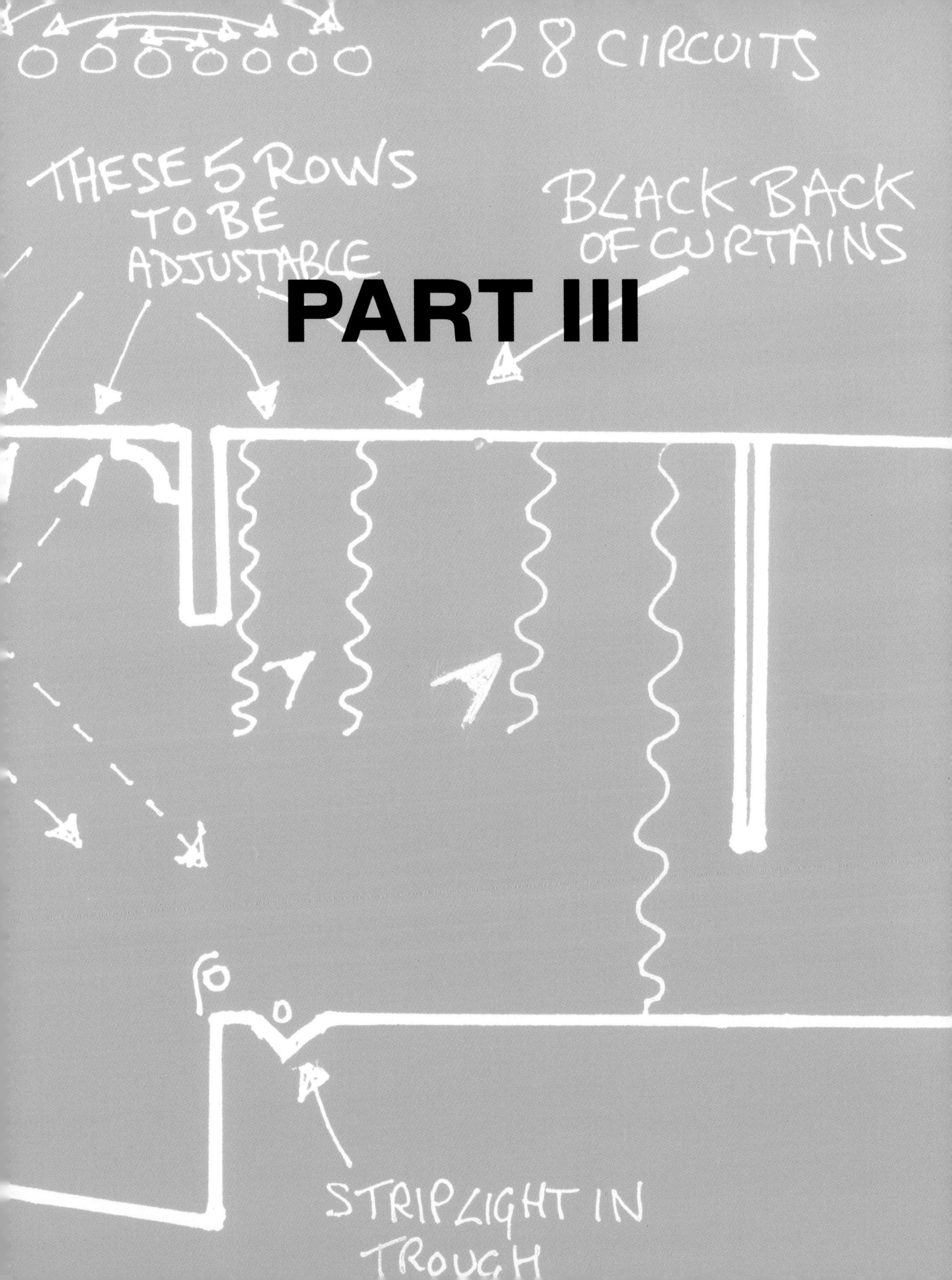

17

O, BROTHER

Do not seek the treasure!

PETE HOGWALLOP, IN *O BROTHER, WHERE ART THOU?*

By accident, rather than design, I'd become something of an expert on prison movies. My next film with Joel and Ethan, *O Brother, Where Art Thou?*, opens with a different picture of prison life. A chain gang sings in the opening shot of the Coens' musical set in 1930s Mississippi, a film that drew on Preston Sturges comedies, traditional American music, regional history, and, providing the spine of the plot, Homer's *The Odyssey*, for which the great author would get a screen credit. It was a typically eccentric mix, and Joel and Ethan were looking for a distinct look to match the material. The phrase "hand-tinted postcard" kept coming up, which seemed like the perfect model. But instead of simple sepia tones they wanted the skies to remain blue and the skin tones to appear natural while shifting the greens and other lush colors to create a more parched landscape. I could picture this. I just didn't know how we'd achieve it.

Finding a solution involved a lot of dead ends and experimentation. Andy Harris, James, and I shot test after test with various types of filtration in front of the lens, attempting to achieve the look photochemically. In discussions with Beverly Wood, our contact at the Deluxe film lab and a former chemist, we considered a bipack process, a technique in which two negatives are exposed on the same positive, allowing a layer of black-and-white to be exposed on top of a normal color pass. Ossie Morris had used a similar technique when he shot *Moby Dick* for John Huston, using the Technicolor dye transfer or imbibition printing process (last used in the United States for the release prints of *The Godfather Part II*). But we wanted to change select colors, not the entirety of the image. Neither Technicolor nor bipack printing, nor any combination of filtration in front of the lens, could achieve this. Perhaps the only solution would be to hand-paint a black-and-white negative, as Georges Méliès had done for his *Le voyage dans la lune* in 1902.

At some point Joel mentioned we might want to look at a technique being used on Gary Ross's upcoming film *Pleasantville*, which John Lindley was shooting. Much of *Pleasantville* takes place in the idealized, black-and-white American world of a 1950s sitcom but would make selective use of color to reflect its setting's shifting reality. The film achieved this effect for the first time using a digital intermediate, by which the camera negative is scanned, and the digital copy of that negative is color-timed (allowing for selective timing not possible with the photochemical process) before being recorded back onto film. Though I was averse to using a digital technique on any film (I am both a purist and hesitant to change), it did sound like the right tool for the job.

To confirm this, James and I took our test footage to Cinesite, a branch of Kodak that had begun putting resources into digital postproduction. The results looked pretty bad. Although the possibilities were obvious, our efforts looked crude. The technology wasn't sensitive enough to achieve what we wanted. Yet. We were told the process was rapidly evolving. In a year it would be perfect for what we needed. We all agreed to take a leap of faith.

The Coens have generous postproduction schedules written into their contracts, which would help, but, in truth, we were still taking a tremendous risk. *O Brother, Where Art Thou?* was an expensive film with big-name actors, including George Clooney. We had no idea what it would look like when we were done, even if we knew what we *wanted* it to look like. While watching dailies in a Jackson, Mississippi, theater I heard Joel telling George and John Turturro, while looking at a fully saturated and lushly green landscape, "It's not going to look like this." I kept thinking, *I hope it doesn't look like this. But what is it going to look like?*

In the meantime, we would be suffering through a sweltering Mississippi summer in which the thermometer rarely registered below ninety degrees. If the actors in the chain gang appear to be suffering from the brutal heat, it's not entirely acting. I think we all started to feel like we were in *Cool Hand Luke*. Happily, Joel and Ethan's working method takes factors like this into account, building breaks into the shooting and, in general, looking after the cast and crew. It has always impressed me that the Coens line up in the lunch queue like everyone else, rather than heading for their trailers and a meal fashioned by a personal chef, as is the habit of some directors. One time I

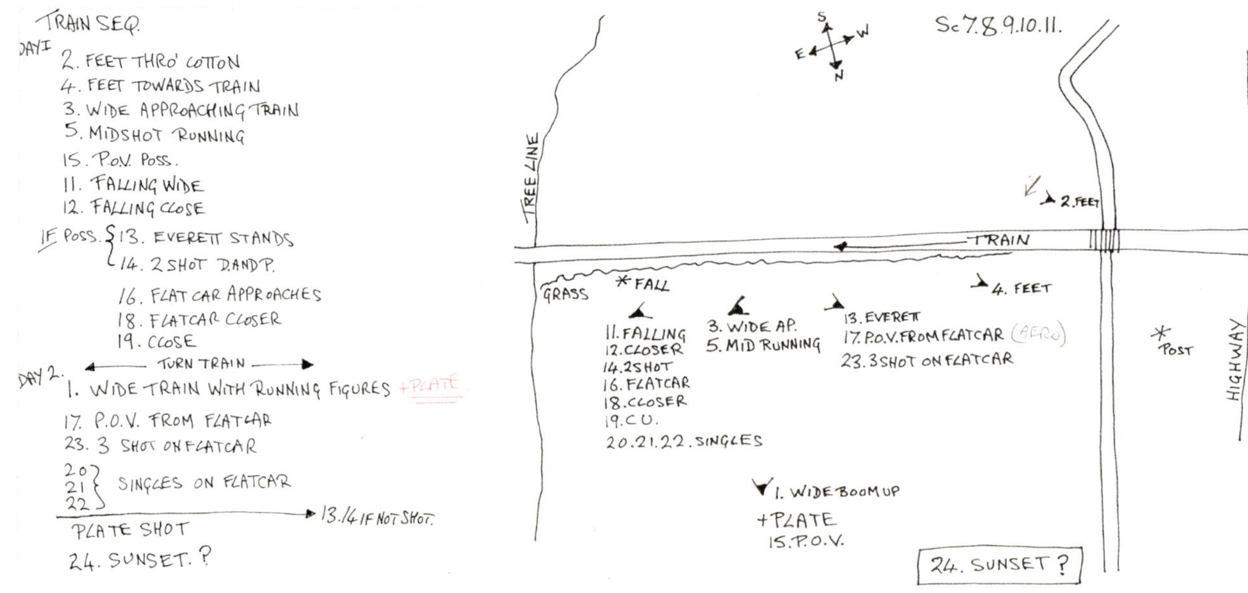

was with Joel in the queue when a crew member asked him what he did. "Oh, I'm the director," he replied without any sense of irony.

On *O Brother*, as on all their shoots, everyone mucked in. For later scenes, as we moved from one wet bayou location to the next, George would carry a tripod on his back, for instance, and Tim Blake Nelson would tote a magazine case. Perhaps it's because George, Tim, and John had all directed films themselves, or planned to, that they understood it made a difference when everyone felt equally involved in the hard work.

Is it because I'm a fisherman that I am always conscious of the weather wherever I am? Perhaps, but it is also crucial to a cinematographer. With assistant director Betsy Magruder, whom I'd first met while making *Sid and Nancy* and had introduced to Joel and Ethan, I'd break down each day of shooting into an order that allowed time for the complexity of each shot while considering the angle of the sun and other factors. For instance, we had two days to shoot the sequence where the film's protagonists make their escape via train, including plates that would form a background to the few shots we had to do with the actors against bluescreen. To get the best from the light on our location we reversed the train overnight to shoot from the opposite direction on the second day.

I draw out similar breakdowns for any complicated exterior work. It's the sort of practical concern that often gets overlooked when talking about filmmaking. You can spend all day setting up one perfect shot, then have no time for the next shot or the shot after that. It's a cinematographer's job to create the right image for a film but also to keep the process rolling. It's important to try not to compromise while keeping to a schedule, knowing that it's inevitable that some compromises will have to be made. Accomplishing both can be done *only* through careful planning and thinking about what needs to happen after a shot's been captured—where the camera goes next, can a camera track be laid in preparation for the next shot without it affecting the present one, what lights need to be moved, how the changing sunlight will affect reflectors, and so on.

Some things fall through the cracks. We filmed the baptism scene at a location called Alligator Lake, though it wasn't the wildlife that nearly derailed us. We'd brought in a seventy-five-foot Akela crane to do an overhead shot, the same crane as we had used in Morocco and to follow that

tumbling tumbleweed. But to achieve the exact camera move the brothers wanted, the base of the Akela had to be mounted on a track and moved during the shot. This would require purpose-made wheels and track to carry more than 5,500 pounds of weight. To say the least, the ground was quite saturated, as we were in a steaming Mississippi swamp, so Mitch Lillian, once again our key grip, decided to bring in some railroad sleepers ("crossties" in American parlance) on which to construct a firm base for the purpose-made track. Everything worked until it didn't. After a few takes, pushing the heavy crane back and forth, the wheels began to fold, and the grips began to sink into the mud—and the crawfish—taking the sleepers with them. But, as luck would have it, we managed to get the shot before everything came apart.

There were crawfish and there were rats. While I was staying in a small motel in Jackson I was woken up in the middle of the night by the sound of scratching. For the first two nights I had been so tired I went back to sleep, but by the third, it went beyond a joke. I traced the noise to the couch. When I bumped this piece of furniture up and down, out popped a very large black rat, more suitable to Winston Smith's nightmares than my own. Once I had chased the rodent out of my clothes closet, through the door, and into the night, I returned to a restless sleep. On my way to work I confronted the manager. "Yes, they will do that," he nonchalantly informed me.

We returned to Los Angeles to finish shooting some of our exterior scenes, including the town square and entrance to Homer Stokes's hoedown. But we shot the hoedown itself, in which the Soggy Bottom Boys would perform and Homer Stokes would be run out on a rail, inside the historic Vicksburg Southern Cultural Heritage Foundation Auditorium, a location that proved challenging. Not only was it a sensitive space to work in, but its low ceiling gave me few lighting options, and there would be no time in our schedule to make changes during the shooting day, no way to light the scene shot by shot.

I planned to boost the footlights beneath the Soggy Bottom Boys and hang two rows of lamps between the drapes above the stage to light the front of the audience. These two sources might have been sufficient in some situations. But here I was looking for the scene to take on a warm glow while concentrating the light on the performances and Homer's antics among the crowd, rather than have it flood the whole auditorium. To combine a soft source with a directional one as I had for *Lebowski*, I again turned to a large array of small Fresnel lamps (though none of the 1Ks I had depicted in my initial plan) instead of household bulbs.

It was a wonder how Mitch managed to tie in a pipe rig against the ceiling without damaging the location. And it was a wonder how Billy managed to fit in forty-eight 650-watt Fresnel lamps (or "Tweenies") so neatly and compactly that we could shoot wide shots of the stage and of the audience without one appearing in frame.

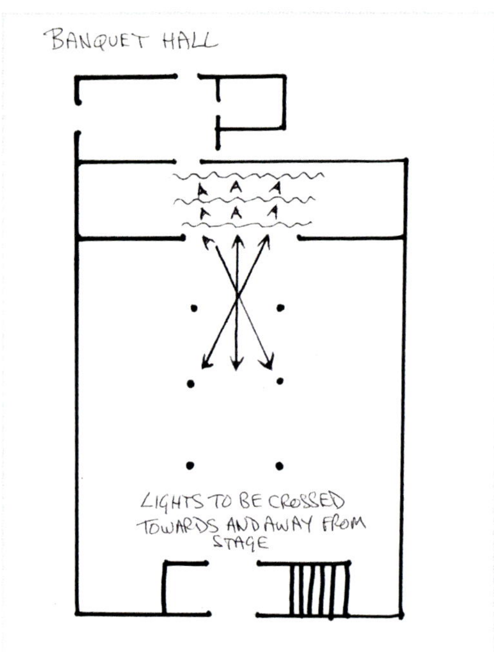
BANQUET HALL
LIGHTS TO BE CROSSED TOWARDS AND AWAY FROM STAGE

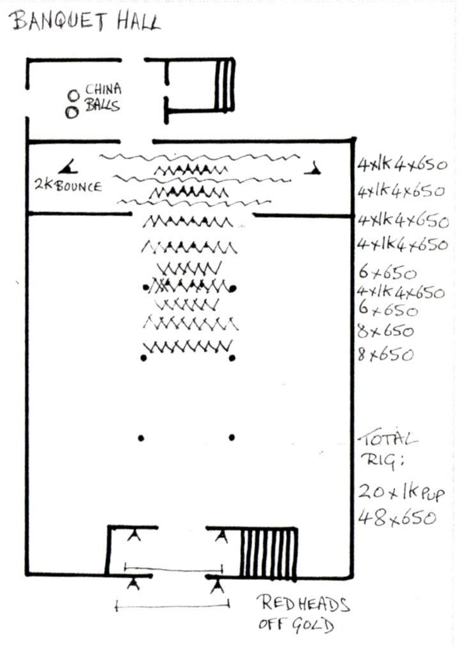
BANQUET HALL
CHINA BALLS
2K BOUNCE
4x1k 4x650
4x1k 4x650
4x1k 4x650
4x1k 4x650
6x650
4x1k 4x650
6x650
8x650
8x650
TOTAL RIG:
20x1k PUP
48x650
REDHEADS OFF GOLD

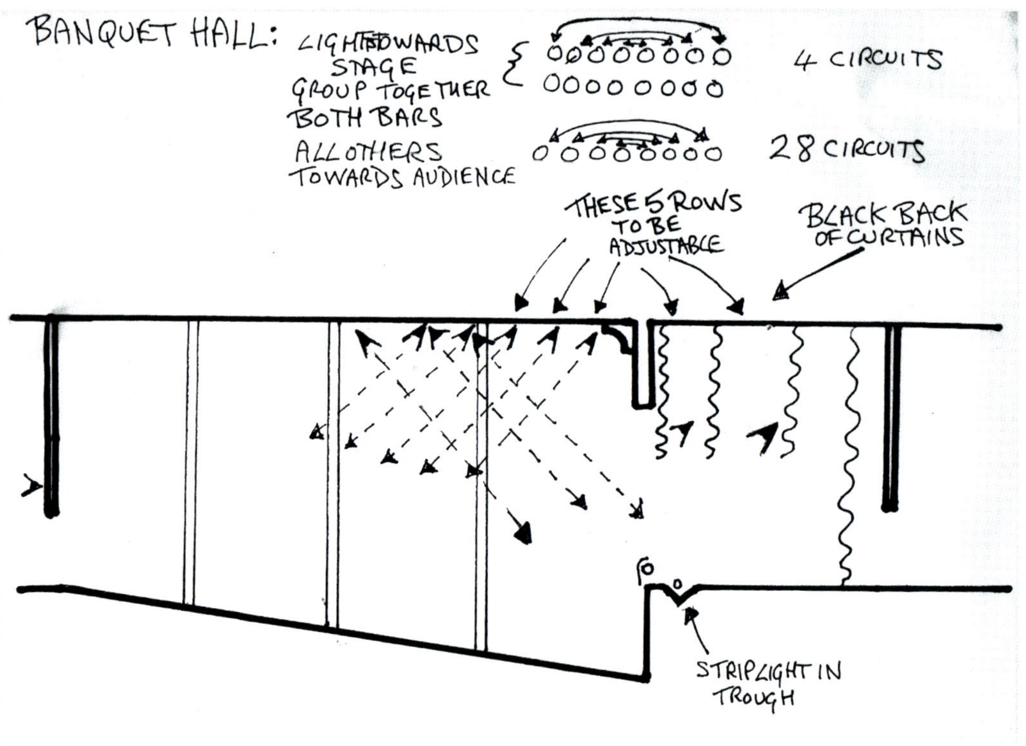
BANQUET HALL:
LIGHTS TOWARDS STAGE
GROUP TOGETHER BOTH BARS
4 CIRCUITS
ALL OTHERS TOWARDS AUDIENCE
28 CIRCUITS
THESE 5 ROWS TO BE ADJUSTABLE
BLACK BACK OF CURTAINS
STRIPLIGHT IN TROUGH

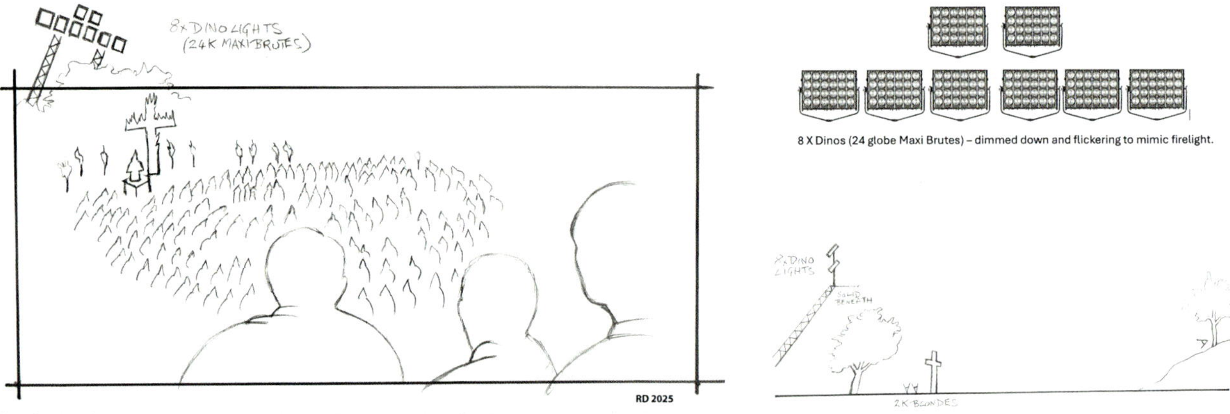

We had based our Mississippi production office in Canton. Because the town had been the site of a recent KKK rally, staging our own there seemed a little inappropriate, to say the least. Consequently, the scene, one of the most challenging in the film, would be staged in a field outside Los Angeles that was surrounded by a wooded hillside. The field was large, as it had to be to accommodate our full complement of hooded extras, and the scene would be lit entirely by the light from a flaming cross.

As with the night scene on the beach in Malindi, I dismissed the idea of a "moonlight" source. And, as in *Mountains of the Moon*, to create a flame effect over a wide area I again turned to Biggles's original suggestion of a dimmed Maxi Brute—in fact, eight dimmed and flickering Maxi Brutes rigged on two large Condor booms. Luckily for me, the field itself was bare but for a single tree that sat alone near its center. This allowed Billy O'Leary to position our lights behind and above the tree, while the cross was some thirty feet in front of it, the tree acting as a cut to the light hitting the ground at the foot of the cross. Only five years in the future, for *Jarhead*, I would be digitally replacing a light source with a flame, but for *O Brother* this was not an option. To overcome the effects of the inverse square law, I needed to project light to the rear of the crowd, where our protagonists entered the action, while making it appear as if it was coming from the fiery cross.

As funny as the scene is, with its obvious contempt for racist buffoons, shooting it had some awkward moments. Not only did the re-creation of something so hateful get to everyone on the crew, one night we saw some people who had stopped their car on the road above our field to watch the "rally." It would have been hard for them to see the camera or the lights from where they stood, and I've often wondered if they thought they were witnessing the real thing—in California.

Damn! We're in a tight spot!

ULYSSES EVERETT McGILL,
IN *O BROTHER, WHERE ART THOU?*

Although nine months had passed since our initial tests, the digital intermediary (DI) process was still in its infancy when we began to color-time *O Brother, Where Art Thou?* Not only was it James's and my first DI, it was also the first for our brilliant and extremely patient colorist, Julius Friede. What we were trying to achieve pushed us to the limit.

We were working with a Spirit DataCine system that output DPX files that could later be transferred back onto celluloid using a Kodak Lightning II recorder. One problem: As we made our

adjustments to its color, the original camera negative would need to be run back and forth through the gate of the DataCine, which scanned it in real time. This goes against the first thing you learn with film—handle the negative as little as possible. Subsequent advances have made digital post routine and less terrifying, but *we* needed to use extreme caution or the resulting damage to the negative could have caused us to lose the entire film. Another problem: Each reel of the negative had to be fully timed before those twenty minutes of cut footage could be scanned and laid down on tape. In an echo of the Heathrow customs official that greeted me on my return from Sudan, nothing existed until we had laid down each fully color-corrected twenty-minute reel—as a power cut was to painfully illustrate when we lost an entire week of work.

This was the first time digital technology had been used to complete every frame of a film. After experiencing it once, I vowed to James that I would never use the process again, a promise that lasted for all of three films. You can't stop progress!

Having spent eleven or twelve weeks in the DI suite staring at the same images, I had a hard time believing *anyone* would choose to go down this route. But some of my fellow cinematographers saw what we achieved on *O Brother, Where Art Thou?* as the opening of Pandora's box. By embracing digital technology, we were cheating. We had destroyed the photochemical process. I didn't know what the future held, and I certainly had no idea that digital tools would take over so quickly and completely. In some ways I was, and still consider myself, a purist. I love film. Even now I shy away from postproduction effects when I believe we can get what we want on set and in camera. But when a director has a vision in mind and asks you to help realize it, you employ any process available. It's the image that matters, not the tools used to create it.

Incidentally, Joel told me that the ASPCA had made a visit to the cutting room. They could not believe the cow that is machine-gunned down by George Nelson and the one on the roof floating with the flood were not real. They were not. Of less concern for them seemed to be Sheriff Cooley's dog, which is seen drowning in the floodwaters. Perhaps the ASPCA had yet to see *Jurassic Park*, which was seven years old at the time *O Brother* was released. And Pandora's box was already open wide.

After all the state-of-the-art experimentation with digital color timing, it was a joy to venture into a world in black-and-white. It was also a rare joy to shoot in LA with James, who, while not on the payroll, was a partner throughout.

18

THE BARBER

Sometimes you look at it, your looking changes it...
The more you look, the less you really know.
It's a fact, a true fact. In a way, it's the only fact there is.

FREDDY RIEDENSCHNEIDER, IN *THE MAN WHO WASN'T THERE*

***The Barber Movie*, as it was originally titled, was inspired by 1950s noir and science fiction. It** was typical of the Coens' work in two ways: It attracted an extraordinary cast (in this case, Billy Bob Thornton, Frances McDormand, Richard Jenkins, Tony Shalhoub, Scarlett Johansson, and James Gandolfini), and it was impossible to classify. My job was to create a look that, to borrow a phrase, tied it all together. I've always loved black-and-white photography and I saw what would ultimately be known as *The Man Who Wasn't There* as the perfect opportunity to blend the naturalism I consider my mainstay with the stylization of film noir.

Joel and Ethan referenced Alfred Hitchcock's *Shadow of a Doubt* when talking of the film's Santa Rosa, California, setting. Others came to mind for me. Robert Aldrich's *Kiss Me Deadly*—described by critic Tim Dirks as "the definitive, apocalyptic, nihilistic, science-fiction film noir of all time"—shot by Ernest Laszlo, is among my favorite films. And I love to revisit the more naturalistic noir of Alexander Mackendrick's *Sweet Smell of Success*, shot by James Wong Howe, and Richard Brooks's *In Cold Blood*, shot impeccably by Conrad Hall. But none became direct photographic references for *The Man Who Wasn't There*.

It's impossible to know how the films you love or the pictures you have seen have influenced your own perceptions. When I'm taking still photographs, I work in black-and-white rather than color. Color can be a distraction when not used purposefully. I love how color is used by painters like Edvard Munch, James Whistler, and Toulouse-Lautrec: sparingly and with extreme deliberation. But I love simplicity, and maybe that is simply why I love black-and-white.

> *In color, I am more worried about the light, the clothes, the setting, etc. It is more complex. In black and white, it's the person who is important.*
>
> **HARRY GRUYAERT**
> **(who is only one of the most influential color photographers on the planet!)**

Though it might seem ironic, after making many tests, Bev Wood, James, and I discovered that our preferred black-and-white look for *The Man Who Wasn't There* could best be achieved by shooting in color. We found a low-contrast color stock, Kodak 5277, that, when printed on a high-contrast title stock, would record a wider tonal range than any traditional black-and-white film emulsion. Since we had a limited budget and I was aiming for a deeper-than-usual depth of field, shooting on 5277, a 320 ASA negative stock, would also be an advantage.

21A

68

72A

Filmmakers often talk about the "key-to-fill ratio" (the contrast between highlight and shadow). Some cinematographers establish a ratio before they begin a project and take a range of meter readings as they light each setup. Personally, I have little idea of what ratio I was using on any shot of *The Man Who Wasn't There*. I don't work like that. I take a meter reading of what I consider to be the primary focus of a shot and judge my exposure from that point. I arrive at the contrast by what I see through the camera by eye, sometimes using my 1970s-era Polaroid camera to confirm my choice.

I used more direct lighting on *The Man Who Wasn't There* than on any film since *1984*—my favorite lamps being the 650 and 1K Fresnel. But there were occasions I used a larger lamp, such as a 6K HMI PAR, to create a shaft of sunlight combined with a small soft bounce source close to an actor's face.

Mixing noir, existential philosophy, quantum physics, and science fiction, *The Man Who Wasn't There* stars Billy Bob Thornton as the barber Ed Crane. To obtain the $10,000 he needs to invest in a dry-cleaning business, Ed decides to blackmail Big Dave (James Gandolfini), for whom his wife, Doris (Frances McDormand), works and with whom she's having a barely concealed affair.

Having returned from a wedding party with his inebriated wife, Ed recounts in voice-over the story of their relationship as he watches her sleep—until he's interrupted by a call from Big Dave. Ed leaves Doris to meet Big Dave in the department store he manages. There is a fight, and Ed

Nirdlingers

kills Big Dave in self-defense. He drives home; for a moment he watches the shadows of the trees blowing in the wind, then enters the house and sits back down in the same spot he just left. As he returns his gaze to the sleeping Doris, Ed completes the story. From this simple scenario, Joel and Ethan conjure up a remarkable combination of image, music, performance, and voice-over. To me this is a brilliant piece of filmmaking, the closest to a perfect sequence I've ever been a part of. Not because of my cinematography, the lighting, or a particular image; the whole mood, the melancholy sadness, it's simply cinema. It makes you feel something in a way that only cinema can.

In shooting this, and all of *The Man Who Wasn't There*, I used specifically chosen practical lamps or direct, hard lights to create the effect of a streetlamp or other justifiable off-camera source. For Big Dave's murder, I needed a lamp that would cast a pool of light on the desk while allowing me to leave James Gandolfini in a deep shadow lit only by the bounce light coming off the paperwork in front of him. As the scene progressed, the lamp, aided by a wire, would fall onto the floor, from where it justified a wide cone of illumination that I enhanced using an open-face fixture, in this case a 650-watt Fresnel without the lens, off camera.

For Doris and Ed's bedroom I wanted a specific weave for the sheer curtains that would allow me to cast a pattern of light across the characters as if from an outside streetlamp. The sheers were dyed a dark gray so that they did not overexpose. To give the whole mood of the scene a slightly eerie feeling, we further broke up the light with the movement of foliage in the wind, a theme that we maintained outside with Ed sitting in the car and when looking at the house from outside.

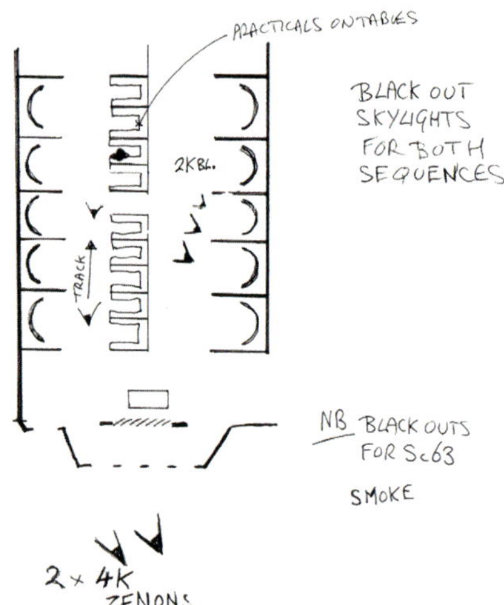

The Man Who Wasn't There's cinematography blended expressionistic touches with naturalism, much as the film balances lurid events with Billy Bob's minimalistic, matter-of-fact performance. It takes place in a recognizable everyday world filled with deep pockets of darkness that threatens. Instead of light we used shadows to limit what the audience could see in the midday restaurant meeting between Ed and lawyer Freddy Riedenschneider (Tony Shalhoub). We shot this at Musso & Frank, a popular and long-lived Los Angeles restaurant that needed little dressing to fit the period. My goal again was to light the entrance as if it were in sunlight as a contrast to the dim interior. I didn't want the audience to struggle to see Billy Bob or Tony, so creating a contrast with the doorway and allowing the characters' lighting to fall off rapidly into the darkness surrounding them created the feeling of a dimly lit space without it actually being one.

I found it a rare occasion when Joel and Ethan would mention a specific light they had in mind for a scene. It was during the last preproduction meeting for *The Hudsucker Proxy* that Ethan suggested we had talked through every aspect of the shoot except lighting, and I had to tell him that we had been rigging the sets for three weeks. It was a bit late to have that discussion. But here, for the scene that takes place in Ed's cell, and in which Freddy suggests arguing Werner Heisenberg's uncertainty principle in his defense, they felt it was the right time for some theatrical lighting.

I took this to our production designer, Dennis Gassner, and asked for a simple small window at the highest level of the cell wall opposite the doorway. I knew this would be our major axis of shooting and that the position of the window would rarely, if ever, appear in frame. I then had a wooden template made for the bars of the window, but instead of fixing it in line with the wall I allowed it to angle down into the set. By positioning the bars at 90 degrees to my light source, the shadow cast would remain more uniform than if the lamp were at an angle to them. While experimenting with the PAR lamp, our rigging gaffer, Chris Napolitano, and I came to the idea that the light pattern should fit inside a circle rather than the more naturally square shape of a window, to enforce the idea that Freddy was performing to an audience.

He told them to look not at the facts,
but at the meaning of the facts.
Then he said the facts had no meaning.

ED CRANE, IN *THE MAN WHO WASN'T THERE*

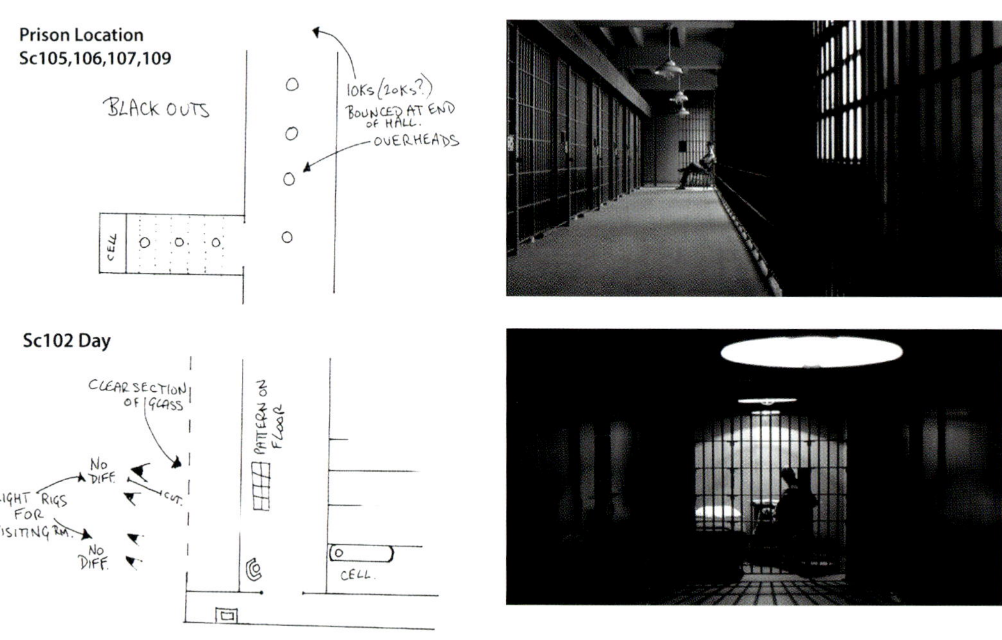

For a later scene, in which Ed walks down a corridor toward his execution, we couldn't afford to build a corridor with any detail, so I suggested using overhead pendant lights. These would focus the light on the center of the corridor and define the walls, which were no more than painted flats, by the shaped pattern they cast. It made for not only a striking image but a cheap one.

Joel and Ethan always imagined *The Man Who Wasn't There* ending with Ed strapped into an electric chair in an execution chamber fashioned to resemble a pure, white void akin to the prison set in George Lucas's *THX 1138* (though this was my reference, not theirs). The set needed to be shadowless, and the walls blend in together. The solution was simple: Stretch a heavy diffusion across the ceiling and evenly light it from above. If the camera caught the ceiling, either directly or in reflection, the diffusion would appear as a flat white and blend with the walls. I find the result, as if Ed is meeting his final moments surrounded by a sea of nothingness, a striking effect in the midst of the film's more shadowed noir atmosphere.

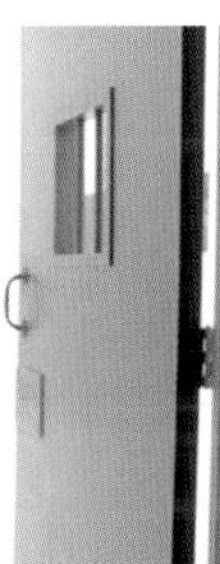
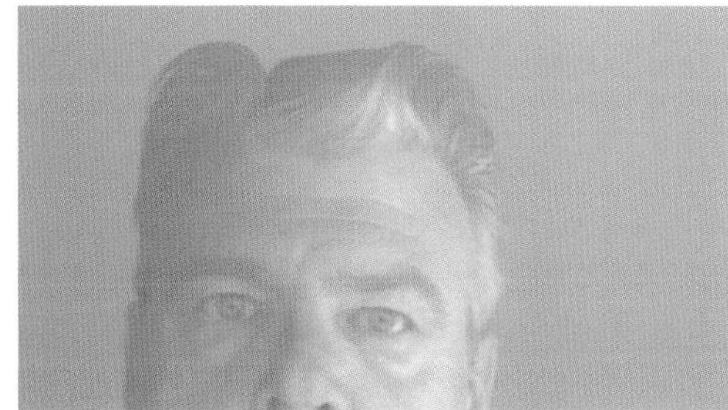

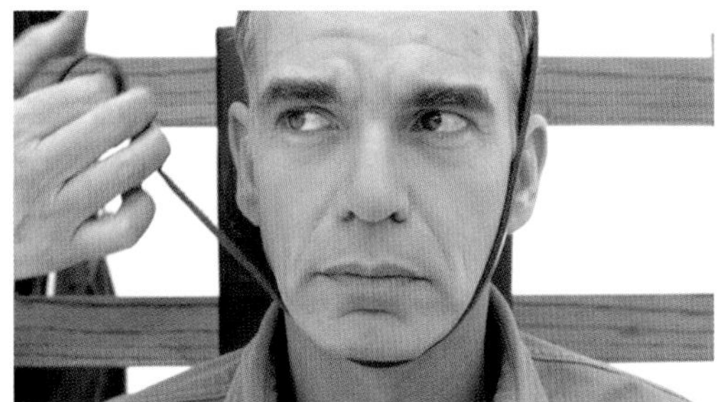

The release of the film underscored the difficulties of exhibiting a black-and-white movie in an era dominated by color. Show prints struck for projection at major venues in Los Angeles and New York were made on a black-and-white title stock, Kodak 5269, which had the contrast and tonal range we wanted, though this had taken some developing magic by Beverly Wood. Most of the general-release prints were struck on a color print stock from a black-and-white internegative.

We'd made a color print, but only to check the negative and with no intention of it ever leaving the lab. But leave it did. After a screening Joel fielded a call from a critic asking why they'd shot twenty minutes of the film, a single reel, in color. What was the significance? As usual, Joel and Ethan kept the answer to themselves, even if they knew it.

We filmed *The Man Who Wasn't There* in the late summer of 2000. In October of that year, Joel, Ethan, producer Jeremy Thomas, and I went to Japan.

We were ostensibly there to promote *O Brother, Where Art Thou?* (a film the locals found more than a little odd), but our main purpose was to scout locations for the Coens' next film, *To the White Sea*, an adaptation of a 1993 novel by the poet and *Deliverance* author, James Dickey. Set in Japan toward the end of World War II, it's the story of an American airman downed over Tokyo the night before the firebombing of the city in March 1945. It becomes a journey into hell as the airman attempts to find his way from Tokyo to Hokkaido and on to the White Sea, off Japan's north shore. As Joel will tell you, I was passionate about this film like few others. It had been a great scout, and it was good to spend time with Joel and Ethan experiencing another country, but it was not to be. The film was going to be beyond the available budget, and on September 10, 2001, Joel called with the bad news. It was a bitter disappointment, but the following day it was one that paled into insignificance.

I would do what many another wouldn't, and the best thing was that I knew I would do it; there wasn't any doubt.

JAMES DICKEY, *TO THE WHITE SEA*

19

MAKING A PLAN

By failing to prepare, you are preparing to fail.

BENJAMIN FRANKLIN

I kept busy during the next few years shooting *A Beautiful Mind* with Ron Howard, *Levity* with Ed Solomon, *House of Sand and Fog* with Vadim Perelman, *Intolerable Cruelty* and *The Ladykillers* with Joel and Ethan, as well as *The Village* with M. Night Shyamalan—a wide variety of projects that involved both location and stage work. For the naturalistic *House of Sand and Fog*, designer Maia Javan built a house onstage so that we could control the fog of the title. Similarly, Dennis Gassner built a full-scale bridge onstage for *The Ladykillers*, and we employed the same sprinkler system to create its misty environment.

The village in the film of the same name was constructed on location so that we could connect all our interiors with the exterior in one composite set, whereas *A Beautiful Mind* shot on a variety of locations, some of them the smallest and most restrictive to work in that I have ever experienced. *A Beautiful Mind* shifts from realism to a more noirish look in depicting John Nash's developing schizophrenia. Some moments recalled a scene in Norman Jewison's *The Hurricane* in which Rubin Carter is hallucinating, referenced in the script as having "visions" of wild animals and so on. Norman and I reduced the scene to Denzel alone in his cell, with no wild animals and fantasy elements, simply cutting between opposing close shots of him talking or boxing with himself. Similarly, Ron and I decided if we shot Nash's hallucinations as if they were real, the audience would be drawn into his world and, through experiencing these visions as he was, only slowly come to understand he was in fact quite ill. Consequently, we drew back from using visual effects and only turned to that more stylized approach when trying to visualize Nash's mathematical process.

Although these were a wide variety of projects with directors who worked in very different ways, my method of drawing diagrams stayed the same. There is rarely a location or a set for which I don't draw a plan.

Though I was wary about working in Hollywood, it did have advantages. These included the opportunity to spend time talking film with some of the greats of cinematography, Vilmos Zsigmond, Owen Roizman, Haskell Wexler, and Conrad Hall, among others. Despite their stature in Hollywood, each of them could be remarkably modest about their own accomplishments. Conrad, for instance, attributed the famous *In Cold Blood* scene, in which the shadow of rain on a window forms "tears" on Robert Blake's face, to chance rather than design, and the bleached exteriors of *Fat City* to a mistake in loading the wrong film stock.

Conrad ended his career shooting two films for Sam Mendes, *American Beauty* and *Road to Perdition*. I'd talked to him about these collaborations, the first films Sam had directed after breaking through as a wunderkind of London theater. When Sam approached me about his third film, I thought I knew what to expect. Conrad had told me that Sam had a dedication to working from storyboards that went beyond most other directors he had worked with. It had frustrated him. He liked to improvise on the day, when the actors were playing their parts on a set and were not just imaginary figures within a pencil drawing.

THE VILLAGE

Sc29
4×MAXIS TO DIM
4×DINOS WARM
4×10K.
1 LIFT. RAKE TREE LINE
ADD "STREET" LIGHTS
STRIPS
RHs
RHs
BLONDES IN SCHOOL HOUSE
2 LIFTS
OIL LAMPS – 600W.
LAMPS ON POSTS. 2K BULBS.
2× FCM'S ON BACK
Sc29
4×DINOS ON BORDER
4×MAXIS BEHIND SCHOOL TO DIM
4×10K BEHIND M.H.
3×4' BATTEN STRIPS ABOVE CENTRE WINDOWS AND DOOR
3×RH
3×RH.
STRIP LIGHTS UNDER AWNING
RED HEADS IN ALL WINDOWS.
DINOS TO FLICKER
Sc43 WALKER CABIN
PORCH LIGHTS LIT EITHER DIRECT LAMPS OR GAG BOUNCE ABOVE DOOR.
TREE LINE
LOW DINO
LIFT IN GARDEN
RAKE TREES
DAPPLE THRO' TREES
USE SINGLE OR DOUBLE DINO!!
WIDE SHOT.
Sc46 EXT. WALKER CABIN
4×DINOS BY TOWER FOR FIRE EFFECT RAKING HILL
TORCHES ON HILL
EXT. HANGING LAMPS GAG BEHIND 600W – REMOVE GLASS ON FAR SIDE.
BLONDES UPLIGHT TREES
WARM LIGHT ONTO GRASS FROM BACK OF BUILDING.
WATCH TOWER
RAKE HILLSIDE
MAXIS ON STANDS WARM LIGHT
Sc48 INT. WALKER CABIN
POSSIBLY HANG RING 4 600W
DOUBLE LIGHT FIXTURE ONE ELECTRIC 500W BULBS
2×500W GAGS IN SHADE
BOUNCE UPSTAIRS
GAGS BEHIND CANDLES
FLOAT
WIDE SLOWMO.
PREP. CEILING PANELS TO FLOAT/FLOORBOARDS
HIDE GAG BULBS BEHIND CANDLES
PREP POWER CABLE ROUTES
Sc67.
LANTERNS TO CARRY 12V×2 BULB
*COLOR HOUSEHOLD BULB TYPE ALSO.
4×DINO LOW IN SETBACK
3×10K + 10 BLONDES ½CTO ON TREES
LANTERNS TO RIG ON POSTS ALL ELECTRIC NEAR CAMERA WITH GAGS.
3×10K UPLIGHT TREES
'STREET' LAMPS FOR BARN.
8 BLONDES (Sc66) ½CTO ON TREES
LIGHTS IN VILLAGE SEP. SHEET
TORCHES AND GAGS
2× MAXIS TO UPLIGHT TOWER
FULL CTO
Sc69 PATH FROM WEDDING.
LIFT LOW LIGHTING HILL BELOW TOWER FULL CTO
MAXIS TO EDGE BUILDINGS
6×MAXIS BEHIND BAKERY – DIMMED
RED HEADS IN WINDOWS
BLONDES/R.Hs TO RAKE OUTSIDES
TORCHES LIT. + BLONDES
3×10Ks TO UPLIGHT TREES
BARN.
FORGROUND LAMPS TO HAVE "GAGS" 600W.
STREET LIGHT BY BARN. 4×BLONDES

A BEAUTIFUL MIND

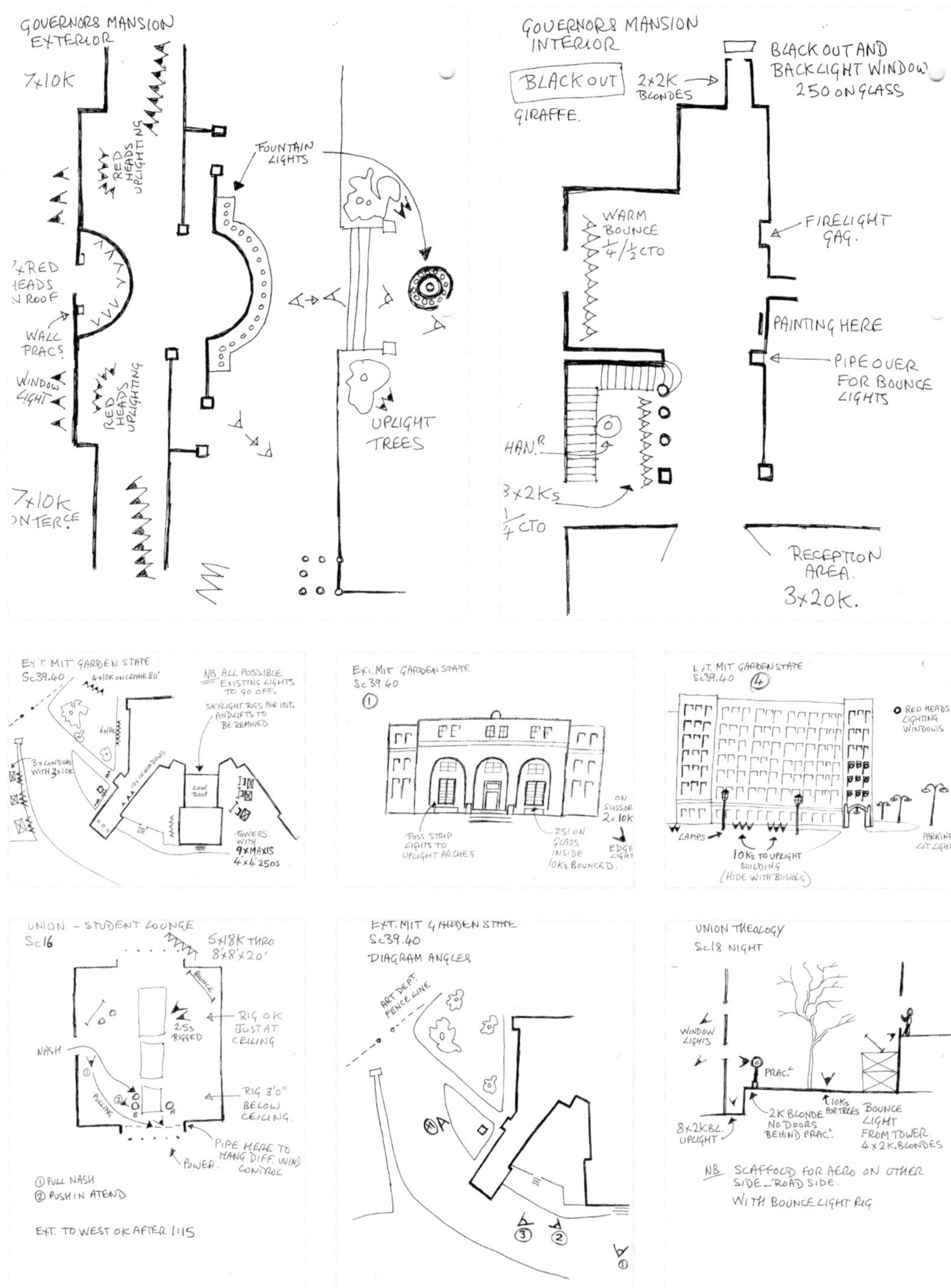

20

"WELCOME TO THE SUCK"

***D.I. FITCH:** What the fuck are you doing here?*

***ANTHONY SWOFFORD:** Sir, I got lost on my way to college, sir!*

JARHEAD

To my surprise, Sam Mendes's approach to *Jarhead* would be altogether different. He planned to make the film with the immediacy of a documentary, shooting handheld and rehearsing on camera. But, unlike a documentary, we could analyze what we had shot and adjust for a take two, take three, or a good many more. We'd, of course, still need to choose locations and design sets to fit both the action and the overall look of the film, but the camera would be free to move wherever the actors would take it as they explored the scene. The more I thought about it, the more intrigued I became. I hadn't shot a primarily handheld film since *Sid and Nancy*. It had made sense on that film, and it made sense now.

Sam wanted to capture in spirit Anthony Swofford's memoir, the story of one soldier's experience serving in the Gulf War. Though trained as a sniper, Swofford would never get a chance to fire his rifle. For both him and his fellow soldiers, the enemy became their sense of futility. Important for Sam was that the film reflected that truth. It's no accident that Swofford, played by Jake Gyllenhaal, can be seen reading Albert Camus's *The Stranger*.

After a while you could get used to anything.

ALBERT CAMUS, *THE STRANGER*

We used many references from actual events to set the look of the film's world and—with shades of Joel and Ethan stripping down *Fargo*'s locations to their basics—leaned away from landscapes with any dramatic features. Sam wanted it to look as if *Jarhead*'s characters were operating in a void, placing them in a surreal empty expanse where the horizon separating earth and sky became almost invisible.

This only sounds simple. Sam also suggested a high-contrast look that allowed viewers to feel the grain of the emulsion as they watched the film. Consequently, his first instinct was to shoot on Super 16 mm since it has significantly more grain than 35 mm, and the smaller cameras would allow for easier handheld shooting. Shooting on 16 mm would have been something of a throwback for me, as I'd have been using the same sort of camera as in my documentary days, one far lighter than the Arriflex 535 35 mm camera that had become my first choice for features since its introduction in 1990. Though a major advance on previous 35 mm cameras, the 535 still weighed twenty-two pounds, twice the weight of the 16 mm Aaton camera. A significant difference when you are shooting handheld across a ten- or twelve-hour day.

Still, I was wary of the limitations of 16 mm's smaller negative, particularly when shooting at night or working under intense sunlight. A 35 mm negative not only would be sharper but would retain more highlight and shadow detail, which led me to consider the 35 mm Moviecam SL (short for "SuperLight"), which I had often used for handheld work, or the recently introduced Arricam Lite, which weighed only eleven pounds. Though I still preferred working with the heavier Arri 535B for some dialogue scenes and less active handheld work (the camera's weight added stability to the shot), for most of the film the Arricam Lite or the Moviecam SL became our camera of choice. However, when we had to run at a gallop to follow the action, times when it became impossible to

keep an eye to the viewfinder, two other cameras, both workhorses introduced decades earlier, came to our rescue.

Our second camera operator, Scott Sakamoto, favored an Eyemo, a lightweight, non-sync 35 mm camera first sold in 1925 that had been much used by newsreel cameramen, while I used an Arri IIIC, an upgrade of the World War II–era Arri IIC. The first spinning-mirror reflex camera, the IIC had been employed for projects as diverse as Robert Flaherty's *Louisiana Story*, Sergio Leone's *The Good, the Bad and the Ugly*, and for other shoots that didn't require sync sound. Like many Italian directors, Sergio Leone had little interest in recording live sound.

For our running shots, Scott designed an old-style parallax sight to help with framing on the Eyemo. When I could not keep my eye to the eyepiece, I simply used the Arri IIIC as a point-and-shoot camera and made a best guess at the frame. The camera motor serves as a pistol grip, which makes it relatively comfortable to hold when running. I remember asking Sam, on a shooting day that cost the production upward of a hundred thousand dollars, what he thought about Scott and me running around with such antiquated cameras. He told me not to worry—if it was right for the film, that was all that mattered.

With those cameras lined up we'd solved how we would be operating, but that was only one problem. Creating *Jarhead*'s overall look involved more film and lab-processing tests than I'd performed for any previous film, including *1984*. We needed to settle on a film stock but also whether to alter the development of the negative, which would have effects beyond the relative

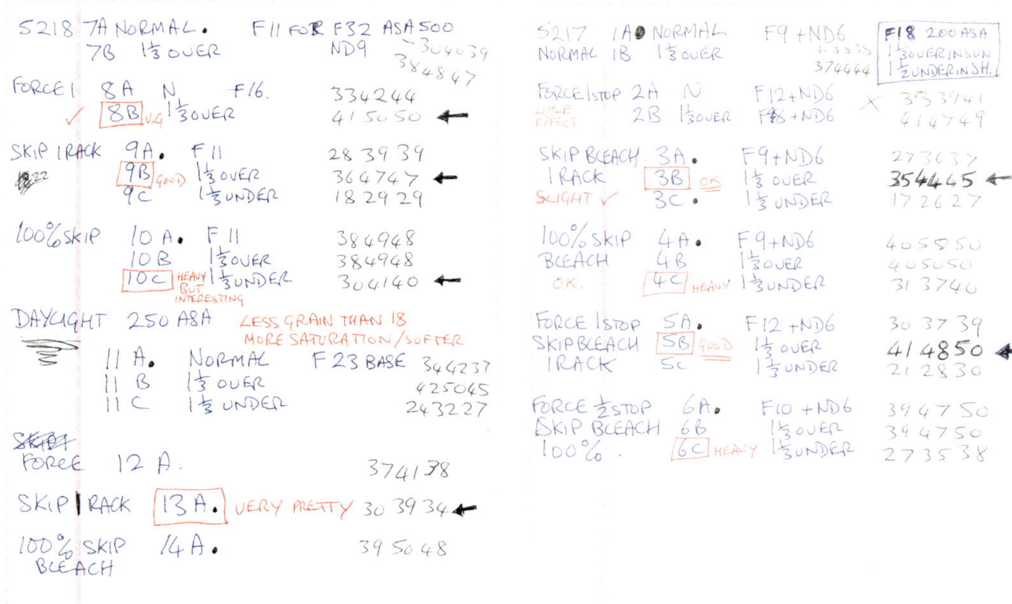

5218 7A NORMAL. F11 FOR F32 ASA 500
7B 1⅓ OVER ND9 304039 384847
FORCE 1 8A N F16. 334244
8B V.G 1⅓ OVER 41 50 50
SKIP 1 RACK 9A. F11 28 39 39
9B GOOD 1⅓ OVER 364747
9C 1⅓ UNDER 18 29 29
100% SKIP 10 A. F11 384948
10 B 1⅓ OVER 384948
10 C HEAVY BUT INTERESTING 1⅓ UNDER 304140
DAYLIGHT 250 ASA LESS GRAIN THAN 18 MORE SATURATION/SOFTER
11 A. NORMAL F23 BASE 344237
11 B 1⅓ OVER 425045
11 C 1⅓ UNDER 243227
FORCE 12 A. 374138
SKIP 1 RACK 13 A. VERY PRETTY 30 39 34
100% SKIP BLEACH 14 A. 39 50 48

5217 1A NORMAL F9 + ND6 F18 200 ASA
NORMAL 1B 1⅓ OVER 374444 1⅓ OVER IN SUN 1½ UNDER IN SH.
FORCE 1 STOP 2A N F12 + ND6 353941
LITTLE EFFECT 2B 1⅓ OVER F8 + ND6 414749
SKIP BLEACH 1 RACK 3A. F9 + ND6 273637
SLIGHT 3B OK 1⅓ OVER 354445
3C. 1⅓ UNDER 172627
100% SKIP BLEACH 4A. F9 + ND6 405550
O.K. 4B 1⅓ OVER 405050
4C HEAVY 1⅓ UNDER 313740
FORCE 1 STOP SKIP BLEACH 1 RACK 5A. F12 + ND6 303739
5B GOOD 1⅓ OVER 414850
5C 1⅓ UNDER 212830
FORCE ½ STOP SKIP BLEACH 100% 6A. F10 + ND6 394750
6B 1⅓ OVER 394750
6C HEAVY 1⅓ UNDER 273538

ASA, or speed, of the film. Both overexposing and underexposing film can alter the grain structure of the emulsion and, with it, the contrast and saturation.

We also had the option of using a bleach bypass. The bypass could now be applied to a film's negative rather than the release prints themselves, and as a percentage rather than by fully removing the bleach bath, as we had done for *1984*. Applying the process to the negative ensured that prints of the film would look the way we intended. Because only *1984*'s print was affected, various full-color versions of the film that looked nothing like what we intended circulated for years on VHS and DVD. It was only a recent release by Criterion that re-created the desaturated look of the original print. A lot had changed in the nearly twenty years since we'd attempted to replicate what Kazuo Miyagawa had done before us, and we now had a number of variants of the process from which to choose.

The process of testing so many combinations on offer can become utterly confusing. Sitting in the projection theater, James and I would sift through the many subtle variations: "This was underdeveloped a stop, but overexposed two stops. So, it's actually overexposed one stop...This one was overexposed one stop, developed normally but with a bleach bypass of 50 percent...And this is the same but now on the slower emulsion. How does that compare with the 5218?"

It was hard to discern any difference between many of the test images while sometimes we (I should say that James and I were again working with the great Beverly Wood at Deluxe Laboratories) felt we had pushed the image too far only to find we *liked* going to such an extreme. We were looking for an image with a visible grain structure and high contrast but nothing so severe it would restrict our latitude in the DI process. Nor could it feel self-conscious, create a layer between the audience and the story.

After a lot of experimentation, we settled on shooting on 5218, a 500 ASA tungsten-balanced film stock, with a one-rack skip-bleach process (in essence leaving a controlled amount of silver in the negative) combined with an overexposure of one and a third stops. It is usually recommended that the negative be underexposed when processing it with a skip bleach to allow for the extra silver left in the emulsion, so we were, in effect, overexposing one and a half stops. My average light for the red, green, and blue of the printing process when shooting on 5218 film negative (my midlight) would usually read as 25-32-27, but on *Jarhead* all three lights would deliberately be ten or twelve points higher.

The DI, the digital intermediary, had become a common part of filmmaking in the years since *O Brother, Where Art Thou?* At the time, the studio standard for this was to work in 2K resolution, which was faster and cheaper than operating in 4K and deemed "good enough" for most movies. *O Brother, Where Art Thou?* had been finished with a resolution of less than 2K, but my *Jarhead* tests revealed that scanning at this level did not clearly resolve the fine details within the emulsion, and the grain, which we had gone through so much trouble to create, looked blurred. Adding grain electronically looked exactly like what it was, electronic noise. In short, using a higher resolution became something of an issue with the studio until James and I screened a 2K and a 4K test side by side in a theater. Then the results were impossible to ignore.

Jake gives a brilliant performance as Swofford, which is fortunate because the film rarely strays from his side. Neither Sam nor I wanted to leave the protagonist's perspective and kept the camera closely focused on the details of his experience. Some shots are literally from the character's point of view, such as when we strapped a gas mask to an Arri IIIC, much as we had a football helmet for one character's point of view in the Coens' film *The Ladykillers*.

Even when not shot in first person, most scenes involved following Swofford wherever he went, on his journey through basic training to Kuwait.

However unlikely it sounds, given the harshness of the film's terrain, some of the trickiest moments came when shooting interiors—particularly one sequence that takes place in the soldiers' barracks at night, which is gradually revealed as Swofford's dream. I felt I had the justification to make this scene graphic and disorientating without stretching it beyond what an audience could believe to be real.

Imagining there were sodium vapor light sources outside the windows, my gaffer, Chris Napolitano, and I chose to use Alpha 4K and Arri X lights. These lamps are essentially bare bulbs with hard reflectors behind them. Consequently, they cast sharp shadows. A photometric chart shows each lamp produces a wide beam and, at sixty feet, a light intensity of around thirty to thirty-two footcandles. At 500 ASA, that would translate to a lens aperture of around 4.0. But, when the daylight blue of the HMI lamps is corrected with an 85 filter on the camera and the lamp itself is warmed by the addition of a ¼ CTO or a ½ CTO gel (Color Temperature Orange), the result becomes less than a 2.8 stop on the lens. In the case of Swofford's nightmare, I would have wanted the highlights to be a little over a mid-exposure, so I would have been shooting at around a 2.2, which is my preferred stop for most night work.

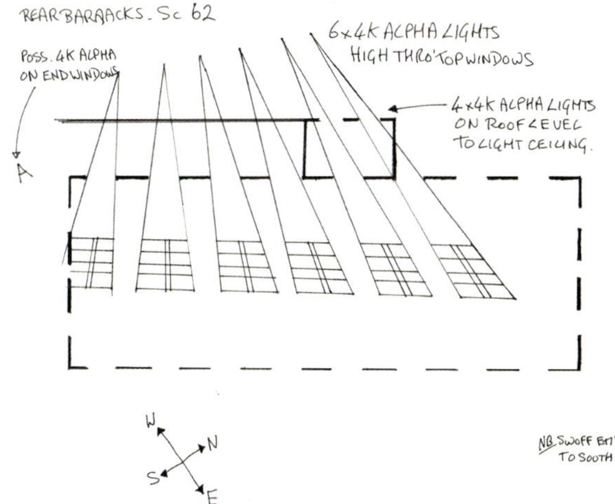

Now, these figures can only be a rough estimate, as it is not certain that a lamp will be exactly sixty feet from the subject. What's more, the age of a metal halide bulb will affect not only the bulb's output but also its color. Where possible, Chris would see to it that the lamps were supplied by the rental house with new bulbs.

The lighting creates a slightly-off reality that only reveals itself as a nightmare when Swofford begins vomiting sand, which is a CGI effect. I asked Jake if he'd consider doing this himself, but he declined!

For some night shoots, inside a tent or when the platoon is building a pyramid out of sandbags in the rain, we used very specific lighting techniques, varying between a group of R40 bulbs set inside aluminum cooking foil to 10K Fresnel lamps shooting directly at the lens through the rain.

The deserts of Arizona and California, as well as the dry lakebed of Laguna Salada in Mexico's Sonora Desert, stood in as Kuwait for our daytime exteriors and gave Chris Napolitano much less to do. I'd asked him to become my gaffer on *House of Sand and Fog*, and he was accustomed to me using large muslin reflectors when shooting under harsh sunlight. But here we *wanted* the harshness, we wanted backgrounds that were *this* close to looking blown out.

Similarly, Bruce Hamme had fewer tracking shots to work on, but he proved an invaluable guide when I was operating handheld, particularly when I had to walk backward or weave around the soldiers as they trudged across the sand or through the infamous "Highway of Death."

As there was no dialogue in these scenes, I would often talk to the actors during a shot, asking them to slow down or speed up whether I was panning off them as if to their point of view or back to them from the background. I'm happy I had someone making sure I didn't fall on my face and close at hand to take the camera from me after a long series of takes.

For daytime shots of the oil fires we filmed outside El Centro, California. Though the deep background remained in full sunlight, Pablo Helman, our VFX supervisor from Industrial Light & Magic, assured us he could deal with this in postproduction. Steve Cremin, our effects coordinator, manufactured a column of smoke to block out the sunlight over a wide area, set up jets of gasoline in the middistance to mimic oil fires, and sprayed black vegetable oil from a crane to envelop both us and the actors.

This all proved very effective, as Scott Sakamoto, our assistants, and I experienced firsthand. We draped ourselves and our cameras in heavy-duty trash bags, leaving only an opening for what the camera was seeing and for our focus pullers to reach the lens. But we still had to contend with an oily mess when we changed magazines for a second take, or a third, or a fourth—as well as when we finally reached our hotel rooms.

We originally planned to shoot night exteriors in the same spot, but the idea of doing this on location made me uncomfortable. *Jarhead*'s night scenes required a particular atmosphere, a sense the soldiers had bivouacked in a hellhole, surrounded by burning oil fires and enveloped in thick smoke. Working at night is always slower and more expensive no matter what the scale of the film, and smoke is hard to control on location, but not onstage.

CGI was still in its relatively early days, but I knew that Sam would be working in post to multiply the extras and add aircraft in a shot or two. So why could we not use a series of lighting rigs to stand in for the oil fires and replace them later with elements we shot separately? I needed a tall unit that would project light in 180 degrees, one that would flicker and glow in the smoky atmosphere as if it were a large column of flame. There was no ready-made unit that remotely resembled what I had in mind, so I decided it best if we made our own using regular household R40 mushroom bulbs. I had plenty of experience using multiples of these bulbs on batten strips for the *Queen Mary*'s ballroom in *Barton Fink*, so I knew it would work. As the production department was not so sure of the concept or of moving the work to the studio, we set up a stage and shot some tests.

For the shoot, Chris constructed a half circle of 6' × 11' wooden battens, each of which held ten 175- or 500-watt R40 mushroom globes. The bulbs were wired into eighteen separate circuits connecting to a dimmer board, each of which would flicker in a different pattern to mimic firelight. We wrapped the whole unit with a ½ CTO gel, keeping it away from the hot bulbs with chicken wire. Secured together with pipe and mounted on a rolling stand, these rigs could easily be moved around the stage and adjusted as the scene evolved.

We shot on two adjoining stages at Universal Studios (the same ones we had filled with mist for the bridge sequences in

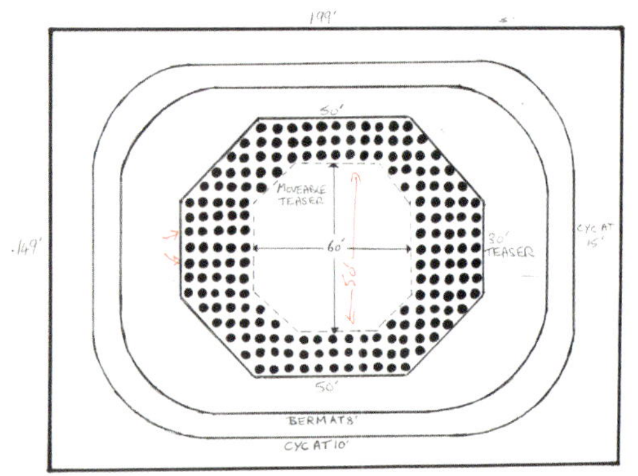
199'
149'
50'
MOVEABLE TEASER
60'
50'
30' TEASER
CYC AT 15'
50'
BERM AT 8'
CYC AT 10'

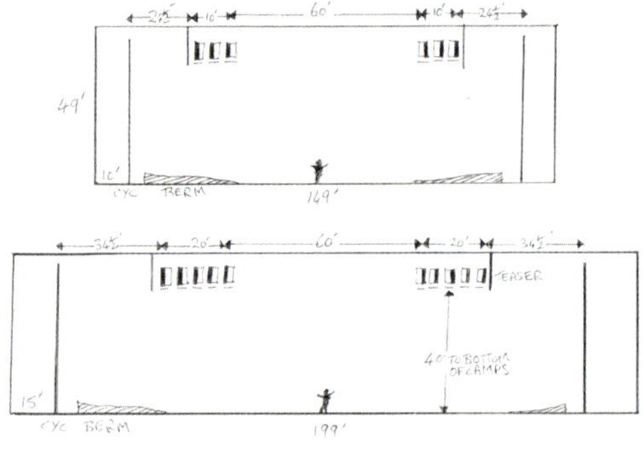
60'
10'
49'
10'
CYC
BERM
149'
20'
60'
20'
TEASER
40' TO BOTTOM OF LAMPS
15'
CYC
BERM
199'

The Ladykillers), and Dennis Gassner imported (literally) tons of sand to create dunes. Taking care to leave a fire lane between it and the sand dunes, we mounted a cyclorama directly against the stage wall, painted as if the landscape continued into the distance. Steve Cremin filled the stages with smoke, controlled the density with a monitor, and I walked around with a handheld camera. It was almost as simple as that.

We drew visual inspiration for *Jarhead* from several sources, including Werner Herzog's 1992 documentary about the Kuwait oil fires, *Lessons of Darkness*, though few sources were as influential as the work of photographer Steve McCurry, particularly his quietly devastating shot of a horse covered in oil. There's an ironic beauty to his image that only underscores its true horror but, like *Jarhead*, it only scratches the surface of what is real.

Our own scene with an oil-covered horse underscored the shoot's difficulty. Though the horse had been trained and spent time on the stage under the lights, we didn't really know what would happen once the camera began rolling. It's a testament to Andy Harris that he held focus as we shot with no rehearsal and with very little depth of field on the lens. When I was shooting handheld and improvising, Andy would always be as close to the lens as possible, just the two feet of his focus whip away, with me talking him through the shot, warning him what my next movement might be.

To create the feeling of the advancing dawn, Chris and I designed a pattern of 164 Spacelights softened with silk skirts. Using solids (black duvetyn), both underneath each lamp and to the sides of the skirts, we directed the light toward the center of the stage. From any point on the stage only the furthest lamps could be seen clearly, while those directly above appeared as if totally blacked out. We gelled the two outside rows of lamps with a ½ CTB filter (a blue gel the opposite of a CTO) and the inner rows with a ¼ CTB to contrast with the warmth of the light from our fake oil fires.

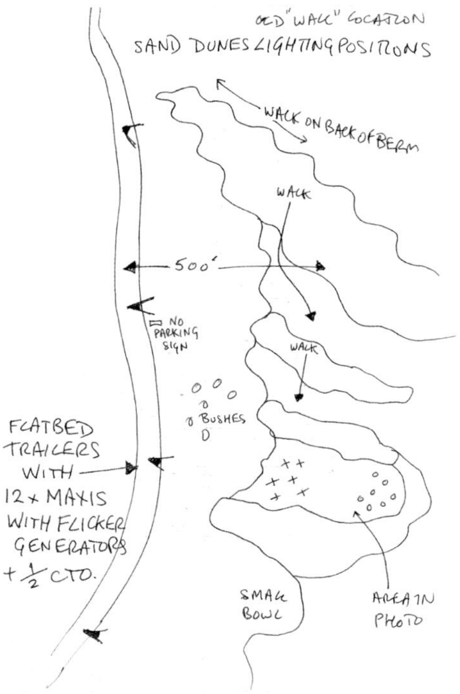

The nights we did shoot in the desert confirmed the wisdom of creating these complicated scenes on a stage. Our location scouts found the perfect spot for the film's final desert scenes within the Glamis Dunes, had it not been for the predicted nightmare of moving our equipment a half mile from the nearest road through deep, soft sand at night. Scouting one weekend, I found an area that provided an equivalent look parallel to a road, so I took some photographs to pitch this alternate option to Sam. It's always good to have an alternative when you want to reject a plan that a director is comfortable with.

As with the stage interiors, to mimic the light from distant oil fires, I intended to use multiple lighting units to create a seemingly soft source but on a much larger scale. Here, it was a pattern of ten or twelve Maxi Brutes, set to flicker through a dimmer and fronted with the warmth of a large sheet of ½ CTO. Our always innovative key grip, Mitch Lillian, suggested we mount our

three rigs—each of which contained a similar array of Maxi Brutes—on flatbed trailers, making them easy to move from scene to scene using farm tractors.

As prepared as we were, we couldn't entirely plan for the forty mph winds that arrived the first night of the shoot on this location, whipping up the sand, stinging our eyes, and ripping apart our gel frames. Mitch and his team persevered, as always, and when we eventually managed to roll film, our efforts proved to be worth the trouble. The wind-blown sand gave our establishing shots an eerie feeling that seemed in unison with the flickering of the lights. It was another happy accident.

The end-of-conflict celebration involved a different location and a total of seventy-two 12-Light Maxi Brutes. These were mounted on a 190-foot platform to softly wash the central action taking place some 700 feet away. A separate line of six 12-Light Maxis side-light Swofford and Troy as they crest the ridge above the celebration and the light from four quarter Dino lights rakes the far background as if coming from a distant oil fire. Shades of the KKK rally on a larger scale.

Making a war film with so little war was always a gamble. *Jarhead*, perhaps predictably, puzzled some, though I thought the characters' remove from the action was the point of the story. I was more confused when I talked to fellow cinematographers and journalists who wanted an answer to the same questions: How long did we shoot in Kuwait? What was it like working under the oil fires?

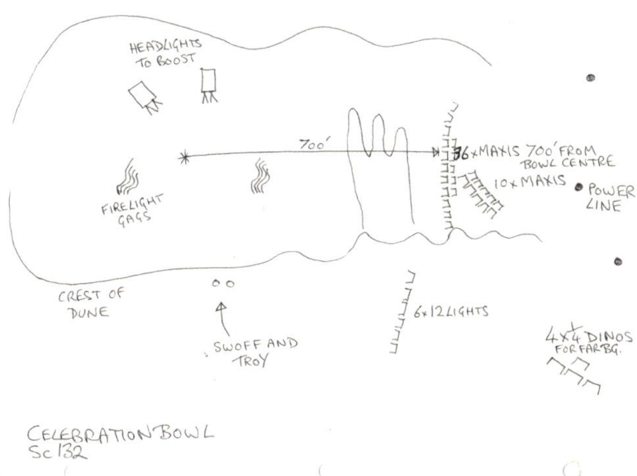

As a lifelong admirer of Westerns, particularly the revisionist Westerns of Sam Peckinpah, I couldn't believe my luck to have a chance to shoot a Western myself, particularly one that was in the spirit of Peckinpah's work in many aspects.

Killing a man isn't clean and quick and simple. It's bloody and awful. And maybe if enough people come to realize that shooting somebody isn't just fun and games, maybe we'll get somewhere.

SAM PECKINPAH

21

THE PREACHER'S SON

Jesse James is like a Leonard Cohen song.

ANDREW DOMINIK

Every director takes a different approach to prepare a shoot, but Andrew Dominik's was detailed in the extreme. For most films the production designer will create what's called a "mood board" that has, among other elements, a color scheme spanning the length of the film. I find these can be useful, but they don't always reflect the lighting I might plan for a scene or the way that might affect the chosen colors. But when mood boards are made with images rather than paintings or color swatches, they can give a more accurate sense of how the movie should feel. For *The Assassination of Jesse James by the Coward Robert Ford,* Andrew, production designer Richard Hoover, and I had created a mood board on steroids. By the time we began shooting, the entire corridor of our film's production office had been lined with film stills, vintage photos, magazine clippings, and Andrew's own Polaroids—anything we all felt could reflect the look and feel of the movie.

One image in particular, a photo Andrew had taken of a tree that become faded and browned at the edges, proved especially influential, as did a portrait of the real Jesse James in the morgue. To accompany the lyrical narration taken from Ron Hansen's beautiful novel and narrated by Hugh Ross (an assistant editor who'd provided a temp track Andrew liked so well he kept it in the film), we wanted to create similar images that recalled early photography and appeared naturally antiquated, with edges that looked like they'd been distorted by the lens rather than created artificially.

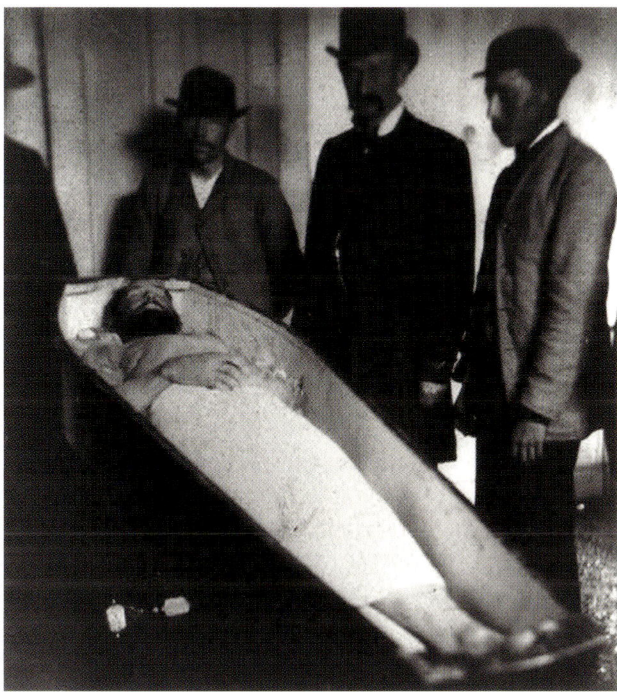

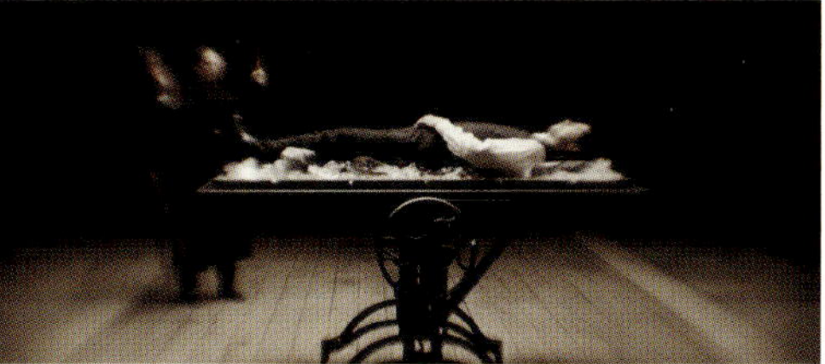

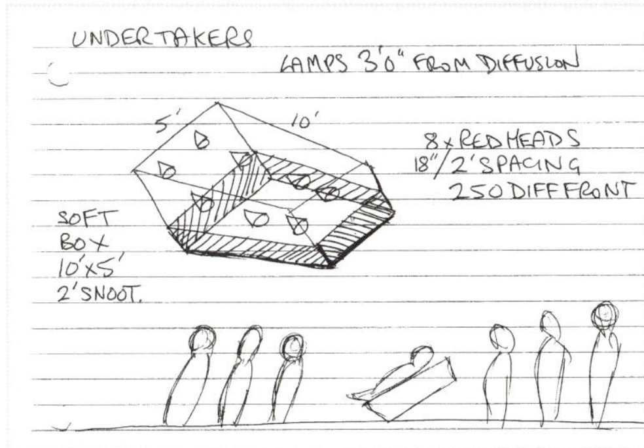

CHICAGO
ALTON

To achieve the vignetting optically, I returned to a technique I'd tried out on a short film in 1981, *Towers of Babel*, which required shots as if through the peephole of an apartment door. My low-tech solution had been to place an element from a still's lens in front of the 50 mm lens of my 35 mm film camera, so I thought to try something similar for *Jesse James*. I worked, as usual, with the Otto Nemenz rental house, who took apart an old wide-angle lens for the experiment. We shot some tests, and they turned out even better than I'd imagined. It appeared as if the image was not just going soft but fracturing around the outside of the frame, producing some lovely and strange color banding in the process—"lens aberration," an effect then impossible to achieve digitally. Otto's completed three different focal length lenses, and, despite some studio pushback, the images shot on these made it into the final film, though both Andrew and I would later wish we'd used them more (the studio had been skeptical of the effect and pressured us to drop it). Since *Jesse James*, Otto Nemenz has rented out these same three lenses as "Deakinizers."

Beyond these lens effects, finding the overall look of the film required more experimentation. Andrew was looking for a desaturated but high-contrast image, one in which the shadows would have a slightly reddish tint. We talked about *McCabe & Mrs. Miller* and mulled over the idea of combining a preflash of the negative with a bleach bypass process. While I felt this look would suit the film, I remembered what a laborious process it had been for Steve Blakely, my lab timer at DuArt, to preflash twenty-eight thousand feet of negative for the opening scenes of *A Beautiful Mind* using an optical printer. For that film, we had flashed the negative—deliberately exposing the emulsion to a low level of light as if fogging it—using a warm light to color the shadow areas of the picture, which was exactly what we were looking for on *Jesse James*. But rather than DuArt and Steve, we'd be using a Canadian lab I'd never worked with before, and instead of limiting the preflashing to a single section of the film, we'd need to flash the entire negative. This felt like a recipe for disaster. So, James and I did some more tests. Through a combination of a photochemical bleach bypass and a subtle digital manipulation of the shadow areas within the image, we achieved a result that Andrew found acceptable, and, important, fit within our budget.

The Assassination of Jesse James by the Coward Robert Ford was a rewarding shoot, but also a long and exhausting one that overlapped with the complicated postproduction of *Jarhead*. James had arranged that the production would work only five-day weeks at the beginning of the schedule, rather than alternating with six, so I could fly to LA from our Edmonton base and continue work on *Jarhead* at the weekends. During the week James would sit with the timer to ensure what I wanted was applied and helped with the postproduction process in my absence. This sometimes required her to fly from LA to Montreal (where timing work on *Jarhead*'s release print was being done), to Calgary, or wherever in Canada we were shooting *Jesse James*. It was a taxing month and a half for both of us.

We began shooting in August 2005 to capture a summertime look for our locations outside of Calgary before traveling to Edmonton for a variety of interior and exterior scenes shot at Fort Edmonton Park. *The Assassination of Jesse James by the Coward Robert Ford*'s most complex sequence, the train robbery, appears early in the film. Andrew, producer David Valdes, and I spent a long time scouting various locations in Canada before settling on three major bases of operation, which seemed to offer us good possibilities for each sequence in the film. Fort Edmonton Park wasn't our first choice for the train robbery, however.

Fort Edmonton has a train track, but one with a narrow gauge. It also has period coaches, but only a small train to pull them. David investigated bringing in a larger train from elsewhere, as had been done on other locations for films such as *O Brother, Where Art Thou?*, but the narrow gauge of the track made this unworkable. We could only use a larger engine at a completely different location, which would require David and our first assistant director, Scott Robertson, to create a new schedule and for the studio to place more money in the budget. Reluctantly, Andrew agreed

to the shoot being in Edmonton with what he called the "toy train" and on the one short section of the track that had a decent approach set between tall trees.

Thankfully, the James Gang performed the Blue Cut robbery at night, which would help obscure the size of the train as well as the limits of the location. And when Andrew said he wanted the scene to feel dark, he really did mean *dark*. I've had the experience of working with a director who agreed with me that a conversation could take place in silhouette, then having him, when viewing dailies the next day, question why the faces of the actors were in shadow. One director's dark is, to some cinematographers, overlighting, so it's good to establish which is which before you shoot the scene. To Andrew, black is indeed black.

Lighting the sequence involved only one traditional lamp. The light that provides the main source for the exterior shots took the place of a dim, kerosene-fueled headlight that lit the train track from on top of the boiler. To make Andrew's "toy train" appear more substantial I needed this to be the most striking element in the shot, something that would itself become a presence and take the viewer's eye away from our diminutive prop. A single tungsten 5K PAR was that light. We also attached a series of dimmed 500-watt bulbs between the front wheels of the train, to enhance the fire from the boiler that naturally illuminated the area below the engine, and which would be especially useful when it let off steam, but the 5K PAR lit the shot.

I had asked our Canadian gaffer, Martin Keough, to provide two small crane arms with two 5K Fresnel lamps in the bucket of each. I intended to cross-light the trees directly in front of where Jesse stood on the railway sleepers to flag down the train, thinking it important that the audience see some texture in the surroundings. However, on the night of the shoot the wind dropped off as we readied to film. That left some atmospheric fog we had spread lightly across the frame lying in a smooth pattern just above the track and directly in the path of the 5K PAR as the train headed toward the camera. The oncoming light was blooming in this haze to reveal the surrounding trees, the train tracks, the sleepers blocking the line, and, finally, Jesse James (Brad Pitt). By hooking up the 5K PAR to a dimmer, I could have the lamp at full intensity as the train first appeared through the trees, then progressively dim it down, so as not to flare the lens, as it approached the camera. Lens flare is a pet peeve of mine. Though I know some cinematographers and directors use it intentionally for effect, I've never been one of them. The Deakinizers being an exception, I rarely like any effect that draws the viewer's attention to the surface of the image rather than immersing them within it.

Realizing that any texture added to the trees was unnecessary, I asked Marty to turn off the other lamps. Then, on second thought, I suggested he pan the lamps away from the shot and toward our catering tent. If production questioned why we had

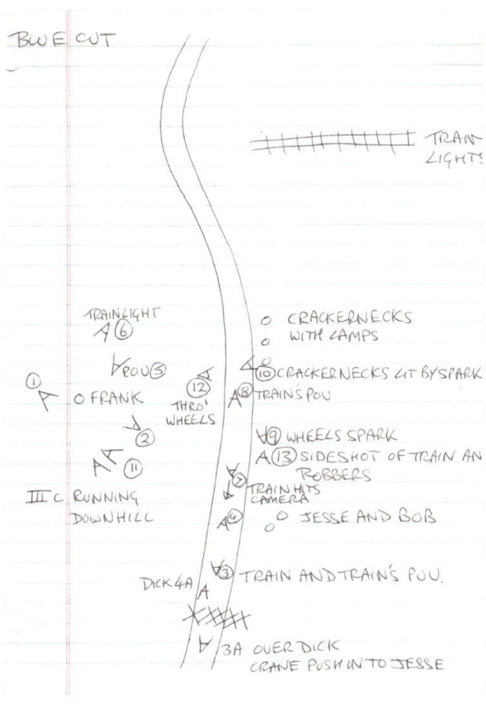

rented the two cranes and the lights, we could at least say they were work lights.

We had five nights to shoot the entire sequence of the Blue Cut robbery, which felt sufficient given the long scene inside the mail car could be blacked out and partly shot during daylight hours. There were two shots that seemed particularly difficult to figure out how to pull off but, ultimately, required a little *less* thought.

The first was a shot of the train reaching the camera, which was then carried along with it as though fixed to the front. We tested several complicated options, including setting a track on a flat car with a jib arm, before it turned dark enough to shoot. But, having confidence in none of them, I suggested we ditch them all and pack the front of the flat car with polystyrene. I would handhold the camera on a square of packaging foam. To light the engine, I had Marty simply handhold a 4' × 4' sheet of polystyrene to catch some bounce from the 5K and light the face of the engine.

We'd solved one potentially tricky situation, but I remained concerned about some shots we were planning of the gang hiding in the trees as the train passed by. They couldn't be lit by their lanterns because they had doused these as the train approached, and I had no intention of bringing in a "moonlight" when I had not used it anywhere else in the sequence. When I noticed how the light from our train would cast interesting shadows through the trees in front of it, I decided to use that as the sole source to light the gang. We'd hard-mounted one 5K PAR lamp to the train, and we would still need this lamp for future shots, but fortunately Marty was carrying a spare. He and Rick Schmidt, our key grip, suggested we use the flatbed and mount our spare on that. This would not only allow us to pan the lamp more easily than the one on the train, but it would be quicker to reset between takes. In reality, the light on the front of the train would never reach so far to the side of the track, but as it sweeps across the gang's masked faces the train takes on a mythical presence, even as it is entirely out of shot. I've never heard a viewer question the authenticity of that effect.

We planned to shoot long Steadicam shots of Frank James (Sam Shepard) moving down the railway carriages, and there would be no place to hide any additional lighting. What appeared in frame would be the only light source. As always, I worked closely with the art department to choose the lamps affixed to the wall or hung above the center aisle of the carriage and boxcar. Each of the wicks or gas mantles within the globes or glass chimneys was swapped out for a 250-watt bulb and wired back to a dimmer board. Inside the shallow conical shades of the hanging practical lights, we mounted an additional four 100-watt bulbs that would project a warm, soft light across the characters below without diluting the shadows to the sides. All the globes were dimmed to between 25 and 40 percent of full intensity to warm their color.

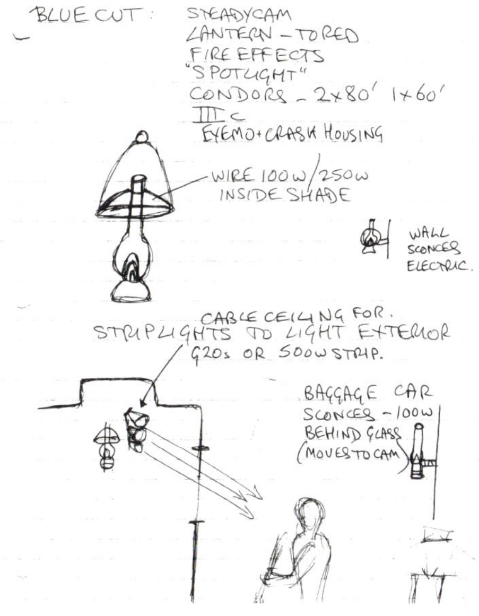

Marty and his electric crew used two miles of cable to rig the train and ensure that both the Steadicam shot that follows Frank down the aisle of the carriage and the intense sequence inside the boxcar could be lit entirely by the light from the practical sources that appear in shot. Other than bringing in a small gold stipple reflector to catch some of that light and bounce it into a character's eyes for a close shot, we used no additional lighting.

Even without the long hours and travel, *Jesse James* would have been a complex job. Having completed our work in Edmonton, we moved back to Calgary, to a remote location we had scouted on horseback (my first and last time on a horse) and where the art department had built the Jameses' "house on the hill," in which Bob Ford would shoot the aging outlaw, as well as a substantial part of the town of St. Joseph sitting in the valley below.

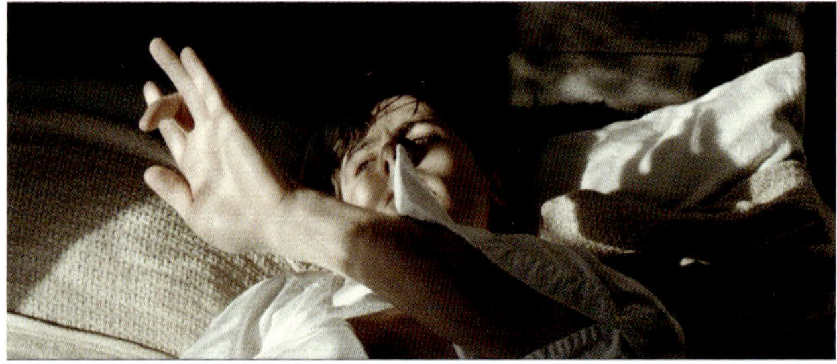

For all the interior scenes, in the kitchen, the bedrooms, and the front room in which Jesse is shot, we worked around the existing daylight. Sometimes we made use of sunlight to create the shot of Jesse in the rocking chair or of Bob lying on Jesse's bed, while at other times we added soft light from outside by bouncing 12K HMIs off 12' × 12' muslin reflectors. Occasionally, we added a light diffusion to a window to "blow out" the exterior when the daylight had faded and we needed to continue shooting. One morning we added a Hampshire Frost filter to a window to hide the fact that it had snowed overnight, but luckily, the snow melted quickly, and it was necessary for only one or two shots.

As with most of the film, the key images were imagined in prep, but we discovered many others as we rehearsed and shot. The montage of Bob pretending he is Jesse was created on the day with Casey Affleck finding things his character might do and taking advantage of the natural daylight. But the death of Jesse James was laid out in detail beforehand. Andrew intended the scene to be like a performance in which each character knows his preordained role.

Specific shots were chosen to enhance this effect: Jesse deliberately tracing the words in the newspaper with his finger, looking at his daughter playing outside and the single shoe that she lost earlier, his face distorted by the window glass, setting his guns down on the couch in the sunlight, and finally placing the chair to stand on as if he were about to hang himself. When Jesse reaches up to dust the picture, he sees Bob Ford raise his gun in the reflection. The intimate point of view of Bob was a shot found on the day and chosen because it reinforces the idea that Jesse is complicit in his own death. But when he falls from the chair, the lens distortion removes the viewer from the scene so that it becomes as if Jesse's death is taking place on a stage, as if we are viewing it from the audience's point of view.

As we had initially intended for all our built sets, the interior of the "house on the hill" combined with the exterior to create a composite set. Harbison Farm proved to be an exception as we had chosen a location that was perfect as an exterior; but because of the marshland around it and its distance from our production base in Calgary, it proved impractical for the interior scenes. Besides, having to visit the location on different occasions for the looks of summer and winter, and to shoot both exteriors and interiors on the same set with all the equipment and lighting involved, would limit our flexibility. Our compromise, though not really a compromise at all, was to shoot the interiors on a set built inside a warehouse, which would not only be more accessible but give us some sorely needed weather cover. This decision would prove fortuitous when many days of heavy rain made the location inaccessible.

Windows and reflections figure prominently in *Jesse James*, and in prep we made a key decision to use handmade period glass. Its wavy imperfections lend a poetic quality to some images, like a poignant shot of Casey as Robert Ford peering at Jesse. But as interested as I was in shooting through the glass, the night work also drew me to it. Projecting light through handmade glass creates a ripple effect that becomes more pronounced the sharper the light source and the further away it is.

For night interiors I used 1K Fresnel lamps without a lens, which in essence become bare bulbs against a hard reflector. In *Jesse James*, there are two lamps, both cooled with a half-blue gel, playing in any one shot: one to create the pattern on the background wall and another for the character light (with a third lamp used occasionally to give a little brighter edge to the characters in wide shots). When lighting with direct sources like this I sometimes use a 2' × 2' polystyrene or loose muslin bounce to bring a little soft light into a face. On a wider shot, when the reflection off the white board is insufficient, I might use one covered in silver stipple or, alternatively, add a small lamp such as a 100-watt Fresnel we call an "Inky." But I try as much as possible to limit myself to the existing light.

In late October we traveled to Winnipeg, which would stand in for our Kansas City exteriors, St. Joseph, a Baltimore street, and the Manhattan Theatre in which Bob and his brother, Charley, reenact the killing of Jesse James for a New York audience. Finally, we returned to Calgary to shoot our locations in the snow.

If the schedule had not already been a challenge for our producer, David Valdes, the final winter sequences were. He had overseen the art department construction of a town in the Rockies, which stood in for the Colorado mining town of Creed where Bob met his death, on a site fifty miles outside Calgary via a winding mountain road.

During the shoot Andrew was under a good deal of pressure from the studio to shorten what was a long script, but although he was forced by our schedule to cut a few small scenes before we shot them, there were a great many we completed but that are not in the final cut of the film. Perhaps the most difficult for everyone involved were those shot in the town built in the Rockies.

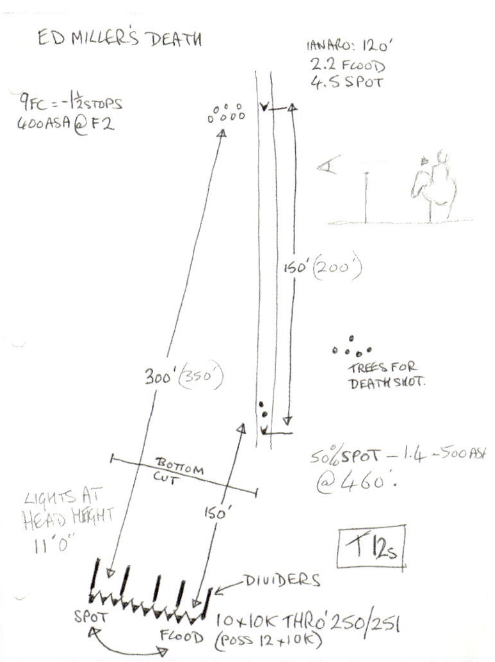

But any compromise, such as shooting an interior onstage instead of on location or the "toy train," only seemed to further Andrew's belief that the production was not on his side.

Nothing could have been further from the truth. During our final days in Canada, David and the art department arranged that the set of Ed Miller's shack be brought into a warehouse overnight when the location it was built on became snowed in. We shot against an exterior made of painted backings, which were still wet as the camera rolled, but we salvaged the scene. And when we couldn't shoot Ed Miller's death in Canada, as that location was also snowed in, David arranged to transfer what was one of the most difficult night scenes to the hills north of LA. There were many compromises, but was the audience aware of them?

We completed shooting *The Assassination of Jesse James by the Coward Robert Ford* in December 2005, but it would not receive a release until September 2007, a year after originally scheduled. James and I saw a first cut of the film with Andrew, and we both loved it. But by this time there was plenty of animosity between Andrew and the studio. His cut, which was initially some three and a half hours long, was deemed unacceptable. It was only Brad Pitt's support that allowed Andrew to complete the film with a much shorter cut. James and I feel the longer version, which included many more scenes after Ford kills James, was better. But we are a little biased.

22

SIGNS AND WONDERS

Chigurh shot him in the face. Everything that Wells had ever known or thought or loved drained slowly down the wall behind him.

CORMAC McCARTHY, *NO COUNTRY FOR OLD MEN*

Joel and Ethan Coen signed on to adapt Cormac McCarthy's 2005 novel, *No Country for Old Men,* not long after its publication, seemingly with no real intent to direct the film themselves. I wouldn't for a moment say I'm responsible for them changing their minds, but I'd loved the book and was passionate in encouraging them to take it on themselves. I knew they could capture the novel's melancholy, metaphysical elements and make it their own.

We all understood *No Country for Old Men* would be less stylized than the Coens' previous work when preparing to shoot the film, even if we never talked about it explicitly. Where the camera had been almost a character in films like *Barton Fink* and *The Hudsucker Proxy*, or more observational on *Fargo*, on *No Country for Old Men* it would be more classical. Though neither Joel nor Ethan referenced Robert Bresson or Jean-Pierre Melville, it was the matter-of-fact minimalism of those two masters that came to my mind. "Understated" probably best describes our approach. The Texas landscape is part of the story, and the characters are part of that landscape, their actions shaped by it. But the bulk of the story takes place in a succession of motels and gas stations, a border crossing and a bus depot, a diner and a trailer park, all evocatively described in Cormac's book. We created the look of the film through the choice of all these individual locations, putting them and the film together, piece by piece.

None of those pieces would prove trickier than the scene in which Moss (Josh Brolin) returns at night to the desolate Texas basin where he previously discovered the aftermath of the aborted drug deal. We chose the location for the daytime view it offered from the bluff and the terrain of the basin below. In that terrain, Joel and Ethan wanted a small hill on which Moss could park his truck above a broad, sloping plain where the main action could take place. The script called for this to lead down to a river, flowing fast enough to sweep away a grown man, but as no single location offered everything in the same place, we filmed the river scenes separately. The one location fulfilled three wishes out of four, and my task was to figure out how to light such a large space at night.

I couldn't get away with lighting only the characters and letting the background fall into complete blackness. What's more, the scene would unfold as dawn broke, and the light would need to reflect this as the action progressed. As there was no other source, it was a given that there would have to be a "moonlight," but creating it would be a challenge. The bluff from which Moss first overlooks the trucks in the basin below offered the best option for a light source, and I made detailed measurements of the distances involved.

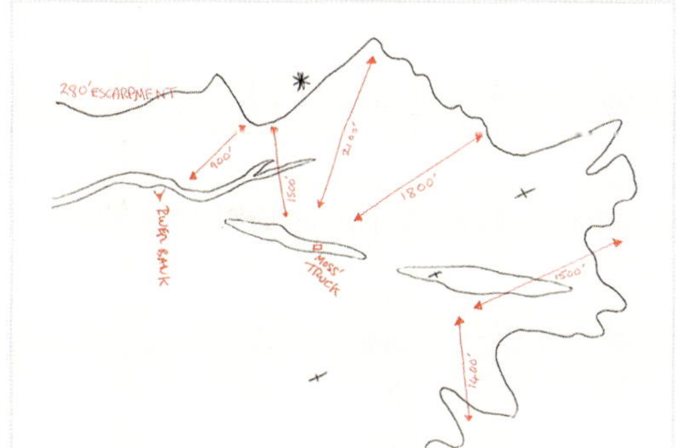

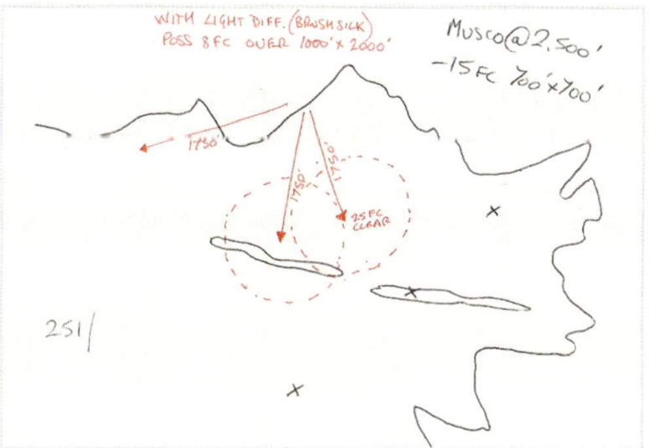

Chris Napolitano and I initially considered using multiple 12K HMI lamps, supported by a tiered scaffold rig, but this would be time-consuming to erect and ultimately more expensive than our chosen alternative. I turned again to Musco lamps, the stadium lighting I'd first used to illuminate an expansive area in *Thunderheart* and, more recently, a tank battle in *Courage Under Fire*, though neither location was on this scale. We'd need three. (Like I said, it took a lot of power to create the illusion of faint moonlight, especially over such a wide area.) It wouldn't be cheap—though I had wanted three we could afford only two—and the summer nights were short.

It would also require some math and another look at the photometric chart for the Musco light. Working from the formula that on 100 ASA stock and with 100 footcandles the lens opening would be 2.8, I knew that at 500 ASA I would require a minimum of 9 fc to shoot in any direction with a shooting stop of plus or minus 2.0. Of course, this kind of calculation is hardly necessary with a digital camera that can be rated at 5,000 ASA or more, but we shot *No Country* on film in 2006.

Luckily for me, at the end of 2005 Arri released their first set of Master Prime lenses. As always with new equipment, James and I tested the Master Primes in the most challenging situation we could imagine: looking directly at the beam of a flashlight in a black space. The best lens will flare in that kind of situation, but the Master Primes were as clean as any lens I had seen. This would be a considerable advantage when shooting toward a headlight or a bright practical as I like to do. And with an aperture of 1.3 they had arrived just in time. Many lenses are marketed as being fast, but when put to the test, they reveal this as only wishful thinking. However, the Master Primes were a true 1.3. Only a few sets of these lenses in a few focal lengths had been made available when we shot *No Country for Old Men*, but I was able to obtain one. The difference between the lens openings may not seem significant on paper, but 1.3 is a full stop faster than a 2.0. At a lens aperture of 1.3, double the light reaches the emulsion and dramatically alters what the camera can or cannot capture—especially when your light source is more than 1,700 feet away from your subject!

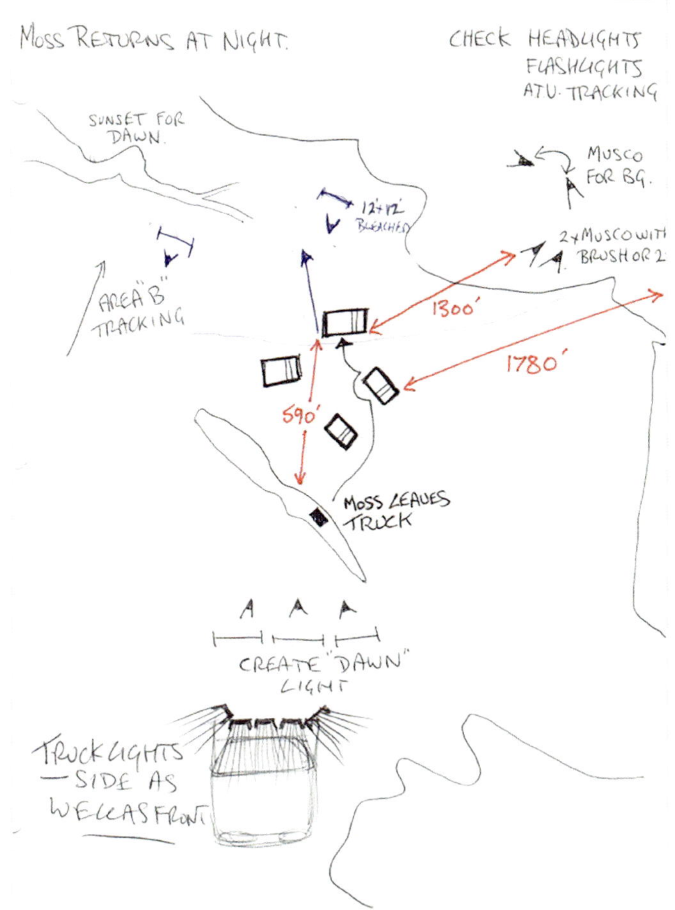

My Gossen Lunasix light meter can record in both a reflected and an incident mode, meaning it's good for measuring both ambient light and specific surfaces. The meter has an extremely accurate readout in low light, so it was especially useful in this situation, working at the edge of what the film emulsion could record. Though to see the needle hardly move on my prelight night did not fill me with confidence. Having been able to afford only two units, Chris and I ditched the idea of diffusing the Muscos' lower lamps, as Billy and I had done so successfully on *Thunderheart*, and we concentrated on working an even spread across the width of the basin, leaving the hillsides to the left and right of the action to fall off into blackness. It was lucky we had a prelight a few days in advance of our shoot as it left time for our rigging crew to bring in two 12K HMIs and two 6K HMI PAR lamps to lift the areas the two Muscos couldn't reach. I sorely missed that third Musco light.

As I do when scouting any location, I noted the path of the sun and the direction in which dawn would break. When Moss looks back toward his truck and sees he has company, I felt it would be more threatening to play his point of view in silhouette, and I asked that this be considered as we laid out the scene on the location. Naturally, we would not have time to shoot all our shots during the first glimmers of dawn, so I would have to come up with an artificial equivalent. We would need a large lighting setup to create what appears as a very dim effect. I had suggested to Chris that we bounce three or four 12K HMIs behind the hill, but without adding smoke or dust into the air,

little light registered. It's always time-consuming to work with smoke and difficult to control it in an open, windy location, so we turned to a direct source. Behind the ridge Chris lined up seven 12K HMIs and pointed them directly at the sky above the camera. Using a long strip of black duvetyn to cut the light off the ridge, we simply illuminated particles of dust that were naturally floating in the air, silhouetting the rise and Moss's pickup truck without the need to add more dust or smoke into the atmosphere.

The scene's sunrise is a cheat in more ways than the lighting. By establishing a false dawn with our array of 12Ks, I could shoot the sequence that follows, the chase to the river and the confrontation with the dog, in the natural light of magic hour. As best we could, we shot toward the dawn or cheated the light by shooting Josh running at dusk. This worked well, but as luck would have it, for the one angle shooting toward my artificial source, as the first glimmers of the true dawn appeared, the sky was overcast. Those seven 12Ks illuminated the air, but the effect could be seen in front of the clouds! Another compromise, though I seem to be the only one concerned by the problem.

As Moss is chased by the dog down the river, we (and by "we," I am including our second unit cinematographer, Paul Elliott) shot during both dawn and dusk, shooting only one or two setups at the beginning or end of night work or before another day. I scouted each point on the river, marking down the best time to shoot, always trying to look toward the light, whether that be the true dawn or dusk.

7:40 5 MINS BEFORE SUNSET T.4.0
7:40 5 MINS BEFORE SUNSET T.4.0

7:40 5 MINS BEFORE SUNSET F 5.6

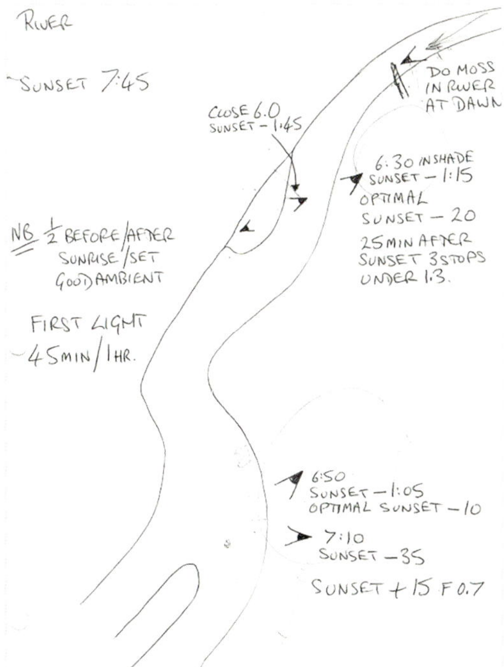
RIVER
SUNSET 7:45
CLOSE 6.0
SUNSET - 1:45
DO MOSS
IN RIVER
AT DAWN
6:30 IN SHADE
SUNSET - 1:15
OPTIMAL
SUNSET - 20
25 MIN AFTER
SUNSET 3 STOPS
UNDER 1.3.
NB 1/2 BEFORE/AFTER
SUNRISE/SET
GOOD AMBIENT
FIRST LIGHT
-45 MIN/1HR.
6:50
SUNSET - 1:05
OPTIMAL SUNSET - 10
7:10
SUNSET - 35
SUNSET + 15 F 0.7

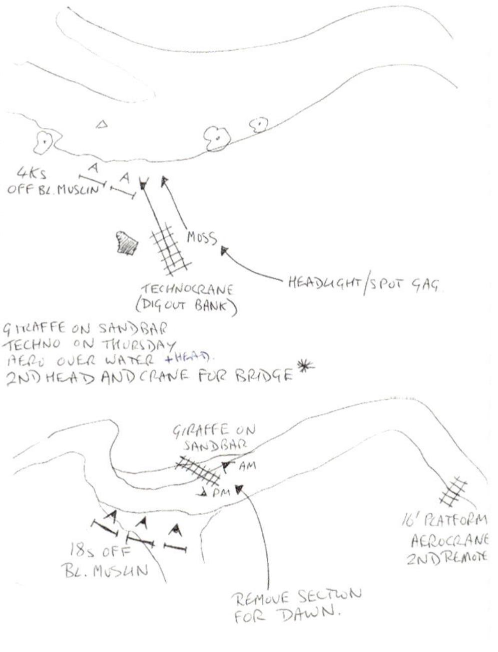
4Ks
OFF BL. MUSLIN
MOSS
TECHNOCRANE
(DIG OUT BANK)
HEADLIGHT/SPOT GAG
GIRAFFE ON SANDBAR
TECHNO ON THURSDAY
AERO OVER WATER +HEAD.
2ND HEAD AND CRANE FOR BRIDGE *
GIRAFFE ON
SANDBAR
AM
PM
18s OFF
BL. MUSLIN
16' PLATFORM
AEROCRANE
2ND REMOTE
REMOVE SECTION
FOR DAWN.

For the film's opening images of the West Texas countryside, Andy Harris and I traveled to Marfa during preproduction to film landscapes at sunrise and sunset. Joel and Ethan told me what they wanted, specifically the feel of the landscape coming alive with the rise of the sun, and I returned with just one or two shots more than those that made it into the final film. The brothers would rarely shoot a shot that was not going to make it into the final cut, so I was not going to behave any differently.

The sequence ends with a shot of a windmill set against an empty landscape of hard caliche, as described so vividly in Cormac McCarthy's novel. This montage would be the only time the film would reflect the landscape in a light that was anything other than brutal. From Marfa to the end of the film, we deliberately shot under a high overhead sun, in light that might usually be called ugly.

Even more than usual when working with Joel and Ethan, location scouts proved important. In Texas we scouted San Antonio and Eagle Pass looking for our streets and border crossing but settled on shooting the bulk of production in New Mexico. As Denis Villeneuve and I were to be reminded while shooting *Sicario*, it was impossible to shoot a border crossing in the real location. The action was just too complex and would take too much time. So, when production designer Jess Gonchor suggested constructing a border post on a freeway overpass, the city of Las Vegas, New Mexico, became our version of Eagle Pass.

We used the historic Plaza Hotel for some interiors and its exterior, as well as four square blocks of the downtown, which we lit to shoot dozens of shots on a short schedule. As intricate as this was, Joel, Ethan, and I had walked the course together, so I knew every angle and could be very specific with how I would light each one. The nighttime streets of Las Vegas offered little in the way of existing lighting, so I made detailed plans for rigging our own lamps on rooftops, cherry pickers, and building facades, and above the few existing streetlights. I did this well in advance of our shooting schedule so that the location department could obtain permits from the city and allow Chris and his crew eight days to put everything in place.

TEXACO
ICE

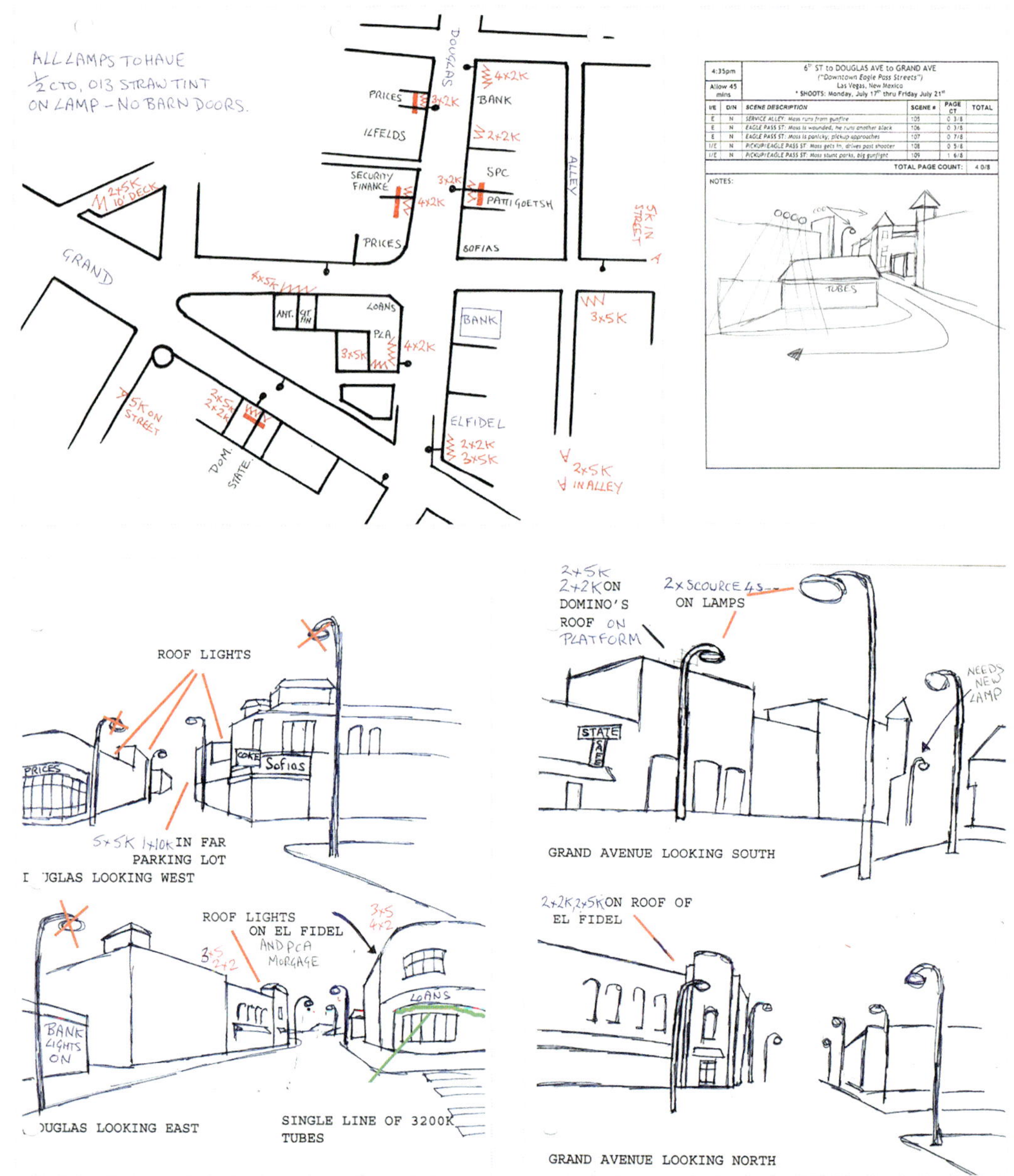

On shoot days we did not use a central dimmer board to control each lamp remotely, as you might these days, but relied on individual hand dimmers dropped to the ground from each lighting position. We used tungsten-balanced lamps and gelled them with a mixture of ½ CTO and 013 straw filters to give the street lighting a warm, sodium tint. Most carried a brushed-silk diffusion on the barn doors as well as the gel. Normally the heat from a Fresnel lamp might burn out a gel pack such as this, but we kept the lamps dimmed down and the nights were quite cold, so this never became a problem. Though Chris did have the rigging crew change the gels every day just in case the color had shifted due to the heat.

The lighting for the Las Vegas streets, the border crossing Jess constructed on the overpass, the trailer park, and the cheap motels would be in stark contrast with the unforgiving sunlight of the daytime scenes. We would light with a wide variety of brightly colored fluorescent tubes, ultrawarm practical bulbs, or streetlights of a mercury cyan or a sodium orange.

We introduced the same threatening sodium orange of the street into the set for the hotel room in which Moss is found hiding out, combining it with the yellow of a shaded practical lamp. And for the exterior of the El Paso motel, in which Moss meets his end, we used a wash of cold blue-green light to contrast with warm household bulbs and the red of the police warning lights.

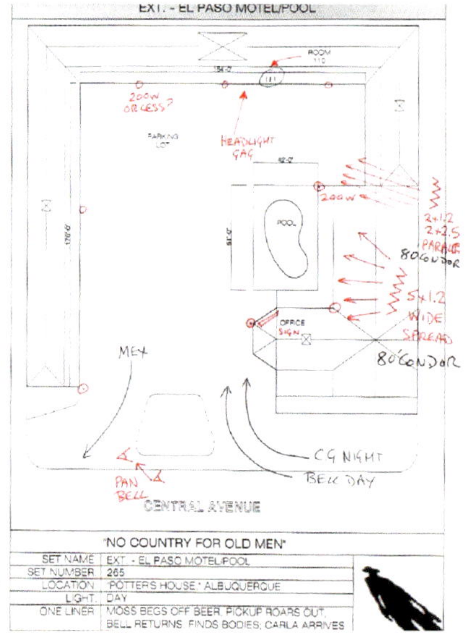

As with *Fargo* and other Coen brothers movies, some striking shots arose by chance. The black scuff marks that pattern the floor of the deputy's office as he is strangled by Anton Chigurh (Javier Bardem) were a product of the actor's rubber footwear and the number of takes that we had to shoot. We completed our tighter coverage first and, to maintain continuity, intended to wipe off the floor for the overhead shots. That was until we saw just how clearly the black scuff marks expressed the brutality of the fight.

Later in the story, the script describes Chigurh looking at his own ghostly reflection in the gray of a TV screen in Moss's trailer, and we added the corresponding image of Sheriff Ed Tom Bell (Tommy Lee Jones) in his cowboy hat doing the same. This shot hadn't originally been planned, but the two characters sitting in the same place, drinking from the same glass of milk, and staring into their own abstractions united them in some strange metaphysical way.

After we filmed the scene in which Sheriff Tom Bell meets the sheriff of El Paso (Rodger Boyce) at a diner, we went outside to shoot them exchanging some final words before going their separate ways. We had an early call the next day and, on top of that, there was the added time pressure of an approaching thunderstorm. To simplify what had been storyboarded as five separate shots, I suggested we play the exchange in silhouette against the rear wall of the restaurant. Joel and Ethan agreed that the scene could work that way, provided we also finish with a close-up of Tommy Lee once he is inside the car. In jest, Joel insisted I be the one to describe the lack of coverage to Tommy Lee and that he would only be seen in silhouette. (He was fine with it.)

From the coffee shop Ed Tom returns to the motel and the scene of Moss's death. This is one of my favorite moments, the only time in the film when Ed Tom and Chigurh are in the same scene. *But are they?* The sheriff can sense Chigurh is in the room, and we see him illuminated by the light kicking off the brass of the empty door lock. But is he really there? Not when Ed Tom enters. I had

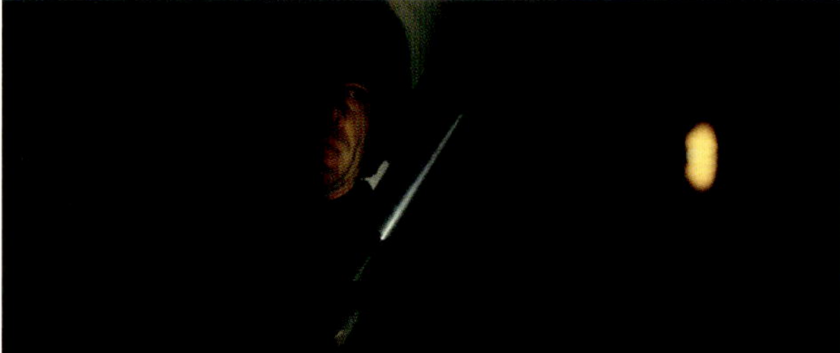

two lucky breaks shooting this scene. First, for the effect of the light bouncing off the brass, Chris and I found that by offsetting the lens of a 150-watt Dedo, its light formed an arcing beam with refracted colors along its edge. Secondly, our storyboard showed Ed Tom standing in the doorway with his shadow cast on the wall by the headlight of his truck. I set a small Fresnel lamp to create a defined shadow, but something bothered me. Though striking, the shot felt more like one from *The Searchers* than *No Country*, and it was only when I placed a second lamp alongside the first—a vehicle has two headlights, of course—that I saw the strength of something I usually go to great lengths to avoid: a double shadow.

No Country for Old Men is remembered as a violence-filled film. That's true to some extent, but the most disturbing violence occurs off-screen. When Carla Jean (Kelly Macdonald) returns home from her husband's funeral, she notices the wind blowing the sheers of an open window and knows then she will find Chigurh. Once again, fate and a coin toss become intertwined. To emphasize that key action and to contrast with where Javier is sitting in the shadows, I projected a fully spotted 12K onto the foreground using the window frame as the cut. Otherwise, the scene is played in simple wide shots in undramatic light. We leave the scene before knowing its outcome. Only when Chigurh appears on the porch outside to nonchalantly look down at the soles of his shoes do we know for certain that Carla Jean is dead. It shows the mastery Joel and Ethan have over the medium that this played in a wide shot of a house that could be anyone's home on anyone's street. The scene is all the more chilling because of the violence we have seen and are about to see. Here it takes place in private.

No Country for Old Men offered plenty of challenging locations to light and wonderful landscapes to point the camera at, but my favorite scene is between two aging men in a dusty cat-filled cabin set out on that hard caliche. Yes, it took a lot of effort for Jess Gonchor to build the cabin in the middle of nowhere—all that existed was a windmill and plenty of dirt, and it took multiple HMI lamps and large bounce sources to balance the interior with the extreme brightness of the exterior. But the scene is pure magic. When you have actors as good as Tommy Lee Jones and Barry Corbin, it is sometimes hard to remember that you are on a set and shooting a performance, an actor saying lines. Did the setting help those incredible performances? Would it have been the same had the set been on a stage and the exterior nothing but a video projection?

The script called for visuals to accompany Tommy Lee's final monologue in the film, images of his character, Ed Tom Bell, as a younger man on a horse accompanying his father, who's holding a flame, as they ride through a snowy night. We talked about staging the scene as if it took place in a kind of limbo, but we were struggling to find a location in which to do it, or for the money to shoot it.

Meanwhile, we visited dozens of rural homesteads looking for our image of Ed Tom's kitchen until we found a perfect match. (I often wonder what the property owner makes of us when we leave shaking our heads. Do they take it personally?) We walked into one ranch house that we warmed to immediately, despite its distance from our production base. The two wizened trees outside the kitchen window seemed to reflect the character of Sheriff Ed Tom perfectly. Tommy Lee's performance, the expression on his face, the sense of finality conveyed by his words, made illustrating the story he told feel unnecessary, maybe even detrimental. I can't remember if it was Joel or Ethan, or both of them together who, after Tommy's first take, said, "OK. Well, that's the end of the film, isn't it?"

As a documentary filmmaker you intrude in other people's lives and sometimes their misery. You take away your trophies in the form of your images and return to your own, probably more comfortable, life. There is an element of voyeurism to this kind of filmmaking that I failed to come to terms with. Similarly, violence in a drama can be just as voyeuristic. But without *No Country for Old Men*'s violent depiction of evil, that final scene, in which Ed Tom bemoans that God has not entered his life, would not have the same emotional resonance. That juxtaposition of ideas, encapsulated in the Coens' storytelling technique, is why I love films and why I love to help build the illusion of life.

You can't stop what's coming.
It ain't all waiting on you. That's vanity.

ELLIS, IN *NO COUNTRY FOR OLD MEN*

23
THE ILLUSION OF LIFE

Animation is about creating the illusion of life.
And you can't create it if you don't have one.

BRAD BIRD

I served as cinematographer for three films in 2008: *Doubt*, *Revolutionary Road*, and *The Reader*, sharing credit with Chris Menges on the lattermost. But it's work on a fourth film released that year that opened another career avenue I've subsequently enjoyed, one that brought me back to watching Mickey and Felix on my dad's projector in the attic. But how things had changed. Shortly after joining the staff of Pixar, after a long tenure working at Industrial Light & Magic, producer Jim Morris reached out to James. "Will you guys come in and do a little seminar?" he asked. I'd conducted lighting workshops from time to time, and this seemed like a pleasant opportunity to do something outside the norm. We agreed, not realizing this seminar would double as an audition.

It was a simple event. Pixar had a small set, a lot of lights, a few electricians, and an Alexa camera with a feed that displayed what the lens was seeing to monitors arranged among the audience. We gave a couple of stand-ins some action, set up a simple two-shot, and began to demonstrate the basics of movie lighting, using a traditional blend of key lights, fill lights, kickers, and backlights with multiple flags to shape the light and create patterns of light and shade on the walls. The audience seemed to be taking it all very seriously but, after about twenty-five minutes, I started to wonder if I'd taken the exercise too far. With so many lamps and stands it was becoming harder and harder to move around the set! I apologized. "I'm sorry. This is how you might think a cinematographer lights, and I purposefully gave you what you expected," I told them, "But it's really a long way from what I do."

I panned the camera around to compose a shot of one of the electricians. He was leaning against a work light, basically a large bare bulb on a stand, and I loved the way the light was catching his face. "*This*," I said, "is what I do. And, even better, the shot is already lit." Thankfully, the audience laughed. "Lighting, to me, begins with the choice of a light source, building from there to create a sense of naturalism. There is no formula you might find in a textbook." I took down all the flags and cutters and continued with the demonstration, only this time lighting the scene as I normally would—with practical lamps and a soft bounce source coming through a window.

It must have gone well, because Jim soon asked us to visit Pixar again. Andrew Stanton, a longtime Pixar creator who'd made his directorial debut with *Finding Nemo*, was working on a new film called *WALL•E*. Andrew and the rest of the team wanted to approach the look of their film (a sci-fi epic as if shot on film in the 1970s) informed by the mechanics and aesthetics of live-action cinematography. *How does a camera dolly move? What is the difference between a zoom and a dolly move? What is the difference between a wide-angle lens and a telephoto? How will the look of a camera move change from a wide lens to a long lens?* Animation can move the camera without worrying about dollies, walls, or any sorts of real-world constrictions. And it can shoot with any length of lens. A 61.2 mm or a 23.75 mm, anyone? This might seem liberating, but there is a well-established film language based on perception, not simply on a random series of choices. An audience may not be able to describe why they're taken out of a scene when the camera makes some physically impossible move, but they feel the effects of that choice.

We began traveling to Pixar and spending a few days at a time working with their layout and lighting teams, a divided structure common in animation. The former places the characters in relation to the camera and sets any move while the latter lights whatever is presented to them, neither one consulting the other. Our greatest contribution might have been suggesting these two teams work more closely together! We put them in the same room and raised questions like "OK, what do you need to see in this scene? What mood are you looking for? Is there a need for close-ups or can the scene play in a wide shot? What focal length lens should we use? If this area is in darkness, how does it affect the composition of the shot? And how about depth of field?" As we explored the language of cinematography with the animators, we also received a crash course in how animation worked.

Most of our work on *WALL•E* concerned the early stages of production, discussing the overall concept for the film as well as creating reference images for the film's opening sequences set on a trash-covered Earth. Putting the sun in the back of the shot and adding atmosphere to the environment, for instance, allowed the piles of trash to hover over our shots like ghosts. I think we helped shape the look of the film, though I can't help but wish we could have spent more time on it and developed its look further.

Got some bad news. Um...Operation Cleanup has, well, uh, failed. Wouldn't you know, rising toxicity levels have made life unsustainable on Earth.

SHELBY FORTHRIGHT, IN *WALL•E*

By contrast, James and I were involved with Gore Verbinski's *Rango* from beginning to end. An oddball take on the spaghetti Western starring a pet chameleon, *Rango* is filled with cinematic references, including the title's homage to *Django*, directed by Sergio Corbucci. Gore felt that to have a cinematographer overseeing the film would take it away from the more conventional look of contemporary animated films being made in Hollywood, and he turned to the prestigious visual effects house ILM, rather than an experienced animation studio, to do the animating.

We began working with Tim Alexander at ILM's studio in San Francisco, as we had on *WALL•E*, by making a series of reference images for situations that would occur multiple times throughout the film—bright desert exteriors, moonlight, a day interior, or a street scene at night. But the film was about more than its environments, and key to it working was testing the rendering of each different character. How, for instance, would Rango's scaly skin look at high noon versus under moonlight? How would a mouse's fur or an eagle's feathers react in those same situations, in the warmth of firelight or in the dim light of an interior? As these are animated characters, it's impossible to determine how their surface textures will react until you light them, especially as the light you are using is only the product of pixels responding to a computer program. Sometimes you get some unexpected results.

As the set pieces of his live-action films suggest, Gore is a genius at designing shots. It was with the lighting that he needed help. As we discovered, what was tricky in live action could also be tricky in animation. Gore wanted the standoff in a dark saloon to recall similar scenes that had been staged in countless live-action Westerns, so we decided to light it with shards of sunlight, as if seeping through holes in the roof. But creating this look in a computer is not the same as working with a physical lamp.

When Rango walks through the desert, we wanted the horizon to blend into the sky, as it does in *Once Upon a Time in the West*. To do this, the atmosphere had to be added using layers in depth so that the foreground would remain clean but the background would be progressively diffused. And it would have been oh so much easier to use moonlight for the scene where Rango crosses the highway at night, but why do that when using the whites of the headlights and the red of the taillights of passing vehicles offered a far more compelling option?

Working in a virtual environment allowed the lighting department to do something impossible in a live-action world: set a sun that would stay in place for an entire scene. On actual locations the order of a day's shooting is chosen with the angle of the light in mind. For example, a scene might have a series of shots backlit against the sun, but to shoot them requires careful planning around the sun's location at each moment during the day. A shoot will follow the sun. (*Robin and Marian*, photographed by David Watkin, has moments like this throughout the film.) Similarly, onstage the key light might be deliberately shifted from one camera angle to another if it better serves the look of a shot and the flow of the scene. Yes, continuity is important and all the shots in a scene should appear to have been taken at the same time and in the same light, but the key words are "appear to." Those shafts of light in the *Rango* saloon could come from anywhere if it helped with the mood of a shot.

No man can walk out of his own story.

SPIRIT OF THE WEST, IN *RANGO*

I've decided I don't want to fight dragons.

HICCUP, IN *HOW TO TRAIN YOUR DRAGON*

After *Rango*, we began a long association with DreamWorks Animation, starting with Chris Sanders's and Dean DeBlois's 2010 film *How to Train Your Dragon*. James and I spent considerably more time working in person at DreamWorks on the three-part *Dragon* series than we had on any previous animated projects, following each film from the first conceptual illustrations, through the story reel process, to animation, layout, and lighting. Sometimes we'd spend the morning moving from one cubicle to the next to discuss lighting with each digital artist, then check on their progress while doing another pass in the afternoon. From the beginning we emphasized, "We don't want to impose our ideas on anything. We're just here to offer advice, give our point of view, and discuss different approaches that might work."

Once again, we felt better coordination between the layout and lighting teams would allow for more possibilities and help create images that were more dynamic. The first scene we lit for the film uses only candles for a conversation between the young hero, Hiccup, and his father, for instance. But where to put the candles? Placed to one side of the scene a candle might rim a character's face and leave the camera side in shadow. And, if the image were to be naturalistic, the light needed to drop off following the inverse square law, even if this left much of the background in darkness. Animators had worked hard on rendering all the detail in those backgrounds, but, as with the opening sequences in *WALL•E*, maybe seeing it all wasn't the best option for the scene. Getting everyone on board with this approach took a while. We screened some initial shots of this candlelit scene, and it was Jeffrey Katzenberg who dismissively commented, "Oh, it's all too dark." But only a few weeks later we screened something similar, and he said, "This might be a bit light." We knew then we'd made a breakthrough.

Still, lighting was often a far more complex process in animation than live action. On a set it's simple enough to project a light onto a white card, or any other surface, and reflect bounced light into a face, but it takes a lot of computer power to achieve the same look in animation (or it used to). So, an important aspect of James's and my work at DreamWorks was talking to programmers about how to bring the real-world physics of light into animation. As the technology grew more sophisticated this became easier. We could soon project light on a surface and have it bounce off without using a separate program to mimic the effect, though for it to bounce a second time remained wishful. But, with time, technology began to drive the lighting.

How to Train Your Dragon: The Hidden World, the final film in the series, includes a scene in a forest. To light it, the team made a 360-degree capture of the light in a wooded area near the studio. When they incorporated this directly into the scene, it didn't look right at all. Had they imposed too much reality on the film's stylized world, created that "uncanny valley," or was their technology just not ready to do what they intended? Either way it didn't look right. But the exercise did give me a chance to explain an idea central to how I approach lighting. Naturalism isn't the same as realism. The goal isn't to mimic how light works in the real world but to use natural-looking light as a form of expression. And what works in live action can work just as well in animation.

As well as the three *How to Train Your Dragon* films, James and I also consulted on *The Croods* and *Rise of the Guardians* during our time at DreamWorks Animation. Each had a different style of animation and different challenges, whether it was the texture of a cloud, the rendition of a volcano, or the color scheme of a dragon. Over the years in their making, we witnessed the constant evolution of technology, though nothing James and I were involved with had yet incorporated artificial intelligence (as far as we knew). After our time at DreamWorks, we became involved with a project at Sony entitled *Vivo*, a colorful animated musical. Production designer Carlos Zaragoza created wonderful color palettes for the various sections of the film. After so much work in telling the story in this vivid chromatic world, it was very disappointing that the film went straight to streaming and was never shown in a theater.

I was able to venture into animation while also shooting live-action films because of the seamless working structure James had created by this point. With the producers of each animated project, James set up virtual network connections that allowed us to be a part of the film's development whatever the location we were currently working on. She was in constant communication with each of the layout and lighting departments to keep apprised of any new material that might be available for us to work on in the evening or over a weekend. As luck would have it, we were working on *True Grit*, a live-action Western with the Coen brothers, while putting the finishing touches with Gore on *Rango*, an animated one.

But before *True Grit* the Coens returned to their roots for "the kind of picture you get to make after you've won an Oscar," as *Variety*'s Todd McCarthy described Joel and Ethan's 2009 film *A Serious Man*. And, unfortunately, he's not wrong. It's a sad indictment of the film industry if that is what it takes. McCarthy's review, like those of most other critics, praised the film while also referring to it as "a particularly personal project" before noting its limited commercial prospects. Drawn from Joel and Ethan's upbringing in the 1960s Minnesota suburbs, it surely *is* the most personal of their films. But it also uses the specific time and place in which it's set to ask more eternal questions about faith and uncertainty. Why do bad things happen to good people?

24

EMBRACE THE MYSTERY

Receive with simplicity everything that happens to you.

RASHI, AS QUOTED IN *A SERIOUS MAN*

Luckily, *A Serious Man* was not set in the depths of winter and had no need for snow. What we did need was a period-correct suburban street that we could make our own, and Joel and Ethan had a very specific look in mind. Also, the main characters' houses had to be opposite each other, and one required a rooftop panorama that could pass for the 1960s without resorting to special effects. (Apart from the wide shot of the shtetl in the opening and the tornado in the final scene, the film has no CGI.) The script also called for interiors that would work with exteriors. Even if the same house didn't work for both, to maximize our shooting time we did need them to be on the same street. After a lot of scouting, we found what we were looking for in Bloomington, a suburb less than ten miles south of Minneapolis that's also home to the Mall of America. We used the roof of one house and the interior of another on the opposite side of the street, to create a composite of the home of beleaguered physics professor Larry Gopnik (Michael Stuhlbarg). Not only did the interior of one work better than the other, but this also allowed me to leave the lighting in place without fear of it being seen in any of our exterior shots.

I'd worked with Joel and Ethan on almost every film they'd made since *Barton Fink*, and I'd never seen such simple and direct storyboards as those created for *A Serious Man*. Apart from Larry's dreams and a couple of scenes shot from the perspective of stoned characters, our goal was either to let scenes play out in a single shot or cut between angles that closed in as the scene progressed, either by using a slow track or, more often, a closer static shot. *A Serious Man* is their most restrained and naturalistic film.

Instead of bounce light, Billy O'Leary and I used mostly lamps projected through large diffusion frames to create a soft daylight source. This served both the mood of each scene and the practicalities of each location, but it was also in sync with the film's relatively low budget. The approach worked well for the scenes set at Larry's house, but for his office I used reflectors, both as bounce sources to light through the windows and, at the same time, as flags to control the natural sunlight.

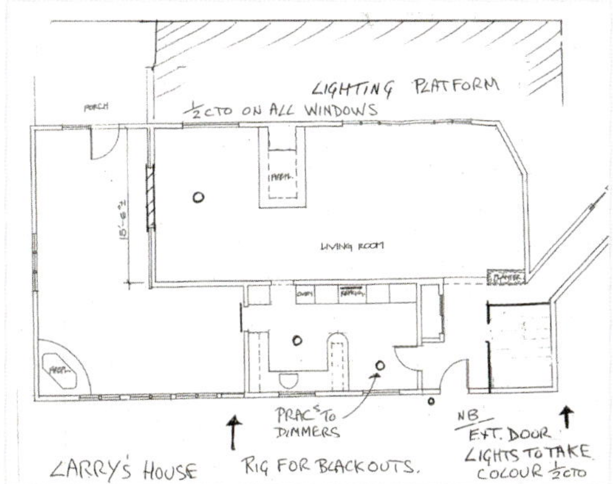

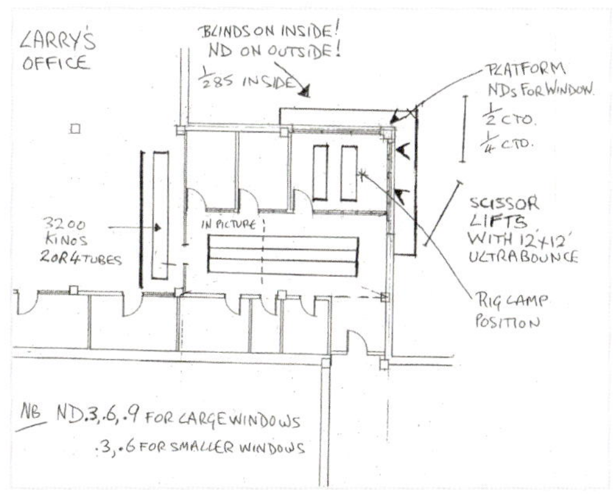

A few locations, such as the opening scene in the shtetl—which was a set but not shot in the Czech Republic as has been quoted—required a very different approach, as did the synagogue.

The synagogue we chose had a stained-glass window that we couldn't use as a source of light, and the few practical fixtures were both dim and randomly set. We had limited time to shoot two lengthy scenes requiring many setups that looked in every direction, so we needed a setup that would work for every camera angle. Further complicating matters: The synagogue did not want us to place lighting stands and other equipment on the floor or touch the walls and decorations. Fortunately, the building's interior had some wooden crossbeams that we were allowed to access, so long as whatever we attached did no damage. I initially considered hanging a tiered set of ring lights, but Mitch Lillian, serving again as key grip, pointed out that they'd be hard to construct and heavy. On the other hand, a hexagon could be made using straight sections of lightweight aluminum joined together with hinges. Other than mounting a porcelain socket every six inches, the hexagons would be simple to make and, being constructed in folding sections, easy to transport and install.

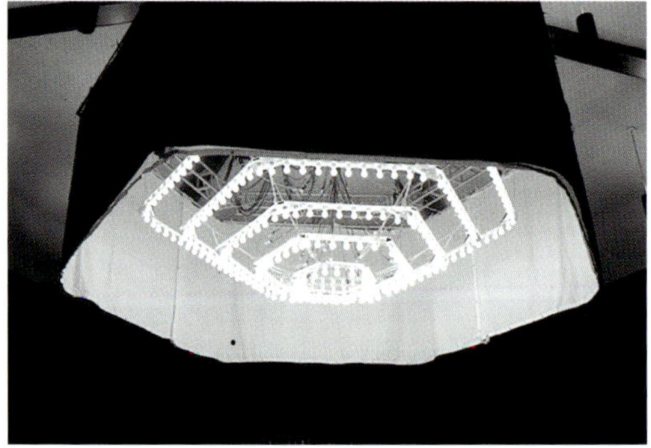

The largest of our five hexagons was sixteen feet across and the smallest about three feet. We filled the center of the light with 100-watt bulbs, the outside with 75-watt bulbs, and separately wired each hexagon to a dimmer. When dimmed in sequence, the overall effect was of a soft, warm light with a brighter and whiter center. We contained the light from our "chandelier" by surrounding it with a larger hexagon of Ultrabounce material, with its white side facing in, and suspended the entire rig using a simple pulley system, which gave us the ability to raise or lower it at any time. Other than covering the window with a ½ CTO, to shift the color of the daylight toward tungsten, this one light served as the only source for the scene. Not only did this rig allow us to shoot quickly, with no lighting change between setups, but it was also a cheap and simple solution to a problem.

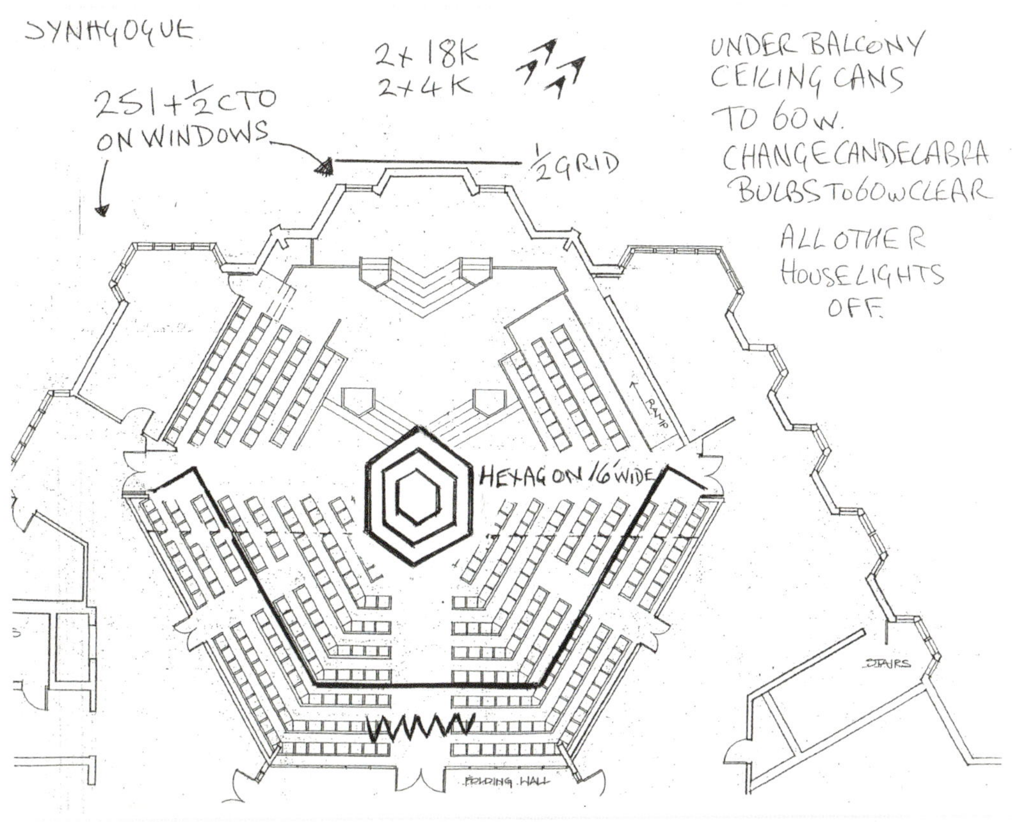
SYNAGOGUE
2x 18K
2x 4K
251 + ½ CTO
ON WINDOWS
½ GRID
UNDER BALCONY
CEILING CANS
TO 60W.
CHANGE CANDELABRA
BULBS TO 60W CLEAR
ALL OTHER
HOUSELIGHTS
OFF
RAMP
HEXAG ON 16' WIDE
STAIRS

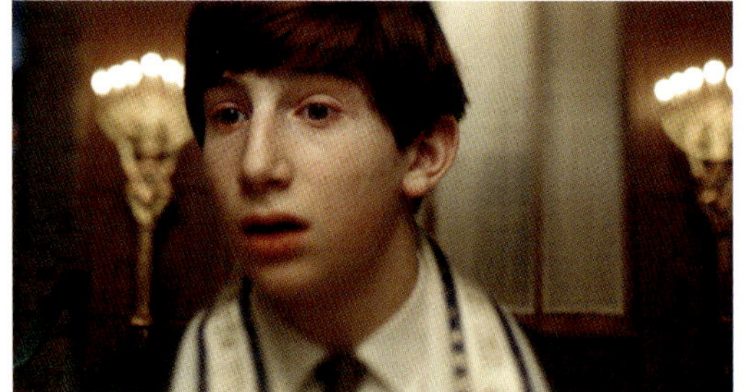

When Larry's son, Danny, is high we chose another relatively simple device I had used on *Jesse James*: a swing-and-tilt lens. These have elements separated by a bellows so the front glass can be shifted in relation to the film plane. The focal plane is usually parallel to the film plane, and focus drops off with distance. Tilting the front element of a lens at an angle to the film plane allows an object in the distance to appear as sharp as one in the foreground or only a small part of the image on the same plane to be in focus. This unexpected pattern of focus registers as a kind of swimming reality, which seemed appropriate for both Danny at his bar mitzvah and Larry as he shares a smoke with Mrs. Samsky.

Danny's still feeling the effects of the joint he smoked when, toward the end of the film, he meets with the head rabbi, a meeting Larry has tried, and failed, to secure for himself almost from the first scene. Filled with lamps, religious paraphernalia, plastic models of teeth, paintings, and many other items, the cluttered study would be disorienting even without cannabis. The only light illuminating the space comes from two small windows to one side of the rabbi's desk. Again,

shooting on a real, if heavily dressed, location, we enhanced the daylight by directing 4K HMI lights through the windows, softening them with a grid cloth diffusion. Projecting two or three smaller lamps through a window rather than a single large lamp allowed me to control the angle and softness of the light more easily. The lamps could be crossed from positions far apart to project light to either side of a window, set close together as a harder horizontal beam, or stacked, one above the other, to create a hard or soft vertical source depending on their separation.

Though we couldn't summon a tornado (this was a CG addition), we did get lucky with the film's final scene, thanks to a well-timed storm. We emphasized the unease of the moment using a handheld camera. When the credits start to roll to the sound of Jefferson Airplane's "Somebody to Love," the audience has been left with a lot of unanswered questions, appropriate for a film so concerned with the unanswerable. As with the box at the end of *Barton Fink* and other moments in the Coens' filmography, it's probably best to take a cue from one of *A Serious Man*'s most memorable lines and "embrace the mystery."

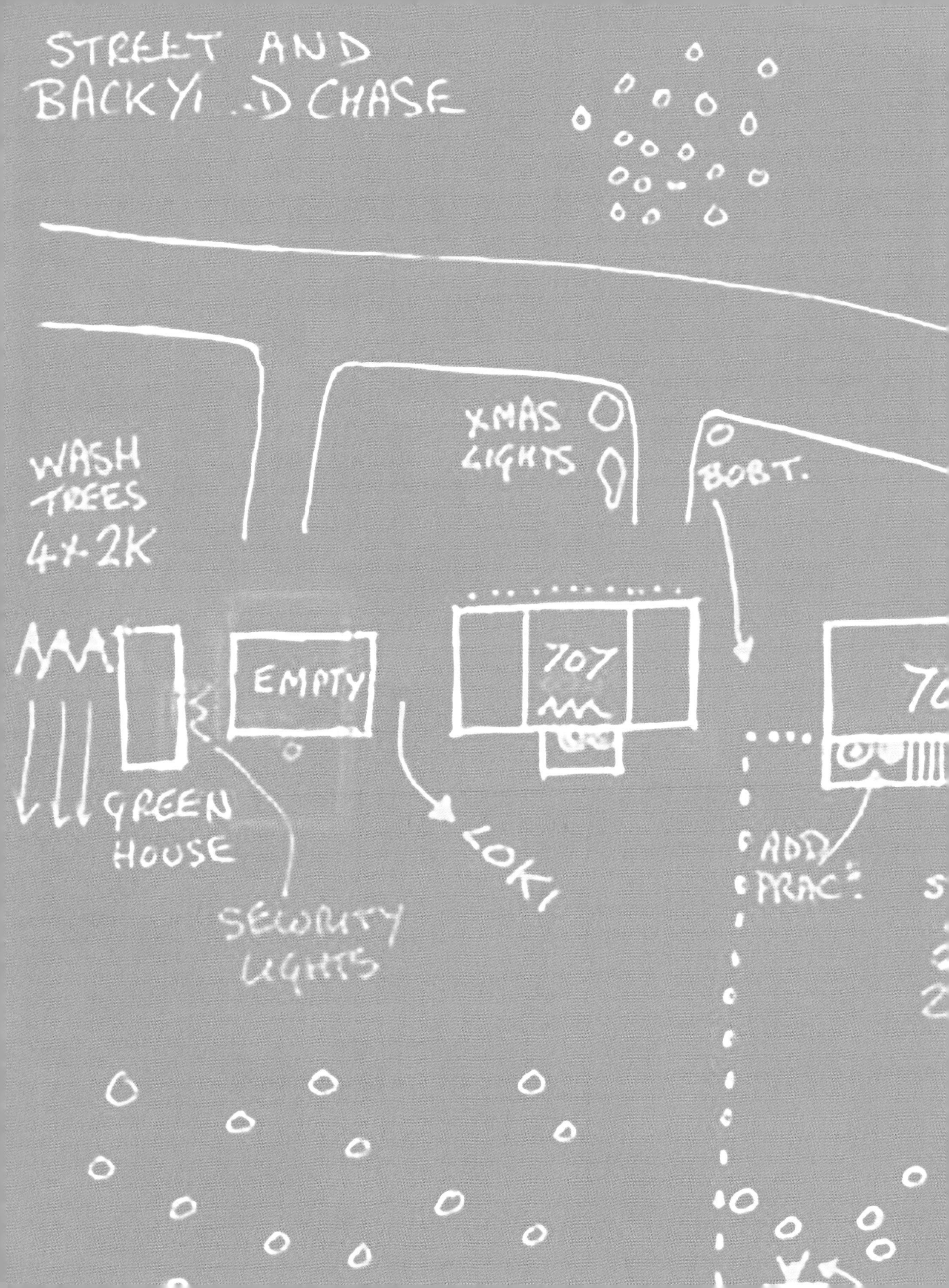

STREET AND
BACKYARD CHASE

XMAS
LIGHTS

WASH
TREES
4×2K

BOBT.

EMPTY

707

70

GREEN
HOUSE

LOKI

ADD
PRAC.

SECURITY
LIGHTS

PART IV

25

PART OF THE ESTABLISHMENT

The ground's too hard. If they wanted a decent funeral, they should have got themselves killed in summer.

ROOSTER COGBURN, IN *TRUE GRIT*

Watching *Guns in the Afternoon or Bad Day at Black Rock* with my father, I could never have imagined working on a Western, let alone being the cinematographer. Yet, if you count the more contemporary *No Country for Old Men* (which I do), *True Grit* was to be my third. Henry Hathaway's 1969 film *True Grit*, starring John Wayne, would be on many short lists of the most famous Westerns ever made. I was a little surprised that Joel and Ethan wanted to remake it. But when I read Charles Portis's original novel, which is more nuanced and darker in tone than Hathaway's film, their interest started to make more sense. When their script arrived, I knew they had a much different sort of film in mind.

The film would reunite the Coens and me with Jeff Bridges, this time casting him as a disparate larger-than-life character, the hard-drinking Marshal "Rooster" Cogburn. Hailee Steinfeld had joined as Mattie Ross, the fourteen-year-old girl who hires Rooster to track down her father's murderer, Tom Chaney (Josh Brolin), and Matt Damon would costar as LaBoeuf, a Texas Ranger also searching for Chaney. Filming *True Grit* turned out to be, as expected, an adventure.

The night shoots for *No Country for Old Men* had been a challenge, but those for *True Grit* were at another level. The location for Greaser Bob's cabin, site of Rooster and Mattie's tense encounter with a band of outlaws, proved hard to find. The Coens wanted a long, deep valley that could snuggle the cabin at one end. The sides of the valley needed to be steep but allow for a trail from which Rooster and Mattie could arrive to see the cabin from above. Furthermore, the valley floor had to have an open end suitable for the bad guys' approach.

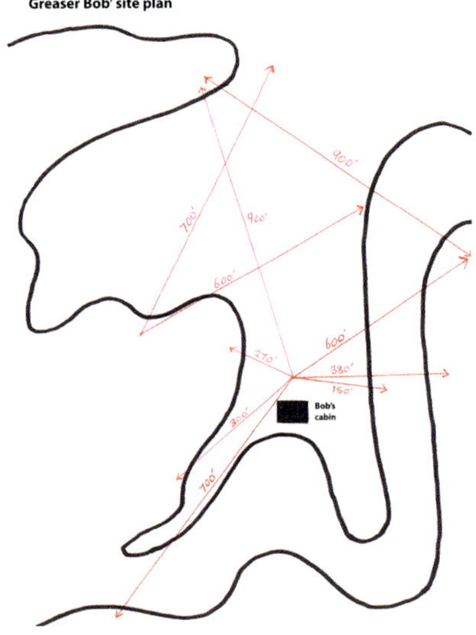

After we settled on some barren land on a ranch outside Santa Fe, gaffer Chris Napolitano and I spent hours hiking around the area to consider what our alternatives might be. Besides the sheer scale of the location and the cost of lighting it, an added consideration was that the axis of the camera would swap between scenes. In the first, Rooster and Mattie approach the cabin to the right, so I intended the light to come from the left. For the shootout that follows, Rooster and Mattie are on the reverse side of the hill looking down at the cabin. Light from one side of the valley would act as a backlight for one scene but become a front light for the other. I needed to light from both angles. After walking through our shots with Joel and Ethan on the location, I constructed the most precise and efficient lighting plan I could think of.

As it was practically impossible to say how much of each scene we would shoot on any one of the six nights we had to complete the work, we needed to be able to move from one lighting setup to the next with minimal loss to our shooting time. Moving lights around the rough hillside in the middle of the night would eat up time and money we didn't have, so my goal was to adjust our lighting with a flick of a switch. This would require more lights, all of which would have to be rigged in advance, but renting more equipment would be far cheaper than losing time on a night shoot.

We returned to the location many times during prep to mark out exactly where each array of lamps would start and end, hopefully making everything clear to our rigging crew, who would be preparing the location later in our schedule, when we would be fully occupied shooting elsewhere. Once rigging began we'd have no time to change the plan, so we needed to get it right.

There was yet another complication! For the shootout we needed to run the camera at high speed and use a long lens to depict Mattie's point of view of the action, both necessitating an increase to the light level required. And that meant more lamps, which meant more cables, which meant more electricians, which meant more generators. Cabling became a major issue as there was no access for our generators other than to the rear of the hillside, resulting in a power loss from the length of the cable runs involved. My plan also required mounting lamps on an unstable rocky terrain during seasonably unpredictable weather and operating them in the dark. Sensibly, Chris Napolitano and Mitch Lillian decided it would be both safer and more efficient to secure platforms to the hillside, thereby mounting each row of lamps on a solid surface. It was a lot of work to be able to shoot at 50 fps on a lens that only opens to 2.8 but, if it was easy…

Why so many lights instead of the Muscos I had used for the night work on *No Country for Old Men* and elsewhere? On first look a large location or set can appear daunting, and it's easy to fall back on what you know. Two factors ruled out the kind of point source lighting the Musco would provide: First, the location offered no access for such a cumbersome piece of machinery. Second, and more important, the script called for snow to arrive at the end of the night. On *No Country for Old Men*, I liked the clean shadows a hard "moonlight" source produced, but here I wanted a softer look, as if the moon was behind a cloud.

Chris, Mitch, and I had a prelight on the weekend before the shoot and, after setting all the lamps, we added double wire "scrims" to the outermost lamps in each row and single wires to

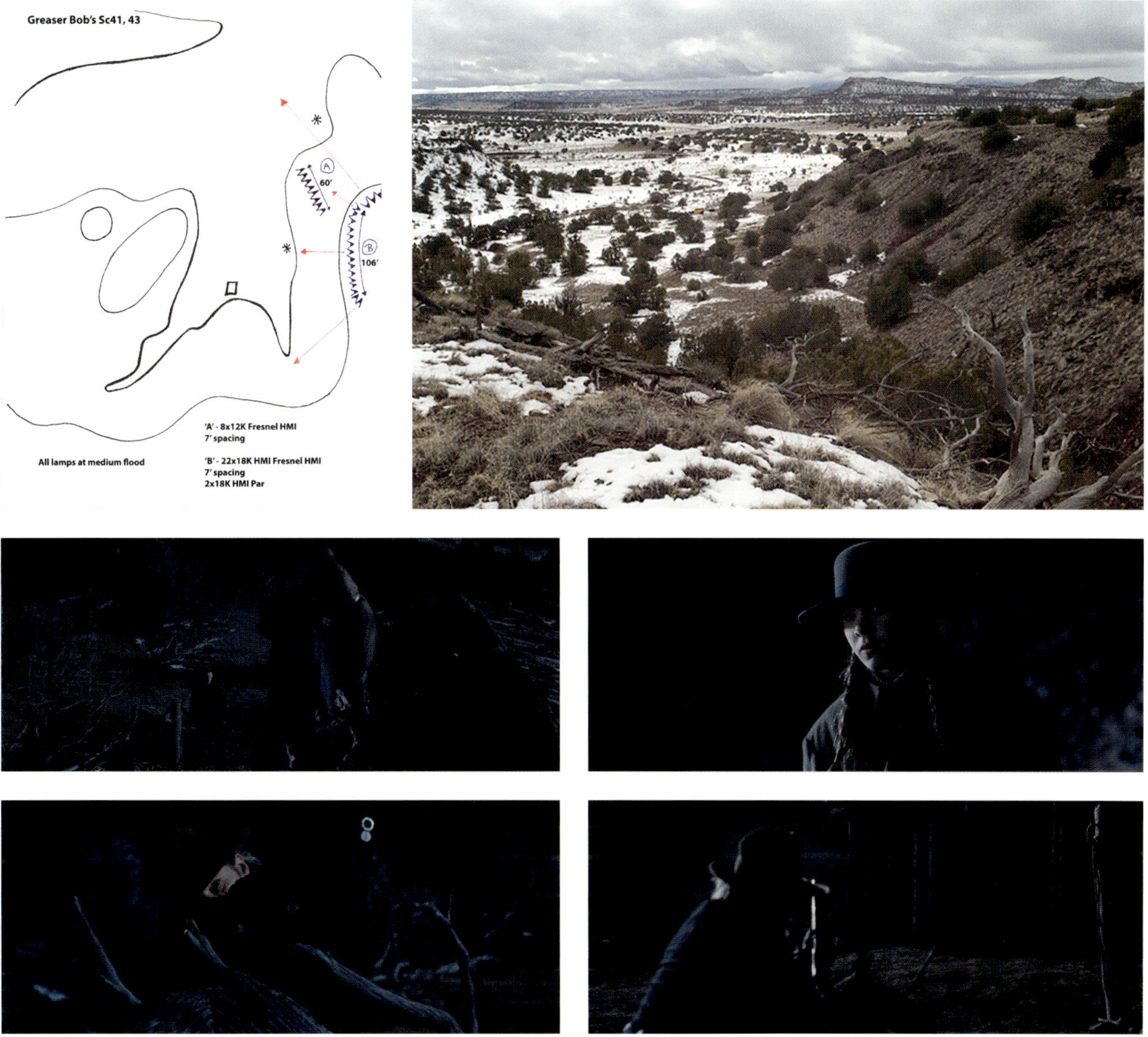

those toward the center of the line. This reduced the light level coming from the ends of the rows of lamps and gave the source a softer edge. I did not add any correction to the HMI lamps as I wanted to contrast the cool blue of the night light (I was shooting on a tungsten-balanced stock) with the warm firelight of the cabin. This set up the illusion of a cozy refuge from the wilderness, though we shot the interiors of the cabin on a stage using 500-watt quartz bulbs to boost the light coming from the fireplace.

We shot the scene that takes place the next morning, as Rooster, Mattie, and LaBoeuf leave Greaser Bob's cabin, on the first day of production, though this was never our plan. Filming was based out of Santa Fe, but because the first day of our shooting schedule was on a distant location,

a ranch to the northeast of Las Vegas, New Mexico, the crew were staying at a nearby motel. That night it snowed, and heavily. After a long drive and having grabbed a burrito each for breakfast, Joel, Ethan, Jess Gonchor (our production designer), and I were standing in the middle of a broad plain up to our knees in snow and wondering what to do—an inauspicious start to the shoot.

We *did* need snow, but only for an entirely different scene and location, the one set outside Greaser Bob's cabin. The problem: Our Greaser Bob's location was eighty or more miles away, south of Santa Fe and down a road we were told was almost impassable. But only almost! Again, a great crew makes all the difference. Mitch managed to free a stake bed truck from a snowdrift, and we stripped down what we needed to the essentials, loaded up, and we were off. We managed to shoot the three shots on our

storyboards in the fading light at the end of the day, and what had started as a disaster turned into a success. And we could check off our one snow-dependent scene, a welcome development since the weather had begun to warm up, while freeing the location for the rigging crew. A lucky break indeed.

We filmed most of our interiors on location. Of these the courtroom proved particularly challenging as it was on the second floor of the Old Courthouse in Blanco, Texas. Joel had given me a brief to hold Rooster, then on the witness stand, in shadow until Mattie moves closer to the front of the spectators to get a better view of him. I decided to create the effect of hard sunlight streaming through the windows behind Rooster, allowing for bounce light to wrap around his face from Mattie's more forward position. Complicating matters, the windows faced south. Ideally, I would need three eighty-foot lifts to raise the lamps and three more to carry 12' × 12' solids to cut the natural sunlight, but to cut down the cost of the rig, I reduced this to a total of four. I worked with Nancy Haigh, the Coens' longtime set dresser, to find the right style, color, and density of material for the window

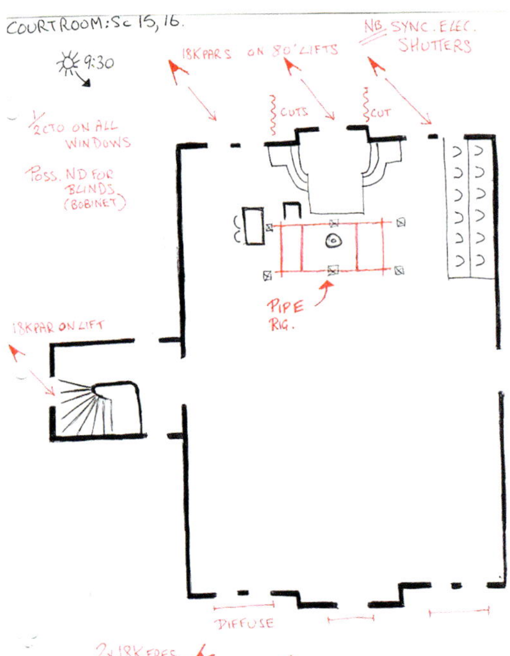
COURTROOM: Sc 15, 16.
9:30
18K PARS ON 80' LIFTS
NB SYNC. ELEC. SHUTTERS
CUTS
CUT
1/2 CTO ON ALL WINDOWS
POSS. ND FOR BLINDS (BOBINET)
PIPE RIG.
18K PAR ON LIFT
DIFFUSE
2x18K FRES.

treatment. The warmth of the yellow cloth we chose enhanced the feeling of the sunlight, and when it was furnished as a roller blind I could restrict the openings through which I was punching the 18K PAR lamps to create the shafts of sunlight (the original plan is a little misdrawn).

Greaser Bob's and the courtroom were two particularly challenging sets to light, but there were so many others. How do you shoot a young girl swimming a horse across a river or galloping through the dark of night on a horse that is called Blackie?

In the end, what we achieved together as a crew worked. For me, *The Man Who Wasn't There* and *True Grit* are the most visually unified films I have worked on. That's not to say that they are the best films, or my best work, just that the images complement the story, set a tone, and flow without distraction. Shooting a film does not just involve perfecting a series of individual shots; each one connects to another, whether it be the one that follows or the one that ends the film.

True Grit enjoyed great popular success without losing the Coens' personal touch or the haunting romance of Portis's book. Joel later mentioned to me that Dick Cheney had announced *True Grit* to be his favorite film of the year. I laughed. I reminded him that he had worried about becoming part of the "establishment" when *No Country for Old Men* won for best picture at the Academy Awards. "What do you have to say now?" I asked.

It was *True Grit* that brought a second letter from Oswald Morris, cinematographer of *Moby Dick*, *Lolita*, *The Hill*, and *The Spy Who Came In from the Cold*. We had met briefly while I was at the National Film School, and he had later written to me to say that he thought I might become a good cinematographer if only I would hire a camera operator (something I have yet to do). Having seen *True Grit*, he wrote to compliment me on, in his opinion, the best-photographed film he had seen in some time and that he now understood why an "A" camera operator was not part of my crew.

I don't always use the same team for every film. Geography and scheduling make this impossible. But I do have collaborators I like to turn to again and again, reliable professionals like Andy Harris, Bruce Hamme, Mitch Lillian, Billy O'Leary, Chris Napolitano, or John Higgins, whenever possible. You can read their names in the credits, but credits don't always tell the whole story. James's name also shows up occasionally, usually as "Digital Workflow Consultant," but she has played an integral role on every job since we met, effectively allowing me to be in more than one place at a time.

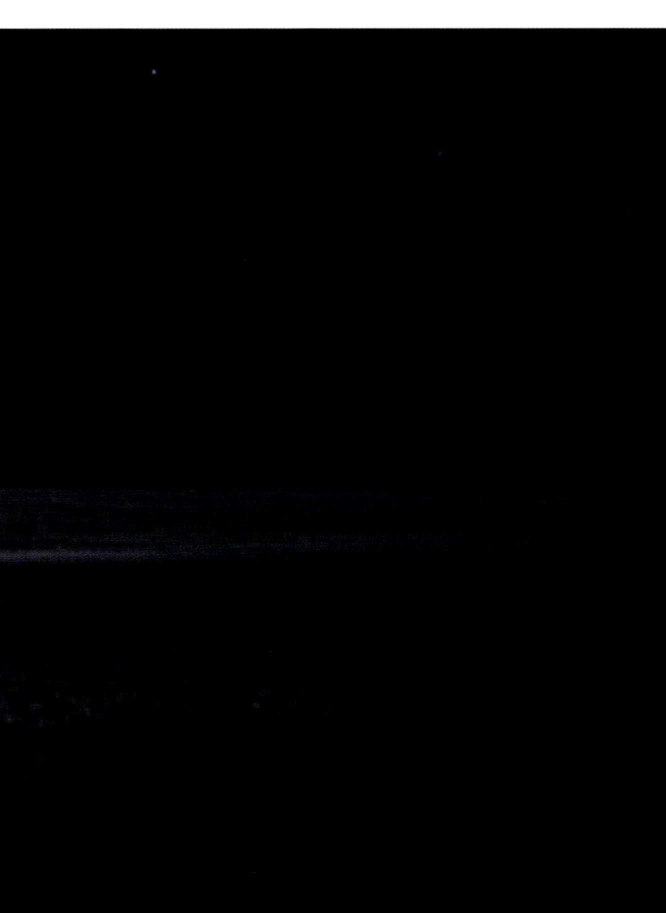

On *The Assassination of Jesse James by the Coward Robert Ford*, for instance, she worked closely with Bev Wood at Deluxe (who'd been with us every step of the way as digital processing became the norm), the effects companies, and the postproduction team. She'd talk to the lab, get a first look at dailies, set up dailies screenings, and oversee every other job that her past film experience and sharp organizational skills make her better suited to do than anyone else. On digital projects, she's the one who makes sure everything runs as it should and the film looks the way she knows I want it to. On *True Grit*, we had digital dailies, which James arranged and oversaw. She supervised the DI process in post and coordinated our *Rango* work with ILM.

Digital tools had become key to our postproduction work while, on the set, I worked in film. The division was clear. Then the sky fell! "Cinematographer Roger Deakins Switching from Film to Digital Camera," read the headline of a 2011 article in the *Hollywood Reporter*.

26

BOND, JAMES BOND

The technology you use impresses no one.
The experience you create with it is everything.

SEAN GERETY

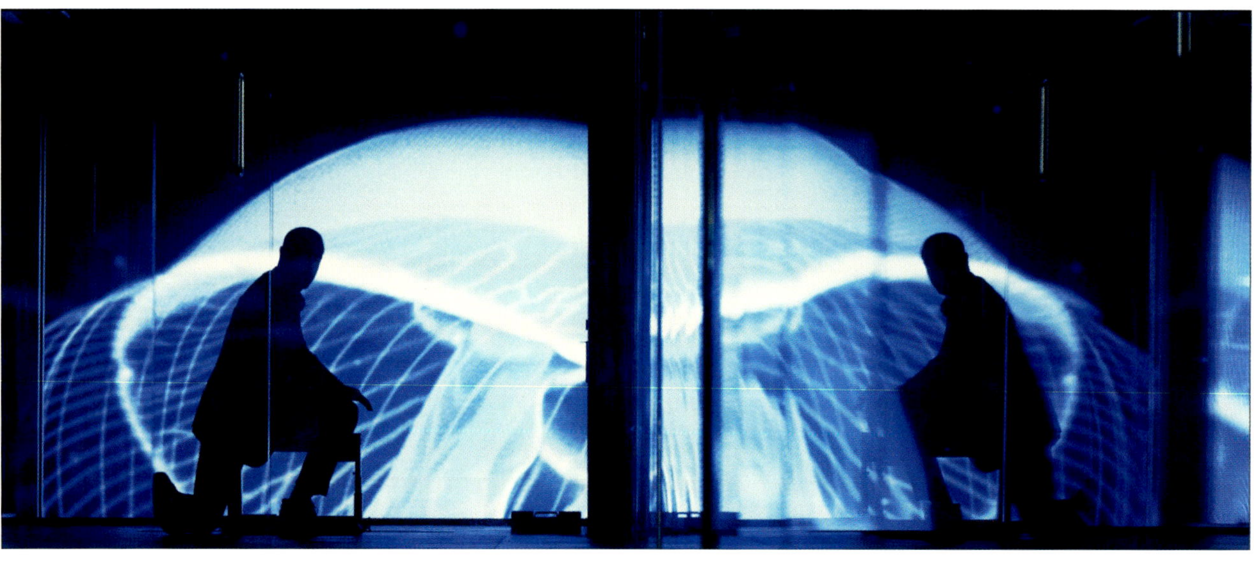

When I made the decision to shoot a movie digitally, I didn't necessarily expect it to turn into a news story. The digital-vs.-film debate had been raging for more than a decade, with proponents dug in on each side. Even as digital filmmaking advanced and became more common, some directors and cinematographers expressed a commitment to shooting on film no matter how good digital cameras became. I was never one to rule out digital capture, but only when I felt there was a reason to embrace it did I make the change. My concern has always been for the image rather than the technology used to create it.

There are Russian spies here now. And if we're lucky, they'll steal some of our secrets and they'll be two years behind.

MORT SAHL

We were in Santa Fe, working on *True Grit*, when, somewhat to my surprise, Sam Mendes called. Anticipating my reaction, the first thing Sam said was, "Don't put the phone down when I tell you what I am doing next." He knew I was not a big fan of action movies and guessed, correctly, I wouldn't respond enthusiastically to the idea of working on a James Bond movie. Though I'd been the right age to be swept up in the popularity of the series, Bond had never really appealed to me. "I'll be in Santa Monica when you finish in Santa Fe," Sam said. "Let's go for a walk on the beach and we'll talk."

When we met, Sam laid out his vision for a Bond film unlike any made before. He wanted to use the franchise to explore what the iconic character meant in the twenty-first century. What if James Bond might be too old to be a spy in a changing world? The film would be messier, brutal, and more morally ambiguous than the typical Bond film, as much a character study as a spy caper. Yes, there would be action and we would need to work with multiple cameras and a second unit, but, Sam insisted, it would be, for the most part, a single-camera shoot. We would work in the same way as we had on *Jarhead* and *Revolutionary Road*.

I joined Sam after he had already begun looking for locations, seemingly all over the world. He had narrowed his focus to shooting in India and China. In a sign of things to come, we'd end up using neither.

In Goa we scouted a railway bridge, high in the mountains, that passes over a waterfall. It looked promising in photos, but as we drove there, we became stuck in a seemingly endless line of trucks—some five thousand, I was told—ferrying bauxite from a Chinese aluminum mine to the dockside. This alone was sure to make shooting impossible, while the bridge, when we finally found it, proved surprisingly disappointing. Moving on to Mumbai, we scouted a large, congested roundabout that bordered the city's main market district, a location that had previously caught Sam's eye. When he asked the policeman acting as our guide if, and for how long, we would be able to shut down the streets, the officer replied, "What would the London police say if you asked to shut down Oxford Street?" Fair comment, I thought.

Despite such frustrations, I find scouting the most enjoyable part of the film process, not just because you stay in a nice hotel and don't have the immediate stress of the shoot, but because it offers precious time that can be spent with a director. Even when a location doesn't pan out, the discussions about what might or might not work for the film are all part of the process. We moved on from India to Turkey and had better luck with an alternative set of locations. Istanbul offered us Eminonu Square, situated by the Bosphorus and beneath the famed Hagia Sophia, as well as a maze of streets we could control for the time needed for our shoot. The eastern city of Adana had a rail line suitable for our opening sequence and, within driving distance, the 332-foot-high, World War I–era Varda Viaduct, in the Taurus Mountains. The coastal resort of Fethiye would replace Goa to become Bond's beachfront hideout and the docking place for the yacht trip to the villain's island.

Cinematography, a military art. Prepare a film like a battle.

ROBERT BRESSON

Robert Bresson talked of filmmaking as "a grand puzzle." Shooting a Bond film proved no exception to that statement. Shanghai was my next stop. In fact, I flew there three times as it was a firm location until close to our shoot date. Yet, in the end, only our second unit actually shot there, and then only establishing shots and plates to use as backgrounds for our work onstage. Other than our weeks spent shooting in Turkey at the end of the schedule, we'd barely leave Britain to create a story that takes Bond around the globe. Javier Bardem, who played the villain, Silva, jokingly commented that he had taken the film expecting to see the world, only for the London Underground to be the furthest he got from Pinewood Studios.

Sam seemed intrigued at my suggestion to shoot *Skyfall* digitally, particularly since the film would feature several action scenes shot at night or in low-light conditions. But he remained unpersuaded, so James, Andy, and I shot some tests that were processed by our digital lab, EFILM. James was now full-time on *Skyfall*. She would arrange for the processing of the camera's higher-resolution digital RAW file and the creation of our LUT (lookup table), and oversee our dailies timing during the production, leaving me free to deal with immediate on-set issues. Digital technology was new to production, but James was, and is, comfortable learning anything that's new and using it creatively. The Arri Alexa camera again proved impressive shooting under minimal light (we had first used the Alexa on Andrew Niccol's sci-fi film *In Time*), but it was finally some close-up shots that sold Sam on going digital. When he viewed a side-by-side test, it was the clarity of an actor's eyes that convinced him the digital image could stand up to one shot on film, if not surpass it. We put this to the test with *Skyfall*'s opening shot, in which Daniel Craig's Bond slowly approaches the camera down a long hotel corridor.

Like all the sets, the hotel room and corridor had been designed around the scene. We had made a rough shot list (not a storyboard) of the entire film during prep, but we chose the final camera placement during a blocking rehearsal with Daniel. To achieve the lighting effect seen in the opening shot, we designed a door with a small glass peephole. It was only on the day of the shoot that I proposed to Sam that we keep the focus on the end point of the shot, pinpointing Bond's eyes, rather than starting on his iconic silhouette.

This first scene established the look of our main character, and it was essential we shoot it before our second unit began work in Turkey on the action sequence that followed. We built the hallway and the room to which it led—where Bond would find a dying MI6 agent he'll be ordered to abandon against his instincts—onstage at Pinewood Studios well in advance of our shooting schedule. This allowed it to serve as weather cover for the first stretch of the shoot.

It was a simple set, but had the weather been uncooperative, it could have been the first scene I would shoot on a Bond movie! To connect the set to the bright light of Istanbul, I wanted to be sure the design would allow for a hard contrast between the exterior and the dark interior, so the size of the windows and their treatments would be crucial. Initially Dennis Gassner (once again our production designer) and I considered using a painted backing outside the window, but settled on revealing the exterior only once Bond exits the building into our Istanbul location. The wooden shutters would allow for shafts of sunlight, via a T12 Fresnel, to light the set while limiting the view outside.

Sam and I had made an animated previsualization (pre-vis) of the opening action sequence that incorporated all of our chosen locations with camera angles and lens choices programmed in. I had never been involved in such detailed animation work on any other live-action production, but it proved essential given the complexity of the sequence and because much of the stunt work would be shot by a second unit being directed by Alexander Witt. Mostly they would shoot using a double, not only for safety reasons but because the stunt team needed time to work out the intricacies of the action.

Though it made sense to shoot the sequence all at once, there were few occasions when Daniel was not busy on first unit, so we were scheduled to work alongside Alex and his crew in Istanbul and Adana before we wrapped production in Turkey. By the time we showed up, both the stunts and effects had been so well rehearsed that we shot more angles with Daniel than we had originally thought possible, leaving fewer effects shots to be picked up in Pinewood at the end of the schedule. These on-location shots only added to the impact of the sequence.

In London, Bond's boss, M (Judi Dench), follows the action in Turkey from the MI6 headquarters. Surprisingly, we were given permission to use the exterior of the real building on the south bank of the Thames. To have an authentic background onstage, we were even allowed to photograph the view from inside the building. And for a night shot we were able to light it, although it was only MI6 staff who were allowed to set our lamps. Later in our schedule, on a Sunday morning, we shut down all of Whitehall, so I guess James Bond has many fans! Though it might have been different had we asked for a week on Oxford Street.

When MI6 is bombed by the cyberterrorist, revealed later as the former agent Raoul Silva (Javier Bardem), the organization is forced to move to its backup headquarters, an underground bunker we're told was used by Winston Churchill during the war. Dennis created this complex

using a combination of locations and sets. For the largest set we used the massive 007 stage at Pinewood, originally built in 1976 for *The Spy Who Loved Me*. The set included a passageway into the main underground space, though the tunnel into which Bond is driven and the unassuming entrance door that leads to the bunker were shot on location in South London. The tunnel was quite short, so we used multiple passes and multiple camera angles to create the sensation of the SUV traveling a much longer distance than reality allowed. The fluorescent fixtures we hung overhead are the same as appear in the main set to imply they were all newly installed.

After entering the tunnel, Bond walks under bulkhead lamps that could be left over from the Victorian era, into which we installed 100-watt tungsten bulbs dimmed down to make them photograph warm and to contrast this space with the cool fluorescent fixtures that Biggles and I had decided to use for the main bunker. (I had last worked with John "Biggles" Higgins on *The Secret Garden*, so it was good to team up with him again.) For this, Chris Lowe, our supervising art director, helped design twin four-foot light fixtures that looked high-tech but were simple to manufacture. At Biggles's suggestion we installed narrow T8 (which are one inch in diameter) fluorescent tubes rather than the traditional T12, because it would make the fixture look even more high-tech but, in multiples, still produce a soft source. The lighting had to fit within Dennis's overall concept for the set, but it also needed to light the scenes. To fulfill both of those requirements Biggles and I worked closely with the art department to come up with a combination of straight rows of fixtures within the larger open spaces and square-shaped fixtures in the smaller confined spaces, such as the interview room.

Because of the large number of bulbs we would need—well into triple figures by the time we finished—we chose a cheaper off-the-shelf brand for all of the location and stage work set within the bunker (even Bond movies need to save money where they can). After testing multiple brands, we settled on a 4,000K tube that we found we could dim to 50 percent of intensity without flicker, and which gave us a cooler look with only a minimal green tint. LED tubes, both expensive and not yet widely available in 2011, don't have any of these problems!

The chase sequence that takes place beneath the city of London was split between locations and sets. Dennis built a curved tunnel for the underground train that Bond only manages to escape at the last second, but we also shot on an actual train and on a disused station platform. Despite all that, Sam felt the sequence lacked one spectacular piece of action, and it was our effect supervisor, Chris Corbould, who suggested that we crash a train through the roof. Chris also said we could shoot it for real—that is, with no model work or CGI. And he was as good as his word. He suspended two sixty-foot carriages beneath a steel beam. He then attached these carriages via a cable system to a truck, which controlled their combined weight of fifteen tons as they were sent to crash through the roof of Dennis's Victorian set and stop as if on a dime in front of one of our eleven cameras, each of which shot footage that was used in the final cut of the sequence. And all in one take.

The London locations came together well, but our plan to shoot in Shanghai kept hitting snags. A sequence involving a power boat race through a complex of canals we had scouted on the outskirts of the city was cut from the script. And a standing set in a Shanghai studio, where we'd planned to shoot the complex Macao casino sequence, was destroyed by a typhoon. So little was left that we decided to create everything in London.

Apart from an exterior shot of the real location, the Kempton Park Racecourse became Shanghai's airport. The scenes of Bond driving through Shanghai's streets were created using a combination of "poor man's process," background plates shot on location, and second unit shots.

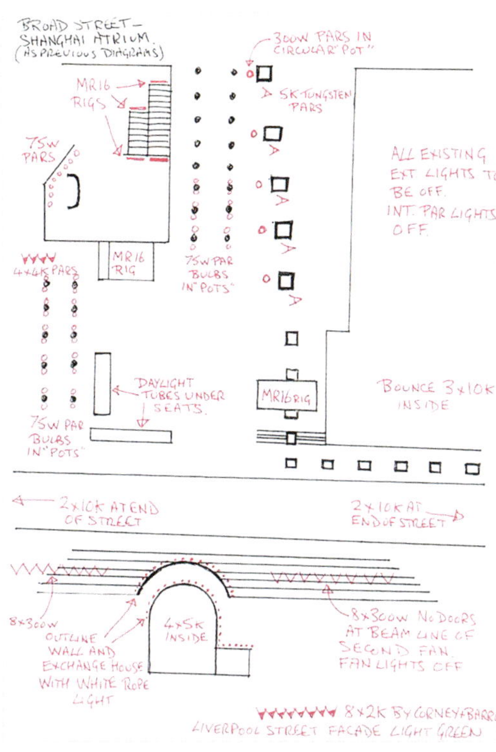

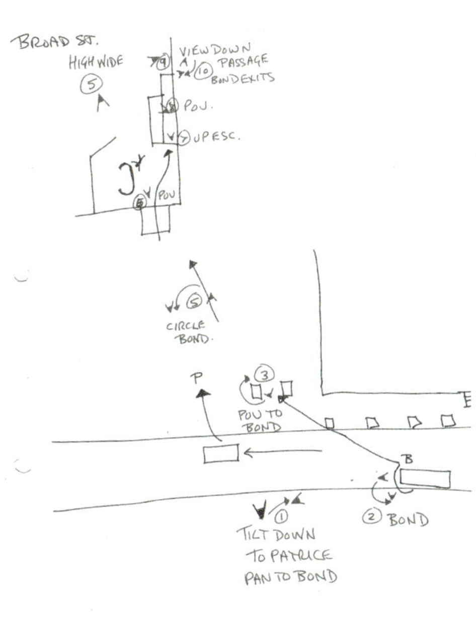

And the location we had chosen in Shanghai as the exterior of the office tower in which Bond finally confronts Patrice became a building close to Liverpool Street station in London. To disguise an area so familiar to citygoers, Biggles lit the back of Liverpool Street station in a vivid green, just part of a color palette more in keeping with Shanghai than London.

After Bond rides an elevator by hanging beneath it—a moment created on set with the help of one of the very few greenscreens we used in the entire film—he walks down a blue-lit corridor into a wide area of glass-walled offices. The production had initially considered shooting this entire scene on location in China, but after I had looked at the scout photographs and voiced some concern, Sam suggested I go there by myself and take a look. There were several options, but none looked out toward Shanghai's famous lit signage, which mostly faces across the Huangpu River toward the Bund.

Sam wanted separate office spaces rather than one open bullpen area. But, enclosed by solid walls, how would the location be lit if not from the city outside? If the lights were on inside the building, wouldn't Bond be in full view of an assassin and, worse still, the assassin in full view of his target? It would be expensive to manufacture an outside source on the forty-seventh floor, and besides that, staring out at nothing but a dark building didn't make much sense to me. As I looked out toward the Huangpu River from the bar of my immaculate Shanghai hotel, I noticed how it and so much of the city around me seemed to be built of glass. Glass filled with reflections!

Before I talked with Sam I met with Dennis. He was our production designer, and I wanted to hear how practical he thought it was to build the set, as a composite of exterior and interior, on the 007 stage at Pinewood. The 007 stage was already being paid for because the MI6 bunker was on part of it. What's more, we could shoot this night scene during the day and in the UK. By building the set, Sam could have total control over the space in which the action was to take place, I could control the lighting, and, even more important to me, we could incorporate large amounts of glass.

Once Dennis and his art director, Chris Lowe, had researched the cost and structural issues involved with the design of such a set, Sam embraced the idea, but he suggested we build a scale model before we finally signed off on the plan. He was rightly concerned that it might make no sense if Bond was chasing an assassin with nothing between them but glass. With a model and some roughed-in lighting, we could study how the backgrounds would react in reflection and if there was space on the stage to separate the office from the hotel room in which the assassin's victim is shot. Though models are not always built for a set, one as complicated as this needed detailed exploration before money was spent. We were freed of the restrictions of the locations, but now we had to create our own version of Shanghai at night. We decided on two large LED playback screens to emulate the copious amount of advertising seen on the city's buildings: one that would silhouette the main action and a second to both side-light the set and add complexity to the reflections. To see how these sources would interact with the glass of our set we used two small iPads, the primary one of which played back a wonderfully incongruous image of jellyfish that the art department had found online. After the design of the set was completed and we settled on the overall stage layout, Dennis turned to Sam and me to ask what we would like on the main LED screen. I remember well we looked at each other and laughed. We had both grown to love those jellyfish!

Meanwhile, Biggles and I studied what LED screens were available and whether they would be bright enough to light the set as we hoped. After shooting some tests with the Alexa to check for unwanted moiré patterns (a product of the two sets of pixels overlapping) as well as light output, we found the one screen that fulfilled both our requirements. We were testing in the late summer of 2011, and it's surprising, looking back not so many years later, there were then so few options available to us. A sectional screen used for rock concerts, our one option, was in high demand and an expensive hire. But it did light the set, so it was more than a prop. The second screen was always going to be seen in reflection or through multiple layers of glass, so this could be a far more industrial type of modular unit and cheaper to hire. Besides, it was on the same plane as the hotel room, so, being that much closer than the "jellyfish," it made sense that we would see more of a pattern and texture in its projections.

An office building, built to appear further away, frames the jellyfish of the larger LED screen. The fluorescent fixtures that light these elements are 2' × T8 tubes, small enough that they help with the false perspective. In the background we placed three nighttime Translite backings; two of them were midground office buildings and the third was the Shanghai Tower. All three were designed in false perspective to give greater depth to the cityscape. The main set stood on a twelve-foot platform so that we could approach the edge without revealing the stage floor. We shot almost everything in camera; only the lower parts of some facing buildings and the moving traffic in the street below were added in post. The glass shattering behind Bond and Patrice is also a CG addition as it was dangerous to do otherwise, but not the glass in the hotel room window shattered by the assassin's bullet. Other than two rows of seven 4' × 4' blue fluorescent fixtures that light the approach to the main bullpen area, the lighting comes entirely from what appears in frame.

We shot the sequence with a lens aperture of between 1.4 and 2.0, rating the camera at 800 ASA. Because the glass was tempered and quite thick, each successive layer took away some exposure. Consequently, the earlier shots in the sequence were more open on the lens than those at the end. Black was the required dress code on set because of the reflective surfaces, and it became even more confusing when the LED screens were running. We moved around with our hands held out before us, searching among reflections that appeared and disappeared on the otherwise invisible glass in front of us, exactly as we wanted the scene to feel.

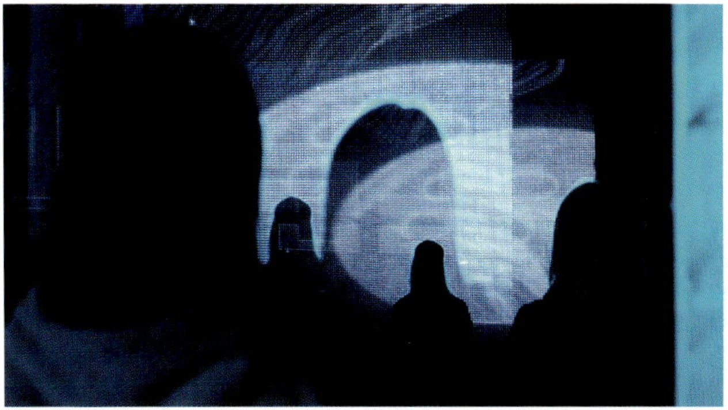

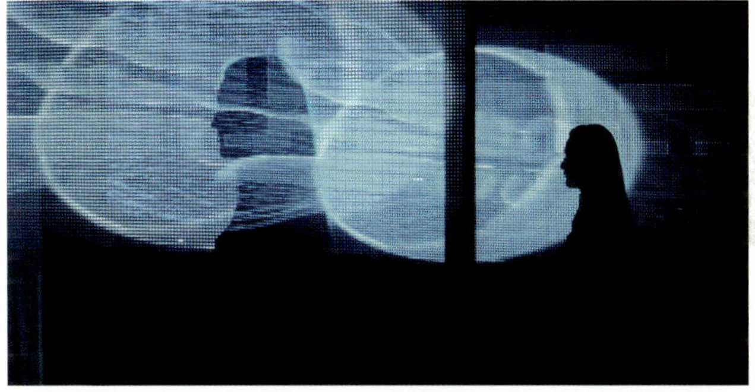

The fight was staged to take place within a single shot, closing in on the silhouetted figures fighting in front of the floating jellyfish before tilting down as Patrice falls over the edge. Sam's choice was formal and controlled, diametrically opposed to the fast cutting of most stunt work (and anathema to our stunt coordinator). In the casino we broke similar action into very specific shots. In contrast to these two scenes, we shot in the burning Skyfall Lodge with a handheld camera and in a very spontaneous way. Sam wanted each action scene within *Skyfall* to have an individual style, or its own point of view.

It wasn't just Shanghai that found an English stand-in. For the exteriors of Macao's casino, we used Pinewood's exterior Paddock Tank, where Dennis created a bridge and island temple based on ones we had scouted in China. While we no longer had to travel, this *did* mean we had to simulate a warm evening in Macao on a cold March night in England. By 10 p.m. the ground froze over but not, luckily, the tank itself. Moreover, the water never started steaming, another potential disaster that almost tripped me up on *Blade Runner 2049*.

We rigged our camera on a 100-foot Technocrane arm raised on a 10-foot-high scaffold platform to the rear of the set. Sam and I had specific shots in mind. Working with our key grip, Gary Hymns, we figured that with a crane of this length we could shoot a majority of our scene with its fulcrum remaining in one position. This was the first time anyone had used the 100-foot Technocrane in the UK, so it became quite a popular shoot that night, with plenty of extra grips "visiting" our set and helping out despite the cold.

Bond arrives at the casino surrounded by a spectacle of different lights. The floating lanterns held 250-watt quartz bulbs dimmed down and flickering slowly to look like flames in a wax lantern. The dragons were built to be translucent, their interiors rigged with an array of regular 100- and 150-watt household bulbs. We hung two lanterns to either end of the boat on which Bond stands to open up Daniel's face. Otherwise, I worked with the art department to outline the roof of the casino using a pattern of low-wattage golf-ball bulbs, a majority of the set being only a flat cutout. The casino and its lighting were then extended in post, as was the sky, the lake beyond, and the silhouette of the far hills. But we captured the bridge, the dragons, the front of the casino, and the large body of water surrounding it in camera, along with many of the fireworks.

Sam decided we would introduce the casino in one continuous shot, following Bond through the main body of the space and to the cashiers' counter. To finesse the camera move and lighting, I rehearsed on a weekend with our Steadicam operator, Peter Cavaciuti. Although we supplemented it, using a 12-foot ring of a dozen dimmed-down 2K open-face Blondes suspended above the gaming floor to give it an overall glow, the main source of light for all our shots came from the practical lamps that appear in frame. The lights that hang above the gaming tables were fitted with 2K quartz bulbs, and the inside of the shades were wrapped with a gold stipple reflective material. Other hanging lights were rigged with 1K bulbs, as were the square walkway lights specially manufactured for this set. We hung a row of paper lanterns to light Moneypenny (Naomie Harris) at the point where she first appears in the shot and rigged a strip of warm fluorescent light above the cashiers' counter. On the tables we placed a variety of glass candleholders that enclosed 250-watt bulbs, and we hid the wires by drilling through the tabletops. On the back walls we rigged small red lanterns to define but not light the walls, which were no more than red drapes hung in place.

The casino bar proved the one exception to the sole use of practical sources elsewhere. Although designed for the set, the lanterns did not, by themselves, light the conversation between Sévérine, played by Bérénice Marlohe, and Bond in an acceptable way—though "acceptable" is a subjective term. To shoot the actors as if lit by these lanterns, we ganged up a series of 2' × 2' gold stipple reflectors to form a U-shaped cove, then bounced 5 × Tweenies (650-watt Fresnel lamps) off them to create a soft but directional wrap of golden light. Once again, the warmth came from a combination of dimming the lamps, the bounce off the gold stipple reflector, and the addition of a light CTO gel to the front of each lamp.

Above the bridge that serves as the entrance of the casino, spanning a pit that's home to an irritable Komodo dragon, we designed a square of bulbs to fit into the ceiling of the set. These would light the final piece of action on the bridge, but the pit concerned me as it had no obvious light source. None, that is, until Dennis suggested he could add a small shrine, and I realized an array of double-wick votive candles might provide a solution. I would not have liked to be the one to light the candles had the dragon been real, but it was only a dummy, a "stuffie," which helped VFX replicate the lighting on their fully animated digital version.

Several scenes justified our choice to shoot *Skyfall* with a digital camera, none more than the casino and the glass offices that looked out on the jellyfish. I know I *could* have shot these on film, but as the Alexa recorded so much more detail in low light, it allowed me to rely far more on practical sources than I had on any previous film. But definition is only one element of image capture. I might have

achieved a similar image quality by shooting in anamorphic or in 65 mm, but both camera systems would have been bigger, heavier, and less easily maneuverable than our digital camera.

We shot *Skyfall* in London and Scotland over ninety-seven days and in Turkey for another twenty. The schedule was only three weeks longer than that for *Kundun*, for example, though it included more travel and complicated action sequences on both stage and location. As James and I soon found out, a Bond film is a roller-coaster ride, and once you start, you just hang on. The hope is that the scene you are shooting one day will seamlessly connect to the one that follows, even though they may shoot weeks apart from one another and, perhaps, in different countries.

The film climaxes at Bond's ancestral home, Scotland's Skyfall Lodge. We used the Highlands for footage of their journey but a moorland area twenty-seven miles west of London for the exterior of the Lodge itself. We had scouted a castle on the west coast of Scotland, but a combination of budgetary limitations, the need to house a large crew on a remote location, and the practical considerations of burning down both a historic castle and the forest that surrounded it led us to look for an alternative solution!

As our alternative we chose an army training area. Like our Salisbury Plain locations for *1917* a few years later, the site provided us with a broad, unspoiled landscape covered at that time of year with browned heather and dried grasses. This matched Scotland well, and a nearby hill bordered by forestry overlooking a flat expanse of moorland worked perfectly for the scripted action. VFX could add the distant mountains and the lake beyond the Lodge later.

Though Dennis built the exterior of Skyfall Lodge on location, the complexity of the action demanded that its interior be a set onstage. The downside: We would have no landscape outside the windows. The upside: We could control the light as the action moved from late afternoon through dusk and into night. Matching the look of our location work with that of our interior set, which was to include action with a helicopter at dusk, would be a challenge. But, by having control of an equivalent lamp, I could more easily time the movement of the beam of its spotlight to the action within the scene.

We first shot the buildup to the action sequence on location, luckily under perfectly overcast skies, before we moved to our stage work. As darkness descends, the view outside becomes less important than what happens inside, so I added some smoke and let the exterior blow out a little. For most of the scene, the windows are seen side on or out of focus in the background, so the slight "blooming" of the light in the smoke felt natural, while the interior felt a little darker in contrast

to the brightness of the outside. On a few occasions, where the windows are in focus and you would expect to see a view, VFX helped by compositing in a background. We never used a blue- or greenscreen for this, primarily because it would have destroyed the way the lighting worked on set, but there was little need as the window frames formed a clear matte line for postproduction work.

As the day turned to dusk, we changed the white backing that hung from the rail to a mid-gray while adding some quarter- or half-blue gel to the barn doors of the bounce lights. As we were using multiple lamps to light the backings, we could, by focusing an individual lamp on a small area of the bounce, control the angle from which the light entered each window. The camera would see the backing as a mid-gray but a lamp, spotted in and panned to the side of the camera's field of view,

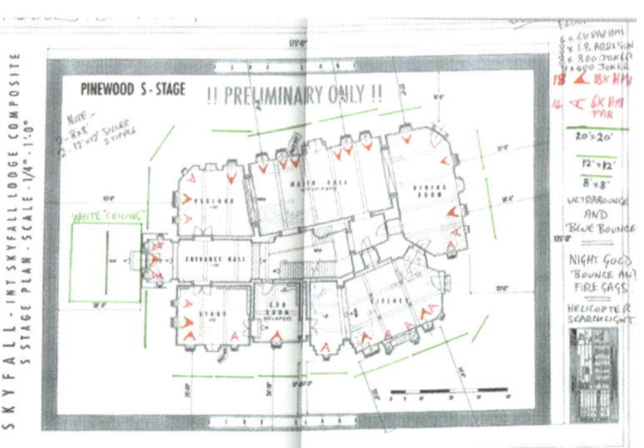

provides the source lighting for the shot. This was similar to the way I would later light Sapper Morton's farm in *Blade Runner 2049*. The camera sees an area that is not burnt-out while the characters are lit from a hot spot to one side.

As night falls and the bad guys enter the building, Biggles and I began adding extra blue gel to the HMI lamps bouncing off the now-gray backing. The shutters on the windows served a central role to both the action and the set design. But, as there was no valid reason for there to be any other source of light inside the building, I didn't want them to cut out all the daylight from the outside. To solve this, we used roughly made wooden shutters and widened some of the slits between the boards of their construction.

The shot of Silva exiting the helicopter and those that follow him were made on our second visit to our exterior set. To create the effect of the helicopter circling Skyfall Lodge onstage, we used a motorized track that carried an HMI 6K PAR lamp, set inside the rail used to hang our bounce material. We mounted the lamp using an underslung Power Pod remote head so that the beam could be panned toward a window and hold on it, as if it were the helicopter's spotlight searching for Bond. I left the camera setting at 4,000K throughout, and changed the blue saturation by using gels on the lamps, so that the color of the helicopter spotlight and the warmth of the firelight remained a constant as the twilight became more saturated.

The cold light of the PAR matched the light on the real helicopter and contrasted with the effects firelight that soon became an integral part of the scene. The explosions and the fires were specifically placed with reference to the overall action we had mapped out in advance. When I needed off-camera firelight, I generally used a flame bar rather than a lamp, as this was quick and easy to add into the mix.

On our exterior location, we filmed several passes with the Chinook helicopter in the very last light of day, shooting handheld as it was impossible to know what the helicopter was going to do or how Javier would react. The wind from the helicopter's rotor was so strong that it once blew out Javier's false teeth—those he wore for the role, I should add! While some of the close coverage of Silva was lit by the actual helicopter, we used a purpose-built lighting rig for other shots. Biggles had a crane constructed inside the shell of the Skyfall exterior able to rotate 360 degrees, while the lamp could be lowered or retracted on a pulley system that suspended it from the boom. The silhouette of the helicopter was later inserted by VFX against the fading light in the sky, and the boom of the crane painted out.

Chris Corbould manufactured a fully controllable fire rig that he had built into the construction of the set, much like the gas lines in the walls of *Barton Fink*'s burning corridor, though on a much larger scale. With this we could shoot all the action on location, including Bond exiting the tunnel with the burning set in the background. Once we had finished shooting with the actors, a second unit and a model unit completed the sequence, as the helicopter destroys Bond's Aston Martin DB5 and meets its own end in a fiery crash.

It always seemed that the sequence that follows Bond across the moor to his final encounter with Silva should be lit by a single light representing the burning Lodge. Talking with Sam, I suggested we could shoot the scene as we had the oil fires in *Jarhead*, and for the same reasons—more control and cheaper. But, with most of the studios in the UK at full capacity, our only viable option was to use a stage space 350 feet long but only about 100 feet wide. Ideally it would have been twice that, but it was the best option, being the only option.

Our characters would be running in a direct line away from the burning Skyfall, and the action was going to take place over some distance. As the inverse square law dictates, to maintain an even falloff between the beginning and end of the action, I needed my source to be as far away as possible. Given the size of the stage, I could afford only sixty feet between my source and the starting point, and the same distance between where it ended and the far stage wall. This left about 230 feet of set in which to stage the scene. Given that we could double back for some shots, this seemed manageable, but I would have to adjust the intensity of the light as the action moved down the "corridor" of our set.

Biggles and I selected twenty-four-bulb Maxi Brutes, Dinos, as our lamps. Arranging these in a pyramid shape allowed us to use the lower section of the rig to light the action at the beginning of the run while adding more intensity, using medium flood and spot bulbs, to the upper tiers of lamps as the action moved further away. We built a large frame of gel to cover the entire pyramid of thirty lamps and, to save a meltdown, secured it eight feet to its front. We cut the gel in vertical sections of ¼, ½, and ¾ CTO in an effort to break up the color and create a variation between the center and the outside.

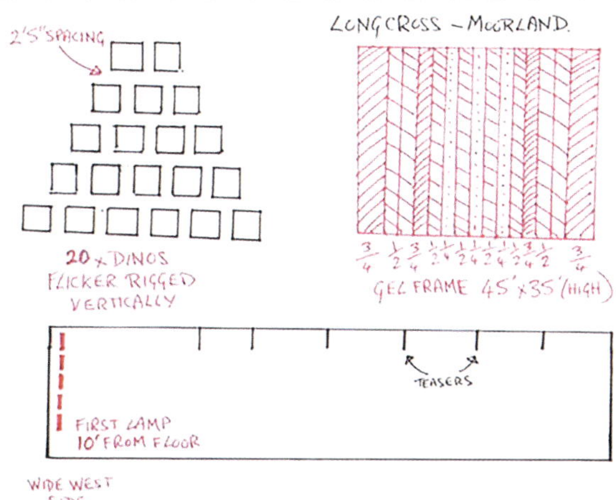

As we had for *Jarhead*, we filled the stage with smoke but restricted it as much as possible to the area around our light source. By using some atmosphere close to the lamps, I could mitigate any flare they might produce in the lens and soften the overall effect of the light. Besides, without the smoke there would have been no silhouette when shooting directly toward the lamps, only bright squares against a black hole.

Peter Cavaciuti was shooting the slower parts of the action on his Steadicam, so to get a little warm light into a character's face, I or an electrician walked backward with him carrying a ring light. This was a three-foot-six ring of half-inch plywood with a crosspiece attached to act as a handle. On the face of the ring, we mounted 40-watt bulbs at six-inch spacing, dimming them down to match the color of the firelight source. A hand-squeeze dimmer allowed us to randomly vary the intensity of the light as if the flicker of the fire.

To shoot some of the running shots we mounted the camera on a programmable wire rig supplied by Gavin Weatherall. This enabled the remotely operated camera to move at the same speed as the action while floating above the uneven ground of our set, a system that would again come in handy when we came to shoot *1917*.

The same night we shot the burning Skyfall on location we filmed the exterior of the church and graveyard. Only a two-wall set, the church stood across the valley from the Lodge at a distance that roughly represented the reality of the script but too far away for the fire to act as a light source (though with today's faster digital cameras that would not be the case). Instead, we rigged a 60-foot line of 12 × 12 Light Maxi Brutes only 250 feet from the church to serve as a stand-in for the burning set. It was a hell of a cheat, but what do you do?

The church interior was a stage set for which we built six 8' × 8' gold stipple reflectors and rigged them parallel to the church windows on the side of the set facing the Lodge. We evenly spaced a row of twelve 2K Blondes beneath the windows and pointed them up toward the reflectors, which were angled at 45 degrees to the set wall. Though the light this created was far too soft to be coming from the burning Skyfall Lodge, which at this distance would have appeared as if a point source, it felt right. I wanted the light to have a romantic quality that would contrast with the violence of the scene, though its deeper red—we had purposely dimmed the lamps for this effect—seemed to be appropriate to that violence. Perhaps I was looking to service two opposing thoughts!

Even now, we occasionally find ourselves talking to someone who can't believe we didn't shoot *Skyfall* on film. In the beginning, Sam and I discussed adding grain in post to make the image look more "filmic." For the same reason, Andrew Niccol and I had planned to add grain while making *In Time* but, on both occasions, we abandoned the plan. But what does "filmic" mean? Even decades after first being asked that question when applying to film school I *still* don't know the answer.

People think far too much about techniques and not enough about seeing.

HENRI CARTIER-BRESSON

27

WELCOME SHADOWS

There are dark shadows on the earth,
but its lights are stronger in the contrast.

CHARLES DICKENS

In 2011, I was asked to introduce the Quebecois director of the Oscar-nominated foreign film *Incendies*, Denis Villeneuve, to an evening gathering of Academy members. Neither James nor I had met Denis, but we'd loved *Incendies* and his previous films, particularly *Maelström*, which is narrated by a fish lying on a fishmonger's slab. We quickly discovered that Denis is passionate about film, highly imaginative, but also thoughtful and calm. He seemed like someone we would enjoy working with, so I asked my agent to put my name in the mix if the chance ever arose.

As luck would have it, Denis planned to make his debut in the United States with *Prisoners*, a dark psychological thriller about the kidnapping of two young girls and the passions stirred in its aftermath. When James and I read the script, we felt the film could be either an over-the-top gothic horror film or an edgy psychological thriller but, based on Denis's earlier work, we had every reason to think it would be the latter. Luck plays such a large part in one's career path, and it was only by chance that Denis was making this film at this moment and had yet to hire a cinematographer. I am always insecure when starting work on any film and especially so when I don't know its director. But sometimes it just seems to fit, and *Prisoners* would become one of my best experiences. I think I could say the same for James, Andy, Bruce Hamme, and gaffer Chris Napolitano, with whom I would be working for a ninth time. It was a bonus that Denis immediately understood the way James and I collaborate on a film.

We would be shooting the film in winter, but on our first scouting trip we found the region bathed in a beautiful, low sunlight. The dappled beams through the trees, the puffy white clouds against an azure sky—it was all quite lovely and exactly what we *didn't* want. But the scout taught us well.

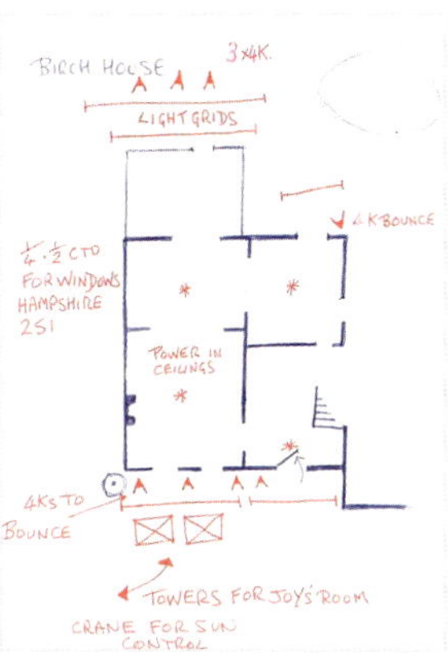

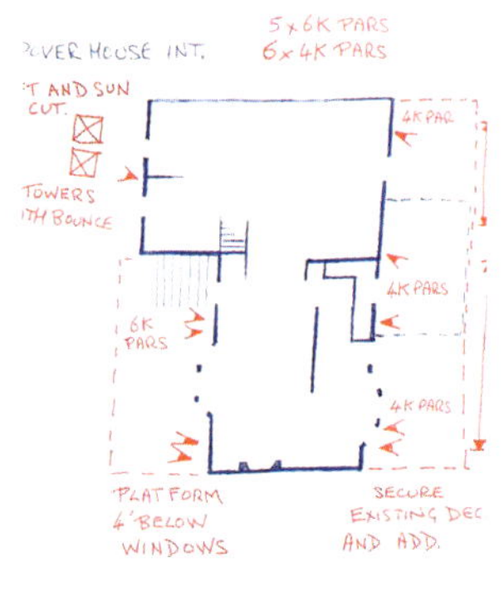

We'd be filming around the weather and our schedule needed to reflect that. Fortunately, the main cast was with us for the entirety of the shoot, which allowed us to have some flexibility. It wasn't quite the same experience as *Another Time, Another Place*, but for a Hollywood production, it came close.

There were other similarities between Mike Radford's and Denis's ways of working. Like Mike, Denis enjoyed the prep period. He was intensely focused on finding the right locations and would set aside time for Canadian production designer Patrice Vermette and me to talk through the script with him and to work on storyboards. Denis and I spent many hours walking through each sequence on location, accompanied by Patrice and our AD, Don Sparks. By the time we started shooting I had a rough sketch of the way Denis imagined staging each scene, and for some scenes we had fully drawn storyboards.

Whatever preparation you might do you can't change the weather, but by finding a small neighborhood on the outskirts of Atlanta that would provide the main settings for the film, we gave ourselves options. On sunny days we headed inside to shoot interiors, which included everything from the homes of the Dovers and Birches—the families of the kidnapped girls—to an abandoned apartment building where suspected kidnapper Alex Jones (Paul Dano) is held captive and tortured.

Each set had its own particular needs. Played by Viola Davis and Terrence Howard, the Birches live in a small house with low ceilings, so my lighting had to come from practical lights or from bounced daylight sources outside the windows. The only interior light I used, other than those seen within the frame, was a twin socket with two 60-watt globes hidden behind the ceiling light in the front room. To remain free to shoot regardless of the weather, I asked the art department to provide sheer curtains that would allow me to diffuse the windows and light through them to replicate daylight.

For the Dovers, played by Hugh Jackman and Maria Bello, we shot inside a different house than the one we used for exteriors. The split made shooting easier as we could light the one set for interior work and hold it in place while we shot exteriors. This would not only provide weather cover but, as it had on *A Serious Man*, allow us to move from exterior to interior without waiting for the set to be lit.

From all our discussions, I made a map of each location denoting the basic angles from which the camera would see the set and my proposed lighting. These were especially useful when Chris and I worked on the extended chase through the backyards of our neighborhood, through the forest and to the freeway. Given my distaste for simulating "moonlight" when there are alternative options and imagining much of the neighborhood bathed in darkness, Chris and I arranged practical lights as if triggered by motion sensors to reveal an intruder on a back porch or a barking dog.

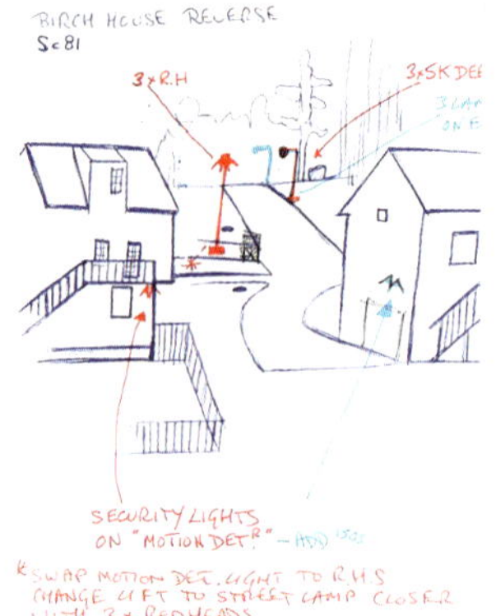

BIRCH HOUSE REVERSE
Sc 81
3 x R.H
SECURITY LIGHTS
ON "MOTION DET^R"
SWAP MOTION DET. LIGHT TO R.H.S
CHANGE LEFT TO STREET LAMP CLOSER
WITH 3 x REDHEADS
STREET LAMP DEEPER WITH 3 x RED HEADS

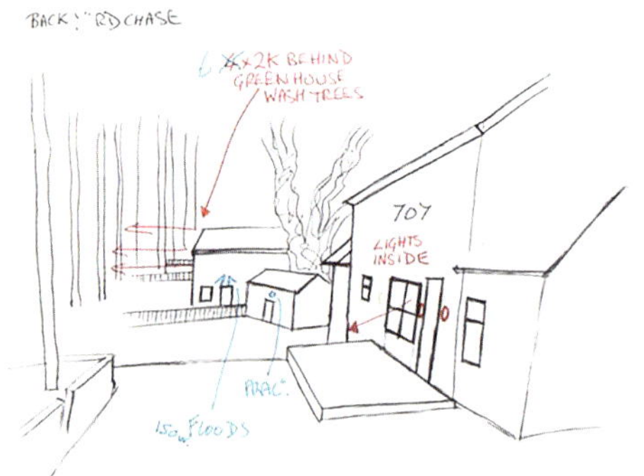

GREEN HOUSE
WASH TREES
707
LIGHTS
INSIDE
PRAC.
FLOODS

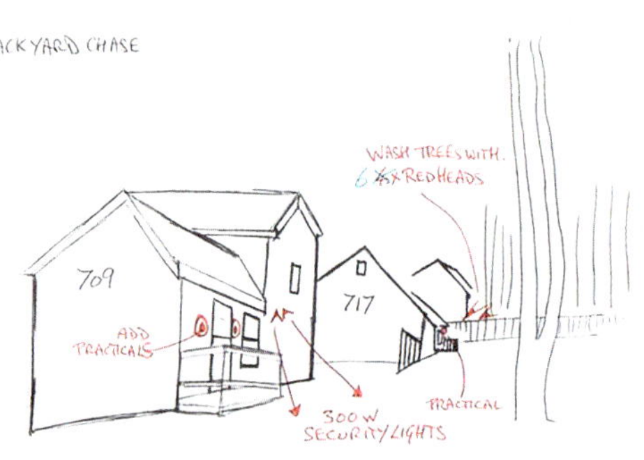

BACKYARD CHASE
WASH TREES WITH
REDHEADS
709
717
ADD
PRACTICALS
300 W
SECURITY LIGHTS
PRACTICAL

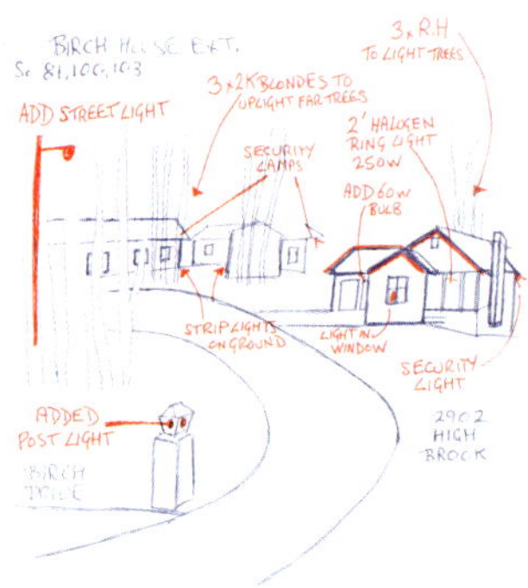

3 x R.H
TO LIGHT TREES
3 x 2K BLONDES TO
UPLIGHT FAR TREES
ADD STREET LIGHT
2' HALOGEN
RING LIGHT
250W
SECURITY
LAMPS
ADD 60W
BULB
STRIP LIGHTS
ON GROUND
LIGHT IN
WINDOW
SECURITY
LIGHT
ADDED
POST LIGHT
2902
HIGH
BROCK

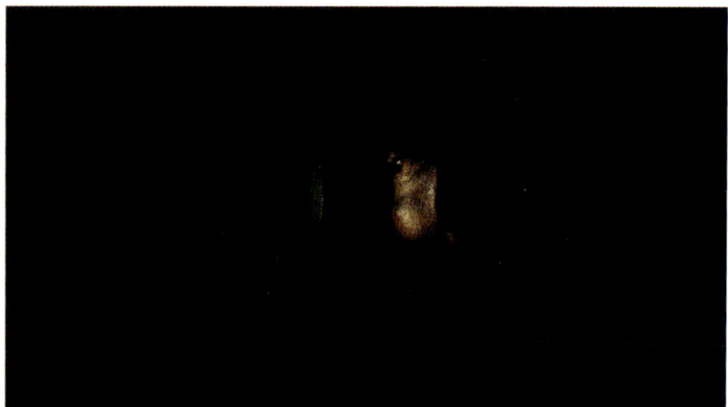

Sometimes you'd never *dream* of using the interiors of a location no matter how perfect the exterior. We did find the perfect abandoned apartment building next to our chosen liquor store's parking lot, but the inside was unsafe for us to scout in, let alone for a crew to work in. The alternative? A standing set that could be lit and ready to shoot, one built inside a warehouse that not only allowed Denis and Patrice to control its layout, but that also served as one more weather cover option.

Although I had not worked with Denis before, I soon realized that he welcomed shadows. He was also willing for a character in the foreground to be in focus as a dark shape or to keep a character out of focus entirely, as can be seen in Keller Dover's dream.

Denis would let a dramatic scene, as when Keller breaks the sink with a hammer, play out in one observational wide shot, giving the audience no escape from the emotion of the moment. Too often a director will use multiple angles in a similar scene, the tension falling away with every edit. Death by a thousand cuts!

Or he might suggest a shot that confounds everyone. While shooting the exterior of the Birch house, and struggling to complete the day's schedule, Denis suggested one last shot—a slow track toward a tree trunk! Despite some protests from production at the lateness of the hour, we completed the shot in the fading light of the day and Denis's idea, which seemed so arbitrary at the time, led to one of the most tense and effective shots of all.

One pivotal location, the gas station where Detective Loki (Jake Gyllenhaal) arrests Alex, presented more of a challenge. The script called for a highway rest stop rather than a brightly lit gas station but, recalling a roadside scene in *Revolutionary Road*, this gave me pause. For the earlier film I had our art department provide three fluorescent-style streetlamps that both appeared in shot and justified the light source. I could do something similar but felt *Prisoners* needed something more graphic, a pool of light surrounded by darkness, with the suspect's RV being parked to one side in the shadows. Searching online, I found an image of a small Hopperesque gas station that seemed an interesting alternative and showed it to Denis. He warmed to the idea but was concerned that the RV be in the shadows close to a wooded area, as scripted. Finding such a gas station with a wooded parking lot, on a road that we could control at night and with space for the cranes we would need for a rain effect, would be a tall ask for our location scouts.

But find it they did. The spot was a little larger than the ideal Denis and I imagined, but with a parking lot bordered by woodland. That the location was virtually lit was a bonus, too. Though Chris did change out some of the mercury vapor lamps above the pumps, which were old and had become discolored, add some fluorescent strips to outline the side of the store, and position a few small HMIs to pick out a billboard, we could save rigging time here and use it elsewhere.

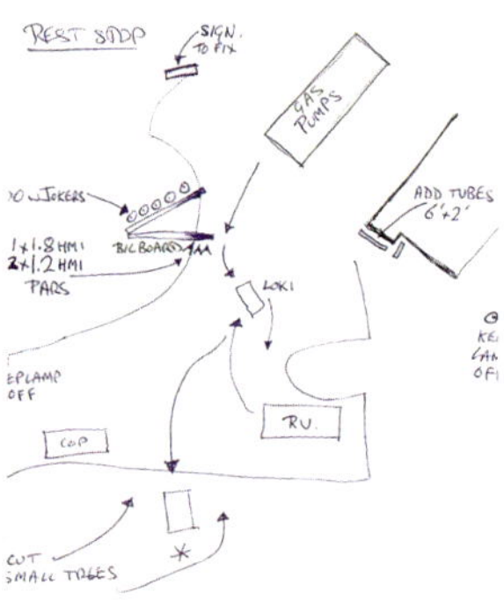

The scenes at the Jones house, where Alex lives with his mother, Holly (Melissa Leo), gave me the most trouble, but it was the sort of trouble that keeps the job interesting. For me, a scene doesn't have to involve spectacular action or a dramatically visual location to offer a challenge. It's the drama within a scene that inspires me, the interplay of the characters with the camera and the light. The street outside had no existing light sources, which can be a blessing or a curse. I added some simple practical sources to the outside of the house and asked the art department to provide a few streetlights to position along the road. I used these only to justify the sickly sodium-colored light I would use to pick out the characters as the isolation of the house was a key element of the story, and the threat implied by the surrounding darkness helped to emphasize that isolation.

The interior of the Joneses' house is a mix of colors, a range of fluorescent lights and old tungsten fixtures, some of which came with the location; others, such as the bare fluorescent tube in the kitchen, we rigged ourselves. To the rear of the house, we used the glassed-in conservatory that faces the abandoned car as the main light source, mounting a double row of cool green fluorescent tubes on the ceiling inside. By using a set of matching tubes, set on stands along the roof line, we were able to "cheat" this source to project a greenish wash of light over the characters at the car that's parked above the pit in which Dover becomes trapped. Other than lighting some trees to create depth, I allowed the backgrounds to go completely dark in contrast to the bright practical sources.

And sometimes just a key fob was enough to light a scene.

For the film's final scene, as the forensic team is finishing and Detective Loki drives up, Patrice and I felt we could justify two banks of work lights. I specifically wanted mercury vapor lights as they would also give a cool, harsh light. As they turn off, Loki is left in silence, with the conservatory now serving as the sole light source. From out of the shadows, Loki finally hears the whistle. At the request of the production company, Alcon Entertainment, we shot two potential endings. In the unused ending Loki joins Keller in the hole. This was not Denis's preferred version as it eliminated any ambiguity, whether Loki would rescue Keller or not. But Alcon, known for the founders Andrew Kosove and Broderick Johnson's strong support of the filmmaker, promised to use whichever ending tested higher. And they stuck to their word!

With our next film, *Unbroken*, James would take on an even bigger role, evolving to deal with the complexities of the digital era. Present every day, she plays many roles and interacts with members of the production at every level, yet it was not until *Sicario* that a producer, who had worked with us previously and knew her role, insisted on adding her to the crew list. With a film negative there are limited ways to print the image, but with a digital file the options are seemingly endless. I had always overseen every step of the photochemical process, but in the world of pixels James oversees what is a far more complex chain of events: first making sure the camera settings and DIT (digital imaging tech) monitors are correctly calibrated, that the digital file is transferred with the correct color space, that the image is timed to reflect what we are capturing on set, and then following that image all the way through post into the DI suite.

We are all visitors to this time, this place.
We are just passing through.

AUSTRALIAN ABORIGINAL SAYING

Unbroken would take James and me Down Under for five months, to film an epic that was scripted by Joel and Ethan but to be directed by Angelina Jolie, who had likened it to *The Bridge on the River Kwai*. It was a challenging project, not least because Australia's box jellyfish can be deadly, and we were attempting to shoot extended sequences in and on the water. Those ended up in a tank surrounded by bluescreen. Our B-24 bomber was purpose-built in Mexico and never left the ground. We staged the Berlin 1936 Olympics in a Sydney sports park and Naoetsu, the notorious Japanese prison camp, on Cockatoo Island, within sight of the Opera House and constantly surrounded by pleasure yachts and sightseeing vessels. Strange things can happen when making a film.

James and I hoped to work with Angelina for a second time on *Africa*, the story of Richard Leakey and the famous paleoanthropologist's crusade to save the wildlife of Kenya. I would have loved to return to Africa with James, to show her some of the continent where I'd worked extensively early in my career, but the familiar "creative differences," this time between Angie and the studio, got in the way. My last visit to the continent, to South Africa and Mozambique with Danny Glover, had been in search of locations for a film about the eighteenth-century Haitian revolution led by Toussaint Louverture. The fortified town and slave port on the Island of Mozambique, once the capital of Portuguese East Africa, proved a perfect fit for our needs, but the project would go no further. Why a film does or doesn't get made is a mystery. As it turned out, James and I were on our way to the Mexican border.

28

THE LAND OF WOLVES

You're asking me how a watch works.
For now we'll just keep an eye on the time.

ALEJANDRO, IN *SICARIO*

As with *Prisoners*, we felt our second film with Denis could have gone the wrong way, had it been another director. Written by Taylor Sheridan, *Sicario* explores the influence of the Mexican drug cartels and the escalating violence on both sides of the border between the United States and Mexico. It's a brutal story that in other hands might have felt exploitative or reactionary rather than becoming the complex, challenging film James and I knew Denis would make.

One of the benefits of working with a director for a second time is that you have a better understanding of his or her process. Denis and I had such a good experience during prep for *Prisoners* that he wanted to repeat the way we had explored the script together on *Sicario*, only this time he might lock his production office door when he didn't want us to be interrupted. Denis loves to think in images, and our discussion would sometimes lead to a scene being dropped, dialogue being cut, or a change of location. Films change from the script, through budgeting, scouting, storyboarding, and rehearsals, and on set when the actors and the day bring their own inspiration. But it's not until the final edit that the film becomes what it is.

Sicario was an unusual film in that it was a story told from the point of view of two characters, Kate Macer (Emily Blunt), an FBI agent still clinging to her ideals as she's drawn into a situation defined by moral compromise, and the enigmatic Alejandro (Benicio Del Toro). Denis was concerned with how the film would transition between one and the other. One scene we shot, for instance, on the beach in Veracruz, establishing Alejandro's identity and his relationship with the CIA operative Matt Graver (Josh Brolin), came too early in the story and was cut. I tell Denis that he cut my favorite scene, but I am joking. It was a great scene, but the film is so much stronger without it.

Denis enjoys location scouting (not all directors do), which, for him, becomes the source of many new ideas. We visited El Paso hoping to shoot on the Bridge of the Americas but, as with *No Country for Old Men*, we needed an alternative for our border crossing. From our storyboards, Patrice Vermette could see that we needed customs booths and a road leading into the United States. He realized the wide shots could be made from a helicopter on the real location while, with minimal CG work in post, he could turn a parking lot, usually used by hot-air balloonists, into a border crossing. In doing so he gave us total control over the scene. Going to Mexico was another problem. But after discussing all the alternatives with the producers, passionately referencing the colorful developing country described in the script and our detailed action storyboards, we were granted shooting time in Mexico City, rather than trying to simulate Ciudad Juarez on the streets of Albuquerque or Fort Lauderdale, as had been suggested. The bodies hanging from the overpass were, however, digital additions and referenced on our shoot with sandbags. The reality of the scene was too vivid a memory for the people living there.

The ordinary-looking suburban neighborhood that now appears in the film's opening scene was a challenge to find. We were based in Albuquerque, one of the fastest-growing cities in the United States, but we needed a specific sort of house, one part of a neighborhood surrounded by the desert but, given the events that are about to be revealed to have taken place inside, also partially removed from its neighbors. We had hoped to find a house that could work for both exteriors and interiors, but our preferred exterior would have involved compromising Denis's idea for the layout of the interior. Also, to shoot inside the location would have involved destroying someone's actual home to make room for all the prop corpses!

As always when shooting onstage, a balance must be drawn between the budget of the film and the desire to see the exterior landscape from inside a set. For *Sicario* this would be particularly important as we were staging action that directly connected the interior with the exterior. Patrice and I decided the best and most straightforward approach would be to use a landscape backing combined with a false perspective version of the backyard that existed on location. The existence of the concrete wall surrounding the yard was a piece of luck as it allowed us to hide the "join" between our three-dimensional onstage set piece and the photorealistic backing depicting the hillside and sky beyond.

It's usually an advantage to have as much space outside a set window as possible, but there is a trade-off between the extent of that space and what the camera will see at the top of frame. Given the height of the stage and what our widest shots would see, we reduced the size of the backyard onstage

by half, placing a scaled-down wall twenty-five feet from the house and the backing another five feet beyond that. This was the best compromise we could find between our need to look out from inside the set and the action to be staged outside the windows.

We used an overhead array of Spacelites to light both the exterior yard and the backing. A front-lit backing, such as we used here on *Sicario*, is best lit softly, and here it required no specific lighting. Chris took six T12 Fresnel lamps to create beams of direct sunlight entering through the tract house windows and hallway skylights. Each lamp had to be separated from the others to avoid double shadows, which was done using extended barn doors rather than flags. We did it this way so that the angle of the lamps could be easily adjusted, as if the sunlight had shifted direction from one scene to another. The windows to the back of the house, which we never saw out of, were surrounded by light grid diffusion frames, covered with a secondary layer of light frost and backlit using an array of 2K Blondes.

Chris Napolitano and I had scouted the exterior location and mapped the sun's path during the day. Having worked with Denis on the storyboards, I could plan our shots so that the angle of the sun would match from the interior to the exterior. For instance, onstage we pan with Emily as she is about to exit into the yard. As she goes through the door the shed explodes and she is blown backward into the set. We shot the explosion at the exterior location. Onstage, we erected a small bluescreen to fill the background, which becomes visible only when the camera looks along the length of the exterior, and we used a charge as well as air blowers to stand in for the effect of the explosion on Emily.

Both before and after the explosion, the scene cuts between inside and out, so it was important that the sunlight on the set was coming from a similar direction as on location.

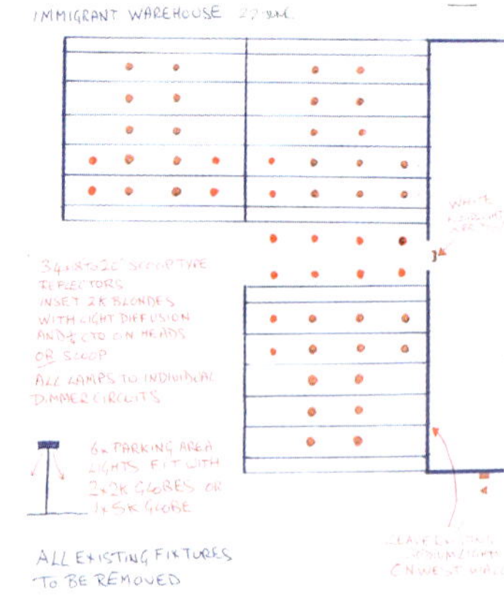

The film follows Kate's journey to places she'd never otherwise see, including a warehouse used as a nighttime holding pen for undocumented immigrants who've been caught crossing the border. When we scouted this location, the building was being used to store fertilizer so, although it had a great look, cleaning it up seemed impractical. But, after much searching, it proved to be our best option. The existing lighting consisted of a few low-wattage mercury vapor lights, nothing I could use to represent a high-security government building.

As always, I wanted to light the space with fixtures that would not only light the scene but appear natural when on camera, defining the space rather than spilling light across the walls and the ceiling. I asked Patrice if we could manufacture some simple aluminum reflectors inside which I could mount a 2K open-face lamp. Using them in multiples, I could create a large soft source that would also be confined to the central area of the location. My concern was the height of the roof and the exposure I could achieve using a minimal number of fixtures. I considered suspending lamps on chains but dismissed the idea. Although it might have looked natural and would certainly have given me a more manageable exposure, I didn't want the lights to distract from the very aspects of the location that Denis and I liked, particularly its openness.

Photometric charts come in handy. Looking at the specs for a 2K Blonde, I could see that a single lamp at full flood from a distance of fifty feet would give me a stop of around 2.0 on the Alexa at 800 ASA. This gave me little room to play with and left me with some real concerns given the size of the space. Our schedule was tight, so Patrice and his art department went ahead with finding a manufacturer to make scoops to house the 2Ks while Chris and I worked on a plan.

The original idea consisted of thirty-four scoop lights, each with a diameter of 20 inches, but following a prelight Chris and I did one night after work, a little more than a week before the scheduled shooting date for this set, we added a few more.

The light from the twenty-four lamps the rigging crew had put in place for our prelight appeared soft, and the multiple shadows from so many single sources were hardly noticeable. But it did surprise me how small the fixtures looked. I had been right to be concerned about the size of the space. I was getting a stop of only 1.4, which would have been fine had I not wanted to add some light diffusion to the face of the scoops and dim them. Our original order expanded to fifty-four lights, giving us a shooting stop of 1.8, which was adequate given we were working with the Master Prime lenses and could rate the Alexa at 1,200 rather than its standard 800 ASA. Adding the diffusion to the face of the scoops not only softened the edge of the beam but allowed the camera to look directly toward the fixtures without any lens flare. And, again, I am not a fan of lens flare!

We never burnt the 2K Blondes at 100 percent, setting the central lamps at around 90 percent and dimming those to the sides to about 70 percent. This filled the space with a warm glow that became both brighter and a little whiter closer to the center. Other than a few small sodium lights we added to the wall outside, the entire scene was shot under this one light source with little additional floor lighting. As with the "chandelier" for the synagogue in *A Serious Man*, this proved to be both a practical and, as it allowed us to shoot the scene quickly, a cheap solution.

Not all our locations needed so much thought. The interrogation room was part of an abandoned military complex, the inside of which was lit by four-foot, stained, yellow fluorescent fixtures. They looked perfect to me (though I'm not sure what the studio executive who called me in Kenya from the Pacific Coast Highway would have made of them). Chris added one more fixture to the ceiling in the interrogation room and, using old diffusers and yellow gel, made sure all the others in the corridor matched the same sickly look.

Some of the most suspenseful scenes in *Sicario* involve a nighttime raid through an underground tunnel used by the cartel to smuggle drugs across the border.

For the opening of the sequence, which sees the team ready themselves for their reconnaissance of the cross-border tunnel, we chose a location facing west, less than a mile from our Albuquerque studio base. This not only allowed us to shoot at the end of a full day of shooting onstage, but also to jump to it when we had the right weather.

When Denis and I discussed the film, and the night work in particular, it became obvious that the audience should not be allowed to see more than the characters, as they were wearing night vision goggles for a reason. To approach the scene as a regular night shoot, with an artificial "moonlight," made no sense. Denis agreed that the sequence could play out as a series of POVs, as if seen through the night vision goggles that all the team members were to wear. His one qualification was to have Alejandro's point of view look different from the others, so that the audience could recognize his specific POV.

The regular image intensifiers that give the grainy green cast familiar to any soldier or hunter, as I'd used on *Courage Under Fire,* were a given.

And, when thinking about Alejandro's POV, I recalled the great Soviet film *I Am Cuba* and the wonderful sequence set on a sugar plantation shot on infrared film stock. Of course, there are plenty of digital infrared cameras on the market that can be used to find a leak or an overheating electrical circuit, all of which produce an array of images in glorious psychedelic colors. But none would give me the resolution I was after, and both Denis and I liked the stark look of black-and-white. To cut a long story short, James did a little research and came across a company called FLIR that had the perfect camera and were willing to go all out to support us.

For the last section of the sequence, which plays almost entirely from Alejandro's perspective, our standby prop heated a pair of boots with a blowtorch before each take. When the lead character walked down the stairs and into the tunnel, his footprints left a heat signal on the ground, which was easily picked up by our infrared camera.

To light for the green night vision, I bounced a 1K Fresnel off a 12' × 12' reflector that was rigged on a fifty-foot crane over one hundred feet from the action. Without *some* lighting the image was

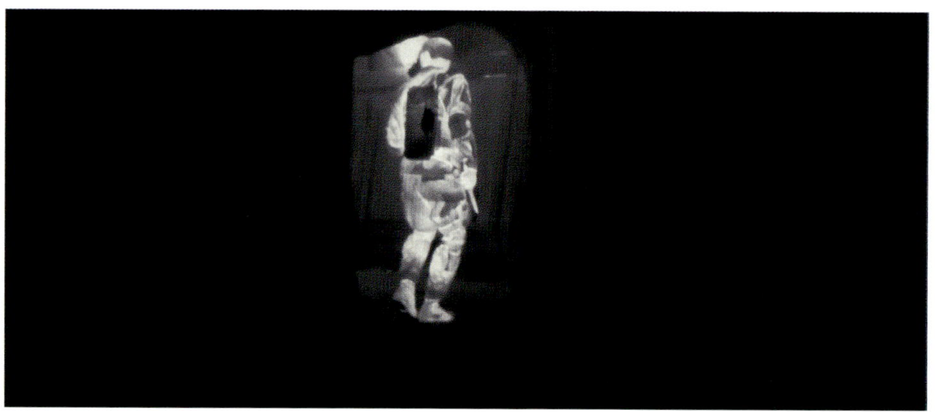

a little too flat and very noisy, so I lit the scene with the most minimal lighting I have ever used at night. Of course, this lighting made no difference to the heat-sensitive infrared camera and hardly helped the actors as their goggles were only props. They were performing in true darkness and doing their best not to trip on the rugged terrain while doing so.

As the Coens and I had done on *Fargo*, we split *Sicario*'s night-driving scenes into those we could shoot onstage and those we really did have to shoot on the road at night. I lit both versions very simply, using a four-foot fluorescent tube sitting on the hood of each vehicle to mimic light from the headlamps bouncing off the road ahead. To get the feeling of movement when shooting Silvio's (Maximiliano Hernandez) police car onstage, we mounted a few lights on dollies and tracked them across the background. The lamps, 150-watt Peppers or 100-watt Inkys ("Inky" being from "dinky," meaning small), were both dimmed and reduced in size to look like point sources far away, although they were only about twenty feet from the car.

Having kidnapped Diaz, Alejandro has him drive to the luxurious villa of his cartel boss, Fausto Alarcón (Julio César Cedillo). For this section of the driving, we used the same technique but with a cool four-foot tube on the hood of his car to differentiate Diaz's vehicle from Silvio's.

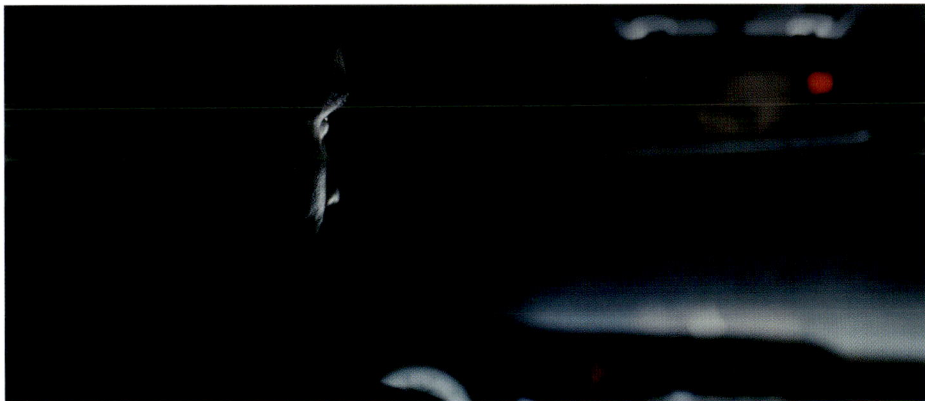

For Fausto's hacienda we were lucky to find a newly constructed building set on a suburban estate that had to be approached via a semiprivate, tree-lined road. This suited our sequence as all we had to do was avoid the surrounding houses to make the road appear as if it belonged to a single property. We would be seeing the driveway and house from a distance as well as from multiple closer angles, so it was obvious that any lighting would appear in picture and would need to be designed into the architecture. It also felt important that the house look a little over-the-top wealthy. Denis had rejected the location at first because it didn't look that expansive and fancy, so, as with Andrew Dominik's "toy train," the lighting would have to help.

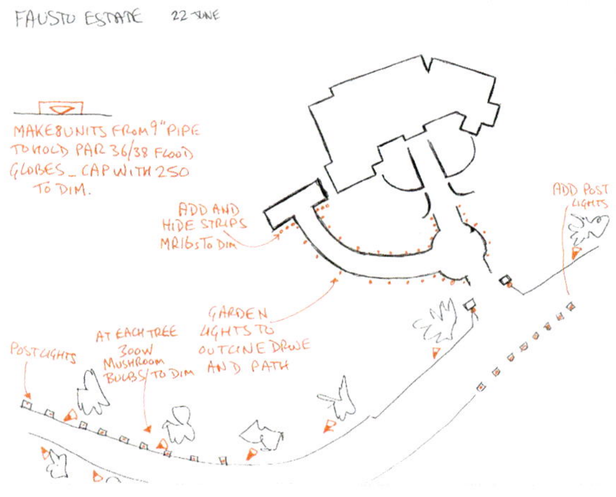

Sometimes you get lucky. When scouting the space with Denis and Patrice we initially dismissed the idea of an open exterior, but all three of us were drawn back to the same space. In the dark and in its own pool of light, it could appear to be a private, sacrosanct family space. I think it was the image of Alejandro stepping out through the screen doors of the main house and walking directly across the lawn toward the family at their dinner that ultimately convinced Denis to use it, even to the point of agreeing with production to reduce the number of our shooting days for the sequence (we would have to shoot at night). Denis felt confident in cutting our shoot time as the scene had been shortened considerably during our storyboarding process. A long conversation was cut from the scene and, instead of Alejandro letting Fausto's children leave the dinner table before he shoots his wife, the scene now plays out a little differently.

To help the shooting go even faster, I had a piece of luck in the form of the temporary lighting the owner of the location had strung up on the ceiling of this "dining room": a simple strand of golf-ball bulbs from Home Depot. It seemed perfect, so we bought another string that matched, and the scene was lit!

The final sequence of *Sicario* is one of my favorites of any film I have worked on. Denis rehearsed at length with Emily and Benicio, both before the day of the shoot and on that same morning, to ensure that the final confrontation between Alejandro and Kate felt right for the moment and in character for each actor. As we had several scenes inside the apartment, and

because the interior of our chosen location had a floor plan that wasn't appropriate for the scripted action, Patrice built a set. For scheduling reasons, the location shots of Emily on the balcony were made more than a week before the interior scenes onstage. But by the time we came to shoot these exteriors we had a clear idea of the angles we wanted and, thankfully, we had a night shoot on the same location. This enabled us to take a late call and shoot our day work in the more dramatic afternoon light typical of New Mexico during, what was by then, midsummer.

The shot from inside the apartment looking out implies someone is watching Kate as she lights her cigarette. Kate turns to the window, sensing something is wrong, but she cannot see inside and just stares at her own reflection. The camera pushes in a little to enhance the moment before it cuts to Kate in close-up, continuing the same slight push in.

Patrice and I discussed using a backing onstage, but as the camera is seeing Kate in a full shot I was not too concerned with the exterior view. Besides, I liked the clear silhouette of the figure against the pattern of the curtains we had specifically chosen for the shot. Perhaps, ideally, I would have liked a vague sense of the trees outside, but there were more important things to spend our budget on, not the least of which was our wish to shoot Mexico for Mexico. This set could be done simply.

When we began to block the crucial scene in the kitchen, what started as complex became quite simple. Instead of standing to confront Emily, perhaps continually moving around her as if studying his prey, Benicio felt his character would appear more threatening if he were relaxed and seated as Kate comes in. Then, to increase the threat, he suggested just the one movement from a stool at the counter to a chair placed opposite Emily at the kitchen table. At the same time, I suggested some adjustments to the positions of the stool and table that I felt would work best for our coverage and for the way the light would fall on each character. I liked that Kate could be sitting with her back to the wall and in a frontal light. She appeared more vulnerable that way and a little trapped. Alejandro would appear more sinister, shadowed and never in full light.

This simple blocking not only focused the camera on the expressions of the characters, it also allowed us to make a slow push in on Kate, which we felt would increase the tension within the scene. We began with a matching move toward Benicio, but Denis felt that, in contrast with Kate, we should remain locked with his character. To do a matching move on both characters, in such a way as allows for fluid cutting between similar-size shots, the timing of the move on one angle needs to match the timing on the other, and to do this the dolly grip has to be almost as familiar with the dialogue as the actors. Bruce had done similar moves a great many times since *The Shawshank Redemption*, but here it became unnecessary, as Alejandro, through his movements, is growing ever closer to Emily and to the camera.

The shot of Silvio's son standing by his father's bed is a deliberate reprise of the earlier scene with his father. We shot on location and, as there was little room between the window and the wall of the next building, I used a mirror to get a longer throw from a 6K HMI PAR and mimic the sunlight that I felt would enhance the sadness of the moment. Later, in the shadow of the border wall (or a CGI rendition of the wall) we see the boy playing football with his friends. While their mothers look on, gunfire rings out and, for a moment, the crowd looks toward the sound. But the violence is just part of life here and nothing has changed with the killing of Fausto. It is, for me, a shot that says everything in a perfectly simple way.

You are not a wolf. And this is the land of wolves now.

ALEJANDRO, IN *SICARIO*

HAIL, CAESAR!

History! Sociology! Politics! Morality! Everything! It's all in a book called Capital*—with a* K.

BAIRD WHITLOCK, IN *HAIL, CAESAR!*

I sometimes take time to consider signing on to a project, but I didn't hesitate with *Hail, Caesar!* Set in Hollywood in the 1950s, the comedy would feature homages to a variety of films from the golden age of the studio system: singing cowboy Westerns, high-society comedies of manners, Esther Williams spectacles, Gene Kelly musicals, and biblical epics, all tied together by the real-life studio Mr. Fixit, Eddie Mannix (Josh Brolin).

Given the period nature of the project, Joel and Ethan wanted to shoot on film, but that didn't help us re-create the different looks of the 1950s. We couldn't, for instance, shoot the elaborate dockside bar dance sequence, featuring Channing Tatum as the secretly communist musical star Burt Gurney, using three-strip Technicolor because the process had not been used in decades. Creating its saturated colors would have to be done in camera, by way of the sets and costumes. For all the movies within the movie, the look would have to be created through the use of traditional styles of lighting I usually eschewed. It was a unique and fun challenge, one that I enjoyed all the more because of the cast and crew that the Coen brothers gathered around them. Nancy Haigh, the Coens' longtime set decorator, Chris Napolitano, and I went to all the Hollywood prop suppliers to pull lamps, stands, dollies, and old pieces of camera equipment out of storage, some that I had never seen and that hadn't been used for years. We even uncovered a backing from *Ben-Hur* to use in a scene depicting the making of the biblical epic that gives the film its title!

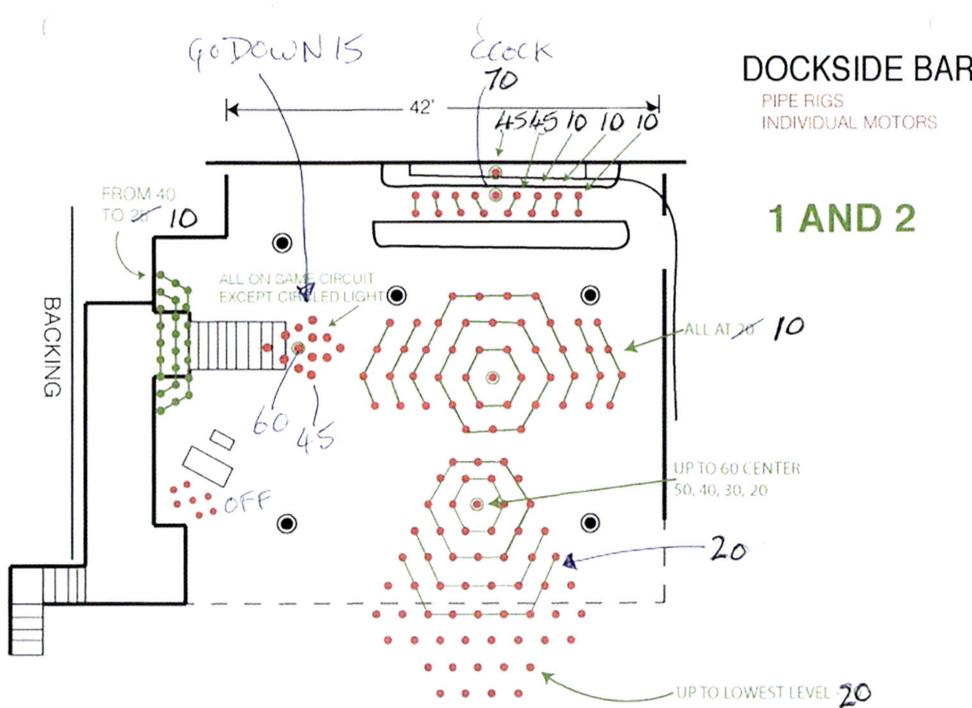

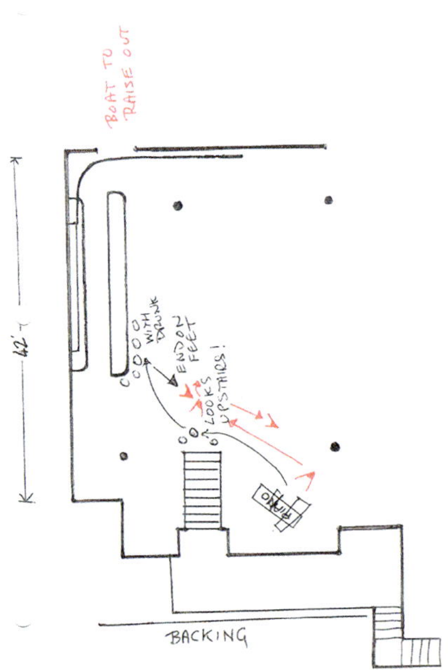

The musical dance routine was a classic of the 1950s, and *Hail, Caesar!* had to have its own. For this Jess Gonchor, our production designer, built a set with a retractable floor and other elements of the traditional way of shooting such a scene. During rehearsals, which were extensive, we broke down the scene into sections and individual shots. From this Chris and I could make our own schematics (there were nine drawings representing each section of the choreography) that laid out the way the lighting would vary alongside the action and camera shots. In this case the lights that appear in camera are only there as props, and the scene is lit using an array of 650 Fresnel lamps (Tweenies), all of which are individually controlled by a programmed dimmer board.

The biblical epic, the military-industrial complex, and the Red Scare: *Hail, Caesar!* touches on them all. But the scene in which Burt defects to the Soviets by submarine is one of my favorites. The commie's escape is part of reality in the story but, like many of the scenes in *Hail Caesar!*, reality starts looking like a movie. Chris and I had a lot of fun working that one out. We shot this on the same 90' × 100' indoor tank as our Esther Williams–inspired swimming routine, on Stage 30 at Sony Studios, the very stage used by Esther in the 1930s. Although none of our rig appears as part of the scene, this being reality, Chris and I decided to use direct sources from an overhead green bed (a lighting platform surrounding the stage), as would have been the practice in the 1950s. Unlike cinematographers of that period, we had the advantage of shooting on a 500 ASA film stock, faster than what would have been available to them, and also with faster lenses. But 500 ASA or not, it still took a lot of lamps to reach a stop of 2.0 on the lens.

We hung three painted backings for the sky behind Jess Gonchor's wooden submarine but not one overlapped another, nor did they make a seamless connection with the water. So, even though we could hide one join behind the conning tower, every shot needed some help from our VFX team. And they did "paint" in the moon (though not exactly in line with my "moonlight" reflection) for the Coens' homage to Leutze's famous painting of George Washington crossing the Delaware!

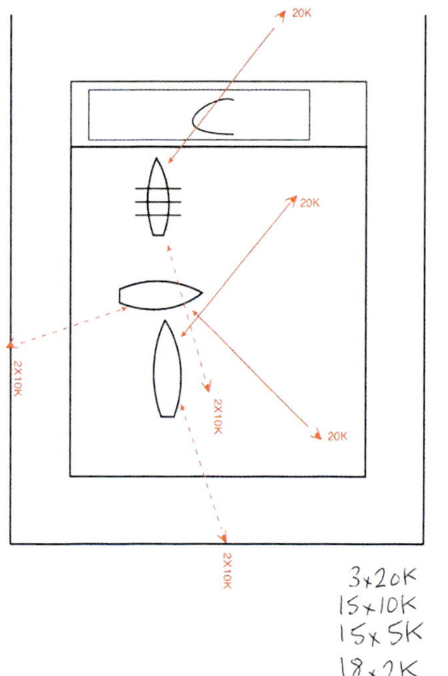
SC. 68 SUBMARINE
LIGHTING DIRECTIONS
20K
20K
2X10K
2X10K
20K
2X10K
3x20K
15x10K
15x5K
18x2K

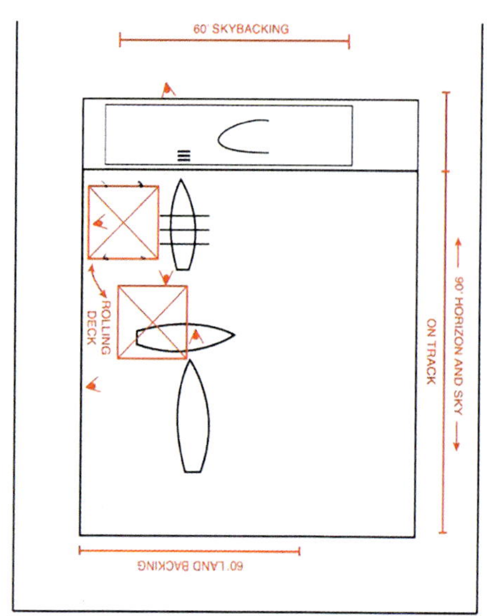
SC 68 SUBMARINE
CAMERA POSITIONS
60' SKYBACKING
ROLLING DECK
90' HORIZON AND SKY
ON TRACK
60' LAND BACKING

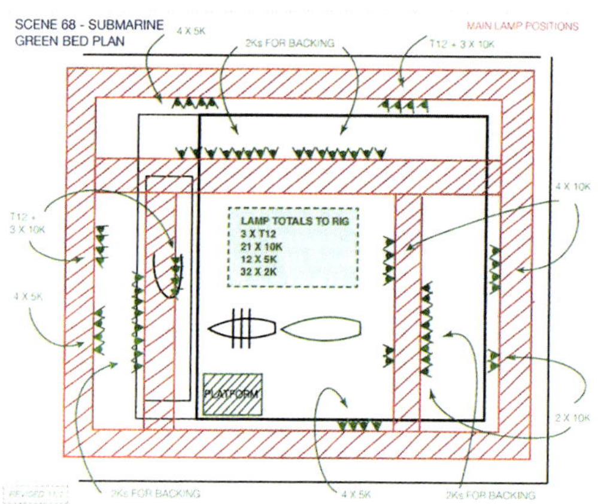
SCENE 68 - SUBMARINE
GREEN BED PLAN
4 X 5K
2Ks FOR BACKING
MAIN LAMP POSITIONS
T12 + 3 X 10K
4 X 10K
T12 +
3 X 10K
LAMP TOTALS TO RIG
3 X T12
21 X 10K
12 X 5K
32 X 2K
4 X 5K
PLATFORM
2 X 10K
2Ks FOR BACKING
4 X 5K
2Ks FOR BACKING

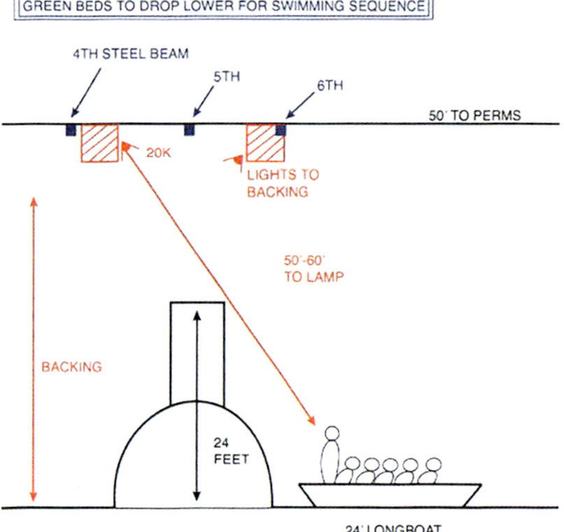
SC 68 SUBMARINE
GREEN BEDS TO DROP LOWER FOR SWIMMING SEQUENCE
4TH STEEL BEAM
5TH
6TH
50' TO PERMS
20K
LIGHTS TO
BACKING
50'-60'
TO LAMP
BACKING
24
FEET
24' LONGBOAT

For both practical and financial reasons, the Malibu house was shot onstage against a greenscreen, and the views outside were inserted in post.

The nighttime exterior plates were shot as "day for night" at the end of our schedule, on the same day as the daytime plates and the introductory dusk shots to the Malibu house. We had scouted the locations beforehand, so I knew the optimal angle of the sunlight that I needed to match on the interior. I wanted the daytime scenes to be lit by a soft sky bounce combined with a hard shaft of sunlight. To create this effect, something that would have been hard to control during the lengthy dialogue scenes had we been shooting on location, Chris and I used T12 Fresnel lamps as bounce sources and 20K Fresnel lamps for the sunlight effect. The T12s were rigged above the set and aimed at white bounce material that hung above the greenscreen backing, while the direct 20Ks were hung on chain motors in front of the greenscreen. As we were dealing with a large glass frontage, the greenscreen was required to separate reflections of the interior as well as the detail in an actor's hair. This was especially true as we were shooting on film.

But, like many of the techniques we used on *Hail, Caesar!*, to surround a set with greenscreen seems like old technology just a few years later. A volume, or virtual reality, stage provides real animated backgrounds that can not only service driving shots but also a set like our Malibu house. Gone is the need for the compositing of a background using a greenscreen, or the array of lamps I used to mimic the natural daylight entering the set and lighting the shot. Of course, you need to shoot background plates in advance, and renting a volume stage is expensive, so there may be a place for a greenscreen, or even a Translite backing, for a few more years. Maybe.

Hail, Caesar! was a fun, sometimes hilarious, reunion with old friends on a film that explored the old-fashioned way (really, several old-fashioned ways) of filmmaking. My next job, however, would find me looking to more cutting-edge technology to help create a vision of a dark future.

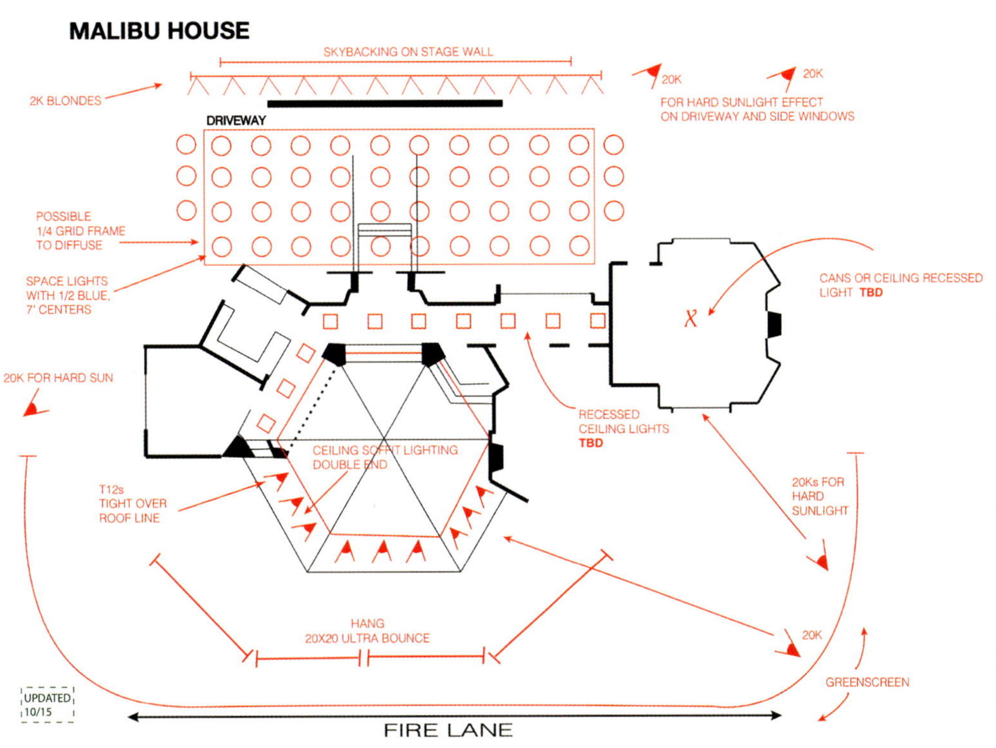

MALIBU HOUSE

CEILING TO FLOAT ALLOW FOR 5'X5" FRAME FOR LAMPS

20'X20' ULTRAS

GREENSCREEN

SPACE LIGHTS AT 7' CENTERS POSSIBLE 1/4 GRID BENEATH

COVE LIGHTS

COVE LIGHTS

T12s

2K BLONDES

ALL THE BEST MEMORIES

To be born is to have a soul, I guess.

K, IN *BLADE RUNNER 2049*

I'd heard rumors of a *Blade Runner* sequel for years, though they never seemed to come to anything. At one point it looked like Ridley Scott, *Blade Runner*'s original director, would take on the challenge, but that changed when he opted to serve as producer instead. So, who *would* direct? I learned the answer while working on *Sicario*: Denis Villeneuve.

Though not successful in its time, *Blade Runner* has emerged as a classic in the decades since. It's at heart a relatively straightforward detective story set in a noir-inspired science-fiction universe, but Denis didn't especially want to revisit what had gone before. Denis planned to make his own film, albeit one that had some connections to the original's story (and the Philip K. Dick novel that inspired it) and set in a similar dystopian universe. His universe would be a twisted version of our world today, reflecting the unpredictable effects of climate change.

I love science fiction. Even if I've worked on only two other sci-fi films, *1984* and *In Time* (and I'm not sure *1984* even counts as sci-fi anymore, but as Philip K. Dick said, the best sci-fi is metaphysics). It's a genre that allows the imagination to run wild but, like any genre, can be used to tell a human story, even if it seldom is.

Expanding on our process for *Sicario*, but starting before we had a production office to interrupt us or a door to lock, Denis wanted to use the months before full-time prep began to visualize the film. James and I joined Denis to work on *Blade Runner 2049* while he was editing *Arrival* in Montreal, working through concepts and visual ideas with his regular storyboard artist, Sam Hudecki. Denis would usually join us at midday for lunch, and through the afternoon we would go over sketches that James and I had worked on with Sam, or we would just sit and bounce ideas around. We were free to put any idea on the table. It was an unusual but highly rewarding process, one Denis referred to as "our chance to dream" before the realities of a budget and a schedule forced compromise.

While looking for studio space in Europe, Denis and I scouted brutalist architecture in London, Hungary, and Slovakia and took the inspiration from our trip back to the drawing board. This went on for weeks until our production designer, Dennis Gassner, could join us and we began to focus more deeply on the sets. After finding only one London stage available to us, and then only for little more than a week, we took Ridley's advice and based the shoot in Budapest. Budapest offered good facilities and, unlike with the overbooked stages of London and Atlanta, we could essentially take over an entire studio while shooting the film.

A cinematographer's challenge with any film is to sustain an aesthetic with consistency from beginning to end. To create the many different looks within *Blade Runner 2049*, while still maintaining a sense that everything was happening in the same world, would prove especially challenging. We had to work within a ninety-one-day schedule, certainly not one of the longest shoots of my career and ambitious for everything we wanted to achieve. To do so would require a great crew. My assistant, Andy Harris, was there right away, as were Bruce Hamme and Steadicam–second camera operator Peter Cavaciuti. Mitch Lillian wondered what he would do by himself with an all-local crew but, thankfully, he was persuaded and brought his best boy, Paul Candrilli, with him. I had not worked with Billy O'Leary since *The Company Men*, but I knew from past experience he would be a perfect fit for the project and with the Hungarian crew. Besides, I wanted to team up with him again. Luckily, he was keen to come on board, as was Josh Gollish, who had been our digital imaging technician since *In Time*. Our line producer was expecting Denis and me to shoot with multiple cameras. That is what you do on major action films, after all. I'm sure it was a shock that we planned to shoot with only one, but it left room in the budget to bring in the people I really needed. Finally, while I had been scouting Budapest with Denis, I met with some Hungarian crew members, and I was confident in my choice of Krisztián Paluch as gaffer and Attila Szûcs as key grip.

As for the look of the film, Jordan Cronenweth's work on *Blade Runner* is remarkable. It's also not how I light. I'd have a hard time replicating what he did even if I wanted to. Denis did, however,

want to draw on some noir influences for *Blade Runner 2049*, but as much as I love noir, I had to find my own way to create a similar mood for what I saw as a naturalistic film. For instance, early in the film, K (Ryan Gosling), the film's replicant blade runner protagonist, visits the farm of rogue replicant Sapper Morton (Dave Bautista), whom he's intent on "retiring." In my opinion, this is the most successful sequence in the entire film, as far as my contributions go.

We wanted to shoot our exteriors on the backlot under cloudy skies, so the interior of Sapper's farm was built on a stage to act as weather cover. The set originally had only two small windows, but I asked for a few more to be placed in strategic spots that would allow me to play the characters in silhouette and lend the interior a more dramatic look, both dark and threatening. It made no sense that there were any interior lights on, other than the one small, illuminated terrarium, so the windows were my sole source. I'd create a noirish feel not by breaking from naturalism but by embracing it. The scene's tension comes from its shadows, wide shots, and long takes. Not every director would have given me the latitude to use so much darkness, but Denis and I had developed a trust over the course of two films together, and it would have been hard to get through such a demanding project without it.

We imagined the film's opening sequence during our "dream time," scouring the internet for contemporary images that would fit into the world of 2049: the black sand beaches of Iceland, the storm clouds over the endless panorama of Mexico City, the greenhouses of Almería, and the solar arrays of the Mojave Desert. Apart from these landscapes, filmed by aerial cinematographer Dylan Goss, whose work had so impressed us on *Sicario*, we filmed *Blade Runner 2049* entirely in Budapest and, for the most part, onstage. Given that, it may sound surprising that we used CG as sparingly as possible. Naturally, sparingly would still be far more CG work than for any other film James and I have worked on, as the scale of Denis's vision would have been prohibitively expensive, if not impossible, to achieve practically. But, whenever possible, we turned to postproduction solutions only when we had no other choice. Take, for instance, the scene where K meets with Joi (Ana de Armas), his virtual

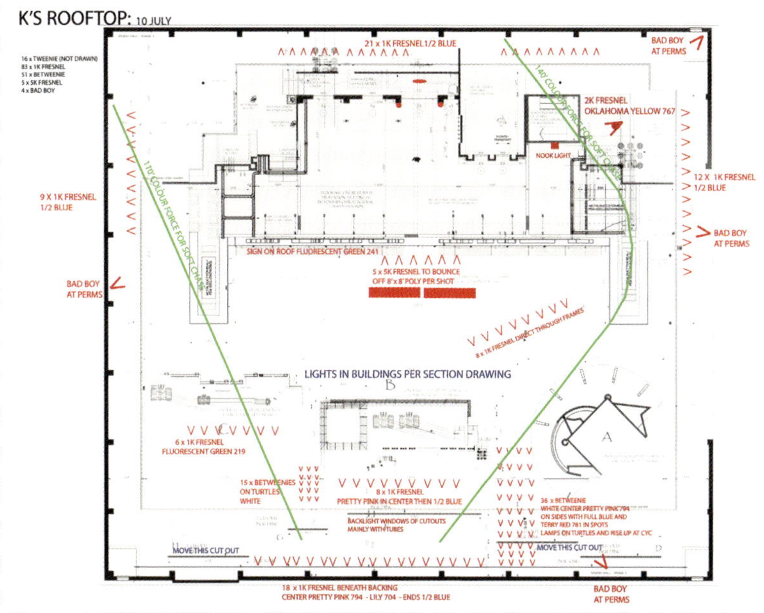
K'S ROOFTOP: 10 JULY
16 x TWEENIE (NOT DRAWN)
83 x 1K FRESNEL
51 x BETWEENIE
5 x 5K FRESNEL
4 x BAD BOY
21 x 1K FRESNEL 1/2 BLUE
BAD BOY AT PERMS
140' COLOUR FORCE FOR SOFT CHASE
2K FRESNEL OKLAHOMA YELLOW 767
NOOK LIGHT
12 X 1K FRESNEL 1/2 BLUE
BAD BOY AT PERMS
9 X 1K FRESNEL 1/2 BLUE
110' COLOUR FORCE FOR SOFT CHASE
SIGN ON ROOF FLUORESCENT GREEN 241
5 x 5K FRESNEL TO BOUNCE OFF 8' x 8' POLY PER SHOT
BAD BOY AT PERMS
8 x 1K FRESNEL DIRECT THROUGH FRAMES
LIGHTS IN BUILDINGS PER SECTION DRAWING
6 x 1K FRESNEL FLUORESCENT GREEN 219
15 x BETWEENIES ON TURTLES WHITE
8 x 1K FRESNEL PRETTY PINK IN CENTER THEN 1/2 BLUE
36 x BETWEENIE WHITE CENTER PRETTY PINK 794 ON SIDES WITH FULL BLUE AND TERRY RED 781 IN SPOTS LAMPS ON TURTLES AND RISE UP AT CYC
BACKLIGHT WINDOWS OF CUTOUTS MAINLY WITH TUBES
MOVE THIS CUT OUT
MOVE THIS CUT OUT
18 x 1K FRESNEL BENEATH BACKING CENTER PRETTY PINK 794 - LILY 704 - ENDS 1/2 BLUE
BAD BOY AT PERMS

girlfriend, on the roof of his apartment in the rain. We had studied images of Beijing in the smog during prep and were struck by the huge, illuminated billboards that glowed in the atmosphere of that city, and these became key references for Denis's LA. During prep we shot a lot of playback material, some of which can be seen on the large LED screen that looks down on the rooftop; for the fog, we used a mister system created by Gerd Nefzer, our on-set effects supervisor. Although I was very familiar with the system, having used misters on *The Ladykillers* and *House of Sand and Fog*, production was, quite rightly, skeptical. But Gerd relished the challenge, and after testing the approach we used it not only for this one scene on the roof but for four larger sets.

The stage we used for K's rooftop was quite small, and Dennis Gassner built to its edges. As the roof had to take up much of the space, Dennis constructed the buildings beyond in false perspective. It made little sense for the light to be coming from above and, with limited workspace below the set, our solution was to rest multiple small units on the stage floor, facing them directly up to create a soft glow as if coming from the street below. We mounted small fluorescent tubes inside the set pieces, panned Big Boy spotlights across the scene as if they were light from passing spinners, and fixed patterns of practical bulbs to the stage wall to resemble more distant lights glowing in the fog. We also rigged two 170-foot spans of Color Force LED battens and programmed in a chase so a beam of colored light tracked across the set. But no stage is ever big enough!

Maintaining the look of our world on location was another challenge. A city block close to the center of Budapest stood in for K's apartment building, and Gerd not only filled this neighborhood with smoke (and, no doubt, most of the city of Budapest) he also used a large crane to add falling

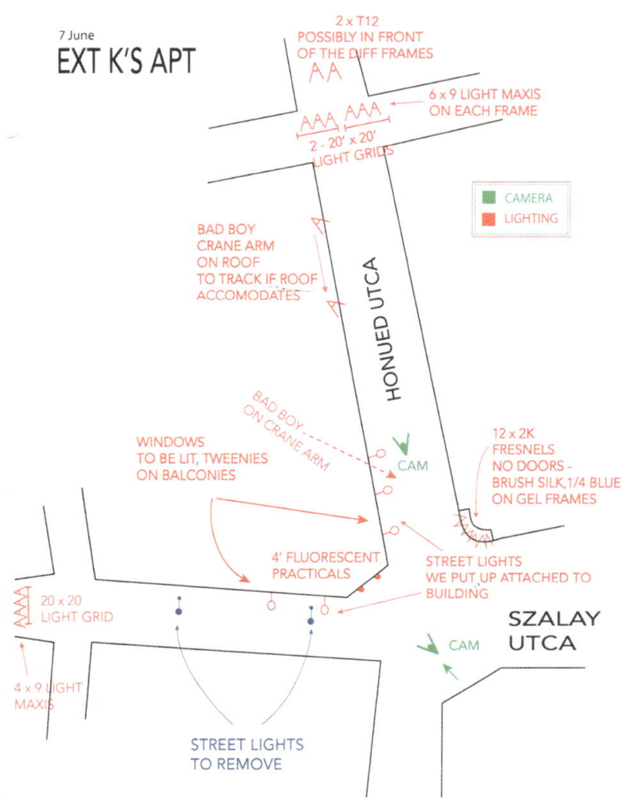

snow. Yes, the look of both the set and location work was augmented in VFX, but shooting the main elements in camera made a difference. You can feel the light interacting with the atmosphere, and that is hard to replicate without a base reference.

Rain, gloom, and artificial light define Denis's Los Angeles, a city of have-nots. But what would Niander Wallace (Jared Leto), a man with infinite wealth, want to set himself apart from the dark, hostile environment surrounding him? Sunlight! That he was blind made the idea seem even more ironic. He could only "feel" the sunlight.

For the office of Wallace's replicant employee Luv (Sylvia Hoeks), Dennis Gassner designed a water tank to fit into the ceiling of the set and connected it with the larger, water-filled environment in which we are introduced to Wallace. To light the office, we simply projected a 10K Skypan and two 2K Blondes through the water to create "caustics," the refraction patterns caused by light interacting with the moving surface of the water. To get the perfect effect, the water had to be agitated at a consistent speed. Too strong, and the pattern would become confused; too slow, it would disappear. To find the sweet spot, one of Gerd's effects team created an electric-powered floating agitator, but in the end, he found he had more control with a small stick and by manipulating it by hand.

Beyond the shimmer created by the water, I wanted the entire Wallace Corporation interior to be a place where sunlight constantly played in motion. For the records library, I drew on an image

I'd seen of sunlight coming through a small window, lighting a room as it bounced off the wall. I wanted to take this idea a little further, creating a moving patch of sunlight to illuminate a much larger space. I imagined the light as if triggered by the motion of our characters. To keep it moving during the conversation in the library might have been distracting and would have required more resources than we had. So, the light stopped when the characters stopped.

The establishing shot of the records room is a composite of a four-by-four-foot maquette and a shot of the two figures, K and the file clerk (Tómas Lemarquis), walking down what looks like a vast corridor between acres of library cabinets. For sheer scale we could only fill their immediate surround.

We lit the maquette simply, with a 1K Fresnel on a wind-up stand, raising the lamp so the square pattern of light would creep slowly down the left-hand wall and allow the "sunlight" to illuminate the interior. The filing cabinets that fill the space in the final image were added by VFX using the light that swept across the floor of the maquette as a reference as well as the cabinets we had

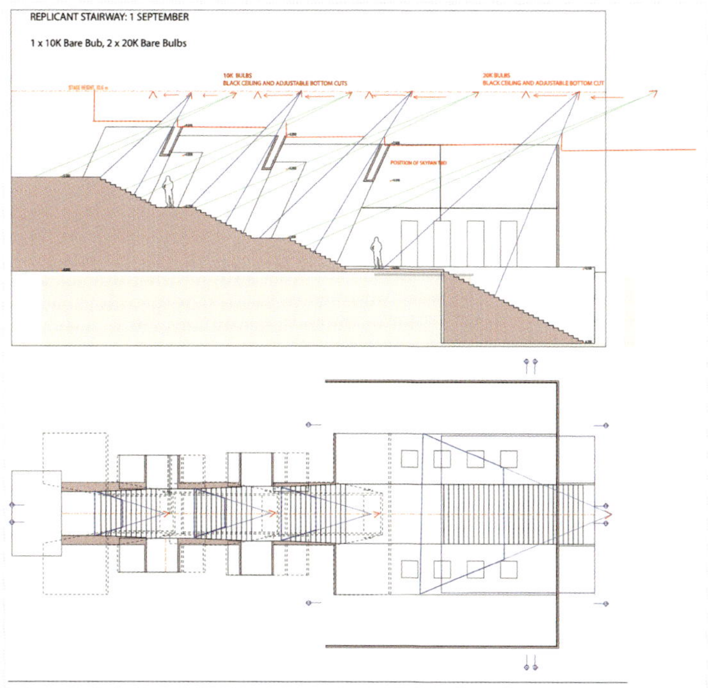

included with the figures. The texture of the maquette was also adjusted to resemble concrete but, in essence, VFX supplemented an in-camera element.

The set seen after the library, the replicant stairway, was one of the last to be designed. Originally a simple museum space displaying replicant designs from previous ages, Denis wanted it to also imply his characters were descending toward the basement of the building. He and Dennis came up with the idea of an Egyptian-style temple with replicants displayed to the sides of what was a larger opening in a narrow flight of stairs. Continuing with the same concept used for the library, I envisioned a single-point source of sunlight passing overhead as if it were following K and Luv as they descended the stairs. A simple concept but not so easy to execute!

Billy had been overseeing the prelighting while Krisztián stayed with me on the floor, and because of the complexity of the sets and rigging, production had allowed for two extra rigging gaffers to join us. One from New York, Richie Ford, I had known since *The Shawshank Redemption*, and the other, Patrick Bramucci, who came in from Rome, had worked with us on *Kundun*. Together they figured out a low-tech solution to the challenge. For the sunlight to follow our characters the bulbs had to travel in the opposite direction so, to cut a very long story short, Billy and his team rigged a series of bulbs, 10K and 20K tungsten globes, on separate skateboard dollies underslung on a rail so that each could

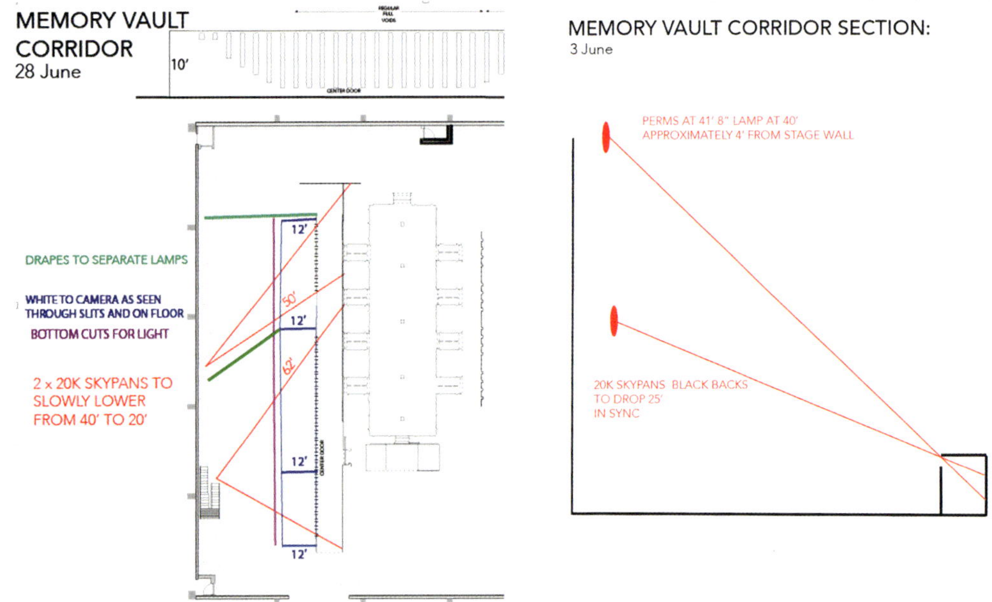

be pulled, by hand, across the individual openings that we had asked to be designed into the ceiling. The trick was to synchronize the movement so when one lamp disappeared behind a cut the next would emerge and take over as one fluid move.

For the next section of K and Luv's journey, I drew on one of my favorite movies, Orson Welles's 1962 adaptation of Franz Kafka's *The Trial*. (I think it's his best film, even including *Citizen Kane*.) In *The Trial*, Welles shoots Anthony Perkins's Josef K. (another protagonist named "K," interestingly) running through a passageway that is defined by slatted shafts of hard light, and the corridor outside Wallace's Memory Vault seemed to offer the perfect chance to steal this idea. Working with art director Paul Inglis, I arranged for one side wall of the corridor to be designed in a series of slats so that two bare 24K bulbs would send a sharp pattern of light across the floor and up the wall when they were lowered on a block and tackle. I wish it had been as simple as that but, in essence, that is what we did.

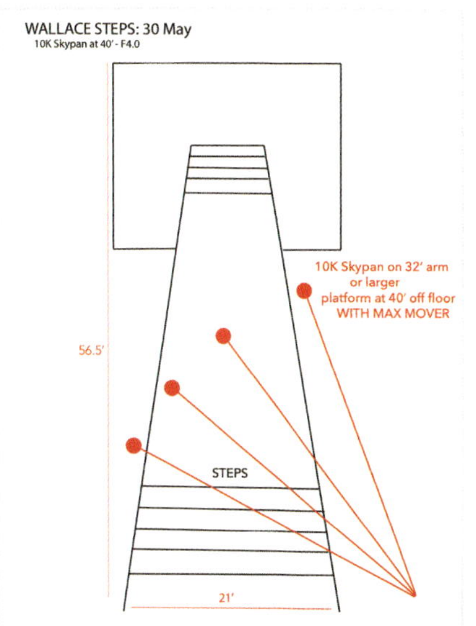
WALLACE STEPS: 30 May
10K Skypan at 40' - F4.0
10K Skypan on 32' arm
or larger
platform at 40' off floor
WITH MAX MOVER
56.5'
STEPS
21'

WALLACE'S OFFICE SC 41: 20 August

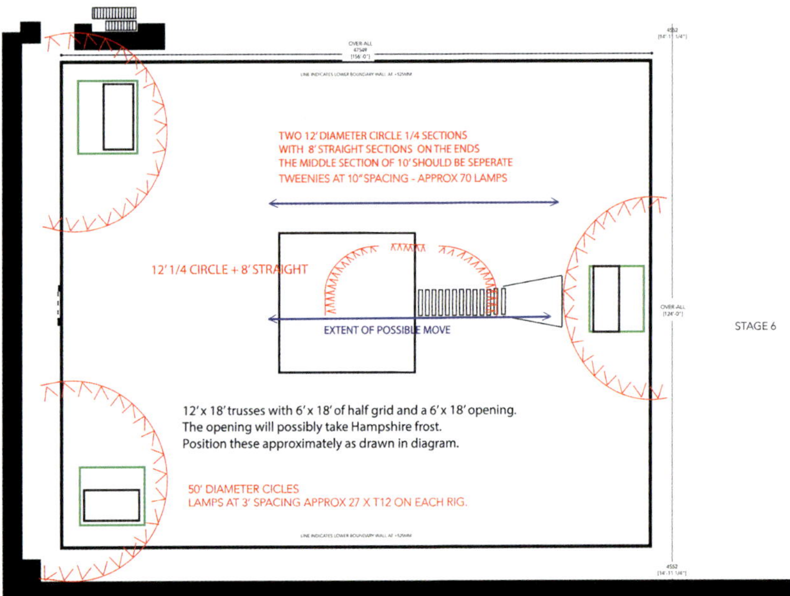

We knew we had to make the film's introduction of Wallace a special moment. Denis had conceptualized Wallace's office as a platform surrounded by water (an idea that I think came to him while he was in a Japanese restaurant with a similar layout), and we had talked about Luv entering as if up some stairs from her office below. The stairway was a separate set, and we lit it quite simply by panning a 10K Skypan, on a thirty-two-foot crane arm, over a water tank that our art department had built into the ceiling.

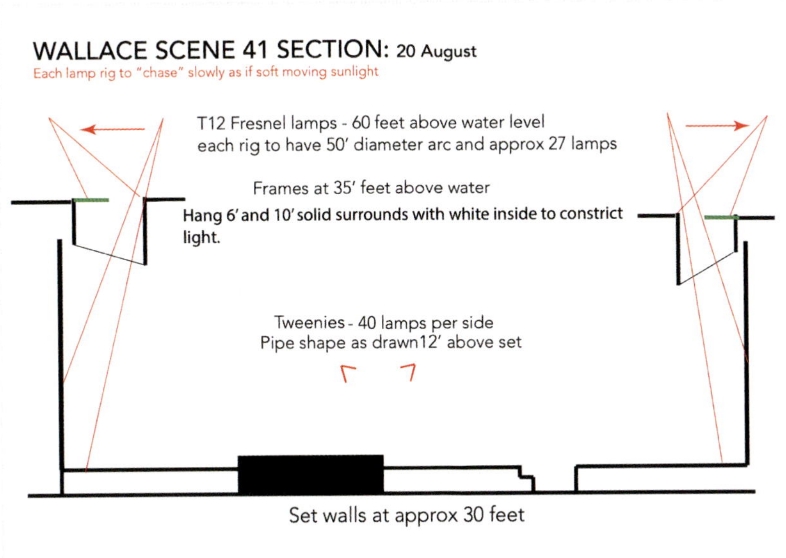

Wallace's office was a far more complex challenge.

I wanted to continue the concept I had used on the maquette of a square pattern, or patterns, of light moving across the walls and allow that to be the sole light source. Denis imagined Jared appearing out of the shadows. If we could sync the light with the action, he liked the concept. My first thought was to rig a single lamp on a rail and track it across an opening that stood in for a skylight, but that proved impractical. There was just no space nor any available technology. So our solution was to rig a circle of 27 × T12 Fresnel lamps and build in a chase, with three or four lamps dimming on and off at any one time, so that it appeared as if a single light was revolving around the circle. To shape the light from the chase, our "skylight" had to be dropped below the lamps and set at an angle to the wall.

For the second scene on the same set, when Deckard (Harrison Ford) is presented with a replicant of Rachael, Denis had suggested a pattern of moving spotlights across the characters. Rather than a random selection of individual spotlights, which might distract from the performances, I felt a more languid movement of a single source would better suit the scene. To reassure Denis and myself that it might just work, we did some tests with a pulse of light revolving around a complete circle of 650-watt Fresnel lamps. Denis liked the test, and Billy and I now had to expand the concept to fit the far larger set. Finally, we settled on two rings of 300-watt Fresnel lamps, "Betweenies," the larger being thirty-five feet in diameter and the smaller twenty feet. Much as we had done with the T12s, the 300-watt lamps were butted together to form an even circle comprising some 283 lamps in total.

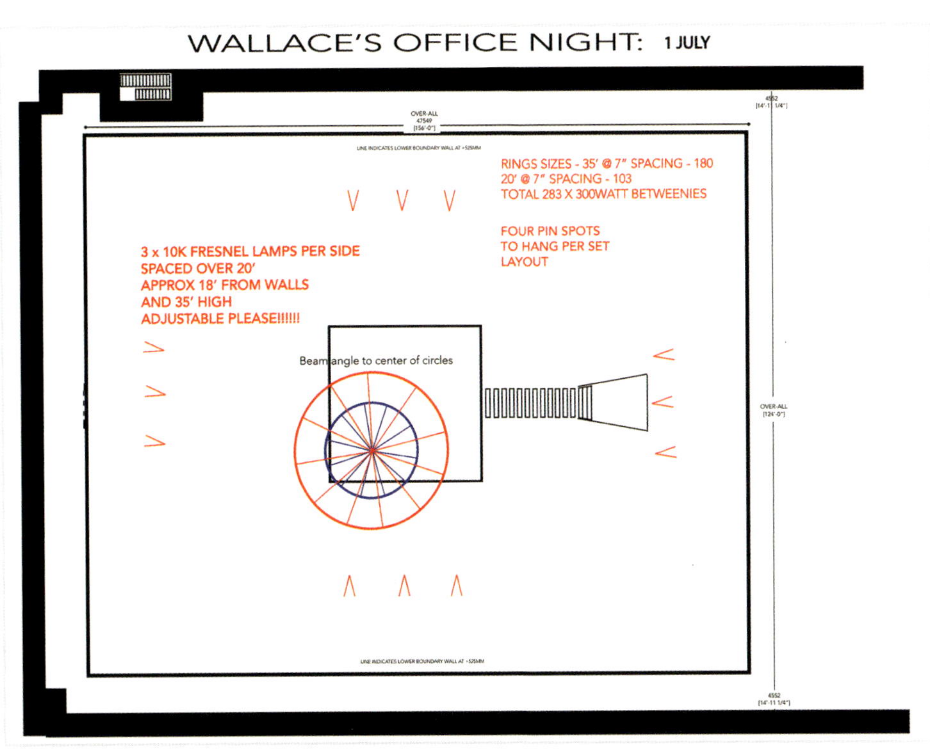
WALLACE'S OFFICE NIGHT: 1 JULY
RINGS SIZES - 35' @ 7" SPACING - 180
20' @ 7" SPACING - 103
TOTAL 283 X 300WATT BETWEENIES
FOUR PIN SPOTS
TO HANG PER SET
LAYOUT
3 x 10K FRESNEL LAMPS PER SIDE
SPACED OVER 20'
APPROX 18' FROM WALLS
AND 35' HIGH
ADJUSTABLE PLEASE!!!!!!
Beam angle to center of circles

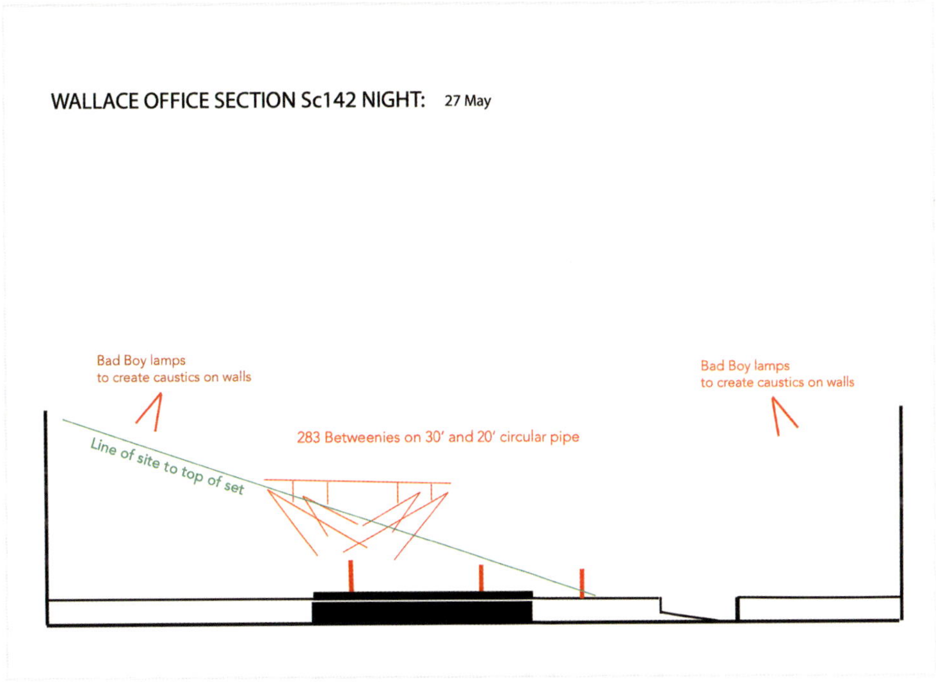
WALLACE OFFICE SECTION Sc142 NIGHT: 27 May
Bad Boy lamps
to create caustics on walls
Bad Boy lamps
to create caustics on walls
283 Betweenies on 30' and 20' circular pipe
Line of site to top of set

The pulse of light we programmed to revolve around the circle consisted of ten to fifteen lamps that slowly faded on or off at any one time, with only the central two or three at full intensity. The result was a soft but directional sliver of light that grew in length and width as the scene built toward the introduction of the replicant Rachael. For the caustic effect on the walls, we bounced 10K Fresnels (not Bad Boy spotlights as it appears in the diagram) off the water and, once again, our effects expert agitated the pond—but now using Gerd's electronic gadget.

On the wide shot, Denis noted it would be simple enough to paint out the entire rig digitally, but I asked him to consider keeping it. "It's going to be weird to have a floating light, isn't it?" he said. But that's why I wanted him to keep it—the moving light source, that is, not the entire rig.

Denis and I had positioned the scene between Deckard and Wallace so the actors' faces would go in and out of darkness as the light revolved around the truss. I had marked the furniture during a rehearsal and was a little freaked when Harrison moved his chair on the day of the shoot.

When he was in conversation with Denis, I moved it back on its mark and, luckily for me, he never noticed. Or maybe he did and knew exactly why. A lot could have gone wrong, not the least because Jared, ever the Method actor, was playing the scene with an opaque set of contact lenses. But, like Wallace, perhaps he could feel the light. Only once did he have to be saved from taking a swim.

The haboobs of North Africa, and a similar dust storm that painted the Sydney Opera House red in 2009, inspired the look of the landscape through which K walks toward the ruins of Las Vegas. Denis had pictured a futuristic city, the Luxor Hotel on steroids, now emptied of people, but he still wanted to retain some of its old-world eroticism. In Budapest, the city has banished all its Soviet statuary to its suburban Memento Park, and our idea was that Las Vegas might have done something similar, but with a different sort of artwork.

The stage was small, but by hanging a gray drape on the walls and filling it with smoke, similarly to what we had done on *Jarhead*, we could create a world that felt as if it went on forever. The lighting rig was a simple pattern of Spacelites, and I used a purpose-made filter on the camera to achieve the otherworldly shade of red. A set of Maxi Brutes, gelled with a light green, backlit the smoke to create a yellowish (the green of the gel plus the red of the filter) hue in the sky, as if

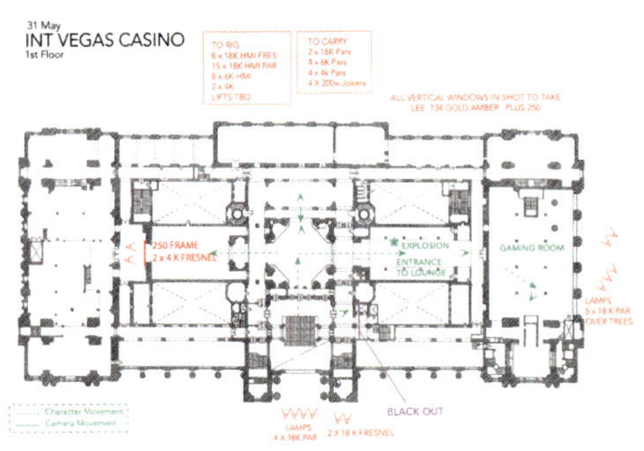
31 May
INT VEGAS CASINO
1st Floor
TO RIG
8 x 18K HMI FRES
15 x 18K HMI PAR
8 x 6K HMI
2 x 4K
LIFTS TBD
TO CARRY
2 x 18K Pars
4 x 6K Pars
4 x 4k Pars
4 X 200w Jokers
ALL VERTICAL WINDOWS IN SHOT TO TAKE
LEE 134 GOLD AMBER PLUS 250
250 FRAME
2 x 4 K FRESNEL
EXPLOSION
ENTRANCE
TO LOUNGE
GAMING ROOM
LAMPS
5 x 18 K PAR
OVER TREES
Character Movement
Camera Movement
LAMPS
4 X 18K PAR
2 X 18 K FRESNEL
BLACK OUT

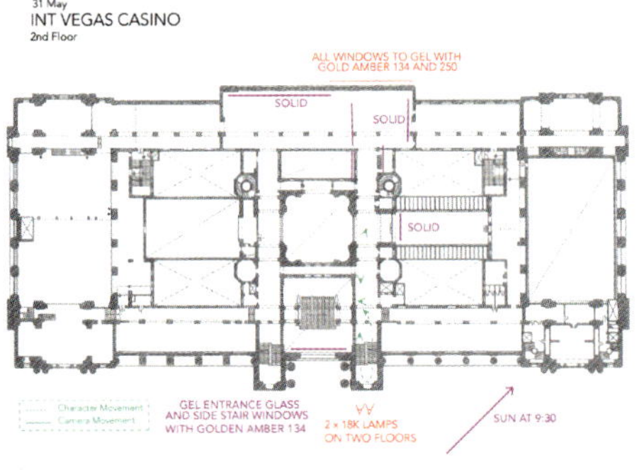
31 May
INT VEGAS CASINO
2nd Floor
ALL WINDOWS TO GEL WITH
GOLD AMBER 134 AND 250
SOLID
SOLID
SOLID
Character Movement
Camera Movement
GEL ENTRANCE GLASS
AND SIDE STAIR WINDOWS
WITH GOLDEN AMBER 134
2 x 18K LAMPS
ON TWO FLOORS
SUN AT 9:30

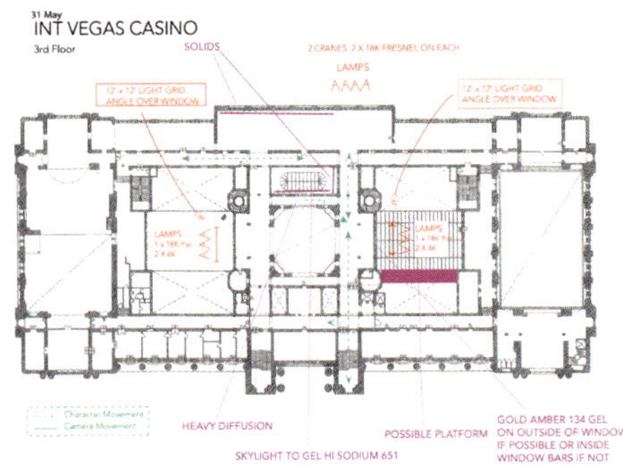
31 May
INT VEGAS CASINO
3rd Floor
SOLIDS
2 CRANES 2 X 18K FRESNEL ON EACH
LAMPS
12' x 12' LIGHT GRID
ANGLE OVER WINDOW
12' x 12' LIGHT GRID
ANGLE OVER WINDOW
LAMPS
1 x 18K Par
2 X 6K
LAMPS
Character Movement
Camera Movement
HEAVY DIFFUSION
SKYLIGHT TO GEL HI SODIUM 651
POSSIBLE PLATFORM
GOLD AMBER 134 GEL
ON OUTSIDE OF WINDOWS
IF POSSIBLE OR INSIDE
WINDOW BARS IF NOT

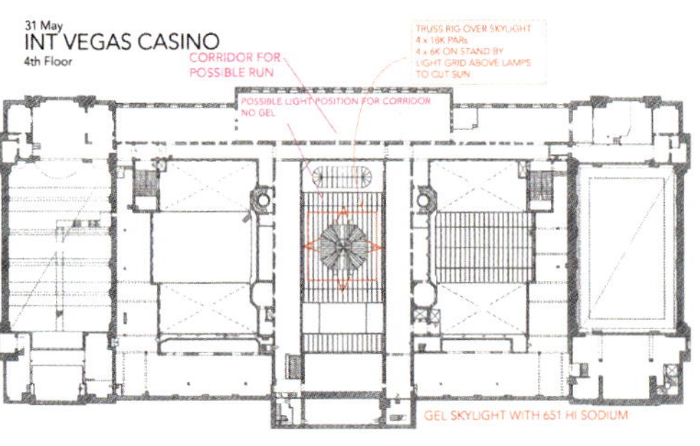
31 May
INT VEGAS CASINO
4th Floor
CORRIDOR FOR
POSSIBLE RUN
TRUSS RIG OVER SKYLIGHT
4 x 18K PARs
4 x 6K ON STAND BY
LIGHT GRID ABOVE LAMPS
TO CUT SUN
POSSIBLE LIGHT POSITION FOR CORRIDOR
NO GEL
GEL SKYLIGHT WITH 651 HI SODIUM

somewhere up there is a sun. For me, it began as a homage to Percy Shelley's poem "Ozymandias": "on the sand, / Half sunk, a shattered visage lies… / Round the decay / Of that colossal wreck, boundless and bare / The lone and level sands stretch far away."

From a small stage we moved to a large semi-abandoned city building for our casino interior. To maintain the reddish color, Billy and Krisztián surrounded the building with large HMIs and we gelled the windows to match the color of the stage work, the higher windows being more yellow and less amber than those on the ground floor. We changed our approach because shooting with a red filter on the lens, as I had onstage, could have created internal reflection problems. When shooting toward a bright light source with a dark surround, light can bounce between the lens and a filter to create a mirror reflection, in this case of a window, on the image. Either approach required adding gel and diffusion to the windows, so shooting with a filter on the lens would not save us the time and money it had onstage. Besides, by gelling the windows, everyone on set would see the color as it would appear in the film.

The Vegas sequence also involved one of the film's most elaborate lighting designs. When K walks into an abandoned casino show floor, he's surrounded by holograms, including an image of Elvis Presley performing "Suspicious Minds" as the sound of the song cuts in and out. The idea

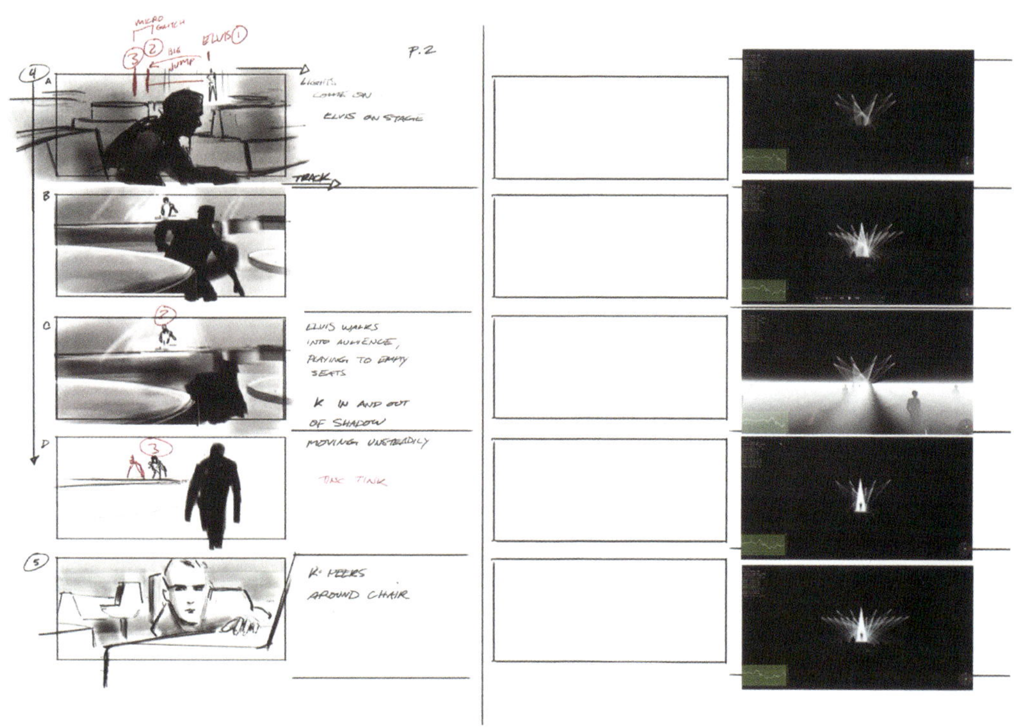
P.2
LIGHTS COME ON
ELVIS ON STAGE
TRACK
ELVIS WALKS INTO AUDIENCE, PLAYING TO EMPTY SEATS
K IN AND OUT OF SHADOW
MOVING UNSTEADILY
K PEERS AROUND CHAIR

FPS : 23
Deferred Shading [High]
Enhanced Visualization: Enabled
Volumetric Beams: Enabled
View Resolution [2116 x 1103]
Number of Objects 981
Number of Fixtures 295
Number of Sources 301
Number of Beams 17
Number of Glowing Screens 0
Number of 2D Reflectors 8
Number of 3D Reflectors 8
Lighting Complexity -> medium
00:18
-02:04

was that malfunctioning display machines had created overlapping shows while the stage lighting moved in unpredictable patterns. It was lighting chaos! I worked with a previsualization team—which I'd done before but never for lighting—at Light Design Kft., a Budapest-based lighting design company, to create a pattern of concert-style lighting that could be programmed to play back in time with the soundtrack and also be easily adjustable if the scene called for it.

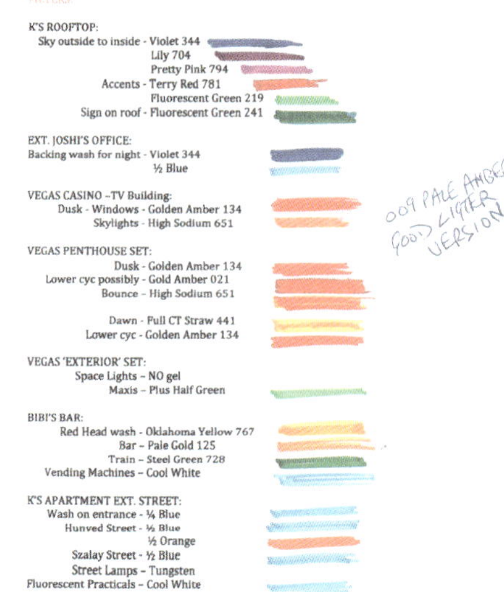

FILTERS:

K'S ROOFTOP:
Sky outside to inside - Violet 344
Lily 704
Pretty Pink 794
Accents - Terry Red 781
Fluorescent Green 219
Sign on roof - Fluorescent Green 241

EXT. JOSHI'S OFFICE:
Backing wash for night - Violet 344
½ Blue

VEGAS CASINO –TV Building:
Dusk - Windows - Golden Amber 134
Skylights - High Sodium 651

009 PALE AMBER GOOD LIGHTER VERSION

VEGAS PENTHOUSE SET:
Dusk - Golden Amber 134
Lower cyc possibly - Gold Amber 021
Bounce – High Sodium 651

Dawn - Full CT Straw 441
Lower cyc - Golden Amber 134

VEGAS 'EXTERIOR' SET:
Space Lights – NO gel
Maxis – Plus Half Green

BIBI'S BAR:
Red Head wash - Oklahoma Yellow 767
Bar – Pale Gold 125
Train – Steel Green 728
Vending Machines – Cool White

K'S APARTMENT EXT. STREET:
Wash on entrance - ¼ Blue
Hunved Street - ½ Blue
½ Orange
Szalay Street - ½ Blue
Street Lamps – Tungsten
Fluorescent Practicals – Cool White

The set itself was a lot simpler than the lighting. By that point in the shoot, other sets had soaked up much of the budget and, during a lunchtime production meeting, I explained how I thought we could deal with the problem: Surround the stage with black drapes, and the lighting could do the rest. All that was needed was a door for Deckard and K to walk through, a stage, and some furniture. It was all about the light!

The interior of Deckard's penthouse apartment, built onstage, included a painted backing which, although digitally augmented in post, allowed the whole environment to be photographed in camera. Using an LED screen was not an option, and I did not want to use greenscreen because of all the glass and reflections. As the view would also contribute to the quality of the light inside the apartment, by far the simplest solution, albeit one that felt quite old-fashioned, was for the art department to paint a canvas backing. I had this done in a range of grays, rather than full color, as we were adding gel to the lamps to create the color.

We lit the backing with 2K Blondes, an inexpensive lamp to hire and that in a multiple of seventy-five we could use to create a wide, soft source. The sun that appears through the red haze is simply a 20K Fresnel spotted onto the canvas. For the light penetrating the windows, we mounted thirty-two T12 Fresnel lamps on the roof of the set, which we had specifically asked construction to reinforce, and bounced them off white reflectors that were hung above the backing, to the very limit of where the camera would see. There was a lot of light on this set as I was intending for a deep focus in this scene, but by the time we added gel to the lamps I was still only shooting at around 2.5/2.8. So it goes!

We used the same set as if it were two different levels of the building, the uppermost being Deckard's apartment and the second an empty floor below. We shot the later scenes later in the schedule so the apartment could be redressed, and Gerd Nefzer had time to rig the gimbal on which he would track Luv's spinner into the room and land. The mechanics were removed and the path of the spinner digitally extended by VFX in post. Both Denis and I felt that shooting as much of the action of the spinner in camera as possible would give it a reality that would have been difficult to achieve on a computer. Perhaps it would be different now.

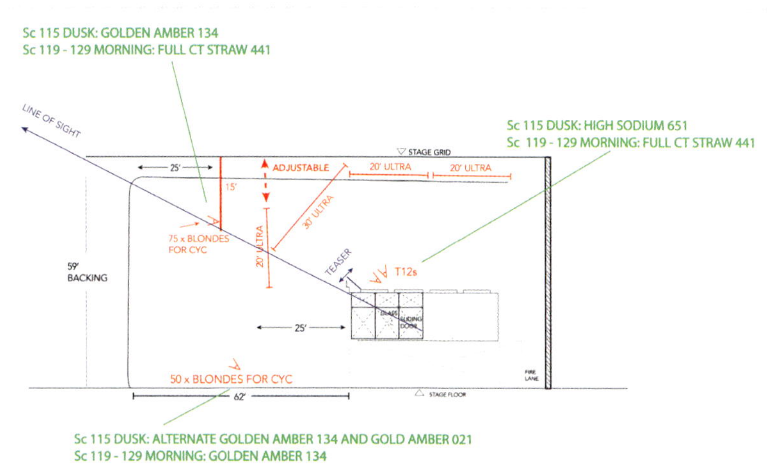

Sc 115 DUSK: GOLDEN AMBER 134
Sc 119 - 129 MORNING: FULL CT STRAW 441
LINE OF SIGHT
Sc 115 DUSK: HIGH SODIUM 651
Sc 119 - 129 MORNING: FULL CT STRAW 441
STAGE GRID
25'
15'
ADJUSTABLE
20' ULTRA
20' ULTRA
30' ULTRA
20' ULTRA
75 x BLONDES FOR CYC
59' BACKING
TEASER
T12s
25'
50 x BLONDES FOR CYC
62'
Sc 115 DUSK: ALTERNATE GOLDEN AMBER 134 AND GOLD AMBER 021
Sc 119 - 129 MORNING: GOLDEN AMBER 134

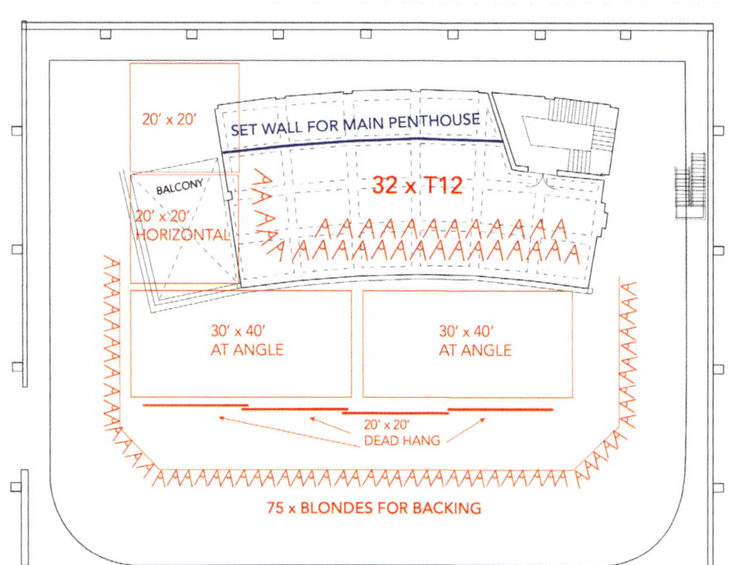

20' x 20'
SET WALL FOR MAIN PENTHOUSE
BALCONY
20' x 20' HORIZONTAL
32 x T12
30' x 40' AT ANGLE
30' x 40' AT ANGLE
20' x 20' DEAD HANG
75 x BLONDES FOR BACKING

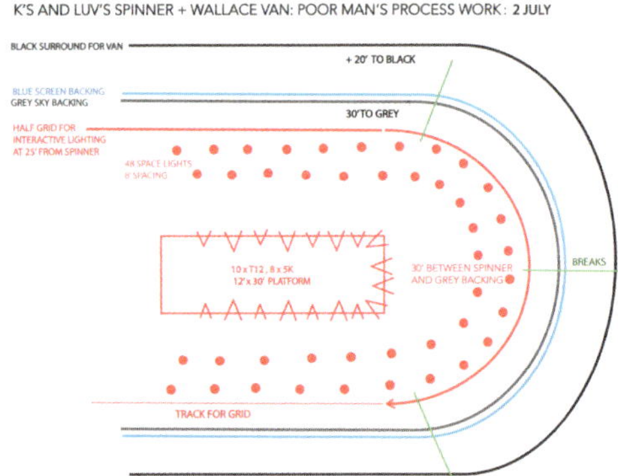

We shot both the interior of K's flying vehicle (his spinner) and the transport vehicle he is pursuing as we had on *Unbroken*, mounted on a gimbal onstage. To create the effect of passing flying machines, Billy rigged a wire across the set and propelled a bulb along it using a strip of elastic.

In the original script the transport vehicle, with Luv and Deckard inside, would crash into the sea, forcing K to jump into the water to effect a rescue. This seemed a very familiar scene. We had a sea wall. Why not use that? So, we designed a wall with a shelf that part of the fight could take place on. Adding to the danger, the transport vehicle could be dragged into the waves and the action continue as it sank. To shoot the scene we considered using a purpose-ready facility in Malta, but it proved to be both cheaper and a better use of our time to build the set in Budapest. And the 150-foot square tank to put it in. This not only removed days that would be lost through travel, but it also gave the art department, the effects department, and my rigging team the time they needed to prepare the set for shooting.

It was quite a number, featuring an array of wave makers, dump tanks, misters, and smoke machines, plus the two platforms for our camera cranes and various underwater housings for our Arri Alexa XTs. We didn't need it all, however. Our purpose-made heated pool created a natural fog as the night became cooler and, although we wanted atmosphere, this wasn't part of the original plan. Production had installed water heaters and told no one that they were set to keep the water at a steady seventy-five degrees. I was shocked as night fell, the air temperature dropped, and an intense mist began to form over the water. And Gert was not responsible. It was nice, but not when you couldn't see the camera, let alone the camera see the set. But Gert set up a bank of fans, and it worked in our favor as there is no substitute for the way light interacts with water droplets.

We used minimal lighting for the exterior, illuminating it with the LED lights we had built into the two downed vehicles and a few small panning spotlights to represent passing spinners. We wanted darkness to do a lot of the work. When we looked at the set during the day, it seemed to be dominated by the mechanics of the process, but when night fell, and the mist started to form, it was surprising how quickly all that fell away to leave just these pools of light.

On *Blade Runner 2049*, as she had on other location movies, James oversaw the creation and running of a "lab" for the dailies, an area where the dailies could be processed and the deliverables made. Most important was a screening room that allowed her to view our dailies every morning, checking that the complex shots had indeed worked and there were no unexpected technical issues. It also allowed us to see some early tests of the visual effects work.

In terms of size and complexity *Blade Runner 2049* rivaled *Skyfall*. But I love shooting and it's not so often you get a chance to delve into so many new possibilities. There is such a buzz on set when things go to plan or when one of those revolving lighting rigs actually works. At times like that, it is not just me that gets a buzz from what I do but also Billy, Mitch, Andy, Bruce, James, and the entire shooting crew. How often does anyone get a chance to work on a film of such scale, with such an inspirational director and such a great team?

You can look at a picture for a week and never think of it again. You can also look at a picture for a second and think of it all your life.

DONNA TARTT, *THE GOLDFINCH*

While we were shooting *The Goldfinch*, directed by John Crowley—one of the best I have had the pleasure to work with—I learned that *Blade Runner 2049* had been nominated by the Academy of Motion Picture Arts and Sciences for its production design, visual effects, sound mixing, and sound editing—and for best cinematography. This was my fourteenth nomination, and James and I had attended every awards ceremony. It was a surprise to be there and an even greater surprise to be called onstage.

The award was for every member of the crew who worked with me on *BR 2049*. Especially, it was for my friends who had been with me for so many years. I hoped I did them proud with whatever I said, which for me disappeared in a haze of smiling faces. But, in the back of my mind, I was thinking about *The Goldfinch* and the next set. *What are we shooting on Tuesday? And how are we going to make the move from New York to Amsterdam to Albuquerque? What have we forgotten? And just how are we going to blow up the Metropolitan Museum?*

31

TO END ALL WARS

Two armies that fight each other
is like one large army that commits suicide.

HENRI BARBUSSE

It's not always easy for me to talk about what films, and which cinematographers, have influenced my work. I can point to many movies I love and cinematographers whose work I admire, even revere. But I'm rarely able to draw a direct line between the images of a particular film and one on which I've worked. For instance, I consider Andrei Tarkovsky's *Solaris* an influence on *Blade Runner 2049*, but my work on that film doesn't, at first glance, resemble Vadim Yusov's contributions to *Solaris*. Just as often, inspiration comes from unexpected sources. *Blade Runner 2049*'s birth scene, for instance, owes a debt to an Italian fashion show for which models were suspended in midair wrapped in plastic. Sometimes it's a single image. When researching *1917* I found myself returning to a photograph of a soldier looking toward the camera with a sad, confused expression.

We'd be shooting the film in color with a dramatically different aspect ratio, but I kept this photo in mind, holding it as symbolic of what we were trying to achieve. I liked the feel of the lens and the relationship of the subject to the camera. But it's the emotions on the soldier's face that I found so haunting. What was his story?

Sam Mendes had contacted us out of the blue to ask if we could meet. We had not spoken since I had turned down the opportunity to shoot his second Bond movie, *Spectre*. He thought I was misguided to choose an "art film," Joel and Ethan's *Hail, Caesar!*, over a huge franchise film like a Bond. What could I say? We left it at that. So it was a little more than a surprise when he called. James and I were planning to be in London and agreed to join him for lunch near the theater where he was in rehearsal for a new play. There, he told us about his next project, a World War I movie inspired by stories he'd been told by his grandfather, who served as a runner in the British Army on the Western Front, carrying messages back and forth between the front lines.

It was only when we received the screenplay that we saw, written on the front page below the film's title, that Sam planned to shoot the film in a single shot. One-shot movies—or movies that appeared to have been created in a single shot—had come into vogue thanks to the success of *Birdman*. We were a bit worried this approach could seem like a gimmick. However, upon reading the script it seemed appropriate to what was a simple story taking place in real time and involving only two main characters. Beyond that, it seemed like a step in the dark.

In our initial meeting, Sam was adamant that we avoid talking about the technical challenge that the one-shot concept would present. We'd treat the film as any other and figure out the rest later. When that "later" came, Sam said, "I know you'll figure it out," but for now, we asked the usual questions. *What do we want the audience to see? Should the camera remain locked on our character's perspective, or do we want it to observe? Is it too claustrophobic to simply pull the characters down a long trench? Is that claustrophobia a good thing? Does the audience see anything more than our characters can see?*

Our references included the great 1985 Soviet antiwar film *Come and See*, directed by Elem Klimov, which depicts real events through the eyes of a young boy, Flyora. Only once or twice does the film leave his singular point of view to show us a horror that he only imagines. We also discussed László Nemes's *Son of Saul*, a 2015 drama set at Auschwitz that stays close to its protagonist as he navigates a horrific environment. Although incredibly effective, Nemes deliberately keeps the surrounding action out of focus and somewhat obscure, whereas we didn't want to put that kind of distance between the characters and their environment. *Son of Saul* had been shot handheld, and, briefly, Sam thought we might approach *1917* as we had *Jarhead*. But as we developed our "shot," the viewpoint shifted between one that was subjective, and close to our characters, to another that was more objective, viewing them from a distance but with the camera always advancing very deliberately forward. This led us to look for a more considered and stable approach to the movement of the camera. Although Sam and I were working without considering the technical challenge posed by our ideas, James and I immediately began to research the equipment we might need.

The long tracking shots of John Huston's classic 1951 film, *The Red Badge of Courage*, were innovative in their time, but it was Garrett Brown's Steadicam system that took the operator off the dolly. In the mid-1970s, *Rocky* and *Bound for Glory* opened an alternative way for the filmmaker to follow action, best described as a cross between a dolly shot and handheld. A Steadicam was a good tool for us, but it was too bulky to fit into our trenches or control at high speed. Now, over thirty years on from *Rocky*, handheld stabilizers seemed to be everywhere.

Most were consumer-based products, but the Stabileye, the brainchild of Dave Freeth and Paul Legall, weighed less than eight pounds, was purpose-built for filmmaking, and could be carried by hand. This became our primary tool. Not only could it be carried by hand, as it was by Gary Hymns and his grip team on the opening, it could be suspended from Gavin Weatherall's wire rig, rigged on a Technocrane, or handed off from one to another to achieve one long continuous move. And, as Peter Cavaciuti (my longtime friend and Steadicam operator) discovered, it could be adapted to fit on a Steadicam arm. With this he could run in front of the actors while shooting back over his shoulder and, given space to accommodate the transition, he could turn around to run behind them in one smooth move. An advantage for Pete was that he did not have to watch the frame line as he would with a Steadicam. The disadvantage for me was that I would have to operate it. The Stabileye was remotely operated off a monitor using a set of wheels and, with Pete running and turning at speed, the movement was far more irregular and abrupt than any I had encountered before. I felt glad to have spent so many lonely hours at the National Film School writing my name with that geared head!

We added one last key piece of equipment to our list.

The Trinity rig is similar in concept to the Steadicam but with a pivoting arm that allows the camera to jib up and down. We knew this would be an invaluable tool if we could find a proficient operator. While we were testing other equipment at Arri rental in London, we were given a demonstration by Charlie Rizek. Although Charlie was only showing off what was a new tool for the camera company, and he had yet to work on a feature film, James and I immediately asked him to come aboard. He was that good.

There could be no discussion regarding whether we shoot on film or digitally, as the movements required of the camera negated the former. The best capture system available was Arri's Large Format camera, which offered not only higher resolution but less distortion and a shallower depth of field, compared to a standard 35 mm format. The look would seem to fit perfectly with that photograph of the young soldier I couldn't get out of my mind. The problem was that the standard version of the LF was too big and too heavy.

As chance would have it, James and I were in Munich leading a seminar at the university, so we took the opportunity to tour the Arriflex factory with CEO Franz Kraus. We had known Franz for many years, and we asked him if, and when, they could provide us with a mini version of the LF. The request obviously took him by surprise and he laughed, until he realized we were serious. By the time we had returned to London, Arri had agreed to provide a camera for our test period and, after a little more friendly persuasion, another two bodies by our shoot date.

Our tests were lengthy and detailed, not only with various camera support systems but to determine the appropriate depth of field of the image. We chose Arri Signature Prime lenses, which were purpose-made to cover the large format. They were fast and sharp, and there was no "breathing" (image shift) when changing focus. Just as important for our style of shooting, they were very light. But what would best reflect the image of that haunted face but not compromise the movement of the camera? Maybe, a 47 mm at F/4? A 40 mm at 3.2? How about a wider lens at a more open stop, a 35 mm at F/2? We settled on a 40 mm, other than for the sequence in the German bunker, which we shot on a 35 mm to emphasize the space. We also attempted to maintain a stop of between a 3.2 and a 4.0 for our day exteriors, though with such long takes and the shifting cloud cover, that was only our aim.

As we normally do, we had set up a mobile lab to time and view our dailies. I always shoot with the idea of not having to do anything major in post, and I treat the DI process as being just about balancing the images. A cut can be quite forgiving, but for a one-shot film it was even more important that there was no visual bump between takes. As she had done many times before, James would view our *1917* footage every morning with timer James Slattery, nicknamed "Eagle Eyes," being especially cautious as our prototype camera had never been "field-tested." That it was a prototype created other issues, particularly because of the various software programs involved in the workflow that wouldn't recognize a camera that, to them, didn't even exist. This time James was asking vendors to update existing digital software so that it recognized "Camera X," as we called our top-secret Mini LF.

One more serious problem! How to connect the camera and its systems to the operating console and its monitor, the DIT monitor, the aperture control, and Andy's monitor and focus control when there was a quarter mile or more between them, and the camera deep inside a trench? James dealt with this as well, finding an expert in Los Angeles ("Noodles") who she had production fly in to address the issue. There were so many elements to coordinate that to have another interruption of connectivity on some of our complex and lengthy shots would have been a disaster. How would we have felt if, after eight minutes, a shot fell apart because a single control system failed?

When we were finally confident in our transmission systems, James introduced a direct line of communication with the grips, Charlie or Pete, or whoever was carrying or operating the camera. While I was on the remote wheels by the monitor, James was on headsets guiding them through the shot and alerting them to their position if it veered slightly off. She knew where I wanted the camera, and by communicating in this way she allowed me to focus entirely on operating, which took every bit of my concentration. We found this system useful for every rig, including one where we mounted the camera on a motorbike.

Once Sam and I had talked through the "shot," it should have been the time to start defining the locations and sets but, on this project, first we needed to rehearse. More than in any film since

I was shooting documentaries, the camera movement in *1917* was a dance, a symbiotic relationship between the camera and the actors. We had an idea of what we wanted the audience to see but, until we rehearsed, it was only drawings on a page.

We were lucky that Sam cast George MacKay and Dean-Charles Chapman as the film's two young leads, Will Schofield and Tom Blake respectively, as both made themselves available when we needed them. By rehearsing with the two of them we could work out the exact timing of the action before Dennis Gassner and his art department began to build a set or dig a trench. We marked out the trench lines in a field and adapted them as the scenes coalesced. When Sam was happy with the blocking, I recorded the rehearsal with a digital camera (one adapted to our format), taking what we had drawn on paper and marrying it with what I saw in front of me. From my recording I could print out a clear visual reference to the shot and the framing from moment to moment. By the time we came to shoot, we knew the abilities of each system and where each would serve us best, and I had overcome most, though not all, of my fear of operating the Stabileye.

The shoot itself was one of the simplest James and I have been on, and if every day had been overcast, I might have also considered it the least stressful. But the weather did present our biggest problem.

The film takes place over the course of a single twenty-four-hour span. To make the join between one shot and another work, the light had to feel consistent. For aesthetic and practical reasons, we wanted to shoot under clouds, and usually England and Scotland can be counted on for gloom. But on the first day of production, we didn't film a frame. There was not a cloud in the sky. I had asked in a production meeting what we would do if, as had been the case the previous year, the UK experienced another warm and cloudless spring. That was *not* the right question to ask! The

second day of the shoot was cloudy, and we managed to do both that day's work and the previous day's as well. We were back on schedule. On some days we'd wait five or six hours for clouds, and at such times Sam would tell me not to stress about it. It wasn't my responsibility. Then why did everyone look to me expectantly until it clouded over?

The opening of the film proved to be one of the most challenging to figure out. Sam and I were trying to design a move that would take our two main characters on a journey from the tree against which they were resting through the "city" that would, by 1917, have grown up behind the front lines. Perhaps we were trying too hard to show a set rather than imply it. What, I suggested, if we simply tracked back? A straight-line pull-back with Schofield and Blake as they returned to the trenches, starting on a field that could be in England (maybe Orwell's and Schofield's Golden Country) to slowly reveal a wall of dirt and sandbags closing in, higher and higher, on either side. I think that one simple move expresses more than the most elaborate set could have done. The idea proved a template for the rest of the film. Occam's razor.

The first question most people ask about *1917* is how we hid the cuts. A couple are obvious, as when Schofield is knocked out. Others, I hope, are not. But none of our methods are particularly high-tech. We'd shoot matching frames for the end of one take and the beginning of the next, cut on a pan or when the camera passes through a crowd, or use the edge of an object as a matte line, many techniques I had become familiar with when working with Joel and Ethan. Sam would have to choose a preferred take on set rather than in the cutting room, as it was crucial for everyone to know the exact frame we were matching to, as well as the speed and angle of the camera, before we moved on. We shot most of the film in sequence, and the opening ten or twenty minutes of footage was set in the trenches. We all had some concern as to whether the uninterrupted "shot" would work, but when it was cut together for a crew screening during the early weeks of the shoot, even without using digital help with the blends, the sequence felt good.

Having our lead actors available during prep proved invaluable to us, but it also helped them prepare for the unusual experience of shooting the film. George told us that because he'd done so many rehearsals with the camera, by the time we came to shooting he was able to forget about it. He was able to repeat his actions precisely and in multiple takes without thinking about it.

The underground bunker in which Schofield and Blake are given their orders was a set built inside a barn and acted as weather cover. Biggles and I used electrified oil lanterns supplied by the art department to light the shot, dimmed to mimic the color of a flame. We had done something similar on many previous occasions, dating back to *Mountains of the Moon*, but here we had two bulbs in each lantern in line with the camera angle, each on a dimmer so that it could be raised or lowered in intensity as the shot reversed direction. The bulb nearest the camera would be dimmed, so as not to flare the lens, while the bulb to the rear would be the one primarily lighting the shot. The camera (and the Stabileye) was mounted on a Technocrane for the main body of the shot, but Gary took it in his hands to make the switch in direction as Schofield and Blake are sent on their way.

For the initial crossing into no-man's-land, Charlie worked with his Trinity, but as the sequence progressed, we would again turn to a Technocrane, a Stabileye in a handheld mode, and a wire rig.

As with Erinmore's bunker, it's not always the big things that present a challenge. Biggles and our practical electrician, Joe McGee, spent weeks finding just the right combination of LED bulb, reflector, and battery for the flashlight that Schofield and Blake enter with in the German bunker. The flashlight had to be period correct, therefore of a certain shape and size, it had to cast a beam of warm light (most bright LEDs at the time were cold) intense enough to light the sequence, and it had to be remotely controlled. The task was a lot harder than it appeared.

ERINMORE'S DUGOUT
40MM
POSS: TECHNO PLUS RETRACTABLE COLUMN
LAMP
E
LAMP
ER. LAST POSITION
LAMP TO HANG
S
B
OVER BLAKE AND SCO TO ERINMORE

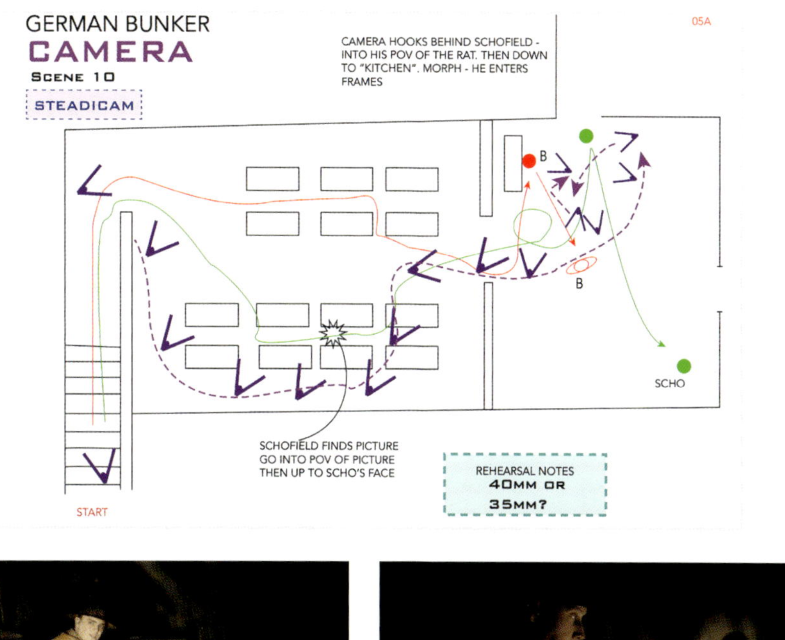

As with every location, we mapped out the shot as a reference for our collaborators in the camera and grip team.

Sam and I scouted locations in France to get a feel of the authentic landscape of the Western Front. But while the art department carved the front line trenches and the shell holes of no-man's-land out of a muddy field to the north of London, we shot much of the film on England's Salisbury Plain, a military training base I'd drive by every time I made the journey from Torquay to London. We had visited a preserved World War I trench system on the Somme battlefield that had been dug in chalk and was snow white, so Sam embraced the same white chalk of Salisbury Plain for the final sequence, though not the live grenades that we had come across in France. We were told that French farmers still get killed to this day from WWI munitions left on the battlefields.

FRONT LINE SCENE 5 • 7 CAMERA

Exit Erinmore's bunker - Stableye

To frontline - Stableye
Paradise to Trinity

Stokes

Corpses

Buchanan

Blend to bunker

Leslie's bunker

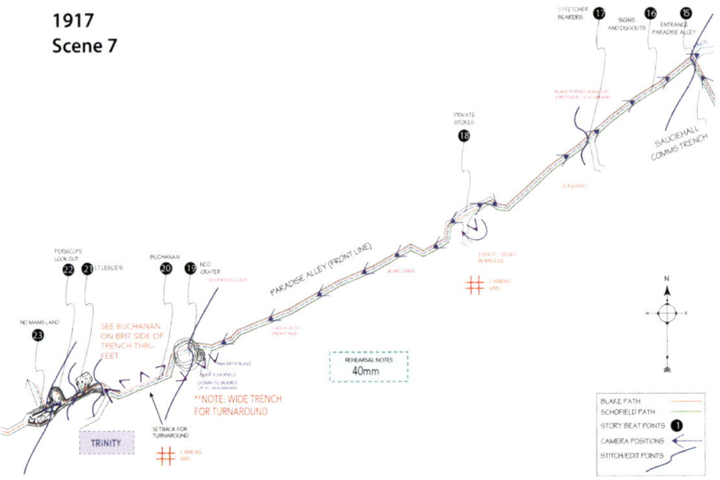

We had searched high and wide for a location in which to shoot the broken canal bridge, at one time even considering digging a canal on the studio backlot, but we eventually settled on Glasgow's historic Govan Graving Docks. As we would have little prep time on-site, we made a full-scale mock-up of the broken bridge, which Dennis Gassner designed for the location, on the backlot at Shepperton Studios. Here Gavin Weatherall could place the four cranes he required for his wire rig in the exact same relationship as he would have room for in Glasgow, while Gary, his grip crew, and I could practice taking the camera on and off the wire to extend the shot before and after the action on the bridge.

The entire action of Schofield crossing the bridge and running to the canal lockhouse was covered in one shot. With the weather in Glasgow a perfect overcast, we finished well ahead of our expected wrap time.

None of this required any lighting, but Biggles soon had his work cut out for him. For Schofield's transit through the French village at night we used every inch of the backlot at Shepperton Studios. This too required rehearsal before we could begin constructing the set. We worked with George to find out the length of his run and at which point we wanted flares to illuminate him. The flares would provide the sole source of light between the lockhouse and the burning cathedral in the town square, so it was important where they fell and just how long they stayed alight. We started laying out the shot on a six-foot model of the entire town (I say "we," but in reality, it was art director Rod McLean), which allowed us, using tiny LED lights as a stand-in, to determine where best to place the flares relative to the action. Effects supervisor Dominic Tuohy came through, finding flares that would be bright enough to shoot by and would burn in the air for the twenty-six seconds we needed, then rigged each on a computer-controlled system of wires to travel in a preprogrammed arc.

As the camera moves through the lockhouse window it reveals a hallucinatory landscape, the look of which we based on aerial footage taken from a balloon of the Belgian city of Ypres in the winter of 1918, just weeks after the war. At the moment when Schofield falls down the stairs and blacks out, there is, hopefully, the only obvious cut in the film. Sam and I felt this moment gave us the license to leave Schofield's perspective, for the camera to take a more objective point of view and enter into what might be his hallucination.

The town was built from our model and the key elements were positioned where they worked best for both the action and the light. Based on the shadows cast by a 60-watt bulb, our burning cathedral, we adjusted the architecture on the model to create structures, such as the colonnade and the arch over the main street. Unlike the Lodge in *Skyfall*, we could not burn its equivalent, the cathedral, on the backlot. Besides, a real fire would not light the set in a controlled way, so I drew on the experience of shooting both *Jarhead* and *Skyfall* to envision a source that could be a replacement for the 60-watt bulb of our model. The result was a rig with five tiers of lights arranged in a circle, each ten feet in height. At fifty feet and comprising something in the order of 2,000 1K bulbs, it was the biggest light I had ever asked for.

Although I was using the entire rig as if it were a single source, it allowed me to control the level of light in any direction. When, for instance, Schofield heads for the basement, I was able to focus a little more light on George as he made his descent, or I could enhance the light coming through the windows of the ruined schoolhouse in a selective way. My only regret is that the rig could not be built to what would have been the full height of the cathedral, as we were limited by Shepperton's proximity to Heathrow and the M3 motorway.

I have included two examples of the schematics I drew for the lighting rig. One is an overview of row two of the tower and the relationship between the Dino lights, the 12-Light Maxis, and the 6-Light Maxis. The other is a front-on view of the pattern of lights on the tower as if seen from the fountain in the town square. I positioned the largest sources to project onto specific areas, while the lights around them just soften the overall effect. All the lamps were on dimmers and rarely burnt at more than 30 percent of full intensity. Mathie (Stephen Mathie, our dimmer board operator who had proved so invaluable on *Skyfall* and *BR 2049*) controlled all this from his iPad, which was a technique that blew me away when I first saw him do it on *Skyfall*. I thought he was texting a friend!

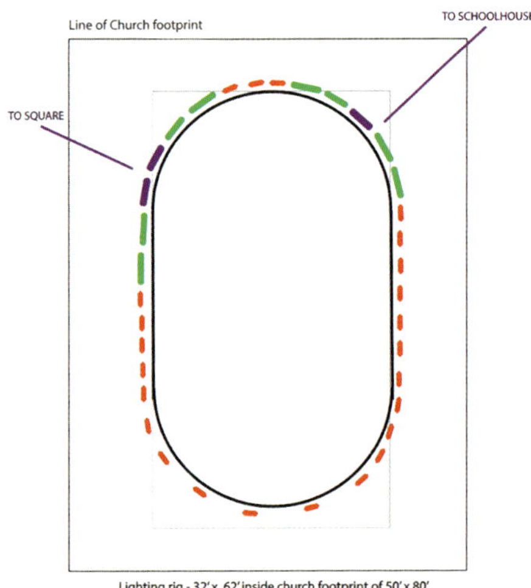

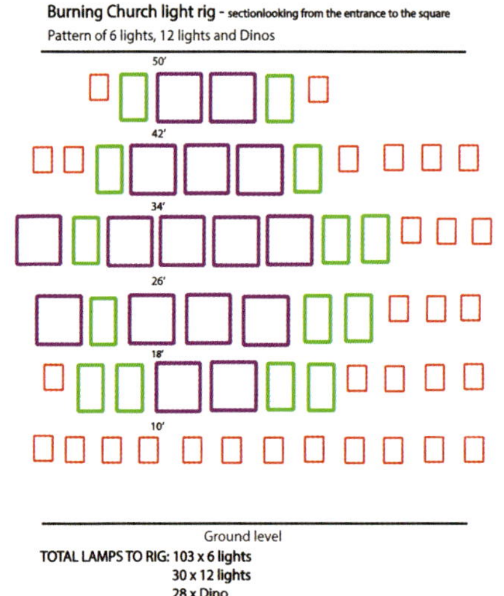

Peter Cavaciuti shot Schofield's encounter with the German soldier in the cathedral square using his Steadicam. It was a difficult piece of timing for Pete. He had to make the transition from walking forward to backward without preempting George's turn away from the enemy soldier, while still having time to find the back platform of the tracking vehicle that he had to step onto. And that tracking vehicle was having to begin moving in order to keep ahead as George burst into his run. We had rehearsed the same kind of moves numerous times during prep, but the pressure is different when it comes to the moment to shoot.

We also had to perform extensive tests to determine the right size, shape, and brightness of the boiler in the basement where Schofield hides with the French mother (Claire Duburcq) and her baby. There was only justification for this one light source, and I felt it important that the light feel romantic and soft. We made a cardboard mock-up of the boiler to study how much of a curve we required to its hearth to reach into the shadows where Claire would be standing and how wide it needed to be to light the scene softly. Mathie and Biggles stood in as we tested the pattern of bulbs we would use within the boiler to stand in for the flames of a fire (twelve double-ended 500-watt halogen bulbs). As with the cathedral, our lights would be replaced by VFX in post. Though a much

smaller set, as well as a simple scene in terms of movement, this proved the most difficult section of the film, both to light and to shoot.

Other sequences that looked hard *were* hard, as when Schofield is pulled down a river after escaping the destroyed village of Ecoust. For this we used a whitewater rafting facility in North Yorkshire, which allowed us to change the intensity of the rapids and use rubber rocks (background elements would be added in post). That was a good find, but how could we get the shot? Sam originally wanted to film from a raft, but I was reminded of how difficult it had been to shoot on a yacht, let alone in a raft. After another crew shot a comprehensive series of tests, we both concluded shooting from the water would be impossible without resorting to multiple cuts. Even if we could have made it work, we would have had to shoot it handheld, which would have been at odds with the rest of the movie. Besides, I still can't swim!

I talked with Gary, and we hit upon the idea of using the telescopic properties of the Technocrane. We put this to the test by mounting it on a tracking vehicle to follow someone walking at a brisk pace, zigzagging back and forth to mimic the motion of a body in a river. It worked and all we'd need to do was build a road, which we did after Sam signed off on the idea. On the day, the camera car driver maintained his position relative to George as he made his way down the rapids, Gary Hymns and his best boy, Gary "Gizza" Smith, held the arm, while Malcolm McGilchrist operated the pickle (a unit that controls the telescopic length of the arm), and I operated remotely while James gave directions to the grips via her radio link. Everyone enjoyed the challenge.

To take Schofield out of the river and through the forest, we used a combination of the Stabileye and the Trinity; as the soldiers are called to the front line, we used just the Stabileye. Charlie and Peter carried the Stabileye to a Technocrane, which then tracked it above the trench line, before Gary removed it from the crane and finished the movement handheld.

We used the same system to shoot Schofield's run from the trench to his encounter with Colonel Mackenzie (Benedict Cumberbatch), only this time the camera was mounted on a Mini Libra head as the motion of our tracking vehicle on rough terrain was too violent for the Stabileye. Gary had to lift the head and camera off a fifty-foot Technocrane arm that had followed George down the trench, carry the camera up and out of the trench, then secure it at the end of a second Technocrane arm, this one twenty-two feet in length, that was rigged on the back of a tracking vehicle. Gary had to be dressed in a soldier's costume (with a 1917 haircut) so he could be lost in the crowd of soldiers running away from the camera after he had played his part in the behind-the-lens action. And his part was merely the start of the shot before the tracking vehicle took over. The shot fully deserved the celebratory high five that everyone joined in once Sam said, "OK, we got that."

Although worked out on paper and rehearsed with George during preproduction, the film's final shot was yet another "happy accident." But maybe you make your own "happy accidents."

The image boards that James and I had made from my rehearsal videos gave every member of our grip and camera crew a clear idea of how we planned to cover the final section of the film. Having practiced the move, Charlie, who was operating the Trinity, needed only a single rehearsal on the day of the shoot, which was just as well as we didn't want to destroy the pristine look of the grass. But the sun was out. The light wouldn't match the previous take, and we waited. And we waited.

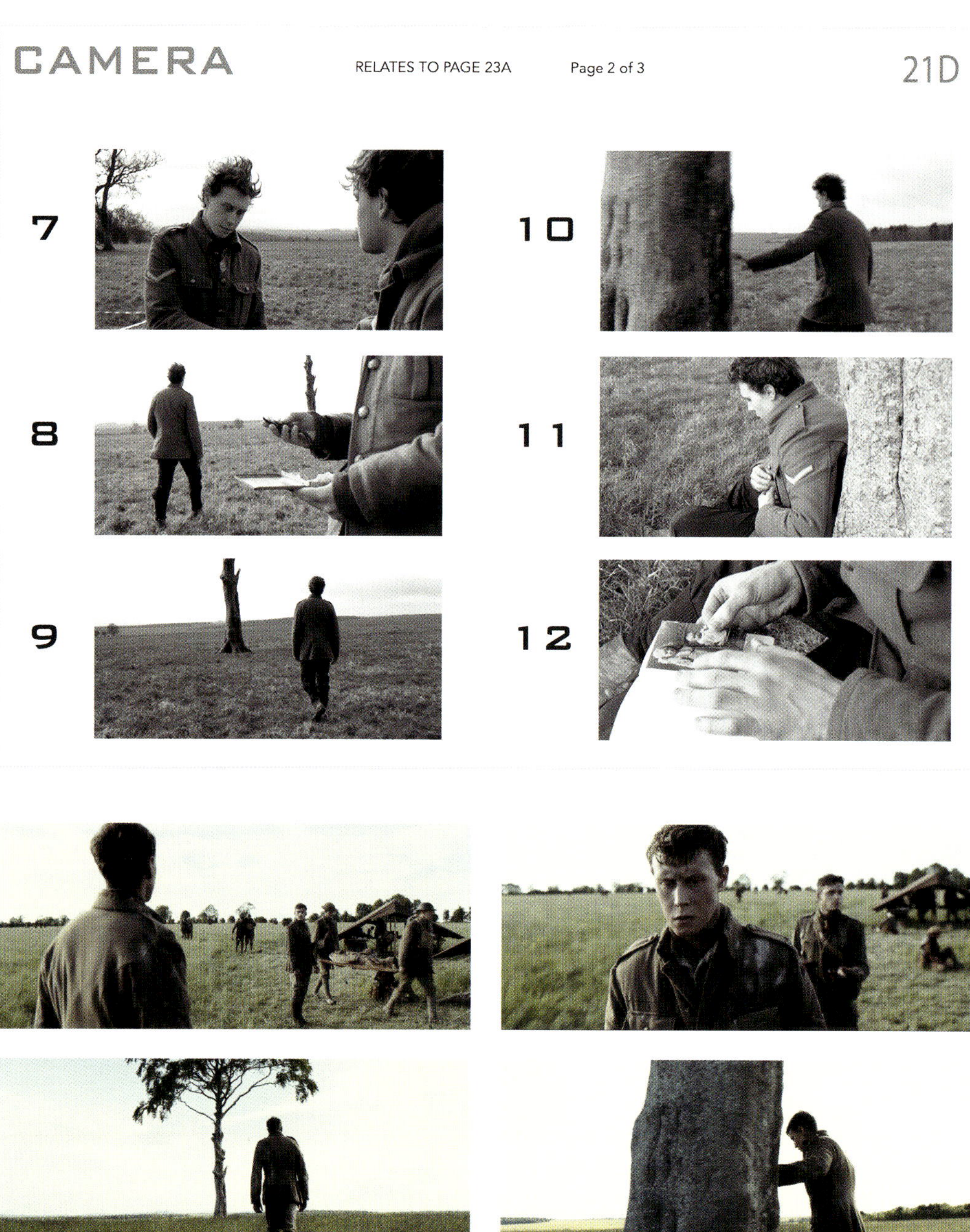
CAMERA
RELATES TO PAGE 23A
Page 2 of 3
21D
7
8
9
10
11
12

The forecast was for a warm front to come in from the west and, sure enough, late in the afternoon, one small cloud seemed on its way to block out the sun. I suspected the overcast light wouldn't last long—maybe only long enough for a single take—so I asked our assistant director, Michael Lerman, to get everyone ready. But what if the sun were to come out in shot? The setup involved a lengthy scene before George would walk to the tree, so judging if and when the sun might come back out was pure guesswork. But ending the film in sunlight felt like a good idea! The sun went in and the light began to match our previous shot. After a brief pause, I nodded to Sam and he called "action." We had waited at least five hours for this moment. If I blew my part, controlling the tilt or the lens iris, the entire shot would be for naught. There was far more pressure on Charlie, who was on the camera, and Andy, pulling focus from a van next to us, over a hundred yards from the scene. But they had been through the same routine for many weeks by this time and had accomplished far more difficult shots than this.

As George settled down against the tree, the sun duly came out. And as Charlie held on what had been storyboarded as the final frame of the film, the photograph in Schofield's hands, I could feel George begin to lean back against the tree. James, who was on our radio connection, whispered to Charlie, "Roger's going to tilt up, so could you move up with him?" As I tilted up, Charlie lifted the camera and George closed his eyes, taking in the warmth of the sun on his face.

What you see in the film is the first take. Though we did several others, the weather front came in and the sun never appeared again that afternoon. A film is about story and character, not lighting or fancy camerawork, and Sam and Lee (Lee Smith, our editor) cut *1917* to performance above all. But Lee felt the first take was the best, the performances felt fresh, and it was the take that captured the emotion of the scene. The sun came out, and that's where the movie ends.

If you want a happy ending,
that depends, of course, on where you stop your story.

ORSON WELLES

32 EMPIRE OF LIGHT

And nothing happens without light.

NORMAN, IN *EMPIRE OF LIGHT*

_1917_ won the award for best cinematography at the BAFTA Awards and at the Oscars. My life might have led me to the stage at the Academy Awards, but that had never been my goal. Neither do I judge my work by the acclaim of others. I know what my contribution might have added to a story. I know where I have failed. Besides, film is a collaborative endeavor. It is hard to say, *I did that*, or *That was the production designer, That was the dolly grip's idea*, or *It was the costume designer's idea*. Of course, I was happy. As I was happy for my longtime friends in the UK, for Biggles and everyone I had known and worked with since my days on *1984*. An award is a recognition that belongs to an entire team.

But then the world changed. COVID-19 had been a small-item news story when *1917* premiered, but by the awards season it began to look like a worldwide problem, and for how long no one knew. Sam sent us his new script in 2021, and we all thought the pandemic would have passed by the time it came to shoot in the following year. How wrong we were.

The town of Margate in Kent, where we filmed *Empire of Light* in 2022, is located five or six hours by car from Torquay, and about two hours from Brighton, where Sam spent much of his childhood. Memories of the cinema unite all three towns. Once Sam had embraced its stark Art Deco style and the more run-down look of Margate, Dreamland, itself a closed cinema from a bygone age, became our stand-in for all such movie palaces. Like *1917*, this was a personal project for Sam. Hilary (Olivia Colman), the film's central character, struggles with schizophrenia, as did Sam's mother. Her affair with Stephen (Micheal Ward), a Black coworker, becomes a focal point for the political turmoil of the Thatcher years of the early 1980s, when Sam came of age.

Having spent weeks searching the country for a cinema on a seafront promenade, Dreamland seemed just too good to be true. Though its appearance was in opposition to the elegant Georgian frontage of the Empire of the script, it had much to offer. The exterior was beautiful in its own way, while upstairs were the remains of a neglected Art Deco ballroom that looked out toward the sea and a rooftop that was the perfect place for our main character to enjoy the new-year fireworks. The lobby, however, which would be the focus of our work, was much too small, with a low ceiling, not at all the luxurious space of Sam's imagination.

When scouting in Brighton, we had considered using the exterior of what was the cinema of Sam's youth, and now a casino, but building an interior on a nearby parking lot with almost the same sea view. It was our luck to find a vacant lot only a few doors away from Dreamland that offered the same opportunity in Margate. A stage set would have required a company move to a major studio and restricted Sam's ability to shoot the film in story order. To be able to walk between Dreamland and one of our most important sets gave us a remarkable advantage.

The entire glass frontage of the lobby opened onto Margate's ever-changing weather, so I needed to build in lighting that I could control, in terms of both intensity and color. Dimming a tungsten halogen bulb warms the color of light it emits, an effect I've frequently used, whether augmenting candlelight or mimicking a burning cathedral. Consequently, to maintain an exposure balance with the approach of dusk, its color moves in the opposite direction to the daylight, which is itself becoming increasingly blue. By dimming tungsten lights, you increase the color disparity. Adding neutral-density filters and CTO gel to the glass doors was an option but a time-consuming one. A recipe for disaster on a film like this. Besides, the doors open in shot. Once again, technology became available when I needed it. LED lighting has been slowly replacing tungsten sources on film production, but *Empire of Light* proved to be the first time that I used the technology almost exclusively.

The lobby was the work of our production designer, Mark Tildesley, in collaboration with our set decorator, Kamlan Man. Specific light sources were either built into the set ceilings or added as practical elements to the walls and stairway. By using bicolor LED strips or Astera LED tubes and globes for every fixture, we could adjust the balance between our set and the daylight without recourse to gels, scrims, or any other traditional tool. Our console programmer and operator, Galo

Dominguez, was able to adjust all the interior light as the daylight shifted, and by separating our lighting into distinct units, he had the ability to balance our sources relative to the camera angle.

The central chandelier, an important visual feature as well as a key lighting element, proved to be a challenge. A period rental, not only did it need to be rewired, but we also needed glass diffusers less opaque than those that came with the fixture and large enough to contain the taller-than-standard Astera bulbs. To light through the false skylight centered above the main staircase as if it were open to the daylight, we used LED panel units. As with all our other LEDs, we were able to balance these to the color temperature of the daylight coming through the doors facing the promenade. The process of filmmaking is always evolving, and I've constantly changed my approach to incorporate new technology, whether involving the camera or in post. This set would have proved even more difficult to shoot in had I been restricted to conventional tungsten or HMI film lighting.

I remembered the promenade lights in my hometown and was struck that those stretching along Margate's seafront had been removed, so when Hilary walks toward her apartment at the opening of the film, there was no source to light her by. Given my aversion to combining "moonlight" with practical lighting, I asked Biggles what he could come up with. Could we line the promenade with a festoon a half mile long? Again, LEDs came to our rescue; festoons came ready-made and far less expensive to power than conventional 60-watt bulbs. With Biggles, his crew, and location manager Emma Pill we pressed the issue, and the lights were ready literally a half hour before the first scene for which we'd need them. Biggles thought it best to leave them on each night and the locals came to love them, but I'm not sure they survived, as they were a cheap overseas brand and began to spark even as we shot the film.

The interior of the main theater proved to be another challenging location. We had scouted in London and elsewhere for a suitable space but, again for practical as well as aesthetic reasons (and Sam's desire to shoot the film in continuity), settled on turning what was now Dreamland's faded bingo hall into a sparkling Art Deco cinema. The problem was that before it became a bingo hall, the upper balcony of the original 1930s theater had been converted into a separate screening room, leaving no space for a projection booth and little space to light. After much negotiation and effort, Biggles managed to install a series of ring lights containing three hundred high-tech Astera bulbs, both a high- and low-tech solution that created a soft source controlled from an iPad. Other than the rings, we rigged four 650-watt Fresnel lamps to highlight the doors and statues, lines of LED strips to outline the walls, and a few front lights for the stage. It was a complex set for everyone but worth

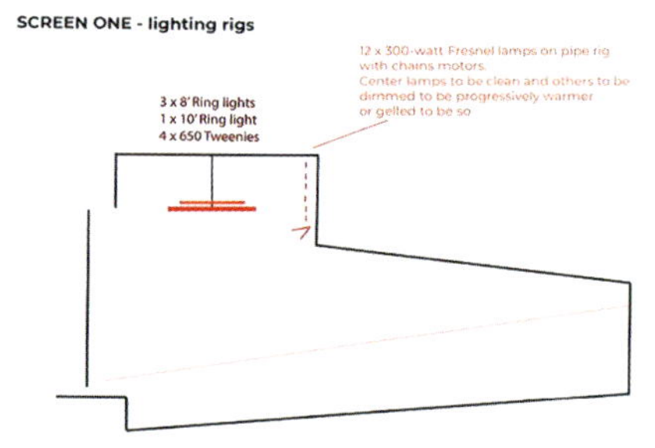

the effort, saving travel time, saving the cost of hiring another location, and allowing Sam to shoot in continuity.

The abandoned ballroom was a real bonus. Mark added the booths, some chandeliers, and panels of yellow gel to alternate windows. For the most part lighting was minimal, just molding the natural daylight using flags and reflectors. We shot the dusk scene over two consecutive evenings, making use of all the advantages of a real location.

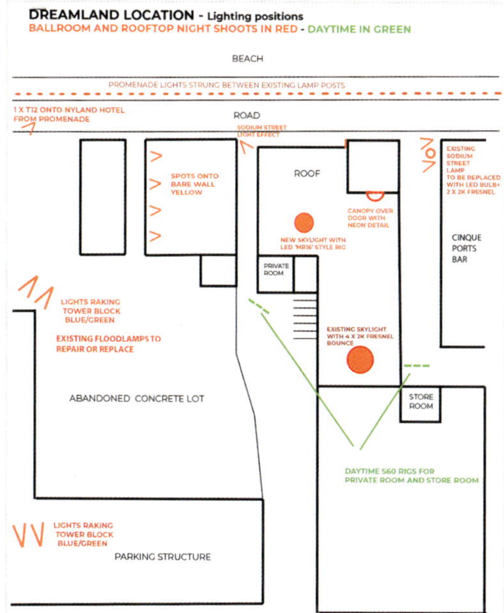

The rooftop of Dreamland looked down on the promenade and out toward the pier and its more modern Turner museum. The festoon would define the bay, and the riggers outlined the pier using a variety of small sources. We lit the imposing tower block that overlooks the roof with large LED panel lights and fluorescent strips, and we detailed a few of Margate's Georgian buildings with open-face 2K Blondes, the cheapest lamps we could get hold of. On the roof, I wanted to play Hilary and Stephen in silhouette as they leaned on the parapet to watch the fireworks. Here, I could light them from below, as if it were the yellow of the cinema's exterior neon, but what to do for their initial conversation in the middle of the roof? And Sam's suggestion that we might see in every direction in one continuous shot posed a real problem. How could you not see any lighting? A false skylight proved the answer. This set piece would emit soft light in all directions from its side windows, via a ring of small LED spot bulbs rigged under the circular roof and bounced off a white reflector on the floor. By positioning it close to where Hilary would set down the champagne bottle, I could light the entire scene using the one element. The fireworks, by the way, were real.

Empire of Light opens with a series of still images of the Empire lobby before Hilary enters from the promenade to prepare the cinema for the day to come. These scenes take place mostly on a set of our creation and with paper pellets standing in for the falling snow. They were shot on a digital camera of the sort unimagined in the film's 1980s and illuminated by newly introduced lighting

controlled by a tablet's touchscreen. The exterior is an old movie palace we'd redressed to suit our needs. The interior is an illusion we created. Movies have changed profoundly since their invention, and some of the most dramatic changes have occurred within the half century of my career. But they've always succeeded through a trick of the light.

EPILOGUE

The end of a picture is always an end of a life.

SAM PECKINPAH

It's over fifty years since I took my first steps into the industry. Along the way the lad from Torquay has been honored with a CBE and a knighthood. It's hard not to become reflective about what my job means and why I do it.

At first my camera was an excuse, my way of avoiding a normal life. But my job behind the camera has also been my education. Perhaps the only things of lasting importance to me are the people I have met and the places I have seen. I have had many experiences, have listened to many stories, and have had a part in telling many more—far more than I have time to recount. It is amazing that I have had the opportunities I have had, given my early life and thoughts.

Film? That's for other people, not me.

Neither am I the most likely individual to be working in this industry. I have turned down many projects. Sometimes I have not connected with the script. Other times I have not connected with a director. Like oil and water, some people just don't mix. I always ask myself, "What is the reason for making this film, other than taking people's money?" To spend three or five months on a film—sometimes longer—I want a script to have more meaning for me than simply offering another paycheck, however welcome that might be.

I want a script to affect me in some way.
I am usually drawn to character studies, scripts about real people
and the world we live in, not some fantasy.

ROGER DEAKINS

Every director I've worked with has had different demands. Some are knowledgeable about every aspect of the process while others concentrate on the script and performance, leaving the choice of shot to their cinematographer. I don't expect a director to know any of the technical aspects of filmmaking, and I've worked with a couple of highly experienced directors who had little understanding of the focal length of a lens or depth of field, for instance.

As a cinematographer, I must be aware of all the equipment that will help me do my job. Then the trick becomes not letting the technology distract from your instinctive reaction to what happens on set. I don't see my role as simply recording what is in front of me. I wouldn't want to be on a film where I could make no suggestions and would only be pushing a button. It's not that I always want to have my suggestions followed. (Most of them are probably best forgotten!) But I'd like them to be acknowledged and for me to be part of the process. Listening to suggestions and making choices with collaborators is the way I light with a gaffer and key grip, and how I work with a camera crew.

People confuse "pretty" with good cinematography.

ROGER DEAKINS

If my work has a signature, the word I would use to describe it would be "simplicity." There is always a temptation to create dramatic visuals because there is so much technology to help you do just that. But why? If you have a good script, you may only be distracting the audience from it by employing an audacious camera move or extravagant lighting. It's easy to be seduced by the beauty of a composition or the light, letting one suffer while drawing attention to the other. A beautiful composition must not be there for its own sake, preferred above one that, while it may appear mundane, contributes more to guiding the audience through the story. Lighting is about framing, and framing is about lighting. I have never been comfortable dividing the two, which is why I have always operated the camera (despite what the union-dictated credits might read). Whether taking a still photograph or operating the camera on a film set, composition is about a feeling, a feeling that you hope will translate to the viewer. There is no formula.

Don't shoot what it looks like.
Shoot what it feels like.

DAVID ALAN HARVEY

Camera movement (or the lack thereof), the choice of when to cut between shots or when to cover a scene in a single wide composition, can create or relieve tension, depending on the moment within the story, the shots that have come before and those that will follow.

Film entertains with different angles, quick moves, like a commercial.
But filmmakers like [Wim] Wenders allow themselves
to observe a subject for a long time without changing an angle,
and allow you to do that along with them.

ANDREY ZVYAGINTSEV

A wide, static image, such as a view over an empty ocean, can suggest tranquility. A fast track toward the same horizon, for example, can shift the mood. With a voice-over cataloging the destructive capabilities of a cruise missile, as it was in one unusual arms manufacturer's commercial I remember seeing, the tranquil view can be transformed into something quite terrifying.

While shooting *Hail, Caesar!* I worked with lighting that was little different than the Fresnel lamps and Brute arcs used by James Wong Howe, Stanley Cortez, or Kazuo Miyagawa in the 1950s. Not only was the style of lighting part of the period look of the film, but the lighting instruments themselves served as part of the set. Not long after shooting *Hail, Caesar!*, I got to experience the other extreme. For *Empire of Light*, Biggles and I explored state-of-the-art LED fixtures, making minimal use of what are still referred to as conventional light sources. To shoot the two films using such different technology emphasized to me why it doesn't matter what you use, you choose the tools for the job. The one-shot concept for *1917* demanded we use cutting-edge camera-stabilizing systems—though the cutting edge has moved on since 2019—and even invent some of our own. Again, the technology served the storytelling. The story was not created to show off the technology.

For a scene in *Skyfall*, production originally intended for a small unit to go to Japan's remote Hashima Island with the lead actors and shoot two or three shots. These would serve as an introduction to the lair of Raoul Silva, the bad guy played by Javier Bardem, but the bulk of the sequence would then be shot on set at Pinewood Studios. These two or three shots would be extremely expensive. I knew there were cuts being made in other areas, particularly to my lighting demands, so I had a chat with Steve Begg, our VFX supervisor, to see what could be done. To cut the story short, Steve translated still photographs, taken by our location scout, into a series of 3D images. These were regular photographs taken on a standard still camera, just location pictures for reference, but the compositions looked great and could be combined with live-action elements of the actors that we shot at Pinewood. Doing this saved production a great deal of money and allowed for more time and energy to be spent on other scenes.

On *Skyfall*, I lit the actors to match Steve's background plates, but today, neural radiance fields derive 3D models from 2D photos in such a way to allow the lighting of objects independently, free from any restriction as to how they appeared when photographed. The object remains photographic in appearance and the result has all the attributes of being lit by "real" light. Rather than a live skill set, lighting can be transformed into a computational technique. Virtual production tools, technology similar to the camera capture systems with which James and I became familiar when working on *Rango* at ILM and with DreamWorks Animation, have broken the remaining barriers between animation and live-action filmmaking. And who knows where AI will lead us? Is already leading us?

People worry that computers will get too smart and take over the world, but the real problem is that they're too stupid and they've already taken over the world.

PEDRO DOMINGOS

And what of cinematography in this brave new world? Will there be a cinematographer, a single "eye" overseeing the "photographing" of a film? In many ways the cinematographer's role is constantly being changed by advances in technology. When once a director would trust a cinematographer to light and expose film emulsion in such a way as fit the story, and the camera operator to capture the performance of the actors with elegant compositions and camera movement, they now view all this in real time on a calibrated monitor. Often a director is not even on the set—in fact, they can be far away from it, so much so that he or she must communicate with an actor via a radio or through the assistant director (though many just shout very loudly).

And what of color timing? I have heard some timers maintain they create the look of a film in their DI suite. *Really?* I view the visual identity of a film as created when it is shot and not one imagined in the DI suite. But have I only myself to blame?

I was one of the first cinematographers to embrace a digital finish, and one of the first to begin shooting feature films with a digital camera. And, yes, digital cameras have democratized filmmaking. Perhaps AI will as well. But as Jim Faris, our anthropologist in Sudan, discovered, time only moves forward. And in the words of the teacher to a young Dalai Lama, "Things change, Kundun."

Obviously, the role of a cinematographer did not exist before the invention of the movie camera, just as there were no still photographers before the development (pun intended) of a light-sensitive plate. When I was at art college photography was considered, by all my tutors other than Roger Mayne, a recording medium and nothing more. But the photographs taken by Roger Mayne, Henri Cartier-Bresson, Josef Koudelka, Larry Burrows, Marc Riboud, Alex Webb, Harry Gruyaert, Gueorgui Pinkhassov, James Nachtwey, and so many more are not simply recordings of reality but images that transmit to the viewer a deeper understanding of it. Cartier-Bresson called it the "decisive moment," life encapsulated by the triggering of the shutter. Now AI can create photorealistic images in many ways indistinguishable from those that are real, but without the human eye are they emotionally sterile?

Whether told in a single frame or through the projection of multiple filmic images, the story remains paramount. Its telling should not be driven by the technology of the day. As I've said, at its best, filmmaking is a collaborative experience. A director can start with a vision but find its full potential by embracing the thoughts and suggestions of their creative team through all the stages of production, until a film evolves that can be so much more than the sum of its parts. Likewise, both James and I are stronger as a team. The sum of our personalities. To form a collaborative working relationship of equals with the person who is closest to you is very special. Since she and I met on *Thunderheart*, I have been able to achieve far more than I could have ever imagined doing alone.

In all my films, it seemed important to me to remind the audience to the fact that they are not alone, lost in an empty universe, but that they are connected by innumerable threads with their past and present, that through certain mystical ways, every human being realizes the rapport with the world and the life of humanity.

ANDREI TARKOVSKY

I left Torquay at eighteen, but I never really left. I kept a small open boat in the harbor for much of my life, just a modest vessel powered by an outboard motor but with a front cuddy to use as a shelter in bad weather. I still have the same boat, although it's no longer in Torquay. There are too many Jet Skis there now, so I have moved on.

One summer a few years ago, I motored out to fish for bass in the tidal flow between Lyme Bay and Torbay. Luke, a friend I had known since I was a kid, was out tending to his crab and lobster pots in the early-dawn light. Luke had been a signwriter, hand-painting the lettering on a shop front, a garden gate, or a billboard until being replaced by stencils and molded plastic. I think he once painted the elegant sign above my father's shop front. When Luke's business began to fail, he transitioned into a full-time fisherman, working his small boat, one hardly larger than my own, around the coast each day no matter what the time of year, the weather, or sea state.

On this particular morning the sea's surface was like glass, broken only by some gulls and the occasional gannet diving on a shoal of brit. Seeing me out on the water for the first time in a while and having just baited one of his crab pots and returned it to the deep, Luke drew up alongside. We chatted about the weather and the scarcity of the mackerel shoals that summer. He said he would often read about me in the local paper, which would rarely fail to mention a film I had worked on or an award that I had been up for, that kind of thing. "It must be an interesting life, Hollywood. But I don't envy you. Why would I want for more than I have here?" he said as he looked out across the bay. "The fishing is not like it used to be, certainly not as good as when we were teenagers, but I still earn enough for a pint in the pub on my way home. That's enough for me." He started up his outboard. "You take care of yourself," he called out as he went off to check on the rest of his traps.

I have thought about that brief encounter quite often. A film set can be a crazy place. On one difficult night shoot, work was held up for over an hour because two lead actors couldn't agree whose trailer would park closest to the set. What complicated matters was that one of them had two trailers, the second containing a personal gym. Once all the egos had been satisfied the equipment trucks could finally park up and unload, naturally, the furthest from the set. On another film and on another set, an actor insisted on shooting a love scene between himself and his costar—for other than creative reasons. And the director acquiesced! At such times, or when a director arrogantly calls me and my idea stupid in front of the whole crew, only to make it their own a few minutes later, my mind wanders back to Torquay. Luke may not ever envy me, but I do find myself envying him.

As a would-be rebellious teenager, I fantasized I was that other Luke, Lucas "Luke" Jackson, so memorably brought to life by Paul Newman in Stuart Rosenberg's *Cool Hand Luke*—although I never did cut down a parking meter. But it was an earlier film, one that starred Paul Newman as a pool player, I thought about whenever a friend and I would challenge tourists in the pub, not at pool but at darts, letting them win a game or two before playing for a round of drinks. Like Newman's Fast Eddie Felson in Robert Rossen's 1961 film *The Hustler*, we just had to show them how good we really were. And we were good. I might have given Eric Bristow or Phil Taylor a run for their money had I not discovered film!

Now there might seem a world of difference between playing pool, signwriting, cinematography, and bricklaying, but there's not if it's a craft you have a passion for, maybe your art, something that gives you pleasure. This one exchange in *The Hustler* has stayed with me since my father first allowed me to see the film. Having played the best pool of his match with Minnesota Fats, before getting drunk and blowing it, Fast Eddie says to his girlfriend, "Just hadda show those creeps and those punks what the game is like when it's great, when it's really great. You know, like anything can be great, anything can be great. I don't care, bricklaying can be great, if a guy knows. If he knows what he is doing and why and if he can make it come off."

Another day, another summer, I was in Teignmouth waiting in line by the beach huts to buy some bait for a day's fishing. Up until recently it was possible to buy live sand eels from the seine net fishermen who caught them at high water in the mouth of the River Teign. But, like many traditional practices, that is now part of history. There were seven or eight anglers standing in line when, from behind me, I heard a man with a thick Devon accent announce, "You were robbed." I turned around, as it seemed to have been directed to me. "Sorry?" "You were robbed. The Oscars. *Jesse James*. It was ridiculous." I chuckled and thanked him. "So, where are you off to?" he asked. "Orestone," I replied. "Any good out there?" "There's a few bass, nothing great." "It's not like it used to be, that's for sure. There's not even that many mackerel around this year," he lamented, an annual refrain.

The seine boats had arrived back at the shore and a fisherman was filling each of the anglers' buckets with a scoop of twenty or thirty eels in exchange for a five-pound note. "Well, good luck. Perhaps I'll see you out there if that easterly doesn't blow up too hard. Should be all right until the tide turns," he suggested as he walked away with his rod and bucket of eels. It was a simple exchange, maybe to some inconsequential, but one that says so much to me.

I was never naive enough to believe that film could change the world, but I always felt that stories mattered, that they could entertain, enlighten, inform, challenge, maybe inspire, just one or all of those things. How could I have ever imagined where my path would lead me and what my part in filmmaking would be? It's not about the awards or the acclaim, but just the one guy who has seen something I have worked on and turns to me, a stranger, and tells me I was robbed. No, I was not robbed. But thanks. Thanks anyway.

As Sarah, played by Piper Laurie in *The Hustler*, says to Eddie, "You're not a loser, Eddie, you're a winner. Some men never get to feel that way about anything."

PHOTOGRAPHY CREDITS

The photographs and diagrams in this book are from the personal archive of Roger Deakins unless otherwise stated.
Photo on page 4 by Kurt Hutton/Picture Post via Getty images
Photo on page 16 by Chris Coles
Photos on pages 35 and 36 by Sarah Errington
Photo on page 38 by Barry Ackroyd

Felix the Cat:
Courtesy of Universal Studios Licensing LLC © 1959 Classic Media, LLC. Felix, its logos, names and related indicia are trademarks of and copyrighted by Classic Media, LLC. All rights reserved.
Page 8

1984:
Courtesy of MGM Media Licensing
1984 © 1984 Orion Pictures Corporation. All Rights Reserved.
Pages 46-57, 60, 61

Sid and Nancy:
Courtesy of MGM Media Licensing
SID & NANCY © 1986 Zenith Productions, Ltd. All Rights Reserved.
&
Used with the permission of StudioCanal S.A.S.
Pages 62-73
BTS shot by Simon Mein

Mountains of the Moon:
Used with the permission of StudioCanal S.A.S.
Pages 74, 78-86

Barton Fink:
Courtesy of Universal Studios Licensing LLC © 1991 Polygram Filmed Entertainment
&
'BARTON FINK' ©1991 20th Century Studios, Inc. All rights reserved.
Pages 92, 94-105
Storyboard drawings on pages 99 and 103 by J. Todd Anderson

Thunderheart:
THUNDERHEART
© 1992 TriStar Pictures, Inc.
All Rights Reserved.
Courtesy of TriStar Pictures
Pages 106, 108, 109
BTS shot by Elliot Marks

The Secret Garden:
Licensed By: Warner Bros. Discovery. All Rights Reserved.
Page 113
BTS shot by Bob Penn

The Hudsucker Proxy:
Courtesy of Universal Studios Licensing LLC © 1994 Warner Bros.
&
Licensed By: Warner Bros. Discovery. All Rights Reserved.
Pages 114-121

The Shawshank Redemption:
Licensed By: Warner Bros. Discovery. All Rights Reserved.
Pages 122-128
BTS shot by Michael P. Weinstein

Fargo:
Courtesy of MGM Media Licensing
FARGO © 1996 Orion Pictures Corporation. All Rights Reserved.
Pages 130-139
Storyboard by J. Todd Anderson

Courage Under Fire:
'COURAGE UNDER FIRE' © 1996 20th Century Studios, Inc. All rights reserved.
Pages 140-142
BTS shot by Merie Weismiller Wallace

Air America:
Used with the permission of StudioCanal S.A.S.
Page 141
BTS shot by Frank Connor

Unbroken:
Courtesy of Universal Studios Licensing LLC © 2014 Universal City Studios, LLC
Pages 143-144, 310

Kundun:
© 1997 Disney
Pages 146-159

BTS shot by Bruce Hamme
Illustrations on page 156 by Roger Deakins, 2025

The Big Lebowski:
Courtesy of Universal Studios Licensing LLC © 1998 Polygram Filmed Entertainment, Inc.
Pages 160-169

O Brother, Where Art Thou?:
Courtesy of Universal Studios Licensing LLC © 2000 Universal Pictures and Touchstone Pictures
&
© 2000 Disney
Pages 174, 176-183
Illustrations on page 182 by Roger Deakins, 2025

The Man Who Wasn't There:
Courtesy of Universal Studios Licensing LLC © 2001 Gramercy Films LLC
Pages 170, 184-193, 195

The Ladykillers:
© 1997 Disney
Pages 196, 205

Jarhead:
Courtesy of Universal Studios Licensing LLC © 2005 Universal Pictures
Pages 200-215
BTS shot by Francois Duhamel

The Assassination of Jesse James by the Coward Robert Ford:
Licensed By: Warner Bros. Discovery. All Rights Reserved.
Pages 216-218, 220-227

No Country for Old Men:
© Paramount Pictures. All Rights Reserved.
Pages 58, 228-245

Rango:
© Paramount Pictures. All Rights Reserved.
Pages 246, 249

How to Train Your Dragon:
Courtesy of Universal Studios Licensing LLC © 2010 How To Train Your Dragon DreamWorks Animation LLC
Page 250

A Serious Man:
Courtesy of Universal Studios Licensing LLC © 2009 Focus Features
Pages 252-259

True Grit:
© Paramount Pictures. All Rights Reserved.
Pages 262-271
BTS shot by Wilson Webb

Skyfall:
Courtesy of MGM Media Licensing
SKYFALL (2012)
Courtesy of Eon Productions and Metro Goldwyn Mayer Studios
SKYFALL © 2012 Danjaq, LLC and Metro-Goldwyn-Mayer Studios Inc.
SKYFALL, 007 Gun Logo and related James Bond Trademarks, M Danjaq. All Rights Reserved.
Pages 272, 274-279, 281-296
BTS shot by Francois Duhamel

Prisoners:
Licensed By: Warner Bros. Discovery. All Rights Reserved.
Pages 298-309
BTS shot by Wilson Webb

Sicario:
Sicario courtesy of Lions Gate Films Inc.
Pages 312-327
BTS shot by Richard Foreman Jr.

Hail, Caesar!
Courtesy of Universal Studios Licensing LLC © 2016 Universal Pictures
Pages 328-337

Blade Runner 2049:
BLADE RUNNER 2049
© 2017 Alcon Entertainment, LLC
© 1992 TriStar Pictures, Inc.
All Rights Reserved.
Courtesy of TriStar Pictures
&
Licensed By: Warner Bros. Discovery. All Rights Reserved.
Pages 338, 340-364

The Goldfinch:
Licensed By: Warner Bros. Discovery. All Rights Reserved.
Page 365
BTS shot by Macall Polay

1917:
1917 courtesy of Content Partners LLC
Pages 368, 370-383
BTS shot by Francois Duhamel
Photos on pages 368, 381 by the author, Optical Support and Francois Duhamel

Empire of Light:
'EMPIRE OF LIGHT' © 2022 20th Century Studios, Inc. All rights reserved.
Pages 384-391

ACKNOWLEDGMENTS

It's been an experience to look back on my life and career and somehow put it on paper. Thankfully, I have not been alone in this task.

I should stress that it was never my intent to write a book. My world has been one of images and not words. Only the enthusiasm of Amar Deol, my editor, convinced James and me that it might be a worthwhile endeavor and of interest to any lover of film. It was his belief in the book that made it possible and his unwavering support that has brough it to fruition. If there is any blame to go round, it is for Amar!

I'd like to give a big shout out to Keith Phipps, who helped take my scattered memories, put them on paper, and give me a firm foundation to move forward. How does one choose one moment from a life while dismissing another? What might be of interest to the reader rather than simply a "favorite shot"? In all this, Keith was my guide.

Thanks are also due to my longtime and longsuffering agent, Peter Franciosa. He truly is a force of nature and has supported us every step of the way. We could not have asked anything more of his commitment to the project.

I am also indebted to Abraham Zeiger, who has worked tirelessly through the many drafts and kept an eye on the details. From the start he has been an invaluable collaborator.

Many thanks to Shubhani Sarkar and Nyamekye Waliyaya for their creative design and contributions to this work. They brought this book to another level with their ideas and hard work.

Thanks to Byrd Leavell and Albert Lee for their advice and patience, and to Eli Idunate for his organization and invaluable contribution.

In many ways I am my own worst enemy and chief critic. I fail to live up to the expectations I have for myself or for my work, rarely feeling satisfaction after a day of shooting or the completion of a film. My support has been in the friendship and collaboration I have experienced with my fellow crew members. Whether someone I have worked with for many years or on a single film, I have been blessed. Collaborating with a team—with a camera crew, electricians and grips, with riggers and standby carpenters, and the many craftspeople on a film—has made it a pleasure to go to work every day—whatever the hour. I trust their work is reflected in this book as much as mine.

And last, but certainly not least, I come to my creative companion and wife, James. We met as strangers on a film crew and have shared our lives and our work ever since. The creation of this book was no exception. She was there from start to finish, both to bounce ideas with and to organize the material, and she was there to deal with the insane number of discussions and phone calls it takes for a book like this to see the light of day. I'm more than grateful to have such a partner in life.

SIR ROGER A. DEAKINS, CBE

Roger A. Deakins, a renowned cinematographer and member of both the American Society of Cinematographers and the British Society of Cinematographers, was born and raised in Devon. He studied graphic design at Bath Academy of Art and, before continuing his education at the National Film School, he spent time shooting still photographs of North Devon, with the intent of capturing the disappearing rural life.

After graduating from the National Film School, he shot a number of documentaries, pop promos (more commonly referred to today as music videos), and dramas before he moved into feature films.

Roger has been nominated 16 times for an Academy Award and won twice for the movies *Blade Runner 2049* and *1917*. He has been nominated 11 times for the BAFTA award and won on 5 occasions, nominated 17 times for the top award of the American Society of Cinematographers and won on 5 occasions—the first time for *The Shawshank Redemption*—and has won the British Society of Cinematographers' award 7 times.

He has been awarded Lifetime Achievement Awards from the American Society of Cinematographers, the British Society of Cinematographers, and the National Board of Review.

He is also the sole cinematographer to have been honored with a CBE, in 2013, and a knighthood, in 2021.

He is also an avid photographer. In 2021, Damiani Books published *Byways*, a monograph of Roger's black-and-white stills taken over the many years since his first introduction to a camera. *Byways* continues to be phenomenally successful and is Damiani's best-selling book to date. Hopefully, there is more to come.